The Future of Pakistan

The Future of Pakistan

STEPHEN P. COHEN
and others

BROOKINGS INSTITUTION PRESS
Washington, D.C.

Library of Congress Cataloging-in-Publication data
The future of Pakistan / Stephen P. Cohen and others.
     p.   cm.
     Includes bibliographical references and index.
     Summary: "Examines Pakistan within the context of current geopolitics and economics,
including specific factors such as impact of foreign and domestic Islamist and other radical
groups on internal and international security; influence of the Pakistani army, civil government, and key regions; nuclear weapons; and relationships with India, China, and the
U.S."—Provided by publisher.
     ISBN 978-0-8157-2180-2 (paperback : alkaline paper)
     1. Pakistan–Politics and government–21st century.   2. Pakistan–Foreign relations–21st
century.   3. Civil-military relations–Pakistan–21st century.   4. Pakistan–Social conditions–21st century.   5. Internal security–Pakistan–21st century.   I. Cohen, Stephen P.,
1936–
    DS389.F88 2011
    303.495491–dc23   2011036940

9 8 7 6 5 4 3 2 1

Printed on acid-free paper

Typeset in Minion

Composition by R. Lynn Rivenbark
Macon, Georgia

Printed by R. R. Donnelley
Harrisonburg, Virginia

Contents

BRUCE RIEDEL

Foreword

Pakistan is a country of growing, indeed crucial, importance to the United States and to the rest of the world. Three years ago President Barack Obama called me a few days after his inauguration and asked me to chair an urgent interagency review of policy toward Pakistan and Afghanistan. He said that no issue on his foreign policy agenda was more important than the fate of Pakistan, which he rightly has described as the epicenter of the global terrorist threat today. Two years later Obama would send American SEAL commandoes into Abbottabad, Pakistan, to kill al Qaeda's leader, Osama bin Laden, in an operation carried out without the advance permission or even knowledge of the Pakistani government and army. It would be a defining moment of the Obama administration.

Pakistan was high on his agenda even before his call to me. The terrorist attack on Mumbai, India, in November 2008, just days after Obama's election, was the first major international crisis on the newly elected president's watch. That attack was staged from Pakistan's biggest city and major port, Karachi. Obama stepped up drone attacks on terrorist targets in Pakistan dramatically right from his first days in office. Today U.S. drones attack terrorist targets inside Pakistan frequently, often twice a week.

Of course, Pakistan is much more than just a problem for U.S. counterterrorism policy. Now the sixth-largest country in the world in terms of population, Pakistan, with its fast growth rate, soon will be the world's fifth-largest country and the largest Muslim country, outpacing Indonesia. No country is more important to the future of America's relationship with the Muslim world. It also has the fastest-growing nuclear arsenal in the world, producing more weapons today, including tactical nuclear weapons, than any other country. It may soon have the fourth-largest nuclear arsenal in the world, outgunned only by the United States, Russia, and China. No country is more important with respect to nuclear arms control, nuclear proliferation, and nuclear war.

The United States and Pakistan have had a very conflicted relationship for over half a century. Some have described it as a roller coaster ride of highs and low, others as a very dysfunctional marriage that goes through courtship, marriage, divorce, and courtship over and over again. Americans have come to see Pakistan as a deceitful partner; many wonder whether Pakistan's spies were clueless or complicit in hiding bin Laden for more than five years just a mile from the country's military academy. Pakistanis have come to see the United States as an unreliable partner at best and an existential enemy at worse. Polls show that Pakistanis' opinion of the United States is very negative.

For most of the last century the United States has been a partner of Pakistan's military dictators, enthusiastically embracing all four generals who have ruled Pakistan. Presidents from Kennedy to Bush have invited them to the White House for state dinners and intimate consultations. We have jointly embarked on great clandestine projects such as the U2 base in Peshawar in the late 1950s; Henry Kissinger's secret trip to Beijing from Islamabad in July 1971; the covert war against the Soviet Union in Afghanistan that helped destroy the USSR in the 1980s; and the battle against al Qaeda in this century. All were done with the involvement of Pakistan's military dictators. Despite our commitment to democracy, we have provided little backing to Pakistan's civilian leaders over the decades. The United States is not wholly responsible for Pakistan's unhealthy civil-military relationship, but it is not innocent of responsibility.

Pakistan was born in great violence, and it is becoming a more violent place. Partition in 1947 led to hundreds of thousands of deaths and millions of refugees. Now Pakistan is wracked by terrorist bombings, assassinations, and even firefights in its major cities, especially Karachi. For years friends of Pakistan have warned that by harboring terrorists, Pakistan risked being devoured by terrorism. Now those fears seem all too real.

For all its importance to so many issues and for all this tangled mutual history, Pakistan is little understood in the United States. There are no think tanks with programs dedicated to the study of Pakistan or institutes for Pakistan studies in America. Pakistan is almost always grouped with its larger neighbor, India, in South Asia programs. This is understandable, given their common heritage in the British Empire, but it often means that Pakistan takes a back seat to its bigger and richer neighbor in American studies. That is a shame; Pakistan is an extremely important country in its own right. If geography had placed it somewhere else in the world, it would be seen as one of the emerging critical nations of the twenty-first century, but geography puts it in the shadow of India. It needs more attention.

Thankfully, this book presents an important and timely group of essays by leading American, European, Indian, and Pakistani scholars trying to fill the gaps in understanding Pakistan's future. My colleague at Brookings, Stephen Cohen, is the dean of Pakistan scholars in America. He has written some of the very best studies of the country in the last decade, especially his masterpiece, *The Idea of Pakistan*. Now he has brought together the best experts available to determine where Pakistan is going. Many of them got together for a workshop in Bellagio, Italy, in 2010 to brainstorm about the key factors influencing Pakistan's future, and they produced the essays that are the core of this book. Other scholars provided essays to fill in gaps and offer additional perspectives.

The result is the best possible guide to the future of this important country available anywhere today. In less than 300 pages the key issues are explored in depth and from many angles. There is no common answer to the impossible question of what the future will bring, but there is more informed commentary and analysis on that question here than anywhere else. This book will not tell you the unknowable, but it will give you a guide to understanding the road that Pakistan is moving along and the various destinations that it may reach in the next five to seven years.

BRUCE RIEDEL
Brookings Institution

October 2011

Preface

Pakistan has become a state in crisis, while its actions have created crises for other states. A short list of Pakistan's new, crisis-defined identity would include the following:

—It has become a violent state, with attacks on its core institutions, notably the police, the army, and the Inter-Services Intelligence Directorate, and assassinations of Benazir Bhutto, its most important politician; Salmaan Taseer, a serving governor; and Shahbaz Bhatti, the only Christian minister in the Cabinet. Moreover, Pakistan has the dubious distinction of being the most unsafe country in the world for journalists and diplomats.

—It is a nuclear weapons state with a very bad record of proliferation and lingering questions about the security of its growing nuclear arsenal.

—Pakistan has, as a matter of state policy, actively supported jihadis and militants in Afghanistan and India.

—Its policies hamper international attempts to stabilize Afghanistan and have contributed to several crises—some of them with nuclear overtones—with India.

—Pakistan's tolerance of or inability to control home-grown terrorists and those who come to Pakistan for terrorist training has worsened its relations with China and several European states, even as Pakistan continues to cooperate in identifying these groups.

—The demographic indicators look bad, and they are worsened by a poor economy—long gone are the days when Pakistan was knocking on the door of middle-income status.

—Finally, Pakistan's economy is stagnating, exacerbated by the massive damage due to the recent earthquake (2005) and floods (2010); this has implications for education, internal migration, and the confidence of Pakistanis in the country's progress, especially when contrasted with India's rapid growth.

Because Pakistan is marinated in crisis, attention is riveted on the latest outrage, disaster, or calamity to occur in the country. At the time of writing, these include the killing of Osama bin Laden in his Pakistani lair and an attack on a major naval base in Karachi; a few years earlier, the sensational news was Benazir Bhutto's assassination, a crisis with India, and earthquakes and floods. All of these events were, in the jargon of the policy world, thought to be "game-changers." By the time this book is in print there will, no doubt, be other equally sensational events.

The often-asked question following such events is whether they will push Pakistan over the edge, "edge" being variously defined—at the minimum, as another military takeover; at the maximum, as the breakup of the state. The cover of this book, which features a puzzle, symbolizes the larger analytical problem: is Pakistan coming apart or is it being put together in some new order?

We do not know the answer to that question. One reason is that both Pakistanis and outside observers were lulled into complacency during the nine years of Pervez Musharraf's rule. He cast himself in the mold of Ayub Khan, even as he repeated many of Ayub's mistakes, and serious thinking about Pakistan came to a halt during his seemingly gentle dictatorship. After Musharraf, there has been one crisis after another.

This book flows from a project that attempts to avoid basing judgments about Pakistan's future on a single recent event or trend. While it is important for policymakers and the public to know if and when a state might collapse, it is even more important to understand the deeper, long-term factors that determine when and how that might happen. Unless the ground has been prepared, complex states and societies do not change overnight. That may also be true of Pakistan.

Many earlier projects that looked at Pakistan's future were cautiously optimistic, although a group of experts convened by the U.S. National Intelligence Council (NIC) was decidedly downbeat. More recent studies are deeply divided along the optimism/pessimism spectrum. Chapter 18 reviews some of these studies.

Pakistan will remain important for the indefinite future. From being one of America's most "allied of allies"—a cliché invoked for decades by frustrated Pakistani diplomats as well as conservative U.S. politicians—it has become a major foreign policy headache for the United States and many other countries, not least its neighbors. Its image in the United States is no longer that of a South Asian friend; India has replaced it in that role. As Lawrence Wright has written, India has become the democratic and tolerant country that the United States tried to create in Pakistan with billions of dollars in aid and three serial military alliances.[1]

This book stems from a project that examined Pakistan's medium-term future, roughly defined as the next five to seven years (2011–17). The components of this project included a summary of past predictions of Pakistan's future; fourteen essays presented at a workshop at the Rockefeller Conference Center, in Bellagio, Italy, in May 2010; two additional essays commissioned from Indian scholars; and my own longer essay on Pakistan's future. The strategy was to approach the question of "Whither Pakistan?" from several perspectives.

All authors were asked to briefly set forth important variables or factors that might shape Pakistan's future and to speculate on the likely outcomes. Some adhered to this request more closely than others, but together these essays offer insights into Pakistan's future that reflect different *national* perspectives, different *disciplinary* perspectives, and of course, different *policy* perspectives. This approach was chosen over sectoral analyses (for example, of the economy, the party system, or the military) to encourage the group to focus on the range and variety of likely futures. There are important variations in their responses, and several participants treated the same events or factors very differently—a result that is instructive in itself. A few contributors were asked to focus on a particular issue, problem, or factor. The essays therefore are not entirely comparable.[2]

My own essay followed the same pattern, but I had the advantage of reading—and partially incorporating—the work of other contributors. My chapter briefly summarizes recent developments, examines a number of factors (distributed among four categories), and then sets forth a number of alternative futures. It also explores the methodological problems inherent in this exercise and discusses policy options, especially for the United States, other Western countries, Japan, and India. As noted, chapter 18 offers a survey of other attempts to predict Pakistan's future.

Predicting the future, which is still more of an art than a science, is very difficult to do responsibly. Yet present actions are based on assumptions about the future. Several of the contributors to this volume wisely note the difficulty of predicting the future of both the state and nation of a Pakistan that is changing so rapidly.

The consensus of participants in this project was that extreme cases could be ruled out for the next few years. Yet uncertainty about Pakistan's trajectory persists and Pakistan's state and society are even less knowable today, partly because conducting firsthand research in Pakistan is now far more difficult than it was even a few years ago.[3]

We have not attached numbers to trends and predictions, but the language should make it clear that the continuation of the current establishment-dominated state—"muddling through," in Jonathan Paris's term—is the most likely future or, more precisely, that several kinds of muddling through are possible, some with a greater likelihood of more extreme and unpleasant futures.[4] Nor am I confident that the United States has "one last chance" to get Pakistan right—but then, in 2003, even that argument was qualified by saying that it "may" have one last chance. The policy implications of this analysis are, however, clear: we know less about whether there will be one last chance than we know about the consequences of failure, which makes a good-faith effort to avoid failure essential. Failure is not an option, even though it may occur despite the best efforts of Pakistanis and outside powers. The usual question is "whither Pakistan," but the real one is "whether Pakistan": what kind of Pakistan will emerge from the current chaos, with recent events, notably the assassination of Salmaan Taseer, highlighting Pakistan's decline as a coherent and purposeful state.

With its declining social indicators, its crumbling infrastructure, and its military's misplaced priorities, Pakistan is a deeply troubled state; were it not for the large number of talented Pakistanis, one would be tempted to judge it to be in terminal decline. This is an important point: although the Pakistani state is enfeebled, Pakistani society is as vigorous as ever, manifest particularly in its provincial cultures and talented elite, but there is a yawning gap between aspiration and actual performance.

On a personal note, I have been studying Pakistan since 1964 and have been visiting the country regularly since then. In my own chapter and other writings I have depended greatly on my Pakistani friends and acquaintances, but even they are at a loss to explain some of the new and more shocking trends now under way in their country. I hope this study does not offend—to paraphrase Arthur Koestler, in the long run a hurtful truth is better than a pleasant lie. In Pakistan's case there have been too many lies—whether by Americans, Pakistanis, or others—and this is the time for some hurtful truths.[5]

I am especially grateful for project support from the Rockefeller Foundation, the Carnegie Corporation, the United States Institute of Peace (USIP), and the Norwegian Peacebuilding Foundation (NOREF) as well as consistent interest and good advice from members of the Norwegian and Pakistani governments, none of which have responsibility for the final product.

The Future of Pakistan project and this book owe much to Azeema Cheema and Erum Haider for their assistance. As young Pakistanis and budding scholars, they offered invaluable insights. Constantino Xavier provided timely help in completing the original project and preparing this volume; he also helped organize the workshop at USIP, where our findings were discussed with a larger audience. Finally, we are especially indebted to Moeed Yusuf, who was not only a contributor to the project but also the host of the workshop at USIP, where he is the South Asia adviser.

As this book was going to press, we learned of the untimely death of Sir Hilary Synnott. From its inception, Sir Hilary was an important part of this project. It owes much to his experience, intelligence, and, at the Bellagio meeting, his practical advice, invariably delivered with wit and good humor. This extraordinary diplomat-turned-scholar will be missed by all of us.

Notes

1. Lawrence Wright, "The Double Game," *New Yorker,* May 16, 2011.

2. The essay writers and conference participants were originally termed a "Delphi" panel, after the methodology used by the Rand Corporation to predict events in the 1960s. However, as one participant wryly noted, the Oracle of Delphi was a woman, and her pronouncements were both cryptic and easily misunderstood, leading to tragic consequences for those who consulted her.

3. Firsthand scholarship on Pakistan has declined as the research environment has become more difficult. See, for example, the case of David Hansen, a Norwegian scholar who was arrested and nearly sent to prison or worse; Hansen's plight is described in his fine Ph.D. dissertation, "Radical Ideas, Moderate Behavior," University of Oslo, November 2010.

4. Jonathan Paris, *Prospects for Pakistan* (London: Legatum Institute, 2010).

5. See the analysis by Howard and Teresita Schaffer about the role that lies and dissembling play in U.S. relations with Pakistan, in *Pakistan Negotiates with America: Riding the Roller-Coaster* (Washington: United States Institute of Peace Press, March 2011).

The Future of Pakistan

STEPHEN P. COHEN

1

Pakistan:
Arrival and Departure

How did Pakistan arrive at its present juncture? Pakistan was originally intended by its great leader, Mohammed Ali Jinnah, to transform the lives of British Indian Muslims by providing them a homeland sheltered from Hindu oppression. It did so for some, although they amounted to less than half of the Indian subcontinent's total number of Muslims. The north Indian Muslim middle class that spearheaded the Pakistan movement found itself united with many Muslims who had been less than enthusiastic about forming Pakistan, and some were hostile to the idea of an explicitly Islamic state.

Pakistan was created on August 14, 1947, but in a decade self-styled field marshal Ayub Khan had replaced its shaky democratic political order with military-guided democracy, a market-oriented economy, and little effective investment in welfare or education. The Ayub experiment faltered, in part because of an unsuccessful war with India in 1965, and Ayub was replaced by another general, Yahya Khan, who could not manage the growing chaos. East Pakistan went into revolt, and with India's assistance, the old Pakistan was broken up with the creation of Bangladesh in 1971.

The second attempt to transform Pakistan was short-lived. It was led by the charismatic Zulfikar Ali Bhutto, who simultaneously tried to gain control over the military, diversify Pakistan's foreign and security policy, build a nuclear weapon, and introduce an economic order based on both Islam and socialism. He failed even more spectacularly than Ayub Khan and Yahya Khan. Bhutto was hanged in a rigged trial organized by General Mohammed Zia ul-Haq, who took Islam more seriously. With U.S. patrons looking the other way and with China and Saudi Arabia providing active support, Zia sought a third transformation, pursuing Islamization and nuclear weaponization. He further

1

damaged several of Pakistan's most important civilian institutions, notably the courts (already craven under Ayub), the universities, and the civil service.[1] Zia was very shrewd—and he was also a fanatic with strong foreign backing because his support for the Afghan mujahideen helped bring down the Soviet Union.

After Zia's death, from 1989 to 1999, Benazir Bhutto and Nawaz Sharif alternated in office during a decade of imperfect democracy, groping toward the recreation of Jinnah's moderate, tolerant vision of Pakistan. In fact, the 1990s, which often are referred to as the "lost decade" in terms of economic growth, witnessed a high rise in urban and rural poverty levels. The growth rate in the 1980s averaged 6.5 percent, but in the 1990s real GDP growth declined to 4.6 percent.

Benazir and Nawaz were unable to govern without interference from the military and the intelligence services, which under Zia had vastly expanded their domestic political role. The army believed that it was the keeper of Pakistan's soul and that it understood better than the politicians the dangers from India and how to woo outside supporters, notably the Americans, the Saudis, and the Chinese. The 1990s—the decade of democracy—saw Benazir and Nawaz holding a combined four terms as prime minister. In this period the press was freed from government censorship (Benazir's accomplishment) and there was movement to liberalize the economy (Sharif's contribution), although neither clamped down on growing Islamist movements nor did much to repair the state apparatus, which had been badly weakened over the previous thirty years. Nor were either of them able to reclaim civilian ground from the military, which by then had developed a complicated apparatus for fixing Pakistan's elections. Benazir invested in education, but the state was unable to implement her policies, and Nawaz turned to the military to exhume the "ghost schools" that Benazir claimed she had built. There were also ghost computers: one of the projects that she liked to boast about involved the wide distribution of computers to schools and villages, which had never happened.

Musharraf: Another Failed General

When General Pervez Musharraf seized power in a bloodless coup on October 12, 1999, he undertook Pakistan's fourth transformation. Musharraf came to power after he launched a politically and militarily catastrophic attack on India in the Kargil region of Kashmir and then blamed Prime Minister Nawaz Sharif for its failure. He believed that the politicians had had their opportunity. Ten years of imperfect democracy had not turned Pakistan's economy around or addressed the country's many social and political tensions, and

Musharraf, fresh from his coup, told me that "this time he would 'fix' the johnnies [corrupt and incompetent politicians and bureaucrats]," setting Pakistan on the right course under the army's tutelage. He rejected my suggestion that corrupt or guilty politicians be removed and that fresh elections be held to bring a new generation of competent politicians to power, the argument being that it takes time to build a democracy and that politicians should be allowed to make mistakes and learn from them. Musharraf would have none of that, as he was confident that with the backing of the military he could launch still another reformation of the Pakistani state and nation. The highlights of Musharraf's domestic reform strategy included

—Fiscal and administrative devolution to the districts, which further weakened the powers of Pakistan's provincial governments; the system was later abandoned.

—Privatization of state-owned assets, which resulted in a huge inflow of money into the treasury.

—Promotion of a poverty-reduction strategy.

—Creation of the National Accountability Bureau, which was extremely controversial; and at one point the bureau was shut down.

—Breaking the monopoly of state-owned media and promoting a free press, although toward the end of his period in office Musharraf declared a state of emergency.

—Empowerment of the Higher Education Commission and establishment of new universities.

—Reservation of seats in Parliament for women.

—Signing of the Women's Protection Bill in an attempt to reform the rigid Islamist-inspired Hudood laws.

—Enacting anti-terrorism measures, which, although they represented a strong public stance against sectarian violence, were in practice ineffective.

—Registration of madrassas and development of new curriculums, which also was unsuccessful.

Musharraf turned to the technocrats for guidance, transforming the system of local government and selling off many state assets (thus improving the balance of payments problem, which always is severe for a country with little foreign investment and hardly any manufacturing capability). He further opened up the airwaves and in 2000 attempted to tame the judiciary, making them take a fresh oath of office swearing allegiance to him. One of Musharraf's cherished goals, often repeated publicly and privately, was to tackle "sectarian violence," the code for Sunni-Shiite death squads and organized mayhem, but it actually intensified. Finally, while having signed up for the G. W. Bush administration's "global war on terror," his government never actually stopped supporting militant and violent groups in Afghanistan, Kashmir, and India itself.

Musharraf did introduce some important changes in relations with India. These were on his mind when he first came to power, and after several years he began to float proposals on Kashmir and a secret back-channel dialogue was established. It was clear from my conversations with other generals at that time that they regarded that approach as naive but were willing to go along with Musharraf to see whether there were any positive results.[2]

Musharraf had an idealized vision of what he wanted Pakistan to become, but he was no strategist. He neither ordered his priorities nor mustered the human and material resources to systematically tackle them one after another. He behaved as president just the way he behaved as a general: he was good at public relations but bad at details and implementation. His greatest accomplishment came when he left things alone—for example, by allowing electronic media to proliferate to the point that Pakistan now has more than eighty television channels, although many of them lack professional standards. On the other hand, his greatest failure—and a calamity for Pakistan—may have been his permissive or lax attitude toward Benazir Bhutto's security. A report issued by the United Nations holds him responsible in part for her murder,[3] which removed the most talented of all Pakistani politicians, despite her flaws, and further undercut Pakistan's prospects.

Musharraf began to lose his grip on power because of his seeming support of an unpopular war in Afghanistan and his strategic miscalculation of Pakistani public opinion, which led him to believe that a public protest movement against his high-handed tactics by judges and lawyers would dissipate. He, like his military predecessors, had to turn to civilian politicians for moral authority after about three years of rule, but doing so failed to generate legitimacy for Musharraf, just as it had failed Ayub and Zia.

In March 2007, Chief Justice Iftikhar Muhammad Chaudhry was summoned by Musharraf and asked to resign. When he refused to do so, Musharraf suspended him (a first in Pakistan's history), initiating a chain of events that eventually led to Musharraf's own downfall. Chaudhry was subsequently reinstated by the Supreme Court in July, which would soon after deliberate Musharraf's eligibility as a legitimate candidate in the elections. Musharraf declared a state of emergency in November 2007, suspending both the country's constitution and the supreme court judges. Because his decisions were fiercely opposed by the community of lawyers, civil society organizations (both liberal and Islamist), and a very vocal population, Musharraf was almost entirely isolated. In 2008, there was civil unrest, rioting, antigovernment protests, and mass support for the lawyers' movement. One leader emerged from this spectacular display of people's power: Aitzaz Ahsan, a Pakistan People's Party (PPP) member and distinguished lawyer. Ahsan, who was not part of the PPP's inner circle or close to President Asif Ali Zardari, has since kept a low profile.[4] Pro-Islamist sentiments were part of the lawyers' movement, which expanded its popular appeal, riding a wave of anti-Americanism.

There were more frequent attacks on U.S. and Western targets by militant Islamists, who made several attempts to kill Musharraf himself. Besides the 9/11 attacks in New York and Washington, there was another momentous development, this one in Pakistan itself: the razing of the Lal Masjid (Red Mosque). The mosque was located in the heart of Islamabad, close to Islamabad's leading hotel, the diplomatic enclave, and the new headquarters of the Inter-Services Intelligence Directorate (ISI). The mosque had close ties to militant groups, some of them patronized by the ISI. The government's attack on the mosque came not at the behest of Washington but of Beijing, regarded by elite Pakistanis as their most reliable supporter. China, like the West and India, was deeply concerned about the growth of Islamist militancy in Pakistan and the training of Chinese Muslims in militant camps. The Chinese ambassador complained publicly about the taking of female Chinese workers as hostages by a women's group associated with the Lal Masjid.

According to military sources, the army's operation killed 102 people, but independent media claim that there were 286 to 300 dead, including many women and young girls. Islamabad residents recalled the stench of rotting bodies.[5] There were other terror attacks by militant Islamists, and Pakistani public opinion hardened against both the United States and Musharraf after Pakistani sovereignty was clearly violated by drone attacks against militants within Pakistan. The army's reputation suffered, and in 2007, officers were warned by Musharraf not to wear their uniforms outside cantonments.

Instances of organized violence, including suicide attacks, have shown no clear trend, but they were more lethal in 2010 than in 2009. There was a major decline in terrorist attacks from 2009 to 2010, with 687 incidents in Pakistan in 2010 (down from 1,915 in 2009) resulting in 1,051 fatalities (down from 2,670). As of December 2010 there had been fifty-two acts of suicide terrorism, down from eighty in 2009, but they were more lethal, with 1,224 deaths in 2010, up from 1,217 in 2009.[6]

Figure 1-1 shows the annual number of suicide attacks in Pakistan from 2002 to 2009, by province. Despite the decline, the figures again ranked the country third in the world in both number of attacks and deaths, after

Figure 1-1. *Annual Number of Suicide Attacks in Pakistan, by Province, 2002–10*[a]

Annual number of suicide attacks by province, 2002–10

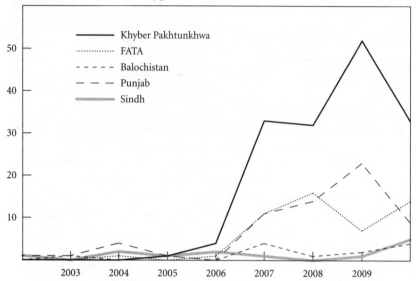

Source: Brookings Institution Pakistan Index (www.brookings.edu/~/media/Files/Programs/FP/pakistan%20index/index.pdf).
a. In addition to the attacks noted above, two additional attacks occurred in Azad Kashmir during 2009, bringing the yearly total to eighty-seven.

Afghanistan and Iraq. Suicide bombing is a relatively new scourge in Pakistan. Only two suicide bombings were recorded there in 2002, but the number grew to fifty-nine in 2008 and to eighty-four in 2009, before dropping to twenty-nine in 2010, the lowest level since 2005. Still, in 2010 Pakistan was the site of far more deaths caused by suicide bombing (556) than any other country and accounted for about one-quarter of all such bombings in the world. The largest number of deaths and attacks took place in the Pashtun belt in Khyber Pakhtunkhwa (KP) and the Federally Administered Tribal Areas (FATA), with Pashtuns killing Pashtuns, whereas the so-called Punjabi Taliban (consisting of Lashkar-e-Jhangvi, Jaish-e-Muhammad, and others) targeted Shiites, Barelvis, and Ahmediyyas as well as Christians.[7]

One Indian observer notes that neither the intensified operations by the Pakistan army in the KP nor U.S. drone attacks have dented the motivation of the Pashtun, both Afghan and Pakistani, nor have they diminished the Punjabi Taliban.[8]

Zardari Treading Water

Benazir Bhutto's widower, Asif Ali Zardari, was elected president on September 6, 2009, with the support of the PPP and in coalition with other secular parties, until the coalition collapsed in January 2011. Politics in Pakistan seems to be reverting to its normal fluid state as parties come and go, leading to uncertain leadership in Sind and Balochistan, in particular. As of 2011 Punjab remains stable, under the leadership of Nawaz's brother, Shahbaz Sharif, but the army seems to be again grooming favored politicians (such as the mercurial former cricket player, Imran Khan) for leadership roles. Being forced to govern in a coalition has its problems, but it has taught Pakistani politicians the virtues of cooperation and some of the "rules of the game" of a democratic political order.

Little was expected of Zardari, a Karachi-born, Sindhi-speaking politician from Punjab's Multan district, but in partnership with stalwart PPP members, his government, led by Prime Minister Yusuf Reza Gilani, has performed better than any prior civilian government—not a great accomplishment, but one that should not be belittled.

The new government's agenda is largely that of Benazir Bhutto: reform and restoration rather than transformation. She had lofty goals, but at the end of her life she understood how badly Pakistan had been governed, even by herself, and she indicated to acquaintances that just as her second term as prime minister had been better than the first, in a third term as prime minister she would have more clarity and purpose. She had the charisma, the international contacts, and the experience of governance that might have given Pakistan half a chance at some kind of success, despite her flaws. That shows that those who killed her knew what they were about, and her death, especially the way that she died, was a tragedy for Pakistan that dramatically reduced the country's odds of emerging from its thirty-year crisis as a normal state.

Zardari lacked his wife's brilliance and charisma. There was a systematic attempt by the opposition and the intelligence services to portray him as corrupt, and his reputation for corruption was one of her greatest political liabilities. Zardari's defense to visitors is that he has never been convicted of any crime, but that, of course, is true of most Pakistani politicians whose reputation for corruption equals or surpasses his. Complaints about corruption have faded in 2011, as the problems facing Pakistan—notably terror attacks—have shifted attention to the military and its inability to control domestic violence.

In the three years of Zardari's presidency, there have been significant changes in Pakistan's constitutional arrangements and an attempt to rebuild some of the badly weakened institutions of the Pakistani state. "Civil society" is booming, the press tentatively exercises its new freedoms (in 2010 Pakistan earned the dubious honor of being the deadliest place in the world for journalists to practice their craft[9]), and growing concern about social inequality, education, and governance has given rise to all kinds of nongovernmental organizations (NGOs), both modernizing and Islamist.

A wide gap remains between the government and the people of Pakistan. Except, paradoxically, for the Islamist Jamaat-e-Islami (JeI), internal party democracy is nonexistent. Distrust still permeates Pakistan's political order, and there remains a deep fear of the security services. The civilian government is still dependent on the military, especially as the internal security situation worsens. Pakistan's foreign friends are as unpredictable as ever.

Zardari's major accomplishments, many of which were the result of cooperation with Prime Minister Gilani, include restoration of the chief justice and deposed judges, unanimous approval by all four provinces of the Seventh National Finance Commission Award, passage of the Eighteenth Amendment to the Constitution, and continuity of national economic policy.

Restoration of the Chief Justice and Deposed Judges. Chief Justice Iftikhar Ahmed Chaudhry and all judges previously deposed by Musharraf were reinstated on March 21, 2009, by Zardari, albeit under pressure from the army. There are indications that the new Supreme Court adheres more closely to international judicial standards than its predecessor.[10]

Agreement on the Seventh National Finance Commission (NFC) Award. The NFC award is the annual distribution by the federal government of financial resources among the provinces of Pakistan, the terms of which have been the cause of bitter disagreement. Under the Zardari government, the Seventh NFC Award was unanimously approved by all four provinces in December 2009 through a consultative process, leading to improved relations between the provinces and to fiscal decentralization. In a distinct departure from policies of the Musharraf regime, the Seventh NFC Award increased the provincial share of the budget from 47.5 percent under Musharraf to 56 percent in the first year of the award (2010–11) and 57.5 percent in the remaining years. The award also includes relief measures for the provinces of Khyber Pakhtunkhwa and Balochistan.

Passage of the Eighteenth Amendment to the Constitution. On April 8, 2010, the National Assembly unanimously passed a constitutional amendment to curtail the powers of the president of Pakistan. In response to some constitutional questions raised by the Supreme Court, the assembly unanimously passed the Nineteenth Amendment in the last days of 2010.

The Eighteenth Amendment reverses the impact of the Eighth Amendment and Seventeenth Amendment, enacted in 1985 and 2003 respectively, which had turned Pakistan into a semi-presidential republic. It places limits on presidential powers, empowering Parliament and the prime minister. It removes articles from the Constitution that allowed the president to dissolve Parliament and suspend the Constitution and removes the two-term limit on prime ministers, thus paving the way for a possible return of Mian Nawaz Sharif. It also removed all formal executive control over judicial appointments.

In addition, legislative authority was decentralized by the removal of the Concurrent List (an enumeration of areas where both federal and provincial governments may legislate but federal law prevails). The North-West Frontier Province also was renamed Khyber Pakhtunkhwa in recognition of the majority Pashtun population, although there were complaints from the province's minority Hazara community.

The passage of these amendments reversed some of the legacies of both General Zia and General Musharraf and re-erected some legal barriers to a return to army rule. The amendments were widely supported by all political parties, and the military allowed the process to move ahead, in part because in its own judgment, it was not the time for it to take an active, public role.

Continuity of Economic Policy. The Zardari government has largely continued the process of both macroeconomic and socioeconomic reform initiated by Musharraf. In doing so the government has been criticized for following an agenda driven by the International Monetary Fund; however, support for the status quo on the socioeconomic side has provided some stability to ongoing processes such as the poverty reduction strategy as well as large social protection programs such as the Benazir income support program.

Trends through 2011

To summarize trends in Pakistan through 2011:

—A number of constitutional changes have theoretically reset the overarching framework of laws and governance, although Pakistan is still in the process of striking a suitable balance among the judicial, the executive, and the legislative branches of government.

—Civilians continue to grope toward a workable constitutional order. Sixty years after independence there is no consensus on the role of major state institutions such as the judiciary, the legislature, the presidency, and the prime minister or on relations between all of them and the military. The relationship between the state and the provinces—and in some cases between provinces—remains unstable.

—The army's role is recessed but not reduced, and the army remains an unelected center of power with its own ties to each of the formal structures of government and to foreign governments. Disgraced by Musharraf's activism and widespread use of its services for nonmilitary activities, the army finds a modest role to be in its interest at the moment, but it retains its distrust and dislike of civilian politicians in general and of Zardari in particular. Two years of seeming stability has not restored army confidence in civilian governance, which is still widely seen as corrupt and venal.

—The media have a new role. Government transparency has increased with intense press and electronic coverage of policies that formerly were made behind closed doors. However, this has not increased accountability, whereby institutions are held responsible for their actions and policies. The media remain vulnerable to pressure from the intelligence services, which have real ways of hurting individuals and private entities, such as corporations or NGOs: by harassment, denial of government contracts, rough treatment, and even disappearances.

—Democracy seems to have returned to Pakistan's political culture, and parties are behaving more responsibly. In earlier years it was possible for a general to joke, without contradiction, that the first priority of Pakistani politicians was that they should be in power but that if that was not possible, they wanted the army, rather than a political rival, to rule. After a few free elections, politicians are now taking their responsibilities a bit more seriously.

—The system has not produced any new leaders. Politics is dominated at the top by two families, the Bhuttos and the Sharifs, and intra-party democracy, which might foster the emergence of new faces, remains absent. Instead, new leadership is rising from within various Islamist and separatist militant groups that seek either to transform Pakistan or to obtain a larger share of whatever spoils there are to be had in this economically stagnating state.

—Pakistan conducts active regional and global diplomacy, and in Afghanistan it has semi-clients, notably the Taliban, that are important to the West. It hopes to be a factor in any Afghan settlement, but that is by no means agreed on by the United States or other supporters of the Afghan government, and Pakistan's relations with both India and Afghanistan are strained at best.

—The impact of foreign governments on Pakistan remains considerable, notably those of the United States and China but also that of Saudi Arabia. The government cannot make any decision of importance without calculating its effect on Pakistan's relations with these powers.

—Anti-Americanism grew steadily in the middle class and the elite during Musharraf's reign and continues to rise, particularly among young people, who constitute an important force given the increasing size of Pakistan's youthful population.

—A few of the home-grown militant outfits have begun to expand their operations, and the Lashkar-e-Tayyiba (LeT) seems to be emulating al Qaeda as it seeks a regional and even global reach with operations in the United States, Great Britain, and South Asia.

—Sectarian violence continues in Lahore and elsewhere in Pakistan, and Karachi, brought under paramilitary control in mid-2011, remains a violent city. It is hard to tell whether the lessening of violence in the capital city is due to increased police surveillance—parts of Islamabad are heavily fortified and secured—or whether a deal has been made with major extremist groups, whose training camps and schools remain untouched.

—The year 2011 began with a commemoration of Benazir's murder three years earlier, interrupted by the assassination on January 4 of her close associate, a secular PPP leader, Salmaan Taseer, the governor of Punjab, who had been outspoken in his criticism of an obscurantist blasphemy law. His security guard shot him down in broad daylight, claiming that Taseer's outspoken comments themselves were beyond the pale. The guard was a member of an elite Punjab security force, and the murder plunged liberal Pakistan deeper into despair, or hiding, or both. On January 26, a U.S. Central Intelligence Agency (CIA) operative killed two Pakistanis in Lahore, precipitating a minor crisis in U.S.-Pakistan relations, and in early May the sole Christian minister in Pakistan's cabinet was gunned down by assassins in Islamabad, raising fresh concerns about the rise of militant Islam.

—Five months later, on May 2, U.S. forces entered Pakistan and killed Osama bin Laden in Abbottabad, a city not far from Islamabad, in a secluded compound very close to the Pakistan Military Academy and other military facilities. It is not clear whether Pakistan (after many official denials that he was in the country) was completely ignorant of Osama's presence, or whether the military and intelligence services had covertly assisted the Americans in locating Osama, or whether they were "stockpiling" him for the moment when they could produce him and claim credit. All three theories put Pakistan in a bad light. Pakistanis were themselves unsure whether they should be more outraged at the Americans or at their own security establishment, but the balance tipped against the government and the military establishment after a successful raid by Islamic extremists, possibly affiliated with al Qaeda, on an important Pakistani navy and air force base in Karachi, which starkly revealed the continuing inability of the military to protect key military facilities and also raised questions about the security of Pakistan's nuclear arsenal.

—There will be more crises and atrocities, but the most recent was the gory murder of a crusading Pakistani journalist, Syed Saleem Shahzad, whose death shocked the media and produced sharp criticism of the ISI and the military.[11]

Analytical Considerations

Three problems need to be discussed as a prelude to examining the factors that will shape Pakistan's future. The first is the rhetoric of hope and failure, the second is sequencing, and the third is the difficulty of "sizing" the problem of Pakistan's future.

Those who make predictions about Pakistan generally fall into two categories: the pessimists, who believe that things will go from bad to worse, and the optimists, who believe that history is about to reverse itself.[12] The Pakistani American scholar Ahmed Faruqui is cautiously optimistic, noting that both France and Britain were mired in "cognitive dissonance" but eventually attained greatness. The consultants involved in the National Intelligence Council study on Pakistan's future were deeply skeptical about Pakistan. Many Indian commentators and some liberal Pakistanis and the Islamic conservatives believe that Pakistan is doomed by its very nature—its cultural DNA—and that transformation must occur or collapse is inevitable. For some, there is a little *Schadenfreude* in their expectations of failure.[13]

On the other hand, most contemporary writers hold out hope; they are cautiously optimistic, although the outright optimists are vanishing quickly.[14] They see Pakistan's known and important assets as evidence of at least the potential for positive transformation. In the words of a distinguished retired Pakistani diplomat, Tariq Fatemi, "Pakistan should be confident of its own abilities and optimistic about its future given its size, location and the qualities of its people. . . . So should the rest of the world, given that Pakistanis have been successful wherever they have gone, and in whatever endeavors they have undertaken."[15]

Hope is neither a policy nor a planning factor, but it is intimately related to success and failure.[16] The hope that things will or can be better is deeply embedded in the human condition, but it also is the mirror image of worst-case thinking, the anticipation of catastrophe. Without hope, there would be little change, in a world dominated by fatalists and pessimists.[17] On the other hand, excessive hope and blind optimism can be the basis for extremist and utopian movements.

Sequencing is yet another important conceptual issue, because it forces one to prioritize. As an Indian Institute for Defence Studies and Analyses study noted, all of the factors or variables shaping Pakistan's future are important.[18] But are any factors more important than the rest? Can we distinguish between those that are important but intractable and those that might be amenable to change? The fundamental question is whether some or all of the variables that will shape Pakistan's future must operate in a certain way to enable something resembling success to occur, but that question is also fundamentally hard to answer. It is evident that there are many factors that qualify as critical to Pakistan's future; none, however, are determinative in their own right. Internal social and economic decay is one factor, but so is the incoherence of the Pakistani political establishment; the political establishment's relations with the military, especially the army; and the role of friendly and hostile outside powers. At least six conditions are *necessary* for a stable Pakistan, but none are *sufficient*, and their sequencing and timing are critical.

My view is that modesty with regard to what can be done is the most appropriate stance because these are events that are inherently difficult to understand. To adapt the words of a former ambassador to the Soviet Union, "I don't know where Pakistan is heading, but once it gets there I will explain to you why it was inevitable."

Finally, there is a "sizing" issue. Scientists talk about sizing a problem—stating its parameters—as the first step toward solving it. In discussing the challenges and capabilities of Pakistan at the Bellagio workshop, Sir Hilary Synnott examined the metaphor of the glass that is alternatively described as being half-full or half-empty, noting that perhaps the real problem is that the glass is too large. That is another way of "sizing": if Pakistan's capabilities are inadequate, it may be because its ambitions are too great. This suggests that priorities are critically important and that Pakistan has to decide which of its challenges are urgent and which are secondary and can be deferred. State capacity then can be directed to the most important problems.

One aspect of this "too-large glass" is that Pakistan carries with it the enormous burden of the past. When it comes to its relations with its most important neighbor, India, and its most important international ally, the United States, its overarching narrative is that of victimhood. Pakistan's perception of itself as the victim of Hindu domination has led to the mother of all "trust deficits," a deficit that can never be eliminated because it stems from the deeply held belief that Indians are dominating, insincere, and untrustworthy. In this view, there is nothing that Pakistan can do to normalize the relationship because Indians/Hindus are essentially untrustworthy and have proven that to be true time and time again. My view is that if trust is a component of the problem, it is an eternal one. There can never be enough "trust" between sovereign states, but sovereign states might think of both trusting and verifying, which in Urdu can be translated as *aitemaad aur tasdeeq*.

With regard to U.S. actions, many Pakistanis believe that the Afghan war in the 1980s, the Pressler sanctions, and other harmful or duplicitous policies were instances of the United States using Pakistan and abandoning it. The war destabilized Pakistan, and the sanctions were imposed because of a nuclear program that Washington had earlier chosen to ignore. More recent examples include the U.S. invasion of Afghanistan to attack the Taliban (which itself had not done the United States any harm), pushing radical elements into Pakistan and further destabilizing the country. The U.S. narrative of all of these events is, of course, quite different, and there is a deep trust deficit between Pakistan and the United States as well as between Pakistan and India. With regard to both sets of relationships, any policy that assumes trust is likely to fail.

Four Clusters

When it comes to Pakistan, everything is important and everything is uncertain. To frame the discussion of the factors or variables that are most important in shaping Pakistan, nineteen of them are grouped into four clusters. The first cluster includes domestic concerns with respect to demographics, urbanization, the economy, and education; these are all closely related, and with the exception of the economy, which is subject to changes in policy, they are less mutable than others. A second cluster concerns the collective identity of Pakistan's people, who identify themselves and act on the basis of their regional, ethnic, and state affiliations. The third cluster concerns the ability of Pakistanis to work for or against a common goal or even to determine what their goals might be. Here are included the bureaucracy and structure of the government; the ability of its officials, notably the military; and the role of the increasingly important electronic and print media. The fourth and final cluster includes the policies and attitudes of important foreign states as well as the phenomenon of globalization. These are the factors that shape Pakistan's environment. Globalization, of course, penetrates into Pakistan in many ways and affects the other factors, shaping economic possibilities, influencing the ambitions and the very identities of Pakistan's citizens, and aiding or undercutting the workings of the state in different ways.

Demographics, Education, Class, and Economics

Demographics. Demographic trends, which are both predictable and difficult to change, are very clear for the next decade or more. They will shape Pakistan in several ways. First, Pakistan is undergoing a population boom, and it will soon have one of world's youngest populations. In some countries where birth rates remain much higher than mortality rates, mainly those in Africa and the Middle East and a few in Latin America and South Asia, growth rates are over 2 percent a year. Pakistan is one of the countries—along with Nepal, Yemen, Afghanistan, and the Democratic Republic of Congo—where the population doubles every generation, or roughly every thirty to thirty-five years.

As a 2009 British Council study noted, half of all Pakistanis are below the age of twenty and two-thirds of those have yet to reach their thirteenth birthday. Birth rates remain high even by regional standards, especially in rural areas. The population, which has tripled in less than fifty years, is likely to grow by another 85 million in the next twenty years. Pakistan's demographic transition from high to low mortality and fertility has stalled.[19] Today, Pakistan has some 180 million people, and the median age of the population is eighteen years. The country's population curve has a classic pyramid shape. For the next fifteen years it will be bottom-heavy. The sheer increase in population will require more food, more energy, and for men, more jobs. Also, an increase in the number of voters places increasing pressure on the state regarding its ability to deliver services, even basic ones such as education, let alone health care or welfare programs.

Second, Pakistan is becoming more urban. The urban population, which amounted to only 17 percent of the total population in 1951, constituted 35 percent of the total population (56 million people) in 2005. However, the rural population is so large and uneducated that some rural cities are not truly urban; they are instead rural or tribal complexes in areas designated as incorporated municipalities.[20] Instead of being calming and socializing, urbanization offers historical rivals a new battleground and in some cases brings previously separated groups into close proximity, where they battle in the urban context. This is especially the case in Karachi, which has strong political parties mobilized to provide resources for city residents and high levels of ethnic tension, with Mohajirs battling Sindhis (displaced from several Sindhi cities, where they used to be the majority population) and both battling the huge influx of Pashtuns, who are migrating from the war-torn provinces of the frontier. In Islamabad mosques such as the Lal Masjid became outposts of radical organizations located in nearby Swat and KP. Radical enclaves have flourished throughout Pakistan, notably in the cities, sometimes co-located with ethnic enclaves. The problem could be managed if police forces were adequate, but they are not. The police therefore find themselves handicapped by the links between politicians and militants and in some cases by the links between militants and the intelligence services.

Third, there is the question of the alleged demographic dividend—whether a population bulge can be used to Pakistan's advantage. The old debate between the Malthusians, who see population booms as catastrophic, and the pro-growth school, exemplified by Julian Simon, who argues that more people may be better, is resolved by the understanding that population growth alone does not cause domestic or internal conflict. Large-scale violence is almost never caused mainly by population growth; population growth is a challenge, not a threat. The critical mediating factors are state capacity and state response.

In this respect Pakistan fares badly. There has been a strong and positive response by the state and by local civil society institutions to demographic expansion in Indonesia, Malaysia, Bangladesh, and India, states that are pre-dominately Muslim or, in the case of India, that have a huge Muslim minor-ity population. These countries have adopted policies designed to foster tolerance and cohesion, although religious interpretative authority still resides within the conservative religious establishments. The conservative establish-ment is strong in Pakistan, and while Pakistan is culturally anchored in South Asia, its religious narrative is increasingly shaped by Islamist narratives derived from the more conservative Arab states and the Iranian revolutionary model.

Education and Youth. Education is the key to taking advantage of the demographic bulge. The theory is that this is an opportunity to educate the young and thereby leapfrog into a more advanced economy, one that features high-level manufacturing and services that can be marketed around the world. Here Pakistan fares worse than even India or Bangladesh, both of which greatly overestimate their capacity to educate the youth bulge.

Only half of Pakistan's children go to primary school, only a quarter go to secondary school, and just 5 percent receive any higher education.[21] There are no plans to create a national educational corps or to mount a crash pro-gram to provide training to the growing number of uneducated youth. It had been suggested that the Army Education Corps be deployed outside of the cantonments to form the core of a national educational system, but that sug-gestion was rejected by the military. Nor are there plans to bring to Pakistan large numbers of teachers and instructors, and the current security situation is such that few would be willing to live in the country if there were. As is well known, the gap has long been filled by the madrassas, religious schools of marginal practical utility in the modern world. Educating the youth bulge is a popular idea, but there has been no effective state action, either at the national or provincial level; instead, young people get whatever education they can. The likely results, as shown in survey after survey, are shocking: the youth bulge will turn into a bulge of the middle-aged and discontented, ill-equipped for the modern world. An important outlet for the ambitious and the adventurous will continue to be extremist movements, which have dis-placed the army as the largest recruiter of young Pakistani men.

The Pakistani government as a whole has been unable to address this fundamental failure of the state; instead, private educational systems flourish with little quality control. The rot starts at the top, where overambitious and unrealistic schemes to produce a flood of PhDs, who presumably would strengthen the overall education and research capacity of Pakistan, were promulgated. Those schemes ran against the political culture of Pakistan, which is decidedly not sympathetic to research, except in a few areas pertaining to national security, nor to mass education. Pakistan has the lowest intake of doctors in the world after Africa, and while the number of students in higher education, mostly funded by foreign organizations (notably the U.S. Agency for International Development) has grown, many of them do not return home when they have completed their studies. Researchers who *do* return to Pakistan do not find a congenial environment, despite some efforts to network them (for example, Pakistani researchers have very good U.S.-funded access to the global library system); therefore they often chose to leave again.[22] Without contact with the region's more dynamic educational institutions, Pakistani scholarship and research will stagnate. At its creation, Pakistan had one university with 600 students; it now has 143 universities with 1 million students. Present-day Pakistan was that part of the Indian Subcontinent where there was no tradition of education; it produced good soldiers and traders, not scholars. As the scholar Hamid Kizilbash observed, in Pakistan the message to scholars has always been "Your work is not important."[23] Kizilbash and others believe that the Pakistani government and the elites see education as a threat to them and to their control of the state. He also notes that there is a lost generation in Pakistan, which did not benefit from the reforms attempted after 2002. One result has been, in his words, "Those who were not privileged are finding different ways of punishing us."

The Middle-Class Myth. Vali Nasr, an American scholar and former U.S. State Department official, argues that the rise of a new middle class in predominately Muslim societies has the potential for a positive transformation of those states.[24] Noting that the vast numbers of Muslims are moderate or conservative in their social outlook, he sees the rise of a new Muslim middle class as leading to a new round of social and economic transformation in states that had been stuck in traditional ways for centuries; in his view, this new middle class could work easily and comfortably with the West. There will be 1 billion middle-class consumers in the Middle Eastern countries, including Pakistan, and they will be a force for openness, trade, and commerce with the rest of the world and within the Middle East itself. Some of this is true in Pakistan, where economic growth has been very limited but where a new middle class has tentatively emerged, energized and given a voice by the rapid expansion of electronic media, which have made the ordinary Pakistani far more aware of the world than before.

The logic behind the middle class as democracy's bastion is that it stands to benefit from political openness, trade, better relations with neighbors, and sympathy with other democracies, including the United States. Jonathan Paris notes that all of those conditions would require greater civilian control of foreign relations and domestic resources.[25] However, there is no inherent connection between an urban middle class and democracy. Middle classes in Europe, Latin America, and Asia have supported autocratic and even totalitarian governments. Pakistan has been no exception, and autocrats such as Zulfikar Ali Bhutto and Ayub Khan were popular in their day.

The growth of a middle class might be a necessary condition but it is not sufficient for Pakistan's democratization. India had (and has) democracy, even though it was one of the poorest countries in the world; China has a growing middle class, as does Vietnam, but the communist parties in both states will fight democratization tooth and nail while allowing consumerism to grow. The Pakistani army serves the same functional role as the communist parties of Vietnam and China: it regulates the system to protect both its own interests and what it sees as Pakistan's vital interests. In Pakistan, the economic base for a large middle class does not yet exist, the economy and society remain very pyramidal, and socioeconomic mobility is obstructed by a culture of feudalism. Above all, hopes for a new and rising middle class must be tempered by the economic facts of life: rampant inflation in Pakistan over the last few years threatens a large number of citizens, making their lives economically insecure just as the physical dangers increase because of rising terror attacks and, for many, the floods of 2010.

Finally, the middle classes, when they are dislocated and threatened, have also formed the basis for revolutionary movements throughout history, and those revolutions have not always been peaceful or democratic. Hope of reform led by the middle class is just that—a hope, not an assured process. Even a cursory example of historical parallels shows that a deprived and angry middle class can easily move into a revolutionary direction that rejects many of Pakistan's policies, embraces some form of extremism, and puts Pakistan on the path of authoritarianism or even disintegration.

The Economy. Countries often choose inappropriate economic strategies or strategies that once were serviceable but were made obsolete by changes in the international environment. Pakistan is no exception. Guided by the thinking of Sir Arthur Lewis, a British-educated West Indian, it opted for a policy of concentrating economic production in the state sector, then spinning the state enterprises off to the private sector. The policy was very successful early on. It created a significant upper and middle class in both East and West Pakistan, and at one point Pakistan was poised at the edge of middle-income status.

Pakistan's strategy ignored land and agriculture. First, it never tried to carry out meaningful land reform, as did many East Asian states and, to a lesser extent, India.[26] Second, there was a consistent policy of keeping wages low, harassing unions, and not investing in basic education.

The lack of education became a crippling problem as globalization intruded and Pakistan could not move up the value chain. The country's position on the Global Competitiveness Index was 92 (among 130 countries) in 2007–08, falling to 101 in 2009–10. The World Economic Forum's latest ranking for 2010–11 places Pakistan at 123 among 130 nations. A recent publication of the Competitive Support Fund notes that while Pakistan's economy grew at a healthy rate of 5 percent a year over the last five decades, that was not the case with the competitiveness of the country's goods and services or the value added of its manufactured goods.[27] Instead, it came to depend on the remittances of workers who found employment elsewhere, notably in the Persian Gulf and other Muslim countries. As a result, very few Pakistanis pay income taxes (about 3 million of a population of over 170 million), and the country's tax-to-GDP ratio is just 9 percent. The Pakistani argument is that that was justified since those few Pakistanis were extraordinarily productive, generating most of Pakistan's wealth and earning most of its foreign exchange.

The growth that *did* take place was misdirected. It favored the rich, with the result that Pakistan did not make the broad social and economic investments that would have prepared it for the onset of globalization, the linking of economies and peoples to the point that, in some respects, the world is truly flat. In Pakistan the educated and well-off urban population lives not so differently from their counterparts in other countries of similar income range.

After peaking between 2005 and 2007, most economic indicators have deteriorated dramatically. Pakistan's GDP growth, which in 2005 had reached a record of 7.7 percent, slowed down to an abysmal 1.6 percent during the recession in 2008 and has been estimated at only 2.6 percent in 2011. After increasing steadily over the last two decades, the economy has proven unable to cope with demographic growth, leading GDP per capita to stagnate at around $2,400 since 2007. In the meantime, further increasing the burden on the population, inflation has skyrocketed; it exceeded 20 percent in 2008. Never before have so many Pakistanis been looking for work; unemployment has now reached a twenty-year record of 14 percent, and it is estimated to continue to increase until 2013 at least. With labor and other productivity indicators having stagnated since 2006, it is not surprising that Pakistan is increasingly forced to rely on external sources. Inward foreign direct investment, which peaked in 2007 at $6 billion, is estimated to stabilize over the near future at $2 billion annually. Pakistan continues to import more than it exports, leading to a current account deficit, which was 2.2 percent in 2009.[28] More important, the country depends increasingly on the generosity of foreign donors. Following the humanitarian disasters of the 2005 Kashmir earthquake and the 2010 floods, external assistance reached unprecedented levels: in 2009 the State Bank of Pakistan recorded a record $4 billion in incoming development assistance, more than half of which came from multilateral organizations and developments banks.[29]

The social consequences of the country's weak and uneven economic growth are very serious. As Anita Weiss notes, the poor and rural inhabitants of Pakistan have been left with limited resources, clamoring for jobs and decent schools for their many children, plagued by inflation, and living—quite literally—in the dark. Pakistan's ranking in the United Nations Development Program's Human Development Index slipped from 120 in 1991 to 138 in 2002 and to 141 in 2009—worse than the Congo (136) and Myanmar (138) and only just above Swaziland (142) and Angola (143), all countries with far weaker economies.[30]

Weiss and other students of Pakistan argue that with greater numbers of people demanding goods and services and most of them living in densely populated cities, Pakistan's government must create economic space for the general population, not just the rich, and give priority to both economic and political justice. As greater numbers of citizens become aware through better education and the expansion of media coverage of what transpires elsewhere in the world, they will naturally expect—and demand—more. On balance, weighing the few positive elements of the economy against the many negatives, it is hard to project that Pakistan will increase its growth rate, that the current maldistribution of income will change, or that the political class will support a higher tax rate. Nor will outside assistance, including the Kerry-Lugar funds, make up the difference.

Pakistan now barely survives on its own income and most social services are paid for by foreign countries. Were aid to cease, the government would again be faced with financial failure. That happened in 2001, and it was only U.S. intervention after 9/11 that came to the rescue of the fiscally bankrupt state. Both Pakistan's leaders and foreign donors know that given its current tax structure and weak export capability, Pakistan will remain dependent on foreign assistance indefinitely.

In the past Pakistan managed because a literate population was not required for the kind of economic development strategy that it had chosen.

Today, however, an educated population can be a greater asset than oil or mineral resources, of which Pakistan has little, in any case. It does not export many high-value products, it provides only very low-level services (mainly through the export of unskilled workers and professionals to other countries), and it missed the opportunity to modernize its agricultural sector years ago. In fairness, its friends and supporters, notably the United States and China, have not been helpful in either assisting Pakistan to develop modern industries or allowing it to export goods and services, notably textiles, free of tariff restrictions.

One major feature of Pakistan's economy is the large share of the budget spent on defense. Pakistan increased its defense budget by nearly 17 percent, to a total $5.17 billion, for 2010–11 to keep pace with inflation and new demand for troops and combat operations in Balochistan, tribal areas such as North and South Waziristan, and Khyber Pakhtunkhwa. Retired general Talat Masood, one of the most respected commentators on security policy, has said that spending on the Eastern (Indian) front remains constant and that the increase is directly related to new counterinsurgency requirements. Since 2001 Pakistan has also received some $15 billion in direct payments from the United States, two-thirds of it related to security measures.[31]

From the mid-1990s, beginning with General Jehangir Karamat, successive army chiefs have been aware that Pakistan's weak economy made it difficult to keep troop levels high, maintain a ready force vis-à-vis India, and purchase sufficient modern equipment. Although wrapped up in the rhetoric that Pakistan will meet every military contingency and that Pakistani courage and skill will compensate for inadequate arms vis-à-vis India, every recent army chief has had to confront the budget problem and some have supported negotiations with India. Budget problems have been further complicated by the advent of nuclear weapons; new combat requirements in Balochistan, Khyber Pakhtunkhwa, and the tribal belt; and the absence of transparency, which rules out informed debate on defense spending—the largest portion of the budget.

Of the factors in this cluster, it would seem that Pakistan's economy would be the easiest for policymakers to shape, as the country has shown high growth rates in the past. That may no longer be possible, as Pakistan may have missed whatever opportunities were present when the world economy started to globalize rapidly. It was unprepared in terms of the skill and educational level of its workforce, its domestic political order was too unstable, and it had little in terms of extractive resources. Pakistan has already slipped behind Bangladesh and India in per capita income, and the gap is likely to grow.

Identity

At their core, nations are ideas and the idea of Pakistan has been in flux since it was first promulgated in the 1930s. We look at three elements of Pakistan's identity: the continuing debate over the meaning of Pakistan and what it means to be a Pakistani, the special difficulty of reconciling this identity with Islam, and regional and subnational challenges to the idea of Pakistan.[32]

The Still-Contested Idea of Pakistan. Different ideas of Pakistan are held by the establishment, the army, different ethnic and linguistic groups, different Islamic groups (especially with respect to internal sectarian disputes), and Pakistan's precariously situated minorities (who favor a secular state). A new challenge comes from an old quarter: the growth of class awareness and differences among Pakistanis, a development that both Islamists and secularists seek to exploit. In many ways the Islamist movement resembles a class revolutionary movement. The avowedly secular Muttahida Qaumi Movement (MQM) claims to be moving out of its urban Sindh and Karachi base into the Punjab and elsewhere, gathering support among Pakistan's middle classes and challenging the Pakistan People's Party. The discussion below deals first with the continuing seventy-year-old debate over what it means to be Pakistani and whether new meanings will drive out what remains of national identity and cohesion and then with identity issues that stem from ethnolinguistic and sectarian challenges to Jinnah's idea of Pakistan.

Among Pakistan's elites there is an intense debate over the purpose and meaning of Pakistan, triggered by the widespread sense that things have gone very wrong. This is notable among Pakistan's young people, who do not share the optimism of their cohorts in other Asian states. The English-language media are filled with laments about intolerance, bigotry, and even racism and the rise in violence directed against religious minorities, foreigners, and linguistic outsiders. Long-time visitors to Pakistan, whether Western or Asian, comment that this is not the Pakistan of the 1970s, let alone of the tranquil 1960s.[33]

Can Pakistan continue with this degree of discontent? It probably can, but the discontent is yet another reason for explosion in the distant future. The new normal is abnormal, and even greater divisions about the purpose and meaning of Pakistan can be expected.

Ethnolinguistic Ambitions. Reports of a new breakup of Pakistan because of ethnic dissent are not to be taken seriously for the next five years.[34] Pakistan is a very diverse state. It contains many groups, as does India, some of which have attributes of nations: their own language, culture, and even identity. Some polls seems to show that Pakistanis regard themselves as Pakistanis first, and Punjabis, Pashtuns, Baloch, Sindhis, or Mohajirs second, although the Pew Global Affairs Project shows that Sindhis have a markedly weaker sense of themselves as Pakistanis than as Sindhis.[35] Polling in Pakistan is suspect, especially on such a sensitive issue, and in any case powerful and disciplined minorities can shape the outcomes of identity disputes no matter what the polls say.

Pakistan's ethnic groups are not quite comparable, but all except Punjabis have faced the wrath of the central government as they generated separatist or autonomist movements.[36] The Baloch are a tribal society, Sindhis are predominately rural, Mohajirs are overwhelmingly urban (and displaced Sindhis are concentrated in Karachi and several cities in Sindh). Until now the army has been used only against these groups, but with the 2010 movement of the army into South Waziristan and other parts of the province of Khyber Pakhtunkhwa (formerly North-West Frontier Province), Pashtuns also have squared off against the military, most importantly in the form of the Tehrik-e-Taliban Pakistan (TTP), the "Pakistan Taliban."

The rise of ethnic consciousness and the more conciliatory position of the current government in Islamabad could, optimistically, sustain a new balance in Pakistan. New provincial centers of power could emerge, each sustained by reinvigorated civil society and expanding media. The 2010 National Finance Commission Award could lead to new rules and procdedures for revenue sharing, returning Pakistan to something resembling its original federal structure. However, few of the provinces—except Punjab—have the administrative capacity to take advantage of their new powers and responsibilities. Should new provinces be created there is a theoretical possibility that Punjab's power will be balanced. Right now it holds a majority stake in the political system: 54 percent (148) of the 272 seats in the National Assembly are reserved for the province. Punjabis, who at 44 percent represent the largest ethnolinguistic group, maintain a central, if not overrepresented, position across a range of indicators: for example, they represent 51 percent of the bureaucracy and 70 percent of the retired officer cadre.[37] Given the disproportionate power of the Punjab, there is unlikely to be a major constitutional adjustment in the next five years, although there is growing support for splitting off parts of the Punjab into separate provinces. That would be an important step toward devolution, and it might have the support of the army if it were, on balance, to reduce the power of the Punjab, thereby strengthening the hand of the army.

In chapter 16 of this volume, Josh White argues that the Pakistani state can contain separatist forces. With the exception of the Bengali uprising in 1971, when West Pakistani elites miscalculated their ability to crush the uprising and did not expect India to interfere militarily to support it, Pakistan's leaders have contained nationalist and separatist movements, albeit harshly at times. Right now there are insurgencies in Balochistan and among the Pashtuns. India is suspected—without much evidence—of continuing support for the Baloch, but the major threat now comes from the Pashtuns. The most potent movements combine religion and ethnicity, and Pakistanis dread the possibility that the combination of religious passion, territorial claims, and linguistic and cultural commonality will appear in the form of the Pashtun–New Taliban movement sweeping KP, with violent echoes among the larger Pashtun population, especially those living in Karachi.

As White notes, the Pakistani Taliban have emerged as a new vehicle for the expression of Pashtun grievances, but they have been careful to portray themselves solely in religious, not ethnic, terms. That is perhaps because they consider religious mobilization to be more effective than ethnic mobilization or perhaps because their ranks are increasingly supplemented by Punjabis from Kashmir and sectarian-oriented organizations.

The Punjab is the only province that has not yet had forces deployed in significant numbers for internal security reasons, partly because the state is heavily garrisoned by military units facing India. The security problem is especially sensitive in Punjab: it is the army's heartland, the country's population center, and the site of the most intense sectarian violence. It also has experienced savage attacks against seemingly innocuous targets, such as the Sri Lankan cricket team in 2009, and against several key state icons: a navy school, the police training academy, and branches of the ISI and other intelligence services. Without improvement in the police force, the army is reluctant to intervene and turns a blind eye, along with the politicians, to the mayhem that has overtaken most of the large cities, notably Lahore. When stories about the mayhem were published in the international press, the government's reaction and that of the military was to blame the *New York Times* and other newspapers for their anti-Pakistan tilt, suggesting that India or other foreign hands might be involved. In fact, some of the stories were leaked to foreign media by the policemen of Punjab, who did not receive support from provincial or national governments, let alone the army.

Radical Islamists and Sectarianism. Islam and "Islamic" grievances such as the Israel-Palestinian dispute have always been at the heart of a country that was founded as a homeland for Muslims. However, three events have accelerated the rise of militant Islam. The first was the Iranian revolution, which provided a potent model for Sunnis as well as Shiites. The second was the expansion of direct support for radical Islamists by the army, both within Pakistan and abroad. The third was the trauma of the U.S. reaction (and that of much of the West) to the 9/11 terrorist attacks and the related invasion of Iraq and Afghanistan.

Those developments expose a convoluted and dangerous relationship between the state and Islam that is not easily resolved. Like Israel, Pakistan was conceived as a refuge for a persecuted religious minority, but it has had difficulty in defining the proper role of religion in the state and the balance between the two. There is no debate in Pakistan on whether there should be a role for Islam; the question is the extent to which religion should regulate personal life and the degree to which foreign policy should be guided by Pakistan's Muslim identity. On both counts, sectarian differences between Sunni and Shia lead Pakistanis to hold different views.

Pakistan has always sought good relations with other Muslim countries and with Muslim minorities (notably in India and more recently in Bosnia), and there is a widespread belief among Pakistanis that Pakistan has a legitimate and natural interest in good relations with Muslim states everywhere. From the beginning it has also supported separatist and independence movements in India-controlled Kashmir and has backed the fundamentalist Taliban in Afghanistan.[38]

The problem is not that most Pakistanis are Muslims and adhere to deep religious beliefs; it is that those beliefs have been exploited by state bureaucracies—notably the army—that support groups whose beliefs they consider ideologically harmonious with theirs and that view militants primarily in instrumental terms, as tools to advance Pakistan's national interests. For those who support such strategies, this is seen as a legitimate expression of Pakistan's Islamic identity, analogous to the support that the West, notably the United States, gives to democratic groups around the world. Thus, support for Islamists in domestic politics as well as abroad is a civilizational responsibility, not an act of terrorism.

It is not Islam or religion that is the problem; it is how religion has been exploited by the state. The genie has escaped, and much of Pakistan's future will be determined by the effort to contain violent and extremist Islamist groups. The most pessimistic of Pakistanis feel that the battle has been lost, and some seek refuge elsewhere. Pakistan is far from a theocracy—the Islamists are at each other's throats too much for that—but they are driving Pakistan toward a different kind of civil war, one in which religion and sectarian allegiances determine which side an individual is on.[39]

Is the process of creeping Islamization irreversible? Pakistanis are saturated with Islamist slogans. The country was always quite religious, and what is happening in Pakistan is similar to the growing religiosity seen elsewhere, not only in the Muslim world, but also in Israel (the second state formed on the basis of religious identification and as a homeland for a persecuted minority) and the United States—although not in Europe, Latin America, or Southeast Asia.

The admixture of religion and politics is potent, but even some of Pakistan's liberals, who despair at the creeping Islamization of their country, retain the hope that the trend is reversible, given good leadership. Pervez Hoodbhoy, the country's most distinguished scientist-commentator, concludes a widely distributed paper by writing:

> I shall end this rather grim essay on an optimistic note: the forces of irrationality will surely cancel themselves out because they act in random directions, whereas reason pulls in only one. History leads us to believe that reason will triumph over unreason, and humans will continue their evolution towards a higher and better species. Ultimately, it will not matter whether we are Pakistanis, Indians, Kashmiris, or whatever. Using ways that we cannot currently anticipate, people will somehow overcome their primal impulses of territoriality, tribalism, religion and nationalism. But for now this must be just a hypothesis.[40]

The idea of a secular, moderate, and democratic Pakistan is under attack from ethnic groups and religious extremists, and Jinnah's vision is not widely accepted, let alone understood, outside the shrinking liberal community. The goal of a more or less secular state, characterized by ethnic tolerance, may be unattainable. Unless there is a radical transformation by the government in the form of a state that supports the Jinnah/liberal idea of Pakistan by word and deed, the erosion of the moral authority of the state will continue and the debate over the purpose of Pakistan will become increasingly fractious.

State Coherence

If nations are ideas, states are bureaucracies. In Pakistan, one bureaucratic organization that neither runs Pakistan effectively nor allows any other organization to do so—the army—has dominated the state. Yet, the actual capacity of the Pakistani state has eroded over the last sixty years. That is evident in comparing Pakistan—the integrity and competence of the state and its supporting institutions, such as the political parties, the bureaucracy, and even the judiciary—with similar states.

Leadership and Political Parties. Pakistan's political parties lack both a democratic process and the ability to aggregate interests; most are only vehicles for individuals or narrow social classes. Even in the largest and most open of the parties, elections within the organization are pro forma. When asked shortly before her death, Benazir Bhutto told me that the Pakistan People's Party was not ready for internal democracy, that it needed a strong leader (herself) to keep its factions together and to develop strategies to protect the party's integrity from assaults by state intelligence agencies. That attitude is not changing. Some of the urban parties, like the Muttahida Qaumi Movement, appeal more to middle-class interests than to clan or family loyalty. But even the MQM has a strong ethnic base in the Mohajirs and their descendants, who are migrants from North and Central India.

Pakistan's political pattern has alternated between weak, unstable democratic governments and benign authoritarian governments, usually led by the army, and that pattern is likely to continue to define Pakistan over the next five years. The present democratic government is not popular, but there is no groundswell for its replacement by either another military leader or a civilian dictator. Periodically, political figures emerged who have been able to inspire and arouse the public to pursue a progressive scenario for Pakistan: for a time in the early 1970s, Zulfikar Ali Bhutto transformed the country's political discourse and reconfigured politics; after 1998, Benazir Bhutto and Nawaz Sharif acquired popular electoral mandates that might have broken the familiar mold of democratic politics; and General Musharraf was initially widely welcomed in the expectation that he would use his presidency to create a fresh political ethos and attract a new breed of politicians. But all eventually forfeited the public's confidence.

As noted by some of the participants in the Bellagio workshop and reflected in their chapters in this volume, a transformation of Pakistan's political system cannot be entirely ruled out. The mass support in 2007 and 2008 for a lawyers' movement that championed an independent judiciary and democratic government suggests that a politically passive population can be mobilized for political action. The judiciary's recent assertiveness, together with newly enacted constitutional changes restoring a parliamentary system, could conceivably lead to a stronger system of institutional checks and balances. Some observers see in these developments an important step toward the realization of a progressive democratic scenario. Others worry that an arrogant, arbitrary judiciary in league with the military or an autocratic party leader can become a powerful instrument of repression.

Class disparities and inequities and the absence of a social safety net leave Pakistan with the basic ingredients for political and social upheaval. Pakistanis have reason to doubt that either the current civilian regime or a military-led government is interested in addressing the causes of their discontent.

An effective leader, with access to the liberalized print and electronic media, could tap into the frustrations that have arisen from severe energy and water shortages, sectarian violence, high food prices, and generalized anger with the United States and the West, not to mention India. High unemployment among the country's youth creates an especially volatile body of participants in extremist movements. For the time being, ethnic differences, persistent patron-client relations, and powerful security forces limit the growth of such national or even regional movements. While that could change quickly as a result of rising extremist forces—or if the military were to be compromised or the middle class to lose its confidence in the system—most Bellagio participants agreed that at least for the next five years, extreme changes are unlikely.

The Military. For years the military's role in Pakistan has been central.[41] It is not only an army of Pakistan but an army of one province, the Punjab, which is grossly overrepresented in both the officer corps and among the *jawans* (rank-and-file soldiers). So when the army intervenes politically, it does not do so merely as a state bureaucracy; any intervention also affects Punjab's relations with all of the other provinces.

Until recently the most vehement critics of Pakistan's military were Pakistani liberals and Indians. Now the Western press also finds fault, in part because of evidence of the army's link to terror groups that operate abroad and because of its support for the Afghan Taliban through the ISI.[42]

Three aspects of the army's centrality are important for Pakistan's future.[43] They are the army's understanding of strategic threats to the country, notably its preoccupation with India; the army's relationship to civilian authority; and, most recently, the army's relationship with militant and extremist groups and radical Islamists, although its use of militants was notable in Kashmir in 1947 and in East Pakistan in 1971.

The Army and India. An obsession with India accompanied the birth of the Pakistan army. Before 1947 its officers and *jawans* and units were literally part of the Indian army, it fought the Indian army in 1947, and it sees India behind every threat to Pakistan. That some threats are real does not excuse the army's collective obsession, which distorts its professional military judgment and shapes its views toward those who do not see India as the central problem facing Pakistan or who believe that a negotiated settlement with India would be Pakistan's best option. That view has never taken deep root in Pakistan, in part because India itself has generally pursued a tough line toward Pakistan.

The Army and Civilian Authority. As Aqil Shah writes in chapter 12 of this book, given history's sticky footprints Pakistan is unlikely to extricate itself from the path-dependent pattern of a military-dominated state with an essentially revisionist foreign policy formed in the country's foundational first decade after independence. The historical sources of this "garrison state," including the perceived threat from India and the powerful (praetorian) military spawned by that threat, will continue to make exits to alternative futures less likely.

Shah and others see several futures ahead, the first one being the "freezing" of the political system in the intermediate, gray zone between full-fledged democracy and military autocracy. While exerting sustained civilian control over the military poses a formidable challenge for any transitional democracy, in this scenario—wherein the civilian government is responsible for and under pressure to tackle broad governance issues squarely (especially the potentially destabilizing economic and energy crises)—the military will continue to operate in the shadows and rattle its sabers at will to prevent undesirable outcomes in domestic politics and foreign policy. New centers of power, such as the judiciary, might exert a countervailing democratic effect and help ensure the rule of law. But the scenario of more military mediation of civilian crises will reproduce the depressingly familiar pattern of civil-military relations under formal elected rule (which is corrosive to democracy).

A second possible future involving the civil-military relationship would be the slow and steady stabilization of democracy, but that would require some agreement between the two dominant parties and an increase in their coherence and ability to govern. Their recent bipartisan efforts to consolidate parliamentary democracy by reversing authoritarian prerogatives in the Constitution—such as the infamous Article 58(2)B, which empowered the president to arbitrarily dismiss an elected government—and conceding substantive provincial autonomy augur well for democratization. The two parties have so far resisted openly "knocking on the garrisons' doors" as they did in the 1990s. Recent reports of an escalating war of words between the two sides that concerns, among other issues, militancy and terrorism in Pakistan Muslim League–controlled Punjab province, may yet erode the uneasy peace. But, on the whole, they appear to have learned from experience that it is better to play by the rules of the game and continue to tolerate each other rather than risk destabilizing the system and losing power to the military for another decade.

On the basis of the experience of the Zardari government, some form of democratic stability is likely if civilians continue to work within a competitive electoral process while slowly reforming the legal and constitutional framework that disfigured the 1973 Constitution. While they continue to defer to the armed forces on critical strategic issues, politicians are acquiring a bit more political space and the now-common practice of working together in coalition governments both at the center and in most of the provinces will strengthen their understanding of how democracies operate.

But the margin for error is thin. It is true that the armed forces do not want to come back to power soon and that civilian governments are strengthened by a new interest in democratic reform by the United States. However, other important backers, such as China and a few of the Gulf states, are not interested in democracy and are not bothered by authoritarian or military rule as long as order is maintained. It may also be that the Islamist parties are being tamed by their participation in local, provincial, and national elections. Twice, once in 1970 and again in 1997, moderate mainstream parties have stalled the Islamists in elections. And while the Jamaat-e-Islami boycotted the 2008 ballot, the relatively more successful Jamiat Ulema-e-Islam–Fazl-ur-Rehman (JUI-F), won only six of the 108 national assembly seats that it contested. However, this moderating trend has to be balanced by the poor economic performance of the Zardari government, the structural problems that it faces in merely governing, and in the growth of extra-parliamentary forces on the right, as evidenced by increased social violence, assassination, and terrorism.

However, as Aqil Shah observes, institutionalization of democracy requires more than balancing just the civilian side of the equation. It also needs a military committed in terms of both behavior and attitude to taking a subordinate role in a democratic framework. The military's behavior appears to have changed since it withdrew from government, but it is important to recall that it did not withdraw to the barracks because of a shift in its core praetorian ethos. Neither the "professionalism" of the army chief, General Ashfaq Parvez Kayani, nor Musharraf's lack of professional restraint can explain the military's recent political behavior. In fact, the Pakistani army's problem has never been "professionalism" per se. Shah is correct when he describes the army as having a particular brand of tutelary professionalism that gives it a sense of entitlement over the polity and structures its responses to changes in the surrounding political environment.

Shah's third and most drastic scenario is that of a military coup d'état followed by military-led authoritarian rule. There are both domestic and international factors that may counteract, if not eliminate, this option. If the past is any guide, the military usually waits at least half a decade or so for its next intervention. Pakistan's revived civil society (lawyers' associations, human rights groups, NGOs, and sections of the media) and more democratically oriented parties will, under an optimistic scenario, probably ensure that the military has no real occasion to openly undermine or overthrow an elected government.

I part company with many in Pakistan who believe that in managing the civil-military relationship, it is wrong to "bring the army in to keep it out" through such arrangements as the National Security Council (NSC). As I wrote in 1985, the army cannot be pushed out of power and be expected to stay there: its withdrawal from politics must be staged, in both senses of the word, and demonstrated civilian competence must replace it gradually as it withdraws from each sector of society.[44] That cannot happen in some spheres, such as natural disaster relief, in which the army is the only institution that has the capacity to manage a crisis. This was the case with the October 8, 2005, earthquake that devastated parts of the NWFP and Pakistan-administered Kashmir; the pattern was repeated with the 2010 earthquake.

Civilian capacity cannot be built up overnight, and adopting an NSC arrangement that has improving the education system and strengthening civilian institutions as part of its core mission would not only solve the serious problem of policy coordination but would also socialize civilians in decisions that had previously been the exclusive responsibility of the armed forces. Senior retired generals and officials have spoken and written about expanding the NSC's role to improve the link between civilian leaders and the army, but nothing has been done to implement those ideas.

The Military and Internal Militancy. Pakistan could, theoretically, be on the path blazed by several countries around the world, most recently in South America. There, the ouster of the military from power and, crucially, the lasting reduction of military autonomy were linked to cessation of the internal threats that had originally induced the military to take control of the political system. But Pakistan's dilemma is not only that are there new and serious domestic threats but also that the external threat remains. The army's first reaction was to see an Indian hand behind domestic terrorist and separatist groups. That was not an implausible response, given Indian involvement in the East Pakistan movement. But the irony is that the Pakistan military fostered many of those groups itself and it now faces a classic case of blowback.[45]

The army is gearing up for a systematic expansion of its counterinsurgency operations[46] after earlier dismissing such operations in favor of its traditional "low-intensity conflict" strategy, which involved quick in-and-out operations. Now the military realizes that it must have a strong civilian component to counter insurgents who are deeply embedded in the frontier, a view that is widely reflected in recent army and military writing on the subject.[47] An even more consequential task, although it has yet to be addressed by the military, is that of containing and eliminating groups that have targeted the state (like the Tehrik-e-Taliban in the frontier) but are based in Punjab. The evidence so far is that the army has avoided doing so, pleading that it is badly overstretched in the frontier as it is. The army has suffered huge casualties there, and it finds itself hard-pressed to fight against a Pashtun enemy with a Punjabi army; as one close observer of the process has reported, officers returning from combat in

Waziristan use the term "invaders" to describe their presence there. They are not proud of their role, but given the open challenge to the state in general and to the army in particular, this domestic insurgency is a more immediate threat than India.

An even greater problem for the army is its continued ties to the militant/terrorist group Lashkar-e-Tayyiba, which it created for the express purpose of pressuring India in Kashmir. While the LeT refrains from targeting the army and the state of Pakistan and the army uses the LeT to balance more radical groups, the LeT itself may be growing in its ambitions and capabilities. It has already conducted one politically catastrophic attack on India in Mumbai (putting the United States more firmly on India's side in the regional terror wars). Senior Pakistan intelligence officials freely admit that the ISI "alumni association" is out of control, a truthful statement but one that is hardly comforting to outsiders.

Basic Governance. One of the most devastating developments in Pakistan over the last forty years has been the systematic weakening of the state itself. This is well-documented, and the trend has not and perhaps cannot be reversed.[48] It is one of Pakistan's critical weaknesses, worsened by the attempts of the army to carry out functions ordinarily executed by civilians. This goes beyond "civil-military relations"; it pertains to the state's capacity to tax, to educate, and to maintain law and order and the ability to make strategic policy, integrating military, political, economic, and administrative concerns through a central decisionmaking process. The state's weakness can be measured in terms of Pakistan's low ranking on almost every governance indicator (crime, corruption, attitude toward the state) and its high ranking on the Failed State Index, where it slipped from twelfth place in 2007 to the current top 10 and "critical" status.[49] Designating Pakistan as "critical" is deceptive; even though the state has lost much of its organizational integrity, it is still a formidable entity, especially compared with states such as the hollowed-out Afghanistan.

Nevertheless, demands on the state are growing as its capacity shrinks, and the population continues to expand at a stunning rate. This could be a race that is already lost. Especially alarming is the incoherence at the very top: in crisis after crisis, especially in security affairs, the state's decisionmaking system has failed. Whether with respect to Kargil, the Mumbai attack, the response to 9/11, or the failed attempt to get negotiations started again with India (which reflects the incapacity of the Pakistan government to demonstrate to India and others that it has its militants under control), there is ineffectiveness. It stems in part from the civil-military divide but also from the loss of a great inheritance from the Raj: a civil service that functioned and a working relationship between civil servants and politicians. The root cause, of course, is the military's supersession of both politicians and bureaucrats; so, again, basic reform has to track back to the military's disproportionate role in governance, which may be very hard to reverse. It will take years, if not decades, and a long period of peace, even if civilian competence is allowed to grow.

The Judiciary and the Lawyers. The judiciary and the legal profession barely qualify as major factors in shaping Pakistan's future. It is true that the actions of judges, especially the chief justice, predicated a crisis in Musharraf's government and that the Lawyers' March contributed to his downfall, but there is no evidence that, as institutions, the courts or the lawyers will not support the establishment mainstream and will not be strongly influenced by army views. While Chief Justice Chaudhry is very popular and he is a true revolutionary in the current Pakistani context and wants to move Pakistan to a normal democracy in one jump, there is no support for that strategy from either the military or the politicians.

Pakistan inherited a great Western legal tradition, and its lawyers are among the best in the world, but they are constrained. They do not have enduring street power and the idea of the law as supreme is not generally respected in a country where force and coercion play major roles. Judges and lawyers have also been at the forefront in rationalizing the army's regime in the name of stability. On occasion they have stood up to individual military leaders but never to the army as an institution.

The New Media. In U.S. Secretary of State Hillary Clinton's felicitous phrase, the new media have created a new global nervous system. For years, Pakistan's governments used state-controlled media to bombard and indoctrinate the public. There was an obsession with Palestine and, closer to home, with Kashmir. Taking an assertive stand on these issues was part of Pakistan's national identity. Before Benazir's reforms, the Pakistani press was tightly controlled and several media outlets—notably television and radio—were state owned and operated.

Now both the medium and the messages are ambiguous. Pakistan is being flooded with confusing and contradictory images, and Pakistan as well as "Islam" have become global media targets. That has affected educated Pakistanis deeply; they feel that the Western media have unfairly singled out their country and that they are victims of a media conspiracy. Pakistan's own media—especially cable television—have not produced quality analysis of important events, and the liberalization of the press, which often is hailed as a sign of the strength of civil society, has an underside in Pakistan. As C. Christine Fair notes in chapter 4, Pakistan's private media appear vibrant and diverse, with networks such as Geo TV being world class, but on issues of national security and contentious domestic affairs, they are heavily self-censored and influenced by commentators with ties to the military and intelligence agencies.

It is evident that new social media and communication methods, such as short message service (SMS) text messaging, are disseminating information quickly and that they help mobilize civil society beyond the grasp of the state, something that senior generals view with frustration and concern. Yet the new mobilization capacity strengthens not only liberal forces—radical and Islamist groups have also used the neutral technology very successfully. The net impact of media liberalization is therefore still unknown, and it is an important question that deserves objective, empirical study.

The press and the new media are thus a pack of wild cards when it comes to mobilizing and potentially transforming Pakistan. The new media and social networks supplant some of the traditional face-to-face patterns of influence and even the impact of Friday sermons in the mosques, balancing traditional Pakistani social conservatism. However, conservatism still reigns in the mosques and madrassas, where the sermons range from the irrelevant to the hard-line.[50]

Transfer of Power. Finally, given the fact that one of Pakistan's core problems has been political instability and its inability to manage an orderly transfer of power (its second free election was not until 1988, the first having resulted in civil war in 1970), it is important to look at the way in which one government or regime yields to another. Both Islamist and leftist critics argue, not without justification, that it hardly matters who governs in Pakistan. But the prospect of an orderly transfer of power, one in which winners and losers accept the results and move on, is at the very core of the process of normal political change, and it has been absent in Pakistan since the nation's formation.

The way that power is transferred in Pakistan seems to have undergone some changes. If the country proceeds along its current path, in which the idea of free elections abiding (mostly) by the law and a more normal civil-military relationship has become entrenched, that would be a major change. In the past, there was only the issue of how much the army would tolerate before it stepped in, followed by the rationalizations of compliant lawyers and politicians eager to claim a tiny place at the political table.

Musharraf's accession to power was in the classic pattern: an incompetent democratic government was displaced by a personally ambitious general, to wide international uninterest and with wide domestic support, both due to Nawaz's transparent incompetence and drive to gain power. He was on the road to becoming a dictator; Musharraf intervened in the name of competent government and then proceeded to imagine himself a latter-day Ayub Khan.

The transition to Zardari also followed a pattern. The army was discredited, as it had been under Ayub, Yahya, and Zia. But this time Pakistan was far more important internationally, and influential outsiders shaped and then bungled the transition. Their intention was not to restore real democracy to Pakistan but to keep Musharraf in power, and the United States and Great Britain worked out an arrangement whereby Musharraf would allow Benazir Bhutto to return to Pakistan, contest the election, and probably again become prime minister, in an arrangement dominated by President Musharraf. U.S. ambassador Ryan Crocker and British high commissioner Mark Lyall Grant brokered the deal, but neither government thought it necessary to include other Pakistani politicians, in effect making Benazir the target not only of those who opposed her but of elements in Pakistan that wanted to force Musharraf out as president.[51]

The result, after Benazir's death and Musharraf's disgrace, was a weak president and a weak prime minister—an outcome that was acceptable to the army and to Pakistan's foreign patrons. However, the Zardari/Gilani government showed by 2010 that even a weak government can initiate major reforms, and in some cases it has received support from opposition parties as well as the army's tolerance.

To summarize, indicators of the competence of the Pakistani state are generally negative. Despite the efforts of the Zardari administration to reform the system, all of the levers of power—the civil bureaucracy, the higher decision-making system, and the public-private interface—are incoherent. The state has yet to regain the integrity that it had forty or fifty years ago, even though it is called on to do much more in terms of economic development and public administration. Corruption is rife, but it would be acceptable if the government were able to deliver the basic services expected of a modern state. The media and the NGO community cannot replace the state; nonetheless, fundamental reform is not supported by the strongest institution of all, the army.

External and Global Factors

While the current cliché seems to be that Pakistanis are ultimately responsible for their own fate and they may have an exaggerated view of the pernicious role of outsiders, external factors do shape Pakistan to an untoward degree. The following discussion treats separately the roles of Afghanistan, the United States, China, and India as well as the impact of globalization and Pakistan's status as a nuclear weapons state.

Afghanistan. There has always been a two-way flow between Pakistan and Afghanistan. For years, Pakistan has played a role in Afghan politics, largely through its support of the Taliban—first overt, now covert—but there is also a reverse flow. Pakistan's future will be shaped by developments in Afghanistan, which track back to Pakistan in three ways: Indian involvement in the country, the U.S. presence there, and the connection between Afghanistan and Pakistan created by the Pashtun population, whose traditional homeland spans the border. Of the states with an interest in Afghanistan, only Pakistan's can be said to be vital because the pan-Pashtun movement challenges the legitimacy of Pakistan's borders as well as the original idea/identity of Pakistan, in which unity among South Asian Muslims is regarded as more important than ethnic parochialism.

Several years ago, in its final published report on Pakistan, the National Intelligence Council (NIC) assessed the country not in terms of its own qualities (about which earlier NIC studies were sharply alarmist) but entirely in terms of its relationship with Afghanistan.[52] That approach reflected changes in U.S. priorities. With the presence of U.S. forces in Afghanistan, Pakistan's stability and its future are important but secondary concerns. According to conversations that I had with U.S. officials in 2010 and 2011, even India's role in Afghanistan—or India-Pakistan relations, which are so vital to Islamabad—are on some vague "to do" list of senior U.S. officials and receive little attention.

Pakistanis are properly concerned about the absence of a clear U.S. goal in Afghanistan. Some Pakistanis believe that the United States is there to balance Pakistani power, perhaps by neutralizing Pakistan's nuclear arsenal, or to support an expanded Indian presence; others think Washington's objective is to contain China, Pakistan's friend. Confused signals from U.S. policymakers exacerbate the problem. Pakistan's minimum goals are to reduce the Indian threat in Afghanistan and to ensure that the regime in Kabul is not hostile to Pakistan—and there is wide consensus that stability in the Pashtun population, which overlaps Pakistan and Afghanistan, is a vital interest.

On June 22, 2011, President Barack Obama announced that a drawdown of U.S. forces from Afghanistan would begin in July 2011, with the expected withdrawal of 33,000 troops by 2012. In White House briefings, administration spokespersons claimed that there will be a long-term U.S. presence for an indeterminate period, at an indeterminate level. That presence will not be a Korea-like, firm alliance—Afghanistan will not become a member of NATO—but neither will it amount to nothing. While intermediate options are being considered, it is very difficult to imagine what Afghanistan will look like even in one year—that is, by mid-2012—as the United States enters into still another national debate about its purpose and goal in Afghanistan, this one influenced by the fact of Osama bin Laden's death.

From Pakistan's perspective, if the Afghan Taliban were to assume power militarily or politically or enter into a coalition with elements of the Kabul government, the odds of a stable arrangement would be slim. If one factors in the Taliban's radical allies—the "syndicate," as a White House official called them in December 2010—then several groups will be competing for influence in Afghanistan, in opposition to the Western-backed government headed by Hamid Karzai. These groups include the Haqqani network; the Afghan Taliban; the Taliban's former ally, al Qaeda; and the Quetta Shura. Most of these groups would welcome a compromise agreement that would allow them greater freedom to operate in Afghanistan. Without that, they and their former mujahideen allies, notably in the Haqqani network and the Hizb-e-Islami, will be ever more beholden to radical Islamic interests outside the region. Their links to al-Qaeda and jihadi organizations in Pakistan remain strong. Together these groups form a network that aims to remove Western influence and create a sharia state in Afghanistan. And there is no reason not to believe that the Taliban would help launch Islamic militants into Uzbekistan and Tajikistan, as they did a decade ago. Most important, a successful Afghan Taliban insurgency is almost certain to energize Taliban forces that seek to achieve a similar sharia state in Pakistan.

Robert Blackwill anticipates the likely failure of the International Security Assistance Force/U.S. counterinsurgency strategy over the next several years.[53] That would almost certainly promote civil conflict in Afghanistan and set the stage for a war among Pakistani, Indian, Iranian, Western, and even Chinese proxies. Ethnic minority Tajiks, Hazara, and Uzbeks in Afghanistan can be expected to resist any outcome that restores the Taliban to power. They learned a decade ago that the Taliban will not be satisfied with control of just Pashtun-majority areas but will seek to extend its authority over the entire country. With Pakistan as the Taliban's patron, Iran, Russia, and the Central Asian republics will similarly seek spheres of influence in Afghanistan. And for all of Pakistan's concerns about Indian influence, a civil war in Afghanistan could increase Indian activity, perhaps with U.S. encouragement. Furthermore, the possibility of Indian military advisers and arms transfer cannot be ruled out, and some Indians speak of using India's massive training infrastructure to train a new, anti-Pakistan Afghan army. Saudi Arabia also would exert influence through client groups, mostly in order to minimize Iranian gains.

A new civil war in Afghanistan would generate millions of refugees, some of whom would flee into Pakistan, putting a new financial burden on Pakistan. In the face of inflation, unemployment, and a weak, corrupt government, civil unrest in Pakistan provoked by extremist groups cannot be ruled out. The most likely outcome would be a full-fledged return to power by Pakistan's military and declaration of martial rule or its equivalent.

A negotiated settlement between the Afghan Taliban and the Karzai government would be the best way for Pakistan to ensure an India-free Afghanistan and also to avoid a civil war. Pakistan's motives closely resemble those behind its efforts in the late 1980s to promote a post-Soviet coalition government in Afghanistan in order to avoid a power vacuum. The case for negotiations with the Afghan Taliban also is an old one. When the Taliban were in power in Afghanistan, Pakistani officials regularly argued that the leadership under Mullah Omar was capable of acting independently and was not necessarily beholden to terrorist organizations such as al Qaeda; allowed to consolidate their power and given international recognition, the Taliban would be anxious to moderate their policies. Then, as now, Pakistan insisted that its influence with Afghan insurgents puts it in a unique position to broker an agreement. That view is strongly contested by several former senior U.S. officials from the Clinton administration interviewed for this project who dealt with the Taliban; they remain unpersuaded that the "new" Taliban are any different.

Of the many difficulties in estimating Pakistan's future, Afghanistan is certainly near the top. It affects Pakistan's relations with the United States, it has a potential influence on Pakistan's Pashtun population, and a victory for the Taliban would be regarded as a civilizational victory by Pakistan's Islamic extremists. Afghanistan is also a field where the India-Pakistan rivalry plays itself out. My conversations with senior Pakistan army leaders in September 2010 indicate that their strategies for a future Afghanistan may be more nuanced. In saying that "we can't have Talibanization . . . if we want to remain modern and progressive," General Kiyani also suggests that Pakistan is better served if the Taliban do not prevail in Afghanistan.[54] The application of his remarks was even clearer when he said that "we cannot wish for Afghanistan what we don't wish for Pakistan." But, in practice, can the Pakistan army control the Taliban? When the Taliban ruled in Kabul, relations between Pakistan and Afghanistan often were difficult. There is no reason why a resurgent Taliban might not target Pakistan itself, riding the crest of a civilizational victory over the West, and the Pakistan army, already targeted by the Pakistan Taliban.

Theoretically, the best option for Pakistan would be strategic cooperation with India on Afghanistan. That seems unlikely, given the deep roots of India-Pakistan hostility and the lack of interest of major powers in promoting such cooperation. A truly regional approach to Afghanistan is also stymied by the apparent impossibility of U.S.-Iran cooperation on Afghan policy, even though the two did collaborate in the aftermath of the 9/11 attack, when Iran assisted the United States in rounding up the Taliban and al Qaeda.

United States. The Pakistani perception is that the United States has repeatedly used, abused, and betrayed Pakistan, beginning with the 1962 war between India and China, when the United States could have forced India to accept an agreement on Kashmir; during the 1965 India-Pakistan war, when the United States cut off aid to a formal ally, Pakistan, after India crossed the international boundary; and in 1972, when it again abandoned Pakistan in the face of Indian military aggression that led to the loss of half of the country.[55] For many Pakistanis, the cutoff of military supplies by the Pressler amendment and the invasion of Afghanistan were only the most recent examples of U.S. betrayal and untrustworthiness. Their view was formalized in the Pakistani lament that there was a massive trust deficit between the two states, and that, as the larger partner, it was up to the United States to demonstrate that it was a reliable and trustworthy friend. This attitude continues today with regard to U.S. Afghan policy and the U.S.-India nuclear agreement. The Pakistani military is not shy about presenting its view of the Afghan situation and of U.S. mistakes.[56]

Under President Bush, the United States separated its India and Pakistan policies—a policy called dehyphenation—arguing that its relationship with each country should be based on its merits alone.[57] That also confirmed the U.S. lack of interest in India-Pakistan relations, other than when they were in crisis. After the events of 9/11, Pakistan again became central to U.S. policy on Afghanistan, but Washington transformed its relations with India. The centerpiece of the new "natural alliance," as it was called, was the U.S.-Indian civilian nuclear deal.

Pakistan viewed this new commitment to India with alarm, seeing it as proof that the United States had chosen India over Pakistan. However, Pakistanis still resist the idea of a close, enduring relationship, remaining convinced that the U.S. commitment to them is short term and linked to the situation in Afghanistan. The U.S. government, however, maintains that the India-U.S. relationship should have no bearing on Pakistan's standing, an assertion that is incomprehensible in Pakistan. Washington has been unable to come up with a central and persuasive theme for relations with Pakistan, as it did for India. Given the diversity of interests embedded in the U.S.-Pakistan relationship, it seems unlikely that the United States can do so. A short list would include Afghanistan, Pakistan's nuclear program, Pakistan-based terrorism, India-Pakistan relations, and the stability of Pakistan itself.

The United States and Pakistan will remain at odds for the foreseeable future. The United States is impatient with Pakistan's corruption, its imbalanced civil-military relationship, its support (or tolerance) for the Afghan Taliban, and its permissive attitude toward terrorist groups based in Pakistan, which, in some cases, are supported by the Pakistani government. The United States and Pakistan continue to engage in a fruitless game of pressure and counter-pressure over Afghanistan. Pakistan's army seems determined to maintain a foothold in the Afghan political theater, and whenever U.S. pressure becomes too obnoxious, Washington finds that its shipments of supplies into Afghanistan are inexplicably interrupted by Pakistan. While dependence on supply routes has been reduced substantially from the 80 percent cited in 2005 and while vital equipment and supplies, such as weapons, are flown in, the ground route is essential for shipment of petrol and bulk supplies.

The ability of Islamists to sell their viewpoint in Muslim societies is closely linked to how those societies perceive Western policies. As Moeed Yusuf argues, if short-term interests continue to dictate the Western agenda and the people of Pakistan see themselves being left out of the bargain, Western policy will continue to fuel the very mindset that it seeks to eliminate. The West's patience, however, may not withstand another terror attack originating in Pakistan and targeting Western property and individuals.

The establishment in Pakistan is skeptical of U.S. policy in Afghanistan and deeply resistant to cooperation on nuclear and intelligence matters. Pakistan believes that close cooperation on intelligence could be turned against it, especially with respect to the security of its nuclear arsenal, or that the United States might share critical and embarrassing information with India regarding terror attacks, as it did by giving India access to David Headley, the Pakistani-American who confessed to being central to the Mumbai attacks.[58] The episode of the CIA officer shooting Pakistanis in Lahore, plus the ease with which Osama's hideout was penetrated by U.S. Special Forces, brought suspicion of the United States to new heights, and relations can easily become much worse.

One event that could cause relations to deteriorate quickly would be an attack on the United States that had its origins in Pakistan, with or without government collusion or knowledge. A successful attack along the lines of the Times Square attempted bombing of May 2010—a plot that was hatched in Pakistan although it used a U.S. citizen and that may have been known to Pakistani authorities—would lead to a powerful popular and congressional reaction to punish Pakistan or at least to stop rewarding it.

A crisis between the United States and Pakistan could also come about for other reasons. U.S. drone attacks against Afghan and Pakistani militants on Pakistani soil (some of them launched from secret bases in Pakistan itself) are a constant reminder of Pakistan's complicity in the war in Afghanistan, even though some of the attacks were directed against individuals and groups that targeted the Pakistan government. There also have been press reports about U.S. plans to send Afghan "militia" groups into Pakistan to attack Afghan Taliban groups operating from Pakistani territory, including the Haqqani network and the former Afghan mujahideen group led by Gulbuddin Hekmat-yar, which, though based in Pakistan, are really part of the Afghan political nexus.

In such cases, lesser grievances—such as the U.S. refusal to grant Pakistan favorable terms for its textile exports to the United States—will become irrelevant and direct U.S. attacks on militants based in Pakistan via drones would be very likely and might signal a shift in U.S. policy toward Pakistan itself.

Yet Pakistan can ill afford to alienate the United States. Although there is talk of a break with America, there is no replacement for U.S. training, advanced weapons, spare parts, and defense budgetary support and developmental assistance. Yet the United States has failed to offer Pakistan a more liberal trade regime, and U.S. patience with Pakistan is wearing thin very fast.

What is euphemistically called a trust deficit has for some time defined the U.S. relationship with both the elites and public of Pakistan, and it will continue to influence the partnership. Conspiracy theories about U.S. collusion with India and Israel to weaken Pakistan and seize its nuclear weapons are widely shared, even at the highest echelons of the army. Despite recognizing the threat posed by the country's militants, most Pakistanis believe that the radicalization of the frontier is a direct result of U.S. counterterrorism policies and military operations in Afghanistan. Less than a tenth of the public holds a favorable view of the United States, and almost twice as many Pakistanis see the United States as a greater threat to Pakistan's security than India.[59] Changing those views is a long-term project that probably has to begin with the United States being willing to offer agreements on trade and nuclear issues, neither of which is in sight over the next several years.

China as a South Asian Power. China has systematically expanded its role in South Asia but nowhere more than in Pakistan, where its popularity among elites and in most of the provinces, its economic penetration, and its comprehensive support for the security establishment in the form of military hardware and nuclear technology mean that its already huge role in Pakistan is growing.[60] That was symbolized by the visit of Chinese prime minister Wen Jiabao in December 2010. Aid and trade agreements worth approximately $35 billion were signed over a three-day period, amid the usual effusive statements from Chinese officials about the importance of Pakistan to China.[61] Almost all media reports and commentaries noted how much easier it was to deal with China than the United States, which made unreasonable demands on Pakistan, including unrealistic requests that Pakistan's overstretched army take on militants in the KP region.

The exaggerated rhetoric used by Pakistan to describe its relationship with China demonstrates both China's importance to Pakistan and Pakistan's distrust of the United States and, of course, India. Further, the Chinese have figured out how to deal with the Pakistanis—through lavish public praise and private warnings about instances in which Pakistani actions endanger Chinese interests, as in the case of training of Islamist militants of Chinese origin. The rise of an assertive and competent China powered by a growing economy, plus the persistence of the Pakistan-India conflict, means that the strategic unity of South Asia, established by the Mughals and maintained by the British, is gone.

Nonetheless, as C. Christine Fair notes in chapter 4 of this volume, despite its rhetoric, China has grown wary of the management of Pakistan's internal security crises. China is currently the largest foreign direct investor in Afghanistan (having, for example, an investment in the Aynak copper mine in Logar Province), and it has made significant investments in Pakistan, Iran, and Central Asia. It is rightly worried about Pakistan's use of Islamist proxies. Moreover, China's own restive Uighurs have received training in Pakistan and Afghanistan. China has simply displaced India as Pakistan's natural trading partner, not on economic grounds but because of political circumstances. Strategically, China is unlikely to abandon its military ties with Pakistan because it believes that balancing Pakistan's capabilities vis-à-vis India helps contain India as a South Asian power. Finally, Chinese officials and business leaders know how to cultivate their Pakistani counterparts. The Chinese, unlike the Americans, voice their criticisms privately, not publicly. Pakistani politicians and generals make frequent trips to Beijing to firm up relations with China. Only in one area do the Chinese suffer in comparison with other countries: few, if any, Pakistanis want to visit or move to China. For most of them, the first land of opportunity remains the Gulf, followed by Europe or the United States.

India. India remains a permanent and likely negative element in affecting Pakistan's future. Pakistan was, after all, the result of a movement by Indian Muslims, and the best historical analyses demonstrate that the creation of the state was almost accidental—which makes Indians less interested in accommodating even legitimate demands and makes Pakistanis even more paranoid about India's intentions.

A majority of Pakistanis still consider India as a major threat and view the United States as an enemy. According to a 2010 Pew survey, they are far less concerned about the Taliban and al Qaeda. When asked whether India, the Taliban, or al Qaeda is the greatest threat to their country, slightly more than half of Pakistanis (53 percent) chose India, 23 percent chose the Taliban, and just 3 percent chose al Qaeda. Roughly 72 percent said that it is important for relations with India to improve, and about 75 percent supported increased trade and further talks with India. Fifty-nine percent of the Pakistani respondents described the United States as an enemy, and only 8 percent trusted President Barack Obama.[62]

Within Pakistan, policy toward India will continue to be dictated by the army, which shows no sign of flexibility on major issues and a great deal of frustration with hard-line Indian attitudes. The army's "India problem" is complicated by the popular view (in the cantonments) that India understands only the language of force, an attitude that led to Pakistan's politically cata-strophic crossing of the Line of Control in the Kargil region in 1999.

It will take the army's compliance, strong political leadership, and res-olutely independent-minded foreign ministers (hitherto conspicuously absent) to secure any significant shift of approach toward India. A true "solu-tion" to the Kashmir issue—or any of the other outstanding disputes between the two states—is nowhere in sight. A reasonable aspiration would be to man-age the issue at the level of a modus vivendi no worse than that of the last few years, but that depends on avoiding new incidents, such as the terror attacks on the Indian Parliament and on Mumbai. If Indian political sentiment were to allow it, there would be scope for rapid adoption of some Kashmir-related confidence-building measures (CBMs). But a real and permanent change of Pakistani attitude will require a radical reduction of the role of Pakistan's army and possibly also a generational shift of sentiment. There is good reason to believe that the Mumbai attack was designed to break up the India-Pakistan dialogue, and the effects of further terrorist incidents like Mumbai would be negative. Indeed, crises strengthen not only nationalist sentiments in Pak-istan but also heighten the credibility of the country's jihadi and other extrem-ists groups. While a new crisis cannot be predicted, neither can normalization of relations. The current situation, characterized by cool hostility and no real progress on a range of issues, is likely to remain the norm.

The management of Pakistan's relations with India has proven to be a source of conflict between Pakistan's civilian and military leaders and a major cause of regime change: the army regarded civilians as too soft toward India on several occasions and considered that justification for their removal. Fur-ther, Pakistan's ethnic cohesion is strained by differences among the provinces in the priority that they give to Kashmir and other issues with India, the Pun-jab being the most hawkish on Kashmir. A humiliating military defeat of Pak-istan's army, as with the loss of East Pakistan in 1971, and an accompanying economic and humanitarian crisis, could test the very integrity of the Pak-istani state, but the fact that both India and Pakistan possess nuclear weapons and the possibility of their mutual assured destruction make such a defeat less likely.

As for the Indian side of the equation, C. Christine Fair, in chapter 4 in this volume, has it about right:

> India demurs from making any policies toward Pakistan that may be conciliatory, including striking a comprehensive settlement between Delhi and Srinagar. India clings to the notion that its varied elections demonstrate that the Kashmir issue is resolved. However, as any visitor to Kashmir can attest, elections have not ameliorated the pervasive discontent and dissatisfaction with Delhi, much less provided a path toward comprehensive reconciliation. India's strategy appears to be to "wait it out" while India ascends and Pakistan weakens.

As some Indian strategists point out, India has been unable to prevent China from expanding its own sphere of influence in South Asia because of India's dispute with Pakistan over Kashmir plus a whole host of other disputes. India's leadership, centered in the Ministry of External Affairs and the army, has inadvertently brought about the destruction of South Asia's strategic unity and ensures that India will forever be paired with a declining Pakistan.

William Milam speculates in chapter 7 about a scenario in which India and Pakistan normalize their strategic relationship, perhaps beginning in Afghanistan. For Milam and many others who participated in the Bellagio meeting, peace and normalization with India is a necessary condition for Pakistan to build itself into a modern society and state. Realistically, however, darker scenarios of India-Pakistan relations are just as likely, including a major crisis within the next dozen years, possibly involving nuclear weapons or, at a minimum, the continuation of the stalemate between the two, to the detriment of each.

With respect to India the biggest questions are whether the Pakistan army will come to have a less paranoid understanding of the Indian threat and whether India itself will take the process of normalization seriously. That would suggest that over time Pakistan acquiesces to the ascent of its larger neighbor but obtains credible assurance that India will not take advantage of its dominant position. In some sense Pakistan would be better off seeking a resolution of this sixty-year-old strategic rivalry now, before it grows weaker and India stronger. But some in Pakistan still believe that the use of terrorism, carried out under the threat of nuclear escalation, will keep India off balance, a strategy that can be traced back many years. That, of course, does nothing to help Kashmiris, solve regional water disputes, or open up transit links to the benefit of both countries. Attitudes toward India have changed more in Pakistan over the last five years than ever before, but there is little sign of this change in the military, even as it grows aware that there is a new domestic threat in the form of the Pakistan Taliban, with its links to many other forces that would like to transform, if not destroy, the idea of a moderate Pakistan.

Globalization and Nuclear Weapons. Two other external trends will influence Pakistan's future. One is globalization—the more rapid and intense movement of ideas, people, and goods—a process that accelerated quickly in the last thirty years. The other is Pakistan's growing nuclear arsenal, which seems unconstrained by financial shortfalls or strategic logic. The two trends are intertwined. Pakistan received almost all of its nuclear technology from other countries and took advantage of globalization to create purchasing networks that stretched around the world; later it used those networks to share its nuclear technology with several customers.

Contemporary globalization is most commonly associated with the huge burst in trade, telecommunications, and movement of people over long distances that began with the introduction of container ships, wide-bodied jets, and instant global electronic communications over the last thirty years. Pakistan was among the states least prepared for this development. It had seriously underinvested in education at all levels, and its economy does not produce many goods or services that are in high demand. Furthermore, it has become the target, transit lounge, and training center for jihadis of all varieties. Pakistan and some of its allies, notably the United States and Saudi Arabia, encouraged those jihadis, many of whom put down local roots. Finally, Pakistan also became addicted to foreign assistance from major countries and the international financial institutions and never really reformed its economy because it did not have to. In this area, Pakistan's friends did it no favor by supporting its addiction.

Along with the burst of movement of people, goods, and ideas came the end of communism. That became an organizing principle for the young and angry, helping to unleash long-suppressed forces. Religious identity became the rallying cry, beginning in Yugoslavia and moving to the former Soviet Union and beyond. Secular revolutionary movements, like the Palestine Liberation Organization, were challenged by Islamist groups. Pakistan, which had religion built into its national identity, moved in that direction. Militant Islamist organizations and parties filled the space created by the absence of the left.[63] Both Pakistan's Sunnis and its Shiites were influenced by the Iranian revolution, the first modern revolution to take a religious, not a leftist, turn. East Pakistan's had been the first successful postcolonial insurgency based on ethnicity, although with substantial support from India. In Pakistan, the Bengalis were followed by another secular separatist movement, this one spearheaded by the Baloch, while Sindhis and Mohajirs still have one eye on the possibility of breaking away from Pakistan.

As for nuclear weapons, given that Pakistan is a state dominated by the armed forces and at near-war with its major neighbor, it is not surprising that changes in the nature of armed conflict have affected Pakistan. Wherever nuclear weapons are involved, war in the form of an organized battle between industrialized states employing the latest and most destructive weapons is hardly imaginable.

Nuclear weapons have not brought about a genuine peace between India and Pakistan, but their presence ensures that no rational leader will ever employ them, and they have effectively ended classic, large-scale, industrialized war. There still remains the outside chance of an accident or of a madman coming to power in a nuclear state, but the greater internal threat is theft and the greater external threat is the conscious transfer of nuclear technology, or even complete weapons, for political reasons or simple greed. Indeed, Pakistan has been a prominent violator of international norms, transferring sensitive nuclear technologies to at least four states.

Nuclear weapons are as valuable to Pakistan as they are to North Korea, both of which (or their regimes) have some kind of survival insurance—a bizarre kind of immortality—because of these weapons. Pakistan, like North Korea, is "too nuclear to fail." That is a fact that those involved in developing the nuclear program frequently and publicly mention, but they ignore "Act two": what a nuclear weapons state does once its gross security problems are alleviated. It is true, as A. Q. Khan and others have frequently said, that no one dares invade Pakistan, but that does not improve Pakistan's economy, lessen its internal strife, or stabilize its politics.[64] Mubakaramand, one of the leaders of the Pakistani weapons design team, noted, probably correctly, that if it were not for Pakistan's nuclear deterrent, "Pakistan would have not survived after Kargil, [or the] Indian parliament and Mumbai incident episodes."[65] These scientists and most Pakistani strategists do not ask whether if Pakistan had *not* possessed nuclear weapons, it would have pursued the provocative strategies that led India to contemplate a military response at Kargil and then go on to promulgate assertive military strategies, such as "Cold Start," that have complicated Pakistan's overall defense position.[66]

Scenarios and Outcomes

Scenarios offer a dynamic view of possible futures and focus attention on the underlying interactions that may have particular policy significance. They can help decisionmakers avoid conventional thinking, which is invariably a straight-line projection of the present into the future.[67] I used this approach in my 2004 book, *The Idea of Pakistan*. Here I present seven scenarios and then discuss the relationship among various factors, noting which might take precedence over others. I also discuss those factors in terms of their criticality. All are necessary to change Pakistan for what we would call the better, but none seem to be sufficient.

Another Five Years: More of the Same

The most likely future for Pakistan over the next five to seven years—but one that is less likely than it was five years ago—is some form of what has been called "muddling through" and what in 2004 I termed "an establishment-dominated" Pakistan.[68] The military will play a key but not necessarily central role in state and political decisions and not necessarily always. This scenario may also include direct military rule. As several of the Bellagio participants noted, it has not made much difference whether the military or civilians are in power, since both have had progressive moments and both have also contributed to the long decline in Pakistan's integrity as both a state and a nation.

In this scenario the political system is bound by certain parameters: the military may take over, but only as a temporary fix; it neither encourages nor tolerates deep reform; and civilians are content with a limited political role. The political system is frozen in an intermediate, gray zone between full-fledged democracy and military autocracy. The state is always in transition, but it never *arrives*, confounding both Pakistan's supporters and its critics. In this scenario the civilian government is under pressure to tackle broad governance issues, especially the sectarian, economic, and energy crises, and military officials continue to operate in the shadows while rattling their sabers to prevent undesirable outcomes in domestic and foreign policy. New centers of power, such as the judiciary, may exert a democratic effect and help ensure the rule of law, but the scenario includes continuing military mediation of civilian crises, which reproduces the depressingly familiar (and democratically corrosive) pattern of civil-military relations under formal elected rule. It also includes the continuation of sectarian and ethnic violence, but neither, apart from other aggravating factors, will drive Pakistan over the edge.

Within those parameters, the economy may improve, democracy may stabilize, and there may be an increase in the government's coherence, but all or some of those factors may also take a turn for the worse. Lurking in the background will be a steady increase in the population, stagnant economic growth, no serious attempt to modernize the educational system, and continued ethnic, sectarian, and social violence. These trends are very hard to alter and impossible to change quickly. Given the military's current campaign, extremist violence might be tamed in KP, but a revival of the insurgency is likely, given the absence of real economic growth and the weakness of political institutions. Absent police

reform and a new attitude toward domestic jihadis, it is doubtful that maintenance of law and order will improve in the Punjab and it will certainly worsen
in KP. Balochistan could again see a revived separatist movement, perhaps with
outside assistance.

In this "muddling through" scenario, similar to General Talat Masood's
"nuanced case," there may be a visible, slow decline of Pakistan's integrity as
a state and further confusion about Pakistan's identity as a nation. One important factor in preserving the current arrangement is that just about every
major power in the world wants to see Pakistan remain whole and stable.
Even most Indian strategists do not relish the idea of a collapsed Pakistan,
although they might want a weak Pakistan, strong enough to maintain internal order but not so strong that it can challenge India. Yet in the face of Pakistan's accelerating decay over the last few years, some Indian strategists are
beginning to consider whether or not it is in their interest to accelerate the
process.

Pakistan could be pushed very far off its present path by regional separatism, sectarianism, a botched crisis with India, or a bad agreement in
Afghanistan triggering new, unmanageable forces or conceivably a counter-
movement toward totalitarianism, authoritarianism, radical reform, or the
rise of a charismatic leader. All are alternative futures for Pakistan, but none
is likely in the near term. Beneath any political developments, demographic
and social change continues, leading mostly in the direction of greater chaos.
This scenario propels Pakistan toward the dismal and chaotic future predicted
in the 2008 NIC study.

Parallel Pakistans

A second future for Pakistan, probably as likely as some kind of "muddling
through" within the next five years and already evident now in some
provinces, would be the emergence of parallel Pakistans. In this scenario the
state carries on with a recognizable central government but some of the
provinces and regions go their different ways, not as separate states following
a breakup but in terms of how they are governed, how their economy functions, how they educate their children, how they tilt toward authoritarian or
democratic traditions, and how they accommodate Islamist, regional, and
separatist movements.

The centrifugal forces in Pakistan are intensifying, and Pakistan is heading
in this direction. Those who oppose democratization do so in part because
they fear the weakening of the state and the unconstrained growth of separatism; those who favor democratization see it as the mechanism by which different and diverse regions and social classes can live together peacefully in the

same state. Current experiments in strengthening provincial autonomy could, if mishandled, have the consequence of tilting the federal balance so that the center loses even more of its authority. Recent decisions to delegate some functions to the provinces might be premature: most of them lack capability already—Punjab excepted—and asking them to do more means, in practical terms, accepting that less will get done in the fields of education, infrastructure building, and social reform, let alone the police and judicial systems.

As the Pakistani state becomes weaker and as divisive tendencies grow stronger, those who favor a strong state will be tempted to invoke the argument that there is an existential external threat to Pakistan that requires the suppression of ethnic, sectarian, and other differences. Such a strategy would do nothing to increase Pakistan's growth rate or address the demographic explosion.

For the near future—over the next five or six years—Pakistan will either struggle on or undergo a more rapid decline, which will be evident in the rise of a more complex and fractious relationship among the provinces and between them and the central government. This will be delayed if the present cooperative arrangement between the politicians and the generals continues, even if there is a change in personalities. General Kayani is not irreplaceable, but the spirit of cooperation with civilian politicians is; similarly, neither President Zardari nor Prime Minister Gilani is indispensable, but their willingness to give the military some political space while attempting to reform Pakistan's government is.

This scenario predicts the emergence of many Pakistans within the framework of an international entity called Pakistan. The army's grip will loosen but not fail, and the problems generated by a bad economy, a bad demographic profile, and bad sectarian relations will deepen. This is not quite the "Lebanonization" of Pakistan, but the rise of the equivalent of Hamas and Hezbollah already has been seen, although their outside supporters are less visible and their impact is not as great as in Lebanon. The army will ensure that the state remains formally intact, but it may be powerless to prevent alliances between and among regional groups and outside powers. China already has considerable influence in Northern Pakistan and is a growing economic factor elsewhere. Some minority sects already look to Iran for protection and inspiration, and Tehran has an incentive to balance out extremist Sunni groups in Pakistan as well as the Taliban in Afghanistan. Some leaders in Karachi and the Mohajir community in particular now look at India from perspectives that are very different from those of their forefathers, who abandoned India, and they talk about an independent Karachi with strong economic and security ties to other countries, just like Singapore. Finally, the Baloch and some Sindhis are utterly disenchanted with Pakistan, and the emergence of hardcore Punjabi leaders allied to the army would further alienate them.

These first two scenarios encompass the likely future of Pakistan. They are, respectively, bad and worse for Pakistan. However, even in the short time frame of five to seven years, other futures are possible. What follows is a list of less likely but still plausible paths that the country might take.

Democratic Consolidation

It seems very unlikely now, but Pakistan could see the slow and steady stabilization of democracy. That would require a greater degree of bipartisanship between the two dominant parties, some increase in their commitment to democratic norms both in and outside the party structure, and recognition by the army that it cannot govern the state effectively and that it must allow (or even assist) a new generation of politicians to come to real power. In 2010 I described this to senior army officers as Pakistan's greatest challenge, even greater than that of India, but their response was muted. Realization of such a future would also require continued support for democratization from Western states, Indian actions to reward Pakistan for moving in this direction, and no Chinese or Saudi actions that rewarded regression to authoritarianism in the name of stability.

The Zardari government, for all of its obvious problems, has put Pakistan on this path, and other mainstream parties have not obstructed its changes. The process seems to have settled into a pattern of one step forward and one step back, or perhaps a hop sideways. A recent clever scorecard of Pakistan's gains and losses in 2010 comes out to about zero.[69] The parties have resisted turning to the military for support, as they did time after time in the past. They appear to have learned that it is better to play by the rules of the game and to continue to tolerate each other than risk destabilizing the system and losing power to the military for another decade. However, the institutionalization of democracy also requires a military that is committed to taking a subordinate role within a democratic framework.

Were Pakistan to move in this direction, it would not necessarily mean that the economy would recover and it certainly would not mean that the social pressures caused by population growth and urbanization would moderate. These are time bombs, buried deep within the Pakistani state, that will present grave problems for a future democratic regime. But such a regime, one that is freer than the current government from the taint of corruption and that makes a more serious effort to improve the functioning of the state, would also have a much greater claim on international resources and help from India.

Breakaway and Breakup

It is misleading to talk of a breakaway of discontented provinces and the breakup of the state, or total state failure, within the next five years. Those who predict such a future soon are patently unaware of Pakistan's resiliency and capabilities, even if it is failing along many dimensions. Ralph Peters, a retired U.S. army officer, raises the possibility of Pakistan being reduced to a rump of Punjab and parts of Sindh, with Balochistan and the Khyber Pakhtunkhwa breaking away.[70] His views have been much cited as evidence of U.S. malice toward Pakistan, and in my own recent visits to military educational and training institutions, his name and the prospect of an outside effort to break up Pakistan came up repeatedly. Peters suggested that Balochistan might become a free state including parts of Iran's province of Sistan and Baluchistan, while the NWFP/KP would become a part of Afghanistan. It seems that retired military officers like this option. In March 2009 a retired Australian officer, David Kilcullen, predicted that Pakistan would fail in a matter of months. These predictions are a result of anger over Pakistani support for the Taliban in Afghanistan and a lack of familiarity with the society as well as the state of Pakistan. In the longer term the breakup of Pakistan is possible, as I discuss in *The Idea of Pakistan*, but any breakup would be preceded by the disintegration of the army, either after a war or because of ethnic and sectarian differences, or by the splitting of the army by some Punjabi political movement. None of that seems likely or plausible at the moment, but the breakup of the Soviet Union was also unexpected and unpredicted by most Soviet experts.

Civil or Military Authoritarianism

Far more plausible than a breakup of Pakistan would be its slide into one or another form of authoritarianism. That could happen at the provincial level if the army permitted it or if it joined with a regional authoritarian movement. Authoritarianism might have staying power in Pakistan, although an authoritarian regime would face the same problems of state competence and national identity as any other kind of regime. There are four authoritarian models; Pakistan might evolve into one or some combination of them.

First, there is liberal authoritarianism, most perfectly embodied in Singapore. Here a dominant party ensures that the state is well run, dissent is carefully channeled, and the economy thrives. Many Pakistanis would opt immediately for a liberal authoritarian system, especially since, as in Singapore, it holds out the hope of further liberal reform while maintaining economic prosperity and social calm. However, Pakistan has no political party capable of running such a state, and the army cannot imagine one because it is preoccupied with defense issues and lacks the secular, liberal bent of, for example, the Turkish army.

Classic authoritarianism, along the lines of Saddam's Iraq, is even less likely. While Pakistan may yet see the rise of a brutal but charismatic leader, it is hard to see how that would work in Pakistan, which lacks the resources, such as oil, to sustain tough authoritarianism.

Moderate military authoritarianism, along the lines of Egypt's, is more plausible. Something like this was tried by Ayub, and even Musharraf might have moved in this direction had he not been so intent on pleasing all of his audiences; he lacked the ruthlessness of a Nasser or a Hosni Mubarak. Such a regime would have the support of China or Saudi Arabia and, if it was effective, of many Western powers. Such a soft authoritarianism would have to be linked to outside assistance to succeed, economics being the driving factor. Here, China could be a major factor, building in Pakistan an acceptable Islamic but authoritarian state identity—just Islamic enough to claim legitimacy in terms of its historical roots but not so Islamic that it would support Islamist movements abroad, particularly in China. Such Islamist exports could be confined to India or other hostile neighbors.

Finally, there are two models of Islamist authoritarianism: Iran and Saudi Arabia. The Iranian model does not fit Pakistan and not only because the very large Shiite minority would not tolerate the imposition of a Sunni state. Iran's population is quite modernized and very sympathetic to liberal values, although power remains with the clerics and the Revolutionary Guards, two institutions that are absent in Pakistan. The Saudi model does not fit at all. There is no monolithic Islamic clergy, and Pakistan has fewer resources and is vastly larger and more diverse than either Saudi Arabia or Iran. More likely would be the emergence of provincial Islamist governments, especially in Khyber Pakhtunkhwa, along with the weakening of the central government. Under the plural Pakistan scenario described above, some provinces could be nominally Islamist and free elections would not be able to remove the Islamists, who would be entrenched in power as in Iran. A provincial government with an Islamist bent (like both the Saudi and Iranian governments) might attempt to export radicalism abroad, and a weak government in Islamabad could claim that the policing mechanisms of the central state were too feeble to prevent such activities.

At the moment authoritarianism would not sit well with most Pakistanis, but if it brought order and a degree of prosperity, it would find a foothold. That is what the Taliban did in Afghanistan, although the prerequisite for such a development would be the collapse of the army, which seems very unlikely under all current circumstances. In addition, authoritarianism does not match up well with Pakistan's diverse religious or social groups or with its deeply complex South Asian culture. Authoritarianism might be an experiment, but an experiment that would be likely to fail in its incapacity to deal with a society that is traditionally averse to centralization. That would be even more likely in the case of any totalitarian movement that might arise in Pakistan. Among other factors, the new media would make it hard for either form of government to establish itself.

An Army-Led Revolution

There is also a remote prospect of an army-led transformation of Pakistan, one in which the generals became true revolutionaries, perhaps along the lines of the Turkish army years ago or, more recently, the Indonesian army. Though unlikely, this is perhaps more likely than the transformation of the civilian elite into a force for modernity. Indonesia is a promising point of comparison, but it differs from Pakistan in that it gave up Konfrontasi, the practice of confronting its regional neighbors and claiming regional leadership. Indonesia then had no external enemy and both its army and its political class could devote their energies to domestic security and reform. The results have been spectacular.

Pakistan's army is attuned to developments elsewhere. Its leadership knows that the country is falling behind its peers, notably India, yet there is no consensus on what has to be done to remedy the situation. It is in the position of being an army that is better than the state that supports it; the strategic challenge is to improve that state without surrendering its own professional status by becoming a political and economic creature. So far the army has become an economic force in Pakistan through its expanding manufacturing and distribution programs, and it remains entangled in mediating domestic crises and enforcing an unviable consensus on foreign and security policy. However, the Pakistan army cannot shoot weapons and think at the same time. While the army is unlikely to return to the Zia experiment, promoting a deeply conservative Islamist reform of Pakistan, it lacks the objectivity to see how it might reduce its own role in the state and thereby contribute to a more normal balance of civilian and military authority. It cannot govern, but it is fearful of civilian governance—and not without reason, given the historical incompetence of many civilian leaders.

Post-Crisis Scenarios

Finally, it is important to note that all calculations about the future of Pakistan can be changed instantaneously should there be another major crisis, especially one with India or now one involving Pakistan's role in Afghanistan and the actions of terrorist groups that have strong links to Pakistan.

Military defeat frequently leads to the erosion of an army's domestic political power, as in Greece in 1974 after the Turkish invasion of Cyprus and in Argentina in 1982 after the Malvinas/Falklands War. In Pakistan, however, defeat in the 1971 war with India did not result in the army's withdrawal from politics and civilian affairs; it only strengthened the army's resolve to take revenge on India and persuaded the army to back the nuclear weapons program. Pakistan's deep involvement in Indian-administered Kashmir and with Indian Islamist groups precipitated a number of crises and earned Pakistan the reputation of being a reckless state. Pakistan's defeat also strengthened jingoistic nationalism, which, under Zia, was encouraged by the state, some elements of which still have close relations with the hypernationalist "Honor" brigade.

For the army to consider complete withdrawal from politics, which would be transformational, it needs at least to be able to claim a draw on the Kashmir problem and to have some assurance that Pakistan's security environment will be stable and normal. Box 1-1 presents a number of other transformation scenarios.

Conclusions

At the most abstract analytical level, the interplay between the contested ideas of Pakistan and the integrity of the Pakistani state will determine Pakistan's future. When a state is unable to protect its citizens and to collect the taxes required for the delivery of basic services, its citizens will regard themselves not as citizens but as subjects. They will try to leave the state, seek to transform the very "idea" that holds them together, or fight the state—or all three at the same time. Pakistan has never had a workable arrangement between the state and those ruled by the state. In the words of Hamid Kizilbash, talking about the upsurge in sectarian and political violence, "The people we ignored are taking their revenge."[71]

Five or six things must happen before Pakistan can be safely put in the "normal" state category. They include developing nearly-normal relations with India, reviving the economy, repairing the state, rebalancing the civil-military relationship, redefining the role of the military in the state, taxing the rich, fighting domestic insurgencies more effectively, and allowing a reshaped police force to emerge. The politicians would have to moderate their disputes, concentrating on issues and reform, not on patronage and corruption. However,

Box 1-1. *Other Transformation Scenarios*

Pakistan is unique, but its core political structure, the role of the military, and potential for revolutionary change can be compared with a number of other historical cases.

In some ways it resembles Czarist Russia, which had a rotting army and was tipped over the edge by involvement in a world war. It differs in that Pakistan's army is coherent, whereas the war destroyed the Czarist forces, which never enjoyed the influence of the court and the aristocracy. The Bolsheviks and others were able to fill the resulting vacuum, in part because they were able to make peace with Germany, but Pakistan's Islamists are unlikely to have such an opportunity as long as the military retains its integrity and might intensify rather than end the conflict with India.

Another case with partial similarities is interwar Japan, where the civil-military relationship resembled that of Pakistan. An aggressive army vied with an aggressive navy to launch Japan on a series of disastrous foreign adventures, leading to its military destruction. Pakistan has nuclear weapons. It can be provocative without fear of retaliation; however, its economic position is much weaker than that of Imperial Japan, and it might collapse even without a war.

Iran and Turkey are sometimes cited as relevant. The Shah's Iran also had the same kind of social dislocation that we now see in Pakistan, but its army was politically weak and its Shiite Islamist movement, led by an organized clergy, was more coherent than anything likely to develop in Pakistan.

Turkey, rescued from a nightmare scenario, has been held up as a model for Pakistan. Vali Nasr writes that Turkey is an exemplary case of capitalist and democratic development, which succeeded "largely with the European Union's help, with the European Union taking the long view in building ties with Turkey, requiring measures on the part of Ankara for it to be further integrated into Europe."[1] Turkish democracy is based on a solid economic foundation, and it has rejected the Islamist revolutionary narrative, which has Israel and the United States at its center. Some of this is still officially part of Pakistan's world view. Pervez Musharraf briefly talked about the Turkish model (he grew up in Turkey), but he retreated from that position even if he personally did not subscribe to the Islamist narrative. However, Pakistan cannot be integrated closely with Europe, let alone the United States. Its natural economic partner is India, although the Chinese exploit Pakistan more thoroughly than any other state. Pakistan's military cannot under current circumstances bring itself to emulate India, the state closest to it in terms of social and ethnic complexity.

Finally, Brazil is the best example of what might have been. With approximately the same population size and level of economic development as Pakistan (both largely agriculture based), Brazil also had an overweening military and at one

(continued)

Box 1-1. *Other Transformation Scenarios (continued)*

time also contemplated a nuclear weapons program. However, it never had the kind of external threat faced by Pakistan. Even though it fancied itself as Argentina's rival, it was able to transform its domestic politics to the point that a normal civil-military relationship emerged, and it was able to focus on filling regional and even global gaps in technology and economics, notably through its success in medium aircraft production and its international role as a sports power. Ten years ago, it was the recipient of the International Monetary Fund's largest-ever loan; today, it is lending money to the IMF.

---

1. Vali Nasr, *Forces of Fortune: The Rise of the New Muslim Middle Class and What It Will Mean for Our World* (New York: Free Press, 2009), p. 231.

---

none of these steps seems to be a *sufficient* factor that trumps all others. In the end, "muddling through" will have at least four or five variations.

Historically, states and empires come and go. The United Nations was founded with 51 states and now has 192. The old Chinese, British, French, Dutch, Austro-Hungarian, and German empires have all vanished or shrunk. The British Indian Raj, of which Pakistan is one of the legatees, has vanished, breaking up the strategic unity of the Subcontinent and pitting the two successor states against each other. The Soviet empire also is gone, there being nothing certain about the future of all or any states and imperial operations. As for states, Yugoslavia no longer exists, nor does Czechoslovakia or East Germany. On the other hand, Poland, which was once partitioned out of existence and then subjected to Nazi and Soviet rule, is now an independent country, firmly fixed in the broader European context.

Pakistan's future is not immutable. Pakistan has lasted sixty years, but in the process it has lost more than half of its population in a breakaway movement and barely resembles the tolerant state envisioned by Jinnah. The territory and the people of what is now Pakistan will remain, even if they are altered beyond recognition by population movement, environmental change, redrawn boundaries, or war. Pakistan's nuclear weapons will also remain, even if they are not controlled by a central government.

All of the participants in this project on the future of Pakistan agreed that the greatest uncertainty facing Pakistan is the interplay between the half-dozen or more critical factors that seem likely to shape the future, which are grouped with other variables into the four large clusters discussed above. That is why few participants were willing to predict beyond a few years and all qualified their predictions. The interplay between critical factors (especially since there was no unanimity on which factors they were or on their order of importance), their sequencing, and their salience in different circumstances are all unknown, and perhaps unknowable. As William Milam writes in chapter 7, most of these factors/variables are both cause and effect; they influence each other and are in turn influenced by other developments. Were the major factors/variables all moving in the right direction, a good-case scenario could not be ruled out. However, as Milam notes, "It will be a long, difficult slog of one or two generations before one could safely wager that Pakistan was going to join the rank of modern societies."

Perhaps the hardest thing for Pakistanis to do is the simplest: to imagine their country as a modern state, meeting the needs of all of its people and escaping from the thrall of religious conflict. Modern states exhibit normal relations between civilian and military elites, and they ensure that state institutions keep up with the legitimate requirements of their people. They do not parody the worst aspects of a colonial empire that vanished sixty years ago. However, achieving modernity is difficult when a state is buffeted by forces of globalization that weaken its institutions and empower separatist and terrorist groups.

Pakistan has resources. It is important in its own right, and because of its nuclearized dispute with India, the international community has a powerful stake in its survival and return to normality. But to move Pakistan ahead will require a concentrated focus on economic and political policies that foster growth and create greater participation of the population in governance. Pakistan's population, which is now regarded as irrelevant by most political leaders, could then become an asset in fighting militancy and ending Pakistan's several insurgencies. Pakistan needs a national debate on what kind of state its citizens believe that they need. In other words, it is critical for Pakistan to set lofty targets for itself and to attempt to meet them with its own resources rather than be subservient to the interest of other states, near or far. Given the short-term perspective of virtually all Pakistani politicians and the institutional obsessions of the military, it is hard to see how such a debate can begin.

Six Warning Signs

I conclude, as I did in 2004, with a list of warning signs. While this project has identified a number of factors, grouped into four clusters, these warning signs point to the immediate and urgent issues, although none alone are sufficient to ensure the normalization of Pakistan.

Unwillingness to Deal Quickly with Economic Issues. Pakistan has fantasized about its economic prospects for years, blaming others for its economic failures and claiming phantom successes, yet it is unwilling to tax the rich, let alone use state money to educate its masses. In the post-Musharraf period a new sense of realism has emerged, but Pakistan is still spending too much on defense and security. If it is to grow in the long term, it must cut its commitments to the military in the short term by building political arrangements that ease the defense problem and by trimming lavish weapons projects and excessive manpower. Economic growth is also the only way to address demographic trends that are creating a large class of unemployed (and unemployable) youth, which in the long run will make Pakistan ungovernable and for some, unlivable.

Unwillingness/Inability to Rebuild State Institutions. It may be that Pakistan is beyond the point of no return with respect to its weakened state institutions, whether they concern education, local administration, or the functions of higher bureaucracies. But these problems are not esoteric, and Pakistan needs help from the international community to conduct a massive organizational rebuilding process. Private organizations and NGOs are not a substitute for functioning state institutions. The army will have to allow civilian competence to develop, but whether it will do so depends on both its willingness to adopt a reduced role and the rise of demonstrated civilian competence. Meanwhile, education and state building should be given the same priority as defense policy.

Absence of Governance at the Top. In all of its recent crises, whether external or internal, Pakistan's government has demonstrated extraordinary incoherence at the top. The Mumbai crisis saw confusion reign in Islamabad, and when one civilian (the national security adviser, himself an ex-general) tried to set the record straight, he was fired. There was and is no coherent system of presenting alterative policies before the government, no systematic planning process, and no effective mechanism for coordinating the actions of different parts of the government. Usually the military has its way, but there is no question that Pakistan's army does not have the strategic capabilities necessary to formulate a coherent strategy on any but the narrowest military issues. It has been unable to develop a response to the domestic terrorism that rages in all parts of the country, especially the government-free zones of KP. If Pakistan does not create such a mechanism, presumably including a National Security Council (unlike the sham NSC created by Musharraf), it will continue to stumble strategically.

The Begging Bowl. Pakistan has fallen into a position of deep dependency vis-à-vis international donors, whether individual states or international lending agencies, and the government is correctly criticized for giving in to them one after another. Pakistan needs to adopt a relationship whereby its dignity and sovereignty are protected. The initiative for assistance must come from Pakistan, not outsiders, as it must from countries that apply for loans from the International Monetary Fund. Pakistan must develop the scope of and criteria for assistance programs and gain the support of donors. The conditions for assistance should come from the Pakistani side, with the acknowledgment that if Pakistan fails to meet those conditions, then the aid or support offered will be correspondingly reduced. Because doing so will require more capacity than Pakistan now has, the government should seek help from competent governments to improve its budget and planning cycle and from the private sector, where there is a great deal of talent. "Tough love" is a suitable standard, and Pakistanis themselves should insist on it.

Fresh Crises with India. A more normal relationship with India is necessary if Pakistan is to avoid further deterioration. Although India does not want to see an assertive Pakistan, a failing Pakistan has the capacity to do India considerable damage. The nuclearization of their sixty-year conflict makes the stakes even higher. Further crises, deliberate or inadvertent, will distract Pakistan from the rebuilding task and endanger India itself. The mechanisms are (or at least were) in place for normalization between the two states. If they move down this path, the process should be encouraged by outside powers and by an endorsement from the United Nations.

Further Appeasement of Islamists. Pakistan is becoming polarized, with liberal elements on the defensive. The global dialogue on reforming Islam has a Pakistani dimension, but much ground has been conceded to doctrinaire Islamists, who receive considerable state patronage. That has already changed Pakistan markedly, and the problem is not just the strength of intolerant and narrow Islamists but also the weakness of the tiny Westernized elite. Pakistan is becoming one of the centers of global jihad.

Policy: Between Hope and Despair

George Shultz once told me that hope was not a policy; when I recounted that conversation to a retired Pakistani diplomat, he countered that despair was also not a policy. The reality is that humans tend to err on the side of hope, and most conversations regarding Pakistan's future invariably try to present a hopeful and optimistic future. This tendency toward optimism and hopefulness is well-documented in the academic literature.[72] However, policy toward Pakistan is permeated by both hope and despair. There are no good policy options. Doing nothing and doing the same thing are both unattractive and problematic approaches, but there are no easy paths to the future, and a strong likelihood of policy disaster remains.

Some members of this project were very pessimistic about Pakistan's future even over the next five years and foresaw greater calamities ahead. One event that the group did not foresee was the massive flooding in July 2010 that submerged a good portion of Pakistan for several months. The flooding was the result of both a freakish weather event (heavy rains fell on the western but not the eastern portions of Pakistan's river system), plus forty years of neglect of the drainage and water management system by both military and civilian regimes. The consequences of the floods are still being debated, but they did not produce the kind of national rally that some hoped for, and they are more likely to turn out to be a negative "black swan" event.[73]

However, two factors give hope, with the caveat that hope is not a policy. First, there is no question that Pakistan has the human capital to reverse its direction. Its tiny elite are competent and there is a middle class that still wants reform. Pakistan needs to experiment with democracy; it cannot be run as an autocracy, whether by a military or a civilian leader, no matter how charismatic he or she might be.

Second, it is now in the interest of the international community that Pakistan succeed, or at least that it not fail badly. No country, not even India, wants to see Pakistan come apart violently, as real failure could spew nuclear weapons and terror groups around the world. That is why the option to break up Pakistan is both impractical and dangerous.

The Western powers, Japan, and India need to have a concerted policy—one that will strengthen reform and democratic forces in Pakistan, encourage the military to adopt a recessed role, improve Pakistan's economy, and generate more resources to address vital domestic needs. But China, Pakistan's closest ally, is no supporter of democratization and favors harsh measures to control terrorist and extremist groups. The parallels with North Korea are striking; by supporting Pakistan and North Korea, China keeps regional rivals off balance while it pursues its narrow economic and strategic goals.

Right now, as far as the West and Japan are concerned, policy regarding Pakistan derives primarily from U.S. and NATO engagement in Afghanistan. A second policy component is support for Pakistan in the battle against its own Taliban and other radical elements. Third, there is unprecedented economic aid, particularly in the form of the Kerry-Lugar bill. The assumption of the Kerry-Lugar initiative is that a failed Pakistan would be calamitous for the United States, given its size, its location, and above all, its nuclear weapons. This is Pakistan as another North Korea—"too nuclear to fail." Few, however, have advocated a massive nation-building program for Pakistan.

If one assumes that Pakistan might be weak and unstable (the worst variant of "muddling through") or holds the view that Pakistan is headed toward greater autonomy for its various provinces, then it makes sense to search for alternative policies. One would be to encourage India to supplant Pakistan in Afghanistan, providing an alternative route to Afghanistan and thus demonstrating to Islamabad that threats to cut off the supply lines can be circumvented. An expansion of this policy would be Ambassador Robert Blackwill's proposal to accept the partition of Afghanistan, throwing U.S. weight behind a Northern Alliance/India group to counter the Pakistan-supported Taliban in southern Afghanistan.

The problem with using India to balance or supplant Pakistan is that it provides negative incentives for the Pakistan army to undertake a program of domestic reform, and it certainly would heighten tensions between India and Pakistan.[74] Those who cling to a reform strategy for Pakistan are unwilling to abandon it for a balancing policy on the grounds that doing so would rule out entirely the possibility of reform.

If one's view, whether based on past Pakistani actions or not, is that Pakistan is not merely a state in trouble but one that will become a rogue state that cannot be reformed, then a balancing policy could be easily transformed into one of containment. That option was rejected by the Council on Foreign Relations task force, but at least one of the members wrote a dissent pointing out that Pakistan cannot be counted on to pursue policies that match up with U.S. interests in a number of sectors, notably relations with India, nuclear policy, and support for terrorists.[75] If one believes that present policies are not working, that aid packages will not have much of an impact, and that Pakistani nationalism trumps Pakistani national interest, then Pakistan should be seen as a threat, not an asset. That view would be confirmed should there be a successful terrorist attack originating in Pakistan against India or a Western country—for example, a successful Times Square bombing that kills many Americans. In that case public opinion would almost certainly demand a reassessment of the U.S. relationship with Pakistan.

Such a reassessment would give India the role of containing a dangerous Pakistan, and it might lead to a policy that placed India at the center of South Asia's geostrategic calculations, with the West working in partnership with New Delhi to "fix" Afghanistan and Pakistan, once and for all. This puts the United States on the side of a rising power, although Indians are deeply ambivalent about undertaking such a regional role.

If Pakistan continues to deteriorate and India does not want to play an active role in containing or balancing a failing Pakistan, then five or six years down the road the United States and its allies might pursue "offshore balancing," an academic/diplomatic euphemism for "cut and run."[76] The columnist Tom Friedman has said that regions such as the Middle East and South Asia eventually work out their difficulties without U.S. intervention.[77] With increasingly scarce resources and unhappy domestic opinion to contend with, the United States and its allies may well decide that the South Asian states can manage their affairs reasonably well and that all they would need to do is to step in every four or five years to prevent a nuclear war. However, the India-Pakistan rivalry involves other states as well, notably China, which has emerged as a significant South Asian power and is itself playing a balancing game with India and Pakistan. Policymakers need to think through carefully whether U.S. intervention would make a difference in the region and calculate the costs of not becoming involved as a facilitator in the stagnant South Asian peace process.

Two other policies need to be mentioned, although each has serious drawbacks. Steve Coll has forwarded the view that Kashmir is at the root of India-Pakistan differences and that if outside powers worked to facilitate a settlement, then the risks of war would be lowered and Pakistan presumably could devote its energies to reconstruction and rebuilding.[78] That, of course, would be opposed tooth and nail by India, but might be workable if, in exchange, there was a settlement of the Kashmir dispute, which Coll believes was almost achieved. Were Pakistan to normalize its relations with India, then cooperation might be extended across the board, restoring the strategic unity of the Subcontinent, which was lost during the 1947 partition. However, India's reluctance to compromise with a failing Pakistan notwithstanding, China would have every reason to oppose normalization, and it could probably offer Pakistan more reason *not* to settle than India could offer Pakistan to settle. Twenty-five years ago, before it went nuclear, Pakistan offered to abandon its nuclear program if the United States were to provide a security guarantee that included protection from an attack from India. The request was spurned; Pakistan went ahead with its nuclear program, and it has now become even more dependent on China. The prospects of restoring South Asia's strategic unity are now low to zero given China's new influence and India's ambivalence over normalization of relations with Pakistan.

So it is back to the current, and perhaps the least worst, cluster of policies. Politics is an experimental, not a theoretical science; we must see how this experiment plays out over the next two years, but it is hard to be optimistic that the West and the United States will get both Afghanistan and Pakistan "right," or that India will suddenly become generous, or that the Pakistani elite, especially the military, will undertake a program of deep reform. Hope for the best, but at least think about the worst.

Notes

1. For the best chronology of this process of state-breaking, see Ilhan Niaz, *The Culture of Power and Governance of Pakistan 1947–2008* (Oxford University Press, 2010).

2. For a recent report based on conversations with a senior retired Pakistani officer active at the time of these initiatives, see Aziz Haniffa, "Musharraf Was Never Close to Solving Kashmir, Says Pakistani General," *India Abroad,* December 16, 2010, p. A-16.

3. See the Report of the United Nations Commission of Inquiry into the facts and circumstances of the assassination of former Pakistani Prime Minister Mohtarma Benazir Bhutto (www.un.org/News/dh/infocus/Pakistan/UN_Bhutto_Report_15April2010.pdf). Other reports, including some U.S. government documents leaked by WikiLeaks, indicate that the army prevailed upon the Zardari government not to follow up on the U.N. report, protecting both Musharraf and perhaps other former officers who may have been implicated one way or another in her murder.

4. For a good overview of his reformist inclinations, see Ahsan's article, "Keep the Flag Flying," *Newsweek Pakistan,* September 13, 2010 (www.newsweekpakistan.com/component/content/article/38-features/108-keep-the-flag-flying-by-aitzaz-ahsan).

5. A close analogy to Lal Masjid was the attack by Indian military forces on the Golden Temple, the Sikhs' holy shrine in Amritsar, in 1984. That also set off a sustained battle between the army and police and Sikh militants, with the latter receiving considerable support from ordinary Sikh citizens who were infuriated by the attack on the temple. Prime Minister Indira Gandhi was eventually assassinated by her Sikh bodyguards, just as the militant Islamists tried repeatedly to kill Musharraf. Although they failed, a number of army officers were assassinated.

6. Amir Mir, "2010: Suicides Drop by 35 pc, Deaths up by 1 pc," *The News,* December 24, 2010 (www.thenews.com.pk/TodaysPrintDetail.aspx?ID=21975&Cat=2 [June 30, 2011]).

7. Two good sources for numbers are the website of the Pakistan Institute for Peace Studies (www.san-pips.com/index.php?action=reports&id=psr_list_1) and the Brookings Pakistan Index, a regularly updated collection of data and figures (www.brookings.edu/foreign-policy/pakistan-index.aspx).

8. See B. Raman, "Is Letting Pakistan Collapse an Option?" *Eurasia Review,* December 26, 2010 (www.eurasiareview.com/is-letting-pakistan-collapse-an-option-2612 2010/).

9. According to the Committee to Protect Journalists, eight of the forty-four journalists murdered around the world in 2010 were Pakistanis, the largest single number in any country.

10. Usman Manzoor, "Incumbent SC Outperforms Dogar Court by 2:1," *The News,* September 19, 2010 (www.thenews.com.pk/TodaysPrintDetail.aspx?ID=692& Cat=13).

11. One of the most remarkable examples is that of Ejaz Haider, a leading journalist who had been sympathetic to the military establishment. See "An Open Letter to General Pasha," *Express Tribune,* June 7, 2011.

12. Ahmed Faruqui, "Reversing History," February 3, 2010, *Outlook India* (www.outlookindia.com/printarticle.aspx?264103).

13. For a critique of the honor or virtue brigade—the *Ghairiyaat*—by a distinguished Pakistan columnist who argues that neither the army nor revolution is the cure

for Pakistan but that its salvation lies in the slow restoration of normal democratic political processes through the ballot box, see Ayaz Amir, "The Gathering Rage of the Virtue Brigades," *The News,* Friday July 23, 2010. Leaders of the *Ghairiyaat* include former ISI general Hamid Gul and A. Q. Khan, the metallurgist who stole centrifuge plans from Holland and persuaded Zulfikar Ali Bhutto that a Pakistani bomb was possible. Khan is one of many who speak approvingly of China as a model for Pakistan and scathingly of current political leaders for their cravenness toward the United States and India. See "Our Leaders Should Learn Lessons from China: Dr. Qadeer," *The Nation,* December 25, 2010 (www.nation.com.pk/pakistan-news-newspaper-daily-english-online/Politics/25-Dec-2010/Our-leaders-should-learn-lesson-from-China-Dr-Abdul-Qadir-Khan).

14. For two relatively optimistic projections, see Maleeha Lodhi, *Pakistan: Beyond the "Crisis State"*(Columbia University Press, 2011), and Anatol Lieven, *Pakistan: A Hard Country* (New York: Public Affairs Press, 2011). For a grimmer assessment, see the book by former U.S. diplomat John R. Schmidt, *The Unraveling: Pakistan in the Age of Jihad* (New York: Farrar, Straus and Giroux, 2011).

15. See Tariq Fatemi's introductory paragraph in chapter 5 of this volume.

16. For an insightful essay on hope in the context of the "failure" of recent India-Pakistan talks, see Mehreen Zahra-Malik, "Hope and Its Discontents," *Friday Times* [Lahore weekly], July 23–28, 2010.

17. For a modern study of disaster and unpredictable events, see Lee Clarke, *Worst Cases: Terror and Catastrophe in the Popular Imagination* (University of Chicago Press, 2006).

18. Institute for Defence Studies and Analyses, *Whither Pakistan: Growing Instability and Implications for India* (www.idsa.in/book/WhitherPakistan).

19. British Council, *Pakistan: The Next Generation,* November 2009, p. iv (www.britishcouncil.org/pakistan-active-citizens-next-generation-report.htm).

20. Irteza Haider and Murtaza Haider, "Pakistan," in Brian Roberts and Trevor Kanaley, *Urbanization and Sustainability in Asia: Case Studies of Good Practice* (Philippines: Asian Development Bank, 2006,) pp. 245–71 (www.adb.org/Documents/Books/Urbanization-Sustainability/urbanization-sustainability.pdf).

21. See the British Council, *Pakistan: The Next Generation.*

22. Athar Osama, "HEC Scholars: Will They Return? And Stay?" Pakistan Research Support Network, August 9, 2008 (http://pakistaniat.com/2008/08/09/hec-pakistan/).

23. Kizilbash's remarks were delivered at the conference "Empowering Faculty and Transforming Education in Pakistan" at the Woodrow Wilson Center, Washington, April 7, 2010 (www.wilsoncenter.org/ondemand/index.cfm?fuseaction=home.play&mediaid=E41FB00A-A2E7-7301-113CE5FEFA3FC864).

24. Vali Nasr, *Forces of Fortune: The Rise of the New Muslim Middle Class and What It Will Mean for Our World* (New York: Free Press, 2009).

25. Jonathan Paris, *Prospects for Pakistan* (London: Legatum Institute, 2010), p. 25.

26. All of this is in dismal contrast to India. At one time Pakistan had a much higher per capita income than the much larger (and generally poorer) India. Today,

with its growth rate of more than 8 percent, India is one of the fastest-growing economies in the world, at the top with Brazil and China. India's WIPRO software company has a bigger market cap than all of Pakistan.

27. See Hussain H. Zaidi, "Only Option," *The News*, Islamabad, September 19, 2010 (http://www.jang.com.pk/thenews/sep2010-weekly/nos-19-09-2010/pol1.htm#5).

28. *Economist Intelligence Unit*, selected country data and estimates for Pakistan, 1986–2013 (www.eiu.com).

29. See "Aid to Pakistan by the Numbers," Center for Global Development (www.cgdev.org/section/initiatives/_active/pakistan/numbers).

30. Data from the U.N. Human Development Index (http://hdr.undp.org/en/statistics/).

31. Zeeshan Haider, "Militancy-Hit Pakistan Ups Defense Spending by 17 Percent," June 5, 2010, *Reuters* (www.reuters.com/article/idUSTRE6541UF20100605).

32. See Stephen Philip Cohen, *The Idea of Pakistan* (Brookings, 2004), and Farzana Shaikh, *Making Sense of Pakistan* (Columbia University Press, 2009).

33. For a vivid comparison of today's Pakistan with Pakistan in the past, see Hajrah Mumtaz, "Pakistan, 50 Years Ago," *Dawn*, June 20, 2011 (www.dawn.com/2011/06/20/pakistan-50-years-ago.html).

34. For an excellent overview of ethnicity in Pakistan, see Alyssa Ayres, *Speaking Like a State: Language and Nationalism in Pakistan* (Cambridge University Press, 2009).

35. Pew Global Attitudes Project, "*Pakistani Public Opinion*," August 13, 2009 (http://pewglobal.org/2009/08/13/pakistani-public-opinion/): "Overall, 89% say they think of themselves first as Pakistani, rather than as a member of their ethnic group."

36. See the references in Cohen, *The Idea of Pakistan*, to ethnolinguistic movements, especially Waseem; for a recent study, see Farhan Hanif Siddiqi, "The State and Politics of Ethnicity in Post-1971 Pakistan: An Analysis of the Baloch, Sindhi, and Mohajir Ethnic Movements," Ph.D. thesis, Department of International Relations, University of Karachi, 2009.

37. Muhammad Mushtaq and Syed Khawaja Alqama, "Poverty Alleviation through Power-Sharing in Pakistan," *European Journal of Social Sciences,* vol. 8, no. 3 (2009), pp. 459–68.

38. Praveen Swami, *India, Pakistan, and the Secret Jihad* (London: Routledge, 2007); Rizwan Hussain, *Pakistan and the Emergence of Islamic Militancy in Afghanistan* (Burlington, Vt.: Ashgate, 2005); Barnett Rubin, *The Fragmentation of Afghanistan* (Yale University Press, 2002); Mariam Abou Zahab, "The Regional Dimension of Sectarian Conflicts in Pakistan," in *Pakistan: Nationalism without a Nation?* edited by Christophe Jaffrelot (London: Zed, 2002), pp.115–28; International Crisis Group, *Pakistan: The Mullahs and the Military*, Asia Report 49 (Islamabad: Crisis Group, March 2003); S. V. R. Nasr, "The Rise of Sunni Militancy in Pakistan: The Changing Role of Islamism and the Ulama in Society and Politics," *Modern Asian Studies*, vol. 34, no. 1 (2000), pp. 139–80.

39. See Pervez Hoodbhoy for a worst-case scenario, "Whither Pakistan" (http://pakistaniat.com/2009/06/16/pervez-hoodbhoy-pakistan-future/).

40. Ibid.

41. The army is central in the papers by Aqil Shah, Hasan Askari Rizvi, and Shaukat Qadir, yet almost every paper presented at the Bellagio workshop commented on the military in one way or another. For the original papers, see www.brookings.edu/~/media/Files/rc/papers/2010/09_bellagio_conference_papers/09_bellagio_papers.pdf; this volume contains all of them in revised form.

42. See the needlessly insulting blog post published by Banyan, "Land of the Impure," *The Economist*, June 19, 2010 (www.economist.com/node/16377259).

43. It is Pakistan's army that is central, not the professional but politically marginal air force and navy.

44. Stephen P. Cohen, *The Pakistan Army* (University of California Press, 1985).

45. The Pakistan army officer corps is not a hotbed of radical Islamic thinking, although it does engage with Islamic theories of war and searches for ways in which Islamic principles can guide it; see Cohen, *The Pakistan Army*. Ambitious officers follow a Western professional model, and many are concerned with blowback from the army's support for radical Islamists. Their own theology is pragmatic, but they have not yet found a strategy to counter true extremism, inside and outside the army, as they distrust "liberal" political and social thought.

46. For two studies, see Stephen P. Cohen, *Mastering Counterinsurgency: A Workshop Report*, based on a conference with the National Defense University of Pakistan, March, 2009 (www.brookings.edu/papers/2009/0707_counterinsurgency_cohen.aspx), and Shuja Nawaz, "Learning by Doing: The Pakistan Army's Experiment with Counterinsurgency," Atlantic Council Report (Washington: February 2011).

47. For recent Pakistan army discussions on regional issues, see, for example, recent editions of *The Citadel*, the journal of the Command and Staff College, Quetta, notably Muhammed Anneq Ur Rehman Malik, "Military Lessons of Operation Enduring Freedom (OEF)," vol. 26, no. 1, (2008); Raza Muhammad, "Indian Cold Start Doctrine: A Brief Review," vol. 27, no. 1 (2009); Saad Mahmood, "Indo-U.S. Nuclear Deal: Implications for Pakistan," vol. 28, no. 1 (2010); Qaiser Ajmal Khattak, "FATA Problem: A Perspective," vol. 28, no. 2 (2010).

48. For a contemporary European study that emphasizes the importance of state governance, see Marco Mezzera, "Challenges of Pakistan's Governance System," NOREF Policy Brief 2, October 2009 (www.peacebuilding.no/eng/Publications/Noref-Policy-Briefs/Challenges-of-Pakistan-s-Governance-System). Numerous academic studies have told of the systematic destruction of state capacity in Pakistan. For a recent comprehensive account that brings the process up to date, see the fine history by Ilhan Niaz, *The Culture of Power and Governance of Pakistan: 1947–2008* (Oxford University Press, 2010).

49. Failed State Index, by *Foreign Policy* and the Fund For Peace (www.foreign policy.com/failedstates).

50. There have been very few attempts to study, let alone measure, the impact of Friday sermons and the mosques on public opinion. For a rare glimpse, see the studies carried out by a group of students and observers by *Mashal*, the liberal publication and

reprint house created by Pervez Hoodbhoy. See "Message from the Mosque," a review of mosque sermons that can be searched by category and topic (http://imams.mashal books.org/).

51. It may never be known whether it was state incompetence or malevolent intent that led to the neglect of her security arrangements. She added to the problem with her belief that the people of Pakistan would protect her from known elements that wanted her dead.

52. National Intelligence Council, *Global Trends 2025: A Transformed World,* NIC 2008-003 (Washington: November 2008), p. 72.

53. Robert Blackwill, "Plan B in Afghanistan: Why a De Facto Partition Is the Least Bad Option," *Foreign Affairs,* January-February 2011 (www.cfr.org/publication/23655/plan_b_in_afghanistan.html).

54. Pamela Constable, "Pakistan's Army Chief Seeks Stable Afghanistan," *Washington Post,* February 2, 2010 (www.washingtonpost.com/wp-dyn/content/article/2010/02/01/AR2010020102506.html).

55. For a comprehensive history of U.S.-Pakistan relations, see Dennis Kux, *The United States and Pakistan, 1947–2000: Disenchanted Allies* (Washington: Woodrow Wilson Center Press, 2001). For a unique study of Pakistani negotiating strategies with the United States, see also Howard B. Schaffer and Teresita C. Schaffer, *Pakistan Negotiates with America: Riding the Roller-Coaster* (Washington: U.S. Institute of Peace Press, 2011).

56. "A Pakistani Response to the U.S. Annual Review," Stratfor, December 21, 2010 (www.stratfor.com/memberships/178428/analysis/20101220-pakistani-response-us-annual-review).

57. See Ashley J. Tellis, "South Asia: U.S. Policy Choices," in *Taking Charge: A Bipartisan Report to the President-Elect on Foreign Policy and National Security*, edited by Frank Carlucci, Robert E. Hunter, and Zalmay Khalilzad (Santa Monica, Calif.: RAND, 2001), p. 88 (www.rand.org/pubs/monograph_reports/MR1306.html).

58. Jane Perlez, "WikiLeaks Archive: U.S. and Pakistan, Ever Wary," *New York Times,* December 1, 2010 (www.nytimes.com/2010/12/01/world/asia/01wikileaks-pakistan.html).

59. BBC, "Global Views of United States Improve While Other Countries Decline," April 18, 2010 (http://news.bbc.co.uk/2/shared/bsp/hi/pdfs/160410bbcwspoll.pdf).

60. For a brief but excellent overview of the value of the relationship to both sides, see James Lamont and Farhan Bokhari, "An Alliance Is Built," *Financial Times,* Friday, July 1, 2011, p. 7.

61. Salman Masood, "China Praises Pakistan's Fight against Terrorism and Vows to Bolster Partnership," *New York Times,* December 20, 2010, p. A8.

62. Nicole Gaouette, "Most Pakistanis View U.S. as Enemy, Want War Over, Survey Finds," *Business Week* (www.businessweek.com/news/2010-07-29/most-pakistanis-view-u-s-as-enemy-want-war-over-survey-finds.html).

63. Even secular democracies also became more "religious," notably the United States, with its angry religious right, and India, with a resurgent Hindutva-inspired Bharatiya Janata Party.

64. Now that the Pakistani courts have ended his house arrest, Dr. Khan comments frequently on nuclear and strategic matters. See his interview in Susan Kolbe, "We May Be Naïve but We Are Not Idiots," Spiegel Online, June 28, 2011 (www.spiegel.de/international/world/0,1518,770746,00.html).

65. Quoted in *Zee News* [New Delhi], May 31, 2009 (http://zeenews.india.com/news/south-asia/pak-would-not-have-survived-after-kargil-mumbai-attacks-without-nukes_535592.html).

66. For a discussion, see Stephen P. Cohen and Sunil Dasgupta, *Arming without Aiming: India's Military Modernization* (Brookings, 2010), pp.66–67.

67. "Mapping the Global Future," Report of the National Intelligence Council's 2020 Project (Washington: National Intelligence Council, December 2004), p. 21 (www.dni.gov/nic/NIC_globaltrend2020.html).

68. As Jonathan Paris has informed me, "muddling through" is not a casual term. See the seminal essay by Charles Lindblom, "The Science of Muddling Through," *Public Administration Review*, vol. 19, no. 2. (Spring 1959), pp. 79–88.

69. See the clever year-end summary by Mahmood Adele, "2010: The Year in Review," a blog post on *New Pakistan* in which he weighs gains and losses in several categories (press, politicians, the military, NGOs, and the economy) and the tally comes out about even (http://new-pakistan.com/2010/12/28/2010-year-in-review/).

70. Ralph Peters, "Blood Borders: How a Better Middle East Would Look," *Armed Forces Journal*, June 2006 (www.armedforcesjournal.com/2006/06/1833899).

71. Speaking at the conference "Empowering Faculty and Transforming Education in Pakistan" at the Woodrow Wilson Center, Washington, April 7, 2010 (www.wilsoncenter.org/ondemand/index.cfm?fuseaction=home.play&mediaid=E41FB00A-A2E7-7301-113CE5FEFA3FC864).

72 For one recent overview see Susan C. Vaughan, *Half Empty, Half Full: Understanding the Psychological Roots of Optimism* (New York: Harcourt, 2000).

73. Stephen P. Cohen, "Lessons from Pakistan's Latest Catastrophe," Brookings, August 17, 2010 (www.brookings.edu/opinions/2010/0817_pakistan_floods_cohen.aspx). For two balanced overviews, see "Pakistan at Risk: Challenges and Opportunities after the Flood," Jinnah Institute Conference Report, September-October 2010 (http://jinnah-institute.org/images/ji%20flood%20conference%20report%20oct 2010.pdf), and K. Allan Kronstadt and others, "Flooding in Pakistan: Overview and Issues for Congress," CRS Report for Congress R41424, Congressional Research Service, September 21, 2010 (http://assets.opencrs.com/rpts/R41424_20100921.pdf).

74. This point was made recently in Council on Foreign Relations, "U.S. Strategy for Pakistan and Afghanistan," Task Force Report, November 2010 (www.cfr.org/publication/23253/us_strategy_for_pakistan_and_afghanistan.html).

75. Ibid. See Michael Krepon's dissent to the CFR task force report, pp. 69–70.

76. For a basic explanation of offshore balancing and other grand strategies, see John Mearsheimer, "Imperial by Design," *National Interest*, vol. 111 (January–February 2011) (http://mearsheimer.uchicago.edu/pub-affairs.html).

77. Thomas L. Friedman, "The Great (Double) Game," *New York Times*, July 31, 2010 (www.nytimes.com/2010/08/01/opinion/01friedman.html).

78. Steve Coll, "Kashmir: The Time Has Come," *New York Review of Books,* September 30, 2010 (www.nybooks.com/articles/archives/2010/sep/30/kashmir-time-has-come/). I think it more likely that India and Pakistan might cooperate on Afghanistan, where both have common interests, but only in the context of a new U.S. and Western policy that returns to the idea of a regional consortium of neighbors. For views on this by Indian and Pakistani writers, see Rudra Chaudhuri, "The Proxy Calculus: Kabul, Not Kashmir, Holds the Key to the India-Pakistani Relationship," *RUSI Journal,* vol. 155, no. 6 (December 2010), pp. 52–59, and Khaled Ahmed, "A 'Doable' Paradigm-Shift," *Friday Times*, September 10–16, 2010, p. 3.

2

Pakistan's Future: Muddle Along

The future of Pakistan is one of the greatest challenges before the international community. It is a country of 169 million people, projected to grow to between 250 and 335 million by 2050, which would make it the fourth- or fifth-largest country in the world.[1] It is riven by internal differences and external worries. It is also wracked by terrorism and, in places, by civil war. Worse still, it has nuclear weapons, which, if they fall into the wrong hands, could lead to regional if not global catastrophe. Where is Pakistan likely to be in the next ten years? I argue that in ten years, Pakistan will be more or less where it is now because there is nothing to tip it into a different state. A muddle-along Pakistan is therefore the future, and from India's point of view, that is better than more radical alternatives. There are several things that India can do to try to help the moderate forces in Pakistan.

This chapter argues that there are six possible futures for Pakistan, three more radical and three more moderate.[2] The three revolutionary futures are a Somalia-like state collapse featuring a Hobbesian "war of every man against every man"; balkanization along regional lines; and an Islamic revolution of the Iranian or Taliban kind. The three more moderate futures are a deepening "liberal" democracy; a complete military takeover as in 1958, 1977, and 1999; and the continuation of the present "muddle along" approach. I suggest that the most likely futures are military rule and an uneasy muddle along, because no person, institution, organization, idea, class, region, or external power is strong enough to bring about a shift from the country's present state. Pakistan is in what economists call a low-level equilibrium trap.

State Collapse

Pakistan could face state collapse in the next ten years, leading to a situation like that in Somalia (or Afghanistan after the Soviet withdrawal), where there is no central authority of any consequence and no actor legitimate or strong enough to ensure order and to govern throughout the country. Powerful warlords and organizations—ethnic, religious—would have sufficient authority and coercive power to provide localized order and government of the most basic, brutish kind.

For state collapse to occur, central authority would have to degrade to the point that it had no effective say in daily life and provincial authority too would be reduced to a nominal existence. Warlords and ethno-religious organizations would extract resources, provide minimal services, and dispense protection and justice. This would be a relatively stable outcome if the various leaders and groups were more or less equal in power. However, any balance of power would exist only to collapse after a period of time, as do balances of power between states in the international system, leading to another round of war. For the most part, there would be a shifting, ceaseless round of fighting and pillaging.

Quite apart from the misery that this would entail for ordinary Pakistanis, a Somalia-like Pakistan would be worrying for the region and the rest of the world. The greatest danger is that among the warlords—or in the interstices between various warlords—there would be Islamic extremists and terrorists who would operate outside the country, against targets in Afghanistan, China, India, Iran, and the West. The greatest advantage of a Somalia-like future is that Pakistanis would be so busy warring against each other that they would not have time to threaten other countries. Afghanistan would not be so lucky, because Pakistanis have kinfolk across the border who would be drawn into Pakistan's internal quarrels.

The chances of state collapse along these lines and the organization of the Pakistani space into one dominated by warlord-led clans and special protection zones seems unlikely, however, for at least four reasons. First and most important, the Pakistani army remains a cohesive enough and militarily effective enough force, particularly with outside assistance, to prevent complete state collapse. Second, the dominance of Punjab and Punjabis means that the country has a strong enough core. Unless Punjab breaks up into warring zones, Pakistan cannot fracture into a Hobbesian state of nature. While there is growing religious violence in Punjab (between Sunni and Shia Muslims, above all) and while Islamic extremists target state functionaries, the province remains intact. Third, Pakistan still has functioning civil services that can and do provide administration. Fourth, Pakistan's political and civil society is not toothless. There are a number of political parties and specifically, two major ones—the Pakistan People's Party and the Pakistan Muslim League–Nawaz. In addition, its media, English and Urdu, while often shrill and irresponsible, continue to provide news and commentary on developments within the country. The media serve to educate and mobilize public opinion and are devoted to the cause of national unity—to "the idea of Pakistan," to use Stephen Cohen's phrase—against the prospect of state collapse.[3]

Balkanization

A second radical future for Pakistan is the balkanization of the country along regional lines, with the unhappy provinces—Balochistan and Sindh in the main, but possibly Khyber Pakhtunkhwa too—breaking away to form separate states and leaving a rump Pakistan in the form of Punjab. Again there would have to be a breakdown of central authority and a decline of central power sufficient to allow these provinces to separate, peacefully or through violence. The result might be a wary, unhappy truce between Punjab and the others, with tensions among the breakaway provinces as well, but a truce at any rate.

There is a less pleasant possibility. Significant minorities exist throughout Pakistan. Because these groups might feel less secure in a balkanized Pakistan than a united but chaotic one, the breakaway provinces in turn might be full of dissent and insurrection, with irredentist claims and counterclaims washing over the new states. In consequence, a Hobbesian future is a darker possibility: each province at war, within and without. If so, the balkanization of Pakistan along regional lines might come to approximate the first future, state collapse and warlordism.

As with the first future, the balkanization future could be a mixed one for the rest of the world. If there is a balance of power between the various provinces and a certain amount of forbearance in respect of neighboring provinces, there could be stability. The worry, again, is that each province, weaker than the erstwhile united Pakistan ruled by a central government, would be unable to stay united and maintain internal order, thus providing a haven for Islamic extremists and terrorists. If there is not a balance of power and irredentist movements proliferate, then the Hobbesian collapse of each province might lead to further fragmentation. Neighboring regional powers might be tempted to intervene in the affairs of the new states and to install proxies and puppets in power. Large population movements might occur, particularly into India and Iran, from Sindh and Baluchistan respectively, reinforcing Tehran's and New Delhi's desire to increase their influence.

What are the prospects for regional balkanization? Two conditions would probably have to be met for the regional breakup of Pakistan. The first is that the largest state, Punjab, loses the will to hold the country together. As long as the army and civil service, both of which are Punjabi dominated, retain their cohesion, Punjab will have the resources to keep unhappy provinces within the fold. If, however, the Punjabis decide that they are paying too heavy a price to preserve the union, then balkanization may occur very quickly. As with the Soviet Union, it is when the more advanced and more powerful part of the union decides to break away that unity collapses.

The second condition for balkanization is outside intervention. If India and Iran or some other powerful state supports one or more of the recalcitrant provinces, those provinces may eventually succeed in separating. Both conditions might occur: outside support to Baluchistan and Sindh may eventually sap the will of Punjab to keep the country together. Punjab may calculate that it is better off without the bother of fighting external and internal foes.

Is this a likely future? Once again, as long as the Punjabi-dominated Pakistani army and higher civil service remain more or less cohesive, it seems implausible that Punjab will secede. Moreover, those who harbor thoughts of secession must be sure that they can remain more than nominally independent in the shadow of India and Iran and must ask themselves whether becoming protectorates of those two countries is to be preferred to Punjabi dominance of Pakistan.

Islamic Revolution

Could Pakistan succumb to an Iranian- or Taliban-style Islamic revolution, led by Sunni clerics? Some might argue that this is a greater worry than either state collapse or balkanization. On the other hand, a strong Islamic government would at least bring order and might give Pakistan an Iran-like coherence and stability. For the international community, a radical Pakistan would be more predictable and in the long run more amenable to socialization in the "rules of the game." Still, a revolutionary Pakistan with nuclear weapons at its disposal and a triumphalist, crusading ideology would cause consternation all over the world, not least in Afghanistan, Central Asia, China, India, Iran, and Russia. It would also send shockwaves through the Muslim world.

At first glance, a number of conditions in Pakistan seem to be conducive to an Islamic revolution. Pakistan has become an increasingly Islamized society, at least from President Zia ul-Haq's time. Sunni Islam is dominant in

Pakistan, and so there is a social basis for a Sunni takeover of the state at some point. In the engulfing chaos that is Pakistan today, fatigue is setting in, particularly in the face of terrorism, state collapse, and regional separatism. Military rule has not brought stability, and the political parties have not been able to make electoral democracy work with any degree of conviction. Corruption, bad governance, inequality, unemployment, inflation, food shortages, disunity, and violence—all that and more still afflict Pakistan, after more than sixty years of military and political party rule. Finally, anti-Westernism and anti-Americanism have never been higher, partly as a result of the global war on terrorism, the war in Afghanistan, the U.S. drone attacks on militants in Pakistan, and perceived U.S. interference in Pakistani affairs.

A Sunni Islamic revolution could come to be regarded as a form of release and redemption from the bad politics that Pakistanis have lived under for six decades. However, several other factors work against those that might push Pakistan in the direction of Sunni rule.

For one thing, because Pakistan already has many features of a fairly Islamized society, a revolution is hardly necessary in order to bring in, say, the sharia and Islamic courts. The success of Islamization over the past four decades, at least since President Zia's days, obviates the need for an Islamic revolution. Perhaps as a result, there is little support for Islamic parties such as the Jamaat-e-Islami, which, in election after election, has failed to garner much of a vote.[4] Nor is there a charismatic figure like Ayatollah Khomeini or Mullah Omar to lead the Sunni clerics and groups—and no sign of any such figure on the political horizon. The leaders of the Pakistani Taliban certainly do not have anything like the respect that accrued to either Khomeini or Omar. The Taliban itself has been seriously hampered if not degraded by both Pakistani and U.S. military operations against it, and the leadership operates mostly from hiding. Finally, Sunni Islam in Pakistan is by no means a united force, partly because of the absence of a popular and charismatic leader and partly because of philosophical and theological schisms within—between Deobandis and Barelvis, between Sufi strains and Wahhabi influences, and so on.

In the end perhaps there is one additional and fairly emphatic reason that an Islamic revolution of the Iranian or Taliban type is unlikely to take place in Pakistan: the negative demonstration effects of those two cases. Both occurred next to Pakistan and therefore are not susceptible to being romanticized by the vast mass of Pakistanis. In the Iranian case, there is a more positive story to tell, in the sense that Iran exhibits greater stability and often a surprising degree of internal political competition. But the puritanical elements of revolutionary Iran and the country's international isolation do not appeal to most Pakistanis. The Taliban's rule in Afghanistan under Mullah Omar is regarded as even more disastrous, with none of the positive features with which Pakistanis might credit Iran. In sum, mullah rule does not appear attractive to Pakistanis despite all the troubles in the country and the increasing political fatigue.

"Liberal" Democracy

The ideal moderate future for Pakistan would be "liberal" democracy. The word has been put in quotes to indicate that Pakistani democracy would not be, in the strict sense, liberal. Pakistan is an Islamic state by constitutional fiat, and any attempt to purge the country of its basic Islamic features and to secularize its politics and society is infeasible. Indeed, there is probably no redder red flag, politically speaking, than the word "liberal." By liberal democracy, we mean here the kind of disposition exemplified by Mohammed Ali Jinnah, the founder of Pakistan, or, to give a more contemporary example, Turkey, where there is a regularly elected civilian leadership, an army that stays in the barracks but keeps a careful eye on things, and fairly widespread public support for moderate Islamic rules and standards in social life.

Is even this kind of liberal democracy a possibility? Pakistan already has liberal democratic elements. The country is in its third year of democracy after Benazir Bhutto's assassination. The military is in the barracks and keeping a watchful eye on things. As for moderation in Islam, daily life in Pakistan is not puritanical in the way that it is in Saudi Arabia or Iran.

On the other hand, in comparison with religion in Turkey, religion in Pakistan plays a far more important and deadly role in politics. There are avowedly Islamic political parties such as the Jamaat-e-Islami (JeI), the Jamiat Ulema-e-Islam–Fazl-ur-Rehman (JUI-F), and several other parties in the six-party coalition, the Muttahida Majlis-e-Amal (MMA), that want much stricter observance of Islam in the country. Pakistan also has very violent and intolerant Islamic groups that operate openly, including the Jaish-e-Muhammad (JeM), the Lashkar-e-Tayyiba (now the Jamaat-ud-Dawa), the Lashkar-e-Jhangvi, the Sipah-e-Sahaba (which is banned), and the Tehrik-e-Taliban Pakistan (TTP). These parties do not get a large percentage of the popular vote—usually single-digit percentages—but they have "street power" and can mobilize from 50,000 to 500,000 people. The extremist groups also can bring large, vociferous crowds out onto the streets. After the assassinations of Punjab's governor, Salmaan Taseer, in January 2011 and of Minority Minister Shahbaz Bhatti in March 2011, the religious parties and groups mobilized crowds in support of the killers and publicly lauded the deaths of both victims. Worse, there is a growing link between the mainstream parties and extremist groups.

The Pakistani military also is not staunchly secular in the way that the Turkish army has been. Indeed, it is the military that gave the religious right the space in which to operate beginning in the late 1970s, when President Zia was in power. Zia's leadership of the military also led to a growing social and religious conservatism within the armed forces.[5] This conservatism has only increased, and there is no prospect of reducing it. The military continues in any case to support extremist groups, against India primarily but also the United States and its Western partners in Afghanistan.

As for public opinion in Pakistan, it would be difficult to describe it as liberal. Liberalism is weak for a number of reasons related to the religiosity of Pakistanis, the state of education, the weakness and corruption of political parties, and anti-Western, anti-American, and anti-Indian feelings. Perhaps the most important reason for the weakness of liberalism, however, is the lack of a sizable middle class. That is not likely to change very quickly. Ironically, the spread of print and electronic media, social networking, and mobile telephones has not strengthened liberal opinion. The more radical Islamic groups have used these communication resources far more effectively to spread their illiberal message.

Military Rule

A return to direct military rule is always a possibility in Pakistan. The military ruled from 1958 to 1971, 1977 to 1988, and from 1999 to 2008, that is, for thirty-three of the sixty-four years since the country came into existence. It has the firepower, clearly, to do so again. Also, given the anarchic and unedifying way in which the political parties conduct themselves, there are bound to be grounds for military intervention in the future. It is a safe bet, in fact, that Pakistan's future is military rule. The average length of government under political parties is 7.5 years. The Pakistan People's Party government has been in power for three years. Going by the average, the military will take over in about four years.

Will the Pakistani military replace civilian rule for any length of time? The average length of military rule in Pakistan is eleven years. Will it return to power by, say, 2015 and stay in the saddle until 2026? If the past is any indication, the odds are in favor. Yet we should be cautious, for at least two reasons.

First, the military has an implicit if not explicit veto in crucial policy areas, in particular the nuclear program, relations with India, Kashmir policy,

Afghanistan, regulating the jihadis and other militants, Pakistan-U.S. and Pakistan-China relations, the defense budget and military procurement, and the military foundations and other privileges. Why rule directly for a long time when it can rule indirectly more or less permanently?

The second and more fundamental reason is that the military faces enormous challenges ahead, in a way that it never has before. Internally, it is worried about the reliability of both the enlisted men and the officers' corps, which has been severely tested in internal security duties, particularly in the anti-militant operations in FATA, where enlisted men have defected to the militants.[6] Morale has also been tested by several very public attacks on the military, including the Inter-Services Intelligence, and by Islamic extremists. In addition, the military faces several strategic challenges: ensuring the safety of nuclear weapons, calibrating the Pakistan-U.S. relationship, plotting the future of Afghanistan, dealing with Indian military power, wrestling the Islamic extremists under control, and squashing secessionism. To run, in addition, the day-to-day affairs of the country in the midst of turmoil and economic bad times is to put the military's image and effectiveness at risk.[7]

Does this mean that the Pakistani military will not intervene and rule? There is a good chance that military rule will resume if the political parties cross certain red lines into veto areas that are "reserved" for the military, as indicated above; if civilian rule again, as in the 1980s, slides into extreme partisanship leading to political paralysis; or if internal violence reaches emergency proportions and the normal functioning of the political system is threatened by massive extremist intimidation and terrorist violence. However, any future intervention is likely to be a short-term measure rather than the decade-long interventions that have characterized earlier instances, primarily because the military faces daunting internal organizational as well as strategic challenges and therefore will want to return to the barracks as quickly as possible.

Muddle Along

A final moderate possibility is that Pakistan will muddle along, more or less as it is today. What is Pakistan today? Present-day Pakistan is a mix of state failure, regional balkanization, Islamic fundamentalism, military domination, and liberal democracy.

Pakistani political life features traces of all five futures simultaneously. Thus, the state in Pakistan is under severe stress, and its authority and power are under challenge as never before. Particularly in Balochistan, there are powerful separatist tendencies, and the autonomous tribal areas are substantially outside central government control. Everywhere in Pakistan, Islamic forces have grown in strength, operating with impunity (calling public meetings, organizing protests, intimidating opponents and the government, collecting and extorting money, imposing religious law, and running schools and training camps for militants) and carrying out acts of terror. The military casts a huge shadow over civilian government and, even when it is out of power, intervenes in politics, exercising a veto over various areas of government policy. Finally, Pakistan has features of liberal democracy even if it is not a liberal democracy. It has elections, a constitution that specifies a set of rights and the rule of law, checks and balances in government, political parties, and a more or less free press.

Why is Pakistan an uneasy mix of these five tendencies? Why has it not turned decisively in one direction or another? I have tried to indicate in my analysis of the five futures why none of them seems plausible in the coming years. In essence, if we abstract from the analysis, we can conclude that there is no person, institution, organization, idea, class, region, or outside power strong enough to tip Pakistan irrevocably one way or other. There is no group or organization that can overwhelm the military, the civil service, the political parties, the media, and the dominance of Punjab to the point of outright collapse. Similarly, although there are separatist forces at work, particularly in Balochistan and the autonomous regions, they are not sufficient to overcome the Pakistani military and the determination of Punjab to hold the country together. Nor is any outside power willing and able to break Pakistan up. As for an Islamic revolution, while there has been a steady growth in Islamization and while violent extremist groups are wreaking havoc, public opinion has not shifted in favor of an overthrow of the present order toward a more radical alternative—the idea of a radical Islamic republic is simply not widespread enough. The Islamic parties have street power, but they cannot win elections. There is no charismatic figure among the extremist groups or political parties that could lead a revolution. Liberal democracy cannot "break out" in Pakistan even though features of a liberal democratic order exist. Pakistani liberals and the middle class are not strong enough to challenge the hold of religion, the illiberalism and interventions of the military, and the extent of anti-Western, anti-American, and anti-India feeling. Finally, military rule, while it is likely to occur again, will not last as long as in previous eras, because the armed forces are beset by a number of internal organizational, domestic security, and external challenges and cannot take on the daunting task of governing full time over many years.

Conclusion: Implications for India

If muddling along and more of the same is the most likely future, what does that imply for India? A Pakistan that muddles along may not be all bad for New Delhi. The present uneasy balance between various entities in Pakistan is not ideal by any means, but it is a situation that Indian decisionmakers understand reasonably well.

Clearly, all the radical futures are negative for India. There are some in India who think that state collapse or balkanization might be in India's interest. That is not the case, for several reasons. There are nuclear weapons in Pakistan. Balkanization might encourage groups in India to think that separatism is plausible and to intensify the fight against the central government. Illegal migration into India and clandestine infiltration across the border might actually increase, and Islamic groups could well find it easier to attack India.

Liberal democracy would, in the long term, be in India's interest. Dealing with a liberal democratic Pakistan on issues such as Kashmir would not necessarily be easy, however—a solidly legitimate government in Pakistan in a liberal democratic order might be a tougher negotiator partly because it would be politically stronger and partly because, in the cut and thrust of domestic politics, it could find it more difficult to push a deal through the legislature. Moreover, the international advantages to India of being democratic, when Pakistan is not, would be lost. As for a military takeover, that would not shock India: for more than half of Pakistan's existence, New Delhi has had to deal with the military regime in charge. It would be more or less business as usual if the military returned to power.

What should India do with respect to a muddle-along Pakistan? Whether India likes Pakistan or not, it is in its interest to ensure that moderate civilian rule in a muddling-along polity continues to grow, however discontinuously and timorously. The following are fairly modest things that India can do to help the moderates, some of which it already is doing (in which case it should stick to them).

—First, New Delhi must remain patient and continue to engage in discussions with Islamabad on the basis of the so-called composite dialogue, which includes the issues of terrorism and Kashmir (even if the term "composite dialogue" has to be shed in favor of something more anodyne).

—Second, India should do what it can to help the civilian government in Pakistan politically. There is not a great deal that New Delhi can do, but it should look for openings. The Manmohan Singh government tried, at the Sharm el-Sheikh summit on July 16, 2009, to give the civilian prime minister something to take home to increase his credibility.[8] In the joint communiqué, India agreed to talk to Pakistan on "all issues, including all outstanding issues," terrorism notwithstanding, and to accept a reference to Pakistan's problems in Balochistan, a decision that was motivated by the desire to help Prime Minister Gilani at home.[9] Recent Indian comments about the possibility of reducing the Indian army's troop presence in Kashmir could also help Islamabad.

—Third, New Delhi should move to resolve at least one or two outstanding disputes. The Sir Creek and Siachen disputes are eminently resolvable. Their resolution would help reduce anti-Indian feeling in Pakistan.

—Fourth, India must expect that there will be terrorist attacks such as in Mumbai in 2008 given that Pakistan is in such a muddle. Indian intelligence and counterterrorism responses must be massively improved to try to handle any future attacks and to reduce the pressure on the Indian prime minister to attack Pakistan in response.

—Fifth, New Delhi should explore the possibility of cooperating with Islamabad on the future of Afghanistan. That may not be easy, but it is not impossible. After the horrors of the first Taliban regime, both India and Pakistan have an interest in a stable, inclusive, moderate Afghanistan. The competition between them is costly, including in terms of opportunities squandered. Afghanistan could be the gateway to Central Asia's energy and markets. India should be able to accept that Pakistan has special interests in its neighbor. Pakistan should in turn be able to accept that India can help Afghanistan in a way that Pakistan cannot (on development issues such as infrastructure and health in particular).

—Sixth, New Delhi should think about how to develop a relationship with the Pakistani military, which has a veto on so many issues of bilateral concern. Building social links between the two militaries,[10] "stroking" the Pakistani military when it fights extremists, and holding talks between India's Research and Analysis Wing and Pakistan's Inter-Services Intelligence[11] are just some of the steps that might help reduce the suspicions and hostility of the Pakistani military.

Can India do much more than this? India has little or no leverage within Pakistan. It has no constituency that it can appeal to or mobilize on its behalf. To be seen to be close to India is the kiss of political death in Pakistan. Any attempt by India to cultivate closer relations with a particular leader, party, institution, or community would be counterproductive. A deal with Pakistan on Kashmir might strengthen the forces of moderation, but the problem for New Delhi is that it has its own domestic politics to worry about on that score. It is far from clear that any Indian government can afford to make concessions to Pakistan on Kashmir—and yet, without some concessions, there is no prospect of a deal.

Notes

1. Population Resource Centre, "Population Projections: Key Facts and Trends" (www.prcdc.org/globalpopulation/Population_Projections [March 26, 2011]). The United Nations is projecting much higher figures. In 2008, it estimated that Pakistan's population in 2050 would be 335 million (this is the so-called "medium variant" projection). See UN Population Division, *World Population Prospects: The 2008 Revision* (http://esa.un.org/unpp/p2k0data.asp [March 27, 2011]).

2. On the perils of futurology and making predictions, see Kathryn Schulz, "Why Experts Get the Future Wrong," *New York Times*, Sunday Book Review, March 25, 2011 (www.nytimes.com/2011/03/27/books/review/book-review-future-babble-by-dan-gardner.html [March 27, 2011]).

3. Stephen P. Cohen, *The Idea of Pakistan* (Brookings, 2004).

4. Hilary Synnott, *Transforming Pakistan: Ways Out of Instability* (Abingdon, UK: Routledge, 2009), p. 26, notes that the religious parties have rarely won more than 4 to 8 percent of the vote. The year 2002 was something of an exception , when the Muttahida Majlis-e-Amal (MMA) alliance of six religious parties, with the help of the Musharraf government, won about 11 percent of the vote. See Synnott, *Transforming Pakistan*, p. 40.

5. See Stephen P. Cohen, *The Pakistan Army* (Oxford University Press, 1998).

6. Defections from the military are noted in Synnott, *Transforming Pakistan*, pp. 114–15.

7. On Pakistan's economic difficulties, see State Bank of Pakistan, *The State of Pakistan's Economy: First Quarterly Report 2010–2011* (www.sbp.org.pk/reports/quarterly/fy11/first/qtr-index-eng.htm [March 27, 2011]). The report projects a GDP growth rate of 2 to 3 percent for 2011, with inflation reaching 15 to 16 percent. See pp. 4–5 of "Economic Outlook and Executive Summary."

8. For the text of the communiqué, see "India, Pak Issue Joint Statement on Bilateral Relations," *Indian Express*, July 16, 2009 (www.indianexpress.com/news/nam-summit-joint-statement-issued-by-indiapakistan/490301/[March 26, 2011]).

9. Pakistan has for some years accused India of fomenting separatist trouble in Balochistan. India's acceptance of the reference to Balochistan was heavily criticized in the Indian press and by the opposition political parties as lending credibility to Islamabad's accusation. See, for instance, "PM Can't Dilute 'Monumental Lapse' in Indo-Pak Jt Statement," *Indian Express*, July 25, 2009 (www.indianexpress.com/news/pm-cant-dilute-monumental-lapse-in-indo/494048/[March 27, 2011]).

10. This is a suggestion that was made several years ago by Bharat Karnad of the Centre for Policy Research, New Delhi. See his "Key to Peace in South Asia: Fostering `Social Links' between the Armies of India and Pakistan," *The Round Table*, vol. 85, no. 338 (1996), pp. 205–29. It is not clear that Karnad would still endorse such a view given what has happened in the meantime and the current state of the Pakistani military.

11. B. Raman has championed the idea of meetings between the two intelligence agencies. For his most recent comments, see "India-Pakistan: Groping for an Alternative," South Asia Analysis Group (www.southasiaanalysis.org/[March 27, 2011]).

LAILA BOKHARI

3

Radicalization, Political Violence, and Militancy

"May you live in interesting times," goes an old saying often attributed to the Chinese. While many people use the phrase casually to describe events in many countries, for Pakistan "interesting times" are almost a constant fact of life. Despite its brief history, Pakistan has seen many interesting times. With attention focused on militancy in the last few years, the country is increasingly viewed as a hub of both local and regional militant groups, and tags such as "the most dangerous place in the world" and "breeding ground par excellence for global jihadists" are increasingly attached to it. Various militant movements are challenging both the state and the very idea of Pakistan, and one of the struggles that has characterized Pakistan and will continue to do so in the near future is the fight for the soul of the state. To change this trend, the foremost task facing Pakistan's leaders is to deal with the problems underlying the tensions and increasing radicalization within its population. Thereafter, much will depend on the ability and willingness of the Pakistani people themselves to stand up to that challenge. Pakistan has over the last years seen increased intolerance, violence, and hatred, oftentimes directed toward minorities, holy places, and even liberal thinkers and activists. Those are all signs of a society that is going though turmoil with respect to itself and its identity.

Pakistan has experienced several waves of political violence, essentially related to various forms of sectarian, ethnic, tribal, and, more recently, so-called global jihadi movements. The fight for different agendas ranges from local sectarianism in Pakistan itself; regional jihads, notably in Afghanistan and in India; and a more global jihad and militant struggle against the West and Western interests.

The core of much of the tension and violence experienced by the country is the key issue that is the very basis of Pakistan—the relationship between the state and religion, the role and place that Islam assumes in Pakistan's society. The creation of Pakistan as a Muslim country, separate from India, a largely Hindu country, formed much of the initial thinking on the idea of the state. The image of Hindu (or rather non-Muslim) India as the "enemy" has been the rationale for many Kashmiri groups, as well as for the Pakistani army. Jihad became a fight against both the Indian army and the Hindu nation over the territory of Kashmir, with its majority Muslim population.

The Soviet invasion of Afghanistan in 1979 gave a whole different tenor and momentum to the many militant groups that were soon to operate in Pakistan. Mujahideen from all over the world passed through Pakistan en route to Afghanistan, and many stayed behind in the region after their victory over the communists. Furthermore, the different schools of Islam present in South Asia, notably such Sunni groups as Deobandi and Ahl-e-Hadith, themselves grew in influence, generating both supporters and rivals at the local and national levels. These groups remain influential, and they are a force that must be reckoned with. Constant rivalries between them, some resulting in violent clashes, persist in Pakistan today.

The 1980s saw the underlying conflict between Shia and Sunni intensify, and groups defining their rationale in forms of sectarian struggles took center stage. The regional battle for dominance in the Muslim world only strengthened these struggles. These groups have taken the biggest toll on the Pakistani people: Sunnis targeting Shia and vice versa. However, in terms of its aims, methods, and rationale, the jihadi landscape of Pakistan is more diverse than suggested by this conflict alone. Recent clashes between Barelvis and Deobandis in both Faisalabad and Karachi and attacks on minorities such as Christians (recently in Gujarat) or Ahmediyyas (recently in Lahore) show there is a broader problem: first is the challenge of religious identity, intolerance, and violence; second is that of state effectiveness (and willingness) to provide security to the Pakistani people. Beyond doubt, Pakistan has been both a major participant in the fight against terrorism and a major victim of terrorism, and the question of whether enough has been done to tackle the issues of radicalization and recruitment to terrorism must be raised.

Thus, different types of militant groups with different agendas and motivations operate in Pakistan today, including the following:

—sectarian groups, for example, Shia and Sunni
—jihadi groups inspired by al Qaeda, often with foreign connections

—Taliban-related groups
—Kashmir-oriented groups, often based in Punjab.
Each of them constitutes a challenge for the Pakistani state.

The Crisis of the State

Several observers point to a fundamental crisis of the legitimacy of the state and its institutions as being the very trigger of these continuous waves of tension.[1] In addition, it is arguably the very writ of the state that is at stake in today's struggles in the border areas with Afghanistan. At the center are questions regarding what structures, if any, fill the void that the state currently is unable to fill. Why is the Pakistani state unable or unwilling to hold onto its authority? The answer can explain much, but not all, of the success of militant groups in various areas over the last few years. Furthermore, the failure of successive regimes in fulfilling their development agendas has created a continuing existential crisis for those regimes. With the energy and economic crises now evident and with their severe consequences for Pakistan's society, the challenges are immense. The weak judicial system and the deterioration of law and order are only the result of the state's failure to fulfill its responsibilities. The unwillingness of the state to take action against attacks on minorities, such as the Ahmediyyas, Christians, or more Sufi-inclined religious practitioners, indicates a fundamental weakness of the state. So does its unwillingness to deal with the many victims in the continuous heated debate on the blasphemy laws.

The Muslim state that the founding father, Quaid-e-Azam Mohammed Ali Jinnah, envisioned before partition in 1947 is very different from the Pakistan that we see today. The process of attempting to define and redefine the state was most apparent in the era of General Zia ul-Haq. The late 1970s and the beginning of the 1980s saw the aggressive promotion of Islamists in the hitherto relatively secular Pakistani army, which was a sign of times to come. The increasing Islamization of both state institutions and general society, coupled with the Afghan war, was a turning point in the role of Islamic orthodoxy in Pakistan. Together they created the very infrastructure of the many militant groups and networks as well as the mindset that we see today.

A more codified and strictly Wahhabi Islam also was exported to Pakistan by its close ally, Saudi Arabia, the guardian of the holy sites. Its effects remain strong and visible in Pakistan today, and it is one reason why the militant infrastructure was embedded in the state. Furthermore, during the 1990s sectarianism flourished, and the decade also saw the growth of Kashmiri jihadi groups and more global groups, in terms of both membership and outlook.

Underlying much of this, as mentioned above, was the country's security buildup against India.

Support of a number of militant movements has been seen as part of a foreign policy tool that has now come back to haunt the Pakistani state apparatus and society.

This question remains a key issue today and for the near future: To what extent, if at all, is the Pakistani establishment willing and able to let go of its old allies, the militant groups that once served its purposes? That question touches on a number of issues relevant to the very identity of the state of Pakistan.

Jihadi Infrastructure

The state of militancy—including both local and international elements—that we see today cannot be understood without taking a look at the framework on which Pakistan was formed and the links between religious identity and politics. Similarly, the buildup of the Taliban in Afghanistan cannot be understood without keeping the Pakistani theater in mind. Pakistani support for the Taliban movement and its offshoots was based on both the ideological wish for a true Sunni Islamic sharia state and the national political aim of establishing strategic depth—physical presence and influence—in the hinterland of the Afghan territory. The roots of the Taliban therefore were watered by the financial, ideological, and logistical support of Pakistani Sunni groups and political religious parties such as the Jamaat-e-Islami (JeI) and the Jamiat Ulema-e-Islam (JUI).

The role and the platform of the religious political parties, in particular the Jamaat-e-Islami but also the Jamaat Ulema-e-Islam, are seen here as vital. While today we see more moderate parties such as the Pakistan People's Party (PPP) and the Pakistan Muslim League (PML-N)—in addition to the provincial, more nationalist and secular Awami National Party (ANP)—at the forefront, the more traditional religious parties do play a role in Pakistani politics. They form a popular front with at times incredible power to assemble people on the street. Traditionally they have run a number of religious institutions and madaris, and they are known to have educated people in ways that may have inspired some to incline toward militancy.[2]

Recent years have seen the various militant groups form a nexus with a focus on Pakistani territory: the Pakistani Taliban has emerged as a power in itself, while the Federally Administered Tribal Areas are seen as the base for much of the Taliban and al Qaeda leadership. Increasingly, links also are seen in the Pakistani "mainland" between Taliban-related groups and more traditional Punjabi militant groups. These links became clear with the increase in attacks and counteroperations in the cities of Punjab in 2010.

In the era following September 11, 2001, Pakistan has witnessed the banning of a number of militant groups and the arrests and targeted killings of key al Qaeda and related militants—a result of both pressure from the international community, most notably the United States, and the domestic realization that the very survival of the Pakistani state itself was at risk. Several failed attempts on the lives of previous prime ministers and the country's president led to increased efforts to clamp down on militant movements in the country. The banning of groups and arrests of key al Qaeda operatives, many of them local militants involved in international networks, has not, however, hindered new groups and factions from appearing and reappearing. Banning led some to change their names while others, such as Lashkar-e-Tayyiba and Jamaat-ud-Dawa, continue their activities more or less openly. Recent years have seen an intensified hunt for certain militants, which public opinion perceives as a massive, U.S.-driven military incursion (including drone attacks) in the tribal areas of Pakistan. The results have backfired—and continue to backfire—on the Pakistani army, through both colossal casualties in the tribal areas and direct attacks against regional and national security forces and military headquarters.

Late 2007 saw the refocusing of many militant movements toward the Pakistani homeland. A strengthened Taliban with a Pakistani flavor appeared on the scene. While Afghanistan and the foreign forces operating there remain as a key frontline, a key enemy, and a raison d'être for the many groups, the aim and agenda of the most vocal and dynamic actors in the Pakistani theater has now shifted to include the army and the so-called "apostate" state and its other institutions as the enemy. That provides the backdrop for the most recent developments, in which the foundations of the state are once again challenged.

Over the last few years, groups and actors operating under the name of the Taliban—with more local Pakistani traits—have increasingly been developing relations with local tribes and gaining ground in new areas, such as the previously peaceful valley of Swat. The question remains of whether this is a temporary arrangement, a result of developments within the groups in recent years, or a more long-term shift. A better and more detailed analysis of recent developments related to the Deobandi umbrella movement, the Tehrik-i-Taliban Pakistan (TTP), and some of its actors might highlight some of the issues at stake here. With the recent NATO-U.S. surge in the region, however, indications of a provoked, stronger, and unified Taliban in Pakistan have appeared, although it may be too early to ascertain.

Absence of National Debate

The political setting in Pakistan is vital to understanding the rise of jihadi groups in the country. Historically, Pakistan served as the key channel for the transmission of resources to the mujahideen resistance during the Soviet occupation of Afghanistan. Its madaris nurtured the core of what was to become the Taliban, and from the mid-1990s until 2001 Pakistan supported the Taliban regime. Some claim that it still supports the Taliban. Pakistan also struggles with severe Shia-Sunni sectarian conflict in addition to intra-Sunni tensions. Furthermore, it is heavily affected by the ongoing Taliban insurgency in Afghanistan, especially in the border regions where popular sympathy for the Taliban is perceived to be high. Finally, Pakistan has its perennial conflict with India over the issue of Kashmir. Since its birth in 1947 Pakistan has had a constant struggle with itself about how being an Islamic state should influence its own identity as a state and its policies. Today, Pakistan finds itself at the forefront in the U.S.-led "global war on terror" as a close ally of the United States, which, in turn, has deepened the cleavages in the Pakistani political landscape, especially in the Federally Administered Tribal Areas over the last year, which arguably took their most serious turn in the spring of 2011.

Much of the academic work undertaken on radical Islamism and terrorism in Pakistan has focused on the historical and political context of the groups and on their infrastructure, ideology, and development and their choice of targets. While much can be said about the political framework, the question of what processes and dynamics make individuals join radical movements is often ignored: What is their reasoning? What exactly happens, how, and why? These questions are also about the larger landscape that encourages radicalization.

Many have underlined the crucial processes of socialization and education. Leaders, trainers, and educators may have a certain amount of influence on the individual. Here are both leaders who may see their role as being to legitimize, convince, and educate and individual men and women who have participated, in some way or another, in the struggle. Both should be part of a debate, which would also be important to defame and "unglorify" the militant jihad.

The lack of a national debate about these issues gives any government more or less carte blanche to act as it pleases. Historically, there has been a relatively high degree of social acceptance of "jihad" as defined by the jihadi groups—that is, violent jihad—in Pakistani society. Furthermore, an unclear or unfinished debate on what Islam should mean to the state is at the center. The country's history with Afghanistan, the jihadist politics of President Zia ul-Haq, and the centrality of Kashmir in its policies, may all offer some explanation for that fact. The recent shift, with the civilian government and the military taking on the militants, is a step in the right direction. Yet much more needs to be done. Questions of why the government and the military are now taking on the militants with a previously unseen degree of force are raised by both critics and realists, who remind the optimists that Pakistan is taking on only the militants that it sees as challenging the state, not those whose support it may need some time in the future. That being the case, the game has not changed.

Government Responses

Two events mark a turning point in the fight against militancy in Pakistan in the last few years. The first event, in the tribal areas bordering Afghanistan, was the Lal Masjid incident in summer 2007, in which several hundred people were killed and others wounded after the government gave the green light to remove the militants at the mosque and madrassa. That set off a whole wave of suicide attacks across Pakistan, targeting state institutions, military and police installations, and the establishment in general. Similarly, the attacks on the military in the tribal areas were severe, and the military suffered great losses.

As the conflict increased on Pakistan's western borders, the Mumbai attack was a reminder that Pakistan fights simultaneously on many fronts. Different militant groups have various agendas, and some aim to hit India. The Mumbai attack reminded many in Pakistan that the state may also have to tackle militant group sympathizers within its own agencies. The banned terrorist group Lashkar-e-Tayyiba (LeT), believed to be behind the Mumbai attack, was once a tool of the country's foreign policy, aided and built up by the Pakistani military to fight India. The question on everyone's mind therefore became to what extent the Pakistani establishment knew about the planned attack.

The government has vowed to "finish off" both the Pakistani Taliban and the terrorists creating havoc on foreign soil (the LeT and others). As previous policies seem to have created a "Frankenstein," the government has come under increasing pressure both from its own population and the international community. In the tribal areas, the military is fighting an insurgency that is more diverse and stronger than previously thought. The strategy there has been two-pronged: military incursions and the negotiation of peace deals. Since 2004, successive local governments and military leaders have signed deals with both tribal leaders and militants, most of which were short-lived and broken by one of the participating parties. Such deals have strengthened the militants, leading to their expansion in terms of territory and resources. At the same time, the ongoing and more successful targeted drone attacks from across the border create a dilemma for the Pakistani leadership. Civilian casualties from unsuccessful drone attacks are increasing anti-Americanism among the population and thereby undermining their aim and purpose. Rather than decreasing militancy, they may actually increase radicalization. As a result, the Pakistan government is blamed for being too lenient toward the Americans.

The Way Forward

Pakistan has a multitude of different political groups, each pursuing its own agenda. Some of them take on a militant shade, increasingly challenging not only the state infrastructure and institutions but also the very identity of the state. Through their successful attacks on both hard and soft targets, they make life in Pakistan insecure for both its leaders and its citizens. The government must show that it has the will and ability to cope with these threats.

Developing a coordinated counterterrorism strategy would be a good start. The National Counter Terrorism Authority (NACTA) was a hopeful beginning, but weak leadership and an unclear mandate have left the institution lame. More than that, developing a counterterrorism strategy is also about securing viable and stable state institutions. Among other things, the development of such a strategy will have to involve a serious national debate about Islam, including extremism and the acceptance of extremist views. Interfaith and intrafaith social cohesion projects and their advancement may be a beginning, but much more will have to be done. Efforts will also have to involve political, economic, and developmental solutions—including quality education, health care, and employment opportunities—and structural reforms, not only for the tribal areas but also for other remote areas and provinces. A serious discussion of what constitutes the basic security of Pakistan will also have to include a regional dimension, looking at the role of India in the region and Pakistan's obsession (and insecurity) with regard to its neighbors.

This is a struggle that Pakistan cannot fight alone, but it is one that Pakistan needs to own and define itself. The future of militancy, sectarian violence, and radical extremism will depend much on the government's capacity to identify the problems it is up against and its willingness to resolve the underlying issues.

Notes

1. For further analysis of these issues, see Stephen P. Cohen, *The Idea of Pakistan* (Brookings, 2004), and Hassan Abbas, *Pakistan's Drift into Extremism. Allah, the Army, and America's War on Terror* (New Delhi: Pentagon Press, 2005).

2. Christine Fair, *The Madrassah Challenge. Militancy and Religious Education in Pakistan* (Washington: United States Institute of Peace Press, 2008), and *Madrassahs, Extremism, and the Military*, ICG Asia Report 36 (Islamabad/Brussels: International Crisis Group, Pakistan, 2002).

C. CHRISTINE FAIR

4

Addressing Fundamental Challenges

Pakistan's problems are as well-known as they are numerous. Pakistan is both the source of terrorists operating throughout the region and beyond (some of which enjoy explicit state sanction) and increasingly the victim of terrorist groups that have emerged from its erstwhile proxies. Despite its mooring as a parliamentary democracy, the state has been dominated by the army, which has governed Pakistan directly or indirectly for most of the state's existence. While democracy has never fully taken root, authoritarianism has never garnered widespread legitimacy. Thus the army always comes to power through the connivance and acquiescence of the broad array of civilian institutions and personalities necessary to provide a patina of legitimacy to its seizure of power. The army enjoys a generally accepted "right to intervene" due in part to Pakistan's origins as an insecure state and the intractable security competition with India, which first centered on the disputed disposition of Kashmir but now derives from India's ascent as an emerging global power. The army believes itself to be the only institution capable of protecting Pakistan, and many Pakistanis share that belief. Because the army sets external policies, including those on the use of Islamist militants, normalized civil-military relations are likely a necessary (albeit insufficient) condition for Pakistan to resolve its security concerns vis-à-vis India. However,

Note that parts of the working paper that this chapter is based on were subsequently accepted for publication. See C. Christine Fair, "Why the Pakistan Army Is Here to Stay: Prospects for Civilian Governance?" *International Affairs,* vol. 87, no. 3 (May 2011), pp. 571–88.

because such normalization would vitiate the Pakistani army's arrogated right to manage Pakistan's affairs, the army itself is an important institutional stakeholder that may subvert normalization.

Pakistan is also riven with ethnic discord, often stemming from strained center-provincial tensions, which include the center's historic refusal to meaningfully devolve power and control of resources to the provinces, consonant with the 1973 Constitution. Pakistan faces numerous governance challenges throughout the country, but these challenges are most acute in the Federally Administered Tribal Areas (FATA). The state has made successive policy decisions to keep FATA beyond the remit of the law by maintaining a draconian, colonial-era legal instrument, the Frontier Crimes Regulation, which facilitates control of the area but not its incorporation into Pakistan's legal structures. To manage both internal and external concerns, the state under both military and civilian leadership has instrumentalized Islam in various ways, to varying degrees, with a variety of outcomes. In short, Pakistanis continue to wrestle with foundational issues, such as the role of Islam in the state, who is a Pakistani and who is not, what relationship should exist between the center and the provinces, where the balance of power should lie, and what kind of Islam Pakistan should embrace as a state.

While these myriad challenges are often evaluated as distinct issues in isolation from the others, I argue here and elsewhere that their origins are fundamentally similar: the failure of constitutionalism to fructify in Pakistan, despite the fact that the country has forged and subsequently abandoned numerous constitutions. Unfortunately, the weaknesses of Pakistan's political and civil society institutions, the groundswell of emergent domestic threats, and the failed institutions of governance and internal security will likely prevent Pakistan's varied polities from forging a consensus on these foundational issues.[1] I further argue that these issues squarely affect domestic and international security. What is most critical for U.S. interests is that Pakistan will not be able to decisively turn against militants targeting the state and those operating in India and Afghanistan until it can resolve these fundamental questions. This suggests that there are no elegant or easy—much less expedient—solutions to the challenges confronting Pakistan and those states seeking to manage the implications of those challenges near and far.

After briefly providing an empirical basis for the above description of the various fault lines that exist in Pakistan, I address structural features and shaping events, focusing first on domestic institutions and development and next on regional and geostrategic factors. I conclude that in the near term (one to three years) and in the mid-term (three to ten years), Pakistan's institutions will be unlikely to resolve the country's foundational issues. While Pakistan will be unable to forge a coherent constitutional rule of law, it will not succumb to its various internal pressures. Wild cards in this trajectory include Pakistan's media, conclusions that the army may have drawn from its various internal security operations in the tribal areas and Swat, and the decisions that international actors such as the United States, India, and China take that influence the Pakistani cost-benefit calculus.

Fault Lines of State and Nation

Polling data obtained in 2009, using a 6,000-person sample drawn from all four of Pakistan's provinces, attest to the pervasiveness of several fault lines.[2]

The role of Islam is contested. While fewer than one in three believed that Pakistan was governed "completely" or "a lot" according to Islamic principles, nearly 70 percent believed that sharia should play a larger role in Pakistani law; one in five preferred the status quo; and only one in ten wanted sharia to play a smaller role. Since most Pakistanis in our poll believed that sharia overwhelmingly meant good governance, large majorities believed that more sharia would translate into better governance (access to justice, reduction of corruption, and so forth). Pakistanis remain torn about the best way to deal with the Pakistani Taliban. Large swaths of Pakistan support peace deals with them, and the Pakistani public is deeply torn on the issue of military force to defeat them.

The kind of government is contested. While most Pakistanis highly valued living under a government of elected representatives (78 percent), only one in two believed that Pakistan was so governed "completely" or "a lot." Similarly high expectations were held for courts independent of political and military authorities, and Pakistanis were similarly disappointed about the courts' actual independence. Yet Pakistanis were fundamentally divided about the nature of governance in Pakistan.

—Fifty-five percent believed that the civilian government should exert "complete" or "a lot" of control over the military. However, 41 percent believed that civilians should exert "a moderate amount," "a little," or even "no control" over the army at all.

—Fourteen percent believed that the president should control the army, and another 24 percent believed that it is the prime minister's job. The largest portion (60 percent) believed that it is the job of the chief of army staff alone.

—Only one in five believed that the military should never be able to take control of the state.

Opinion diverges on what to do about FATA. Pakistanis believed that Pakistan's interests would be undermined if FATA remained autonomous. A majority favored negotiating with the Taliban in one way or another. While support for military operations in FATA was generally low, support for political reform in FATA was high.

Pakistanis overall do not support the numerous militant groups operating in Pakistan, but important minorities do. Support was strongest among proponents of democracy, and opposition to militant groups was most intense among the urban poor.[3]

Constitutions and Constitutionalism

The current Constitution, adopted in 1973, remains the lodestone of legitimacy, but it has been mangled by civilian and military regimes alike. The country has tended to be governed by a strong president, with a pliable Parliament and prime minister, with interludes of parliamentary democracy, as called for in the 1973 Constitution. Until Pakistan can resolve its varied foundational issues through a process of constitutionalism, the country will likely continue to lurch from one crisis to another. Many of the internal security issues that Pakistan confronts stem from the failure of the process of constitutionalism. Pakistan's contentious center-province relations, which have often spawned ethnic-based rebellions; the country's failure (or unwillingness) to extend the writ of the law to all of Pakistan's territories, such as FATA; the failure of civilian institutions to exert control over the military; the argument over what kind of government Pakistan should have and the role that Islam should play in the state as well as within Pakistan's social and cultural fabric all exemplify this. As noted above, Pakistanis themselves are deeply divided on these key issues.

What then are the prospects for resolving these issues, which I contend is key to stabilizing Pakistan? Several types of institution are necessary to resolve these concerns, each of which will be addressed briefly below: political parties; civil society institutions; domestic security institutions; and the state governance apparatus. This list is not comprehensive, but it does illustrate key institutions and their limits.

Political Parties

A comprehensive assessment of Pakistan's political parties is beyond the scope of this short chapter. However, Cohen, among others, has documented their organizational strengths and shortcomings.[4] Most of the parties are vertically integrated personality cults that aggregate highly localized interests. That is true of the regional and religious parties discussed below, as well as of the so-called "mainstream" parties: the Pakistan Muslim League–Nawaz (PML-N) and the Pakistan People's Party (PPP), of which only the PPP has any modicum of national standing. While the PPP may have a more expansive presence across the country, its core remains in rural Sindh. Similarly, the PML-N has its strongest hold on Punjab's urban centers.

In addition to these purportedly mainstream parties, Pakistan has numerous parties that are based on ethnic and/or provincial ties, such as the Awami National Party, which represents a slice of Pashtun interests in Khyber Pakhtunkhwa (KP) and, in recent years, in Karachi. Balochistan hosts a number of Baloch ethnic parties with little reach beyond Balochistan. The Muttahida Qaumi Movement (MQM) represents what is perhaps the closest thing to a secular movement in Pakistan, but it represents the interests of Pakistan's Mohajir community and is essentially a political movement formed from an organized criminal organization. In addition to these parties, Pakistan has several Islamist parties, which garner few votes in free and fair elections but nonetheless have a power and influence in the army and in the street that is disproportionate to their showing at the ballot box. Curiously, one of these parties—the Jamaat-e-Islami—is the only party to elect its leaders democratically and until recently had been the only party to operate a think tank, the Institute of Pakistan Studies, in Islamabad, to generate policy options.

The fundamental problem with Pakistan's political parties is that they fail to aggregate national interest (with a few notable exceptions) and pursue deeply personal rather than collective agendas. Parties tend not to develop robust party platforms; indeed, they are more interested in developing and servicing patronage networks than promulgating and shepherding effective policies. The failure to pass sensible tax reform policies remains one of the most illustrative examples of the negative role in state building that Pakistan's patronage-driven politics plays. The state's ability to raise revenues through taxation and redistribute those revenues as services is a fundamental democratic transaction that binds the governed to the government. Yet the self-serving political class will never enact such legislation as it would be tantamount to taxing their own interests, literally. Similarly, any meaningful efforts to establish more normalized civil-military relations are undermined by the simple fact that many politicians benefit from the status quo, whereby they can use the army to undermine their political opponents.

Any renewed process to establish constitutionalism, forging a new contract between the government and the governed, and to address the above-noted foundational issues (including the role of Islam in the state) requires party leadership and effective aggregation of interests. Unfortunately, that appears to be beyond the capacities of the political parties for the foreseeable future due, among other shortcomings, to the parties' deeply nondemocratic nature and the limits of civil society to pressure parties to act.

Civil Society Institutions

Given the pervasive structural problems with Pakistan's political parties and inadequate demands for reform from within, what are the prospects for pressure for reform from without? Historically, Pakistan's civil society institutions have been weak in contrast to those in neighboring India and even Bangladesh. In recent years, civil society organizations have evolved, but not all will be forces for liberalism or even for resolution of fundamental questions about the state and its polity. Arguably, the ways in which civil society organizations are evolving augur more—not less—division across Pakistan.

On one hand are human rights organizations, civil society organizations (CSOs), and the lawyers' movement, which have pressed for greater adherence to democratic practices but have a very limited base of support across Pakistan. After all, by their nature CSOs attend to deeply localized issues and their constituents. (While at first blush it may appear attractive to the United States to invest in these institutions, studies of CSOs find that they become less effective when they receive international aid, in part because they stop answering to their members and become increasingly oriented toward meeting the demands of their funders.)[5] On the other hand are civil society organizations that are antiliberal and pursue an explicitly Islamist agenda that, at best, seeks to use democratic processes to undermine democracy. Others do not even entertain the rhetoric of democracy and explicitly state their goal of Islamizing Pakistan (as a variously construed Sunni entity). These civil society forces take the guise of Islamist parties such as Jamaat-e-Islami and evangelical revival movements such as Tanzeem-e-Islami and Tablighi-Jamaat. Others include movements such as al Huda, which targets women and couches adherence to orthodox Islam in feminist and liberationist terms.[6] The types of future of Pakistan that these forces are fighting for are orthogonal to each other.

The wild card in mobilizing Pakistanis is the press. Pakistan's private media, at first blush, appears vibrant and diverse, and on many measures that characterization is accurate. However, on issues of national security and contentious domestic affairs, Pakistan's media censors itself heavily and is deeply influenced by establishment commentators with strong ties to the military and intelligence agencies. Many, according to Pakistani journalists known to the author, are explicitly paid by Pakistan's intelligence agency, the Inter-Services Intelligence Directorate (ISI); therefore, their ability to resolve some of these issues may be very limited by design. However, it is likely inevitable that new social media and the novel use of cell phones to disseminate information quickly may help transform and even mobilize civil society beyond the grasp of the state. As noted above, any mobilization need not be for greater liberalism in Pakistan; it is equally likely to be geared toward greater Islamism of state and society. Whether or not mobilization, liberal or its obverse, can effectively pressure Pakistan's political and other governance institutions remains an important empirical question for the near, mid-, and even long term.

Domestic Security Institutions

The army believes that it is—and is believed by many Pakistanis to be—the only institution capable of protecting Pakistan. The army is able to sustain that claim principally by convincing Pakistanis that India, and to a lesser degree Afghanistan, pose existential and enduring threats to Pakistan's integrity and by reinforcing the popular belief that the army alone can contend with these foes. Pakistan's armed forces (as well as civilian leaders) have relied on instrumentalizing Islam to manage Pakistan's security and to protect what has been called the "ideology" of Pakistan,[7] which has resulted in a complex and dangerous relationship between the state and Islam that is not easily disentangled. Pakistan, conceived as a home to South Asia's Muslims, has yet to resolve the role of Islam within the state; what is not at question is that there is and will be a role of Islam in the state. Few people are demanding a secular Pakistan. Pakistan couches its "natural power projection" throughout Central and South West Asia in terms of its Muslim-ness, and it claims to have some responsibility to protect India's Muslims. For a number of well-documented reasons, Pakistan has come to rely upon Islamist proxies to prosecute its interests in the region, beginning in 1947 in Kashmir and in the 1960s in Afghanistan.[8]

In recognition of these realities, some interlocutors have argued that Pakistan will not be able to give up its militant proxies as long as security competition exists with India. Indeed, Pakistanis say that their concerns in Afghanistan stem from their fear of India and that if Pakistan's issues with India (Kashmir) could be resolved, their need for the Afghan Taliban would abate. However, a counterargument can also be made: until Pakistan is ready to give up its commitment to instrumentalizing Islam for domestic and external purposes, Pakistan will never be able to resolve its existential and neuralgic issues with India. Because neither a durable resolution with India nor abandonment of Islam as an instrument of policy is on the horizon, Pakistan is likely to continue using militant and Islamist groups to manage an array of domestic and external challenges.

India, for its part, is appallingly shortsighted. India demurs from making any policies regarding Pakistan that may be conciliatory, including by striking a comprehensive settlement between Delhi and Srinagar. India clings to the notion that its varied elections demonstrate that the Kashmir issue is resolved. However, as any visitor to Kashmir can attest, elections have not ameliorated the pervasive discontent and dissatisfaction with Delhi, much less provided a path toward comprehensive reconciliation. India's strategy appears to be "wait it out" while India ascends and Pakistan weakens. Unfortunately, in the mean-time, India forgoes important opportunities to contend with this important domestic issue among its own Kashmiri populations. In the meantime, the "Kashmir issue" increasingly has merged with larger Hindu-Muslim discord throughout India. Pakistan-backed militant groups have leveraged the dis-cord to develop Indian assets to conduct operations with Indian personnel in order to increase the plausible deniability of Pakistan's involvement. The Kash-mir issue, which has largely centered on both countries' national narratives, has now become a strategic issue centered on regional water supplies. If India could resolve its issues with its own Kashmiri citizens, it might diminish any space that Pakistan and its militant proxies have to maneuver on the issue. However, India's inability to decide what kind of neighbor it wants to have and to effect policies that make one outcome more likely than another has only exacerbated Pakistan's existential crises and concomitant security challenges.

State Governance Apparatus

While Pakistan's army generally takes the lion's share of opprobrium for its intervention in the managing of the state, the army always comes to power with the assistance of virtually every civilian and political institution.[9] The process is predictable. The army chief steps in, suspends the Constitution, disbands the Parliament, promulgates various legal orders, and requires the Supreme Court justices not only to validate the move but also to take an oath to support the new government. Most justices, in the principle of self-interest, do so, violating the very Constitution that they previously took a vow to pro-tect; those that demur are simply replaced. Thus the military regime is able to construct a compliant judiciary. Since persons from the judiciary may become members of the independent election commission, they also play a critical role in the inevitably problematic elections that ensue.

As authoritarianism enjoys little outright support in Pakistan, the army-chief-cum-president has a limited time to cobble together a democratic face for his regime. Using the intelligence agencies, the regime is able to forge a "king's party" through a combination of enticement and coercion of members of extant parties. Once the party is assembled, invariably flawed elections are held, in which the king's party comes into power at the center and provinces, perhaps in coalition with opposition parties of choice. The opposition party of choice is usually a coalition of Islamist parties, which the army chief uses to offset any challenges to his regime from Islamist quarters. The Parliament that emerges rubber stamps the various orders of the military regime.

This arrangement sustains itself until the Pakistani public becomes exhausted with army rule and increasingly vexed with the army itself. At that juncture, the army moves against the president in an effort to protect its own standing among the people. The army then returns to a watchful role as an invariably problematic and ineffective democracy emerges until once again, the public turns against the political class and again welcomes the army into power. Needless to say, with each round of military interventions, the political and bureaucratic institutions become ever more ineffective and the debate on the modalities of government (prime minister versus president, president versus Parliament) becomes ever more tendentious.

This process has played out more or less consistently four times, under generals Ayub Khan, Yahya Khan, Zia ul-Haq, and Pervez Musharraf. None of the civilian entities or persons that aided and abetted the regime has ever been punished. Until 2008, no army chief was even threatened with punishment, even though the coups are, according to Pakistani law, a capital offense. (In April 2008 Musharraf resigned under threat of impeachment, which was utterly unprecedented.) Until the judiciary and the political parties punish members of the same institutions for undermining democracy by legitimizing military takeovers, what can put an end to this predictable cycle? Judicial reform and accountability is clearly needed to intervene at several nodes in this process. However, as the last several years have shown, the judiciary seeks to secure its own independence of action and the political parties seek to politicize the judiciary for their own purposes. Thus the likelihood of developing institutions of rule of law nears zero in any meaningful time frame.

Internal Security

Pakistan has long contended with ethnic challenges in the Pashtun areas of the frontier, in Balochistan, and at times among Muhajirs and Sindhis in Sindh. It also managed complex, urban, low-intensity conflict in Karachi. In recent years, it has confronted a complex insurgency that has organized under the banner of the Tehrik-e-Taliban Pakistan (TTP). While the TTP is based in Pashtun areas of the FATA and parts of Khyber Pakhtunkhwa, the TTP comprises several Deobandi-affiliated organizations that draw their members from a raft of other Deobandi militant groups, such as the Sipha-e-Sahaba Pakistan (SSP), Lashkar-e-Jhangvi (LeJ), Jaish-e-Muhammad (JeM), and Harkat-ul-Jihadi-e-Islami (HUJI), among others. Almost all of the groups are based in the Punjab, and none are new, with LeJ and SSP having formed in the Punjab in the late 1970s and early 1980s. Equally important are the ties that bind these Deobandi militant organizations to the Deobandi Islamist political parties. The parties comprise the various factions of the Jamiat Ulema-e-Islam (JUI) organized around specific individuals, such as the JUI-F of Fazl-ur-Rehman and the JUI-S of Sami ul-Haq.[10]

Pakistan acknowledges that part of the TTP is an enemy of the state and has engaged in military operations to target TTP bases in much of FATA and Khyber Pakhtunkhwa. However, Pakistan's ability to decisively eliminate these groups is limited by the fact that Pakistan still seeks to protect groups like Jaish-e-Muhammad. Pakistani security managers believe that the group will reorient against India and again become an ally one day rather than remain a potential foe of the state. Indeed, JeM's leader, Masood Azhar, freely roams around Bahawalpur, where an entire army corps is stationed.[11]

The implications are clear: if Pakistan cannot abandon Islamist militancy as a tool of external power projection, its ability to eliminate its internal threat will be very, very limited. Since the TTP has overlapping networks with the Afghan Taliban and al Qaeda, Pakistan will come under increasing pressure to act against the TTP while preserving its interests in JeM.[12]

While it is popular to argue that only the military has espoused the policy of reliance on militant proxies, the realty is quite different. Both the PPP and the PML-N have supported the jihadi groups operating in a variety of theaters. The purportedly secularly inclined PPP has even allied with groups such as LeJ and SSP. A return to civilian-run government therefore is not necessarily tantamount to a reversal of these dangerous polices.[13]

So far, the United States has done little to push Pakistan on Lashkar-e-Tayyiba (LeT), now operating under the name of Jamaat-ud-Dawa (JuD), out of fear that Pakistan may diminish its cooperation with the United States in Afghanistan. From Pakistan's point of view, LeT/JuD does not threaten the state because it has never acted against targets within Pakistan. Indeed, Western and Indian intelligence officials note that Pakistani state support to LeT has increased, not decreased, since the LeT attack in Mumbai in 2008. LeT also has operated against the United States and its allies in Afghanistan with increasing frequency. Fortunately for U.S.-Pakistan relations, the failed New York City Times Square bomber was trained by the TTP, which Pakistan and the United States see as an enemy, rather than the LeT.

While Pakistan's commitment to its external Islamist proxies diminishes the country's ability to act against its internal Islamist foes, Pakistan's inability to promulgate effective institutions of governance and the rule of law further hinders its ability to manage its internal security issues. For a host of institutional reasons, Pakistan has not invested in its police. First, the army seeks to be the primary guarantor of Pakistan's security and is loath to delegate that authority and responsibility to civilian entities, including the police. Recent army involvement in low-intensity conflict throughout Pakistan appears to have convinced some military personnel of the need for more effective police agencies. However, it is far from obvious that this view has greater currency across the army. Second, the intelligence agencies undermine local police. For example, in Bahawalpur, the police would like to act against Jaish-e-Muhammad's leadership but are prevented from doing so by the ISI. The police routinely pick up militants only to have the ISI arrange their release. Third, the political class has also been an enormous obstacle to police reform. To date, politicians have used the police as their own private thugs; the politicians therefore have posed the greatest challenge to legal reform of policing.[14]

Fourth, given the pay structure of the police, corruption is institutionalized. As evidenced by the Motorway Police, when police are given real wages and rigorously held accountable, they actually perform their job admirably. Similar efforts have been made with the Islamabad and Lahore traffic police, with surprising success. Unfortunately, such programs are inherently not scalable. They skim the "cream"—the best police—from the various police structures. Without system-wide pay reform and accountability measures, effective policing will remain elusive in Pakistan.

Similarly, judicial reform currently has few takers. There are too few justices and even fewer good justices. In real terms, their salaries are lower than they were under the British. However, the justices can augment their salaries with bribes to hear cases with inordinate expedience, providing justice for those who can pay. There are no quick fixes here either, as justice reform will likely have to be a part of the larger and more difficult challenge of civil service reform, for which there are few proponents.

Arguably, the failure to provide good governance, to diminish corruption, to provide easy access to justice, and to provide security is at the core of the security challenges in FATA and Swat. Why would anyone oppose the TTP when, purportedly without corruption, it offers access to some form of justice, provides services, and can threaten violence when the state is not there to protect people from the same?

Regional and Geopolitical Factors

Pakistan's domestic and external challenges do not exist in isolation. Several factors beyond the capacity of the Pakistani state will likely have import for

Pakistan's precarious path, including U.S. relations and engagement in the region, India's rise, and the eventual position that China takes toward Pakistan.

The first of these factors is the way in which the United States has chosen to interact with the region. The United States, under President Bush, pursued a policy of dehyphenation, first articulated by Ashley Tellis in 2000.[15] Tellis argued that the United States should pursue policies with India and Pakistan that are consonant with the merits of each country, irrespective of U.S. relations with the other or the continuing security competition between the two. Tellis argued that India, as a rising power, deserves an increasingly strategic relationship with the United States to help manage China's rise, to contend with terrorism, and to provide energy security, among other regional and international security affairs. In contrast, Pakistan should be prepared for a "soft landing."[16] After the events of 9/11, given the centrality of Pakistan, the soft landing was deferred. However, Washington transformed its relations with India under the umbrella of dehyphenation. The centerpiece of this has been the U.S.-Indian civilian nuclear deal.

Pakistan has viewed Washington's commitment to help India become a global power with unease. Its discomfiture has not been alleviated by the massive infusion of military assistance and lucrative reimbursements that Pakistan has received since 9/11. (It should be noted that Pakistanis believe that Pakistan has suffered a net loss because the reimbursements and other forms of assistance are inadequate to cover Pakistan's losses due to economic volatility, domestic terrorism in response to the U.S.-led war on terror, political instability, and so forth. U.S. officials reject that view, noting that Pakistan is reimbursed for costs that it invoices through the Coalition Support Funds program.)

The United States has sought to induce Pakistan into greater cooperation by offering Pakistan a "strategic dialogue." However, the relationship that the United States has tried to offer has few takers in Islamabad. The United States has generally maintained that the Indo-U.S. relationship should have no bearing on Pakistan's standing. However, that view is incomprehensible in Pakistan. The United States has been unwilling to forge a "new big idea" for Pakistan as it did for India. That is unfortunate. Until Washington develops the political will to put forward new and meaningful (likely political) carrots and effective sticks, the United States will likely be unable to positively influence the arc of Pakistan's development.

The U.S. relationship with Afghanistan as well as with India and Pakistan will influence Pakistan's domestic and external affairs. While Pakistanis opine that they distrust the United States and must prepare for any eventuality, they are fundamentally bothered by the fact that the Americans cannot articulate a desired end state for Afghanistan, much less a strategy to achieve that state. (Pakistanis are not alone in that frustration.) However, Pakistan's interests remain stable, and thus policy continuity will persist under civilian or military leadership. Pakistan will continue to work toward diminishing India's influence in Afghanistan and securing a regime that is minimally hostile to Pakistan if a friendly regime cannot be secured. Above all, however, Pakistan wishes to retain primacy in the region as a security manager. (In this capacity, Pakistan may also receive payments from Washington and others as a positive externality.)

The second factor, related to the first, is the rise of India. India seeks to be an extra-regional power and, according to some, a global power. Right-wing Indians associated with the Bharatiya Janata Party (BJP), for example, believe that India already is a global power. As such, India continues to develop relationships in Pakistan's near and far neighborhood that serve both to deny Pakistan the possibility of developing a positive influence in and access to the same countries as well as of developing commercial and other economic interests throughout the region, including hydrocarbon resources. As India continues its ascent with U.S. assistance and continues to develop ties to its neighbors, such as Iran and Afghanistan, Pakistan will likely turn more toward Islamism and militancy and redouble its efforts to regain control of its various militant proxies, some of whom have turned against the Pakistani state or who are, at least for now, operating with greater independence from it.

It is also possible—albeit less likely—that the Pakistan military will eventually conclude that Islamist proxies are dangerous to Pakistan. If so, they will see these proxies as unmanageable as a tool to contain India over the long term. That would suggest that over time Pakistan acquiesces to the ascent of its larger neighbor and seeks some accommodation with it. In some sense, that response would be rational, as Pakistan would be better off seeking a resolution today before India grows stronger and Pakistan grows weaker. However, it is doubtful that the army would buy into such an approach, as doing so would be to concede its massive powers of influence across the state.

A third issue factor China. In recent years, China has grown ever more wary of the management of Pakistan's internal security crises. Because China currently is the largest foreign direct investor (in the Aynak copper mine in Logar) in Afghanistan and has made significant investments in Pakistan, Iran, and Central Asia, it is rightly worried about Pakistan's use of Islamist proxies. Moreover, China's own restive Uighurs have received training in Pakistan and Afghanistan. While China increasingly views India with concern, it is also aware that India offers more opportunities than Pakistan. Any reorienting of China away from Pakistan—be it political, diplomatic, or economic—may be an important wake-up call. However, China is unlikely to abandon its military ties with Pakistan because China believes that balancing Pakistan's capabilities vis-à-vis India serves its objectives with respect to containing India as a South Asian power. Unfortunately, the United States has not made significant outreach to China as a regional partner.

Similar other wild cards are Saudi Arabia and the other Arab Gulf states, as well as Iran. While the Sunni Arab Gulf States are in a strategic competition with the Shia Iranian regime, these states all have one thing in common: a fear of Pakistan's expanding Sunni militancy affecting them at home. Pakistan and Iran have had a low-profile rapprochement. Iran has accused Pakistan and the United States of supporting Jundullah, a Sunni terrorist organization targeting the Iranian state, despite the fact that Pakistan was recently involved in the capture of Jundullah's leader, Abdolmalek Riga. Pakistani intelligence officials told me in June 2010 that Iran has also been helpful in limiting the movement of Indian assistance to Pakistan's Balochistan province. The Sunni Arab Gulf states have sought to influence Pakistan's domestic forces by funding Islamic institutions such as mosques and madrassas and by providing various forms of economic support. However, it is beyond my capacity to undertake a comprehensive disaggregation of these varied states' interests and options.

Conclusions

In brief, Pakistan's political and civil society organizations are too weak and/or self-interested to forge a new consensus on the nature of the state of Pakistan and its relations with Islam, among other issues. Political and bureaucratic institutions are too weak to address both the causes and the manifestations of Pakistan's decrepit internal security situation and inadequate rule of law institutions. Without resolving foundational issues about the state and its citizenry, the army will likely continue to dominate state decisionmaking with no diminution of reliance on Islam and Islamism as tools of policy. Therefore the threat posed by Pakistan's domestic Islamist militants will be difficult to contain as Pakistan continues to nurture their co-sectarian members who purport to operate within India and Afghanistan. Over time, these groups will continue to develop greater autonomy, seriously challenging South Asian stability. Will India hold Pakistan accountable in the future as these groups develop independence? Will India develop new military postures and doctrines and invest in further force modernization to tackle this threat?

At the same time, as Pakistan's varied civil societies struggle over the Pakistan that will emerge, the attempts to find consensus on who is a Pakistani and on what basis the state exists will become more, not less, contested. It is entirely possible that two Pakistans will exist in an uneasy and unstable equilibrium with each other. On one hand will be the Pakistan of forward-looking, modernizing Pakistanis, who want to free the state of its reliance on dangerous proxies. On the other hand will be the Pakistan of those who view Islam and Islamism as the only meaningful antidote to the various pressures bearing on the state and its polities.

Notes

1. C. Christine Fair and others, *Pakistan: Helping to Secure an Insecure State* (Santa Monica, Calif.: RAND, 2010).

2. This section draws from C. Christine Fair, Neil Malhotra, and Jacob N. Shapiro, "Islam, Militancy, and Politics in Pakistan: Insights from a National Sample," *Terrorism and Political Violence*, vol. 22, no. 4 (September 2010); C. Christine Fair, Neil Malhotra, and Jacob N. Shapiro, "The Roots of Militancy: Explaining Support for Political Violence in Pakistan," working paper, March 10, 2010 (www.princeton.edu/~jns/papers/FMS_2009_The_Roots_of_Militancy.pdf) ; C. Christine Fair, "Pakistan's Own War on Terror: What the Pakistani Public Thinks," *Journal of International Affairs*, vol. 63, no. 1 (Fall–Winter 2009).

3. Graeme Blair and others, "Poverty and Support for Militant Politics: Evidence from Pakistan," May 2, 2011 (http://papers.ssrn.com/sol3/papers.cfm?abstract_id=1829264).

4. Stephen P. Cohen, *The Idea of Pakistan* (Brookings, 2005).

5. Masooda Bano, "Dangerous Correlations: Aid's Impact on NGO's Performance and Ability to Mobilize Members in Pakistan," *World Development*, vol. 36, no. 1 (2008), pp. 2297–313.

6. Sadaf Ahmad, *Transforming Faith: The Story of al-Huda and Islamic Revivalism among Urban Pakistani Women* (Syracuse University Press, 2009).

7. Cohen, *The Idea of Pakistan*; Husain Haqqani, *Pakistan: Between Mosque and Military* (Washington: CEIP, 2005).

8. C. Christine Fair, "The Militant Challenge in Pakistan," *Asia Policy*, vol. 11 (January 2011), pp. 105–37; Praveen Swami, *India, Pakistan, and the Secret Jihad* (London: Routledge, 2007); Rizwan Hussain, *Pakistan and the Emergence of Islamic Militancy in Afghanistan* (Burlington, Vt.: Ashgate, 2005); Barnett Rubin, *The Fragmentation of Afghanistan* (Yale University Press, 2002); Mariam Abou Zahab, "The Regional Dimension of Sectarian Conflicts in Pakistan," in *Pakistan: Nationalism without a Nation?* edited by Christophe Jaffrelot (London: Zed, 2002), pp.115–28; S. V. R. Nasr, "The Rise of Sunni Militancy in Pakistan: The Changing Role of Islamism and the Ulama in Society and Politics," *Modern Asian Studies*, vol. 34, no. 1 (2000), pp. 139–80.

9. See the divergent accounts in Ayesha Siddiqa, *Military Inc.: Inside Pakistan's Military Economy* (London: Pluto Press, 2007), and Shuja Nawaz, *Crossed Swords: Pakistan, Its Army, and the Wars Within* (Oxford University Press, 2008).

10. Fair, "The Militant Challenge in Pakistan," pp. 105–37.

11. Ibid.

12. Ibid.

13. Ibid.

14. See C. Christine Fair, "Security Sector Governance in Pakistan?" *Current History*, vol. 110, no. 735 (2011), pp. 136–43.

15. See Ashley J. Tellis, "The Merits of Dehyphenation: Explaining U.S. Success in Engaging India and Pakistan," *Washington Quarterly*, vol. 31, no. 4 (2008), pp. 21–42.

16. See Ashley J. Tellis, "South Asia: U.S. Policy Choices," in *Taking Charge: A Bipartisan Report to the President-Elect on Foreign Policy and National Security—Discussion Papers*, edited by Frank Carlucci, Robert E. Hunter, and Zalmay Khalilzad (Santa Monica: RAND, 2001), p. 88 (www.rand.org/pubs/monograph_reports/MR1306.1/MR1306.1.sec3.pdf).

TARIQ FATEMI

5

Looking Ahead

Pakistan should be confident of its own abilities and optimistic about its future, given its size, location, and the qualities of its people, who now number over 170 million. So should the rest of the world, given that Pakistanis have been successful wherever they have gone and in whatever endeavor they have undertaken. Yet it is not only scholars and political analysts who are convinced that Pakistan faces an uncertain future; many Pakistanis too are worried about the destiny of their country.

What explains this phenomenon, when much smaller and weaker countries appear far more confident about themselves and do not arouse similar worries and fears? The factors are many and go as far back as the unusual circumstances surrounding the birth of Pakistan, which cast a deep shadow on the state's future conduct and behavior. Upon emerging from colonial rule, Pakistan's political leadership and its elite lacked adequate resources for spending on important social sectors, such as health and education. Instead, priority had to be accorded to ensuring the country's safety and security, in view of the hostility that it faced from its much stronger and far bigger neighbor, India.

Even if some of Pakistan's concerns may have been exaggerated, India's leaders left no stone unturned to increase the pressure on Pakistan. India went so far as to assuage the hurt pride of its citizens at the Subcontinent's partition by assuring them that the newly established state would be a short-term experiment and that sooner rather than later, its people would seek to rejoin the "motherland." Thereafter, a host of problems cropped up between the two neighbors, including the issue of Kashmir, which has been the primary cause of the three wars and numerous confrontations between them. In fact, this issue should not be seen merely as one relating to a disputed territory, for it has impacted the hearts and minds of Pakistanis who cannot visualize their country without this strategically important Muslim-majority area, which had always figured in demands for a homeland for the Muslims of the Subcontinent. Not surprisingly, this lingering dispute continues to cast an ominous shadow on relations between the two South Asian neighbors, while also influencing Pakistan's domestic policies.

In this context, one may refer to "The Geopolitics of Emotion," a book by the French scholar Dominique Moisi.[1] In it, he asserts that contrary to common perception, emotions and symbols do play an important role in international relations and that this role is much more evident in the case of India and Pakistan. When discussing complex legal matters, both sides give primacy to historic memories and cultural beliefs rather than to strategic interests based on reason and logic. The skill and resourcefulness of South Asians is evident in their success in foreign countries, which only proves how sentiments and emotions have impeded their political development at home. In Moisi's words, the policymakers of the region should strive for the right balance between good and bad emotions, and he recommends that the two countries resolve those issues that are easily amenable to solution while leaving the intractable ones on the back burner.

There is no doubt that the two nations' inability to resolve their differences provided Pakistan's military, intelligence, and security organizations the opportunity and legitimacy to seek a "special role" for themselves in national affairs. Over a period of time, they came to assume the role of the protector of the nation's geographical borders and guardian of its ideological frontiers. That role became more pronounced during the rule of General Zia ul-Haq, but it had been in evidence since the country's early days. Consequently, in external relations, Pakistan's major motivation became the search for external "props," both in terms of economic assistance and military arms, to help deter the perceived designs of its much larger and inimical neighbor. That led Pakistan in the early 1950s to the United States, which was already looking for friends and allies in what it rightly anticipated would be a global confrontation with a militarily powerful and ideologically formidable foe—the Soviet Union.

There was another feature of Pakistan's political development that was not only unusual but also harmful to the growth of its national politics. It arose from the fact that the most vigorous and sustained campaign for an independent Pakistan was carried out in the Muslim-minority provinces of undivided India, as a result of which the Muslim League was better organized in those areas. Consequently, it was from these provinces that Pakistan's first political leaders and senior civil servants were drawn, and they staffed various government departments and agencies. Even the business class consisted primarily of migrants from the state of Gujarat and the cities of Bombay and Calcutta. But the domination of the migrants, or Muhajirs as they became known in popular parlance, coupled with their inability to relate to popular sentiments and needs, soon began to be resented by the locals. An unfortunate chasm was therefore inevitable between the rulers and the ruled.

On the other hand, the only institution that remained predominantly "local" was the armed forces, in particular, the army. That made the army conscious of the fact that it best represented the ethos of the people and encouraged it to seek a stronger voice in national affairs. Eventually the army carved out a unique role for itself as the guardian of the national interest, not only with respect to the country's sovereignty and independence but also with respect to its ideological moorings. That came about gradually at first, but then much more forcefully under Zia, who shamelessly exploited the faith of the majority to lay claim to a virtual "divine" right to maintain his stranglehold on power. In such an arrangement, it was inevitable that the authoritarian regime would prefer to deal with people who were neither popular nor principled. In fact, with brief interludes of civilian government, Pakistan has been ruled for more than half of its history by military dictators who had little interest in promoting democracy or the rule of law and even less in formulating policies that would cater to the needs of the common people. The long spells of authoritarian rule destroyed the institutions of the state, promoted sectarian and ethnic organizations, and encouraged fissiparous tendencies. More important, they ignored the interests of smaller and less influential communities and classes, which led to a sense of deep cynicism and foreboding among millions of common citizens and eventually to the country's breakup in 1971.

The country's strong alliance with the United States has also had an enduring influence on the state and its institutions and their political evolution. And yet this relationship has never enjoyed popular support, viewed as it has been as another effort by the country's elite to protect its entrenched interests. This view is confirmed by the fact that close cooperation with the United States and promotion of the elite's interests appeared to coincide with the advent of military regimes in Pakistan. Lacking legality, these authoritarian regimes sought to establish their credibility at home and legitimacy abroad by seeking sustenance and support from foreign powers, even if it meant becoming their willing tool in ventures that were not in the interest of Pakistan's people and that sometimes were undertaken without their knowledge. Over a period of time, that led to a disconnect between the rulers and the ruled, giving rise to the perception that the common man mattered little in the national scheme of things, which in turn led the poor and disenfranchised to believe that they had no stake in the country's future.

There has, however, been a welcome recent change in U.S. attitude, as evident in the Obama administration's decision to engage in a strategic dialogue with Pakistan. The United States is now proposing cooperation in many diverse fields rather than focusing on the single-item agenda—the war on terror—that had been the feature of U.S. policy during the Bush administration. There is also a distinct change in the U.S. attitude toward Pakistan's nuclear program, confirmed in President Obama's remarks at a press conference on April 13, 2010, at the conclusion of the nuclear security summit, when he rejected a journalist's insinuation that "it appears that Pakistan is playing by a different set of rules." Instead, Obama categorically stated: "I have actually seen progress over the last several years with respect to Pakistan's nuclear security issues. I feel confident about Pakistan's security around its nuclear weapons program." Then, in a rare show of humility, Obama observed that "it is important to note that every nuclear power, every country that has a civilian nuclear energy program, has to take better steps to secure these materials. We are not, either." He is also reported to have assured Prime Minister Gilani: "I will take it [bilateral relations] to the heights, where it has never been taken before."[2] Whether the United States succeeds in attaining that goal is difficult to predict, but even the articulation of this objective is commendable, as it has helped to inject greater cordiality and trust in the ties between the two nations.

However, for the relationship to become truly meaningful, the United States will have to focus on building broad ties with the people of Pakistan rather than merely confining the relationship to a few individuals and focusing on a couple of agenda items. Those ties should include regular and continuous cross-sector dialogue and engagement between the political leadership and the civil and military bureaucracies of the two countries, which should help reduce the trust deficit between them.

Moreover, the numerous legal and administrative steps taken by Pakistan with respect to nuclear material and technology appear to have finally convinced key members of the international community that the country's nuclear program was secure. There also appears to be a better appreciation in Washington of Pakistan's legitimate security requirements, which include its nuclear program. Linked to that is a grudging acknowledgment that the United States cannot remain totally indifferent to the failure of India and Pakistan to engage productively in the process of normalizing their relations. There is also the realization, especially in the Pentagon, that Pakistan's complete and unambiguous cooperation in the war against the militants is essential for success of the U.S. strategy in Afghanistan. These considerations and others appear to have had a profound impact on how the Obama administration currently sees Pakistan. Far from viewing Pakistan as a failed state, the Obama administration favors a comprehensive, productive, and meaningful relationship with this important South Asian country.

Meanwhile, the abysmally inadequate allocation of resources over the years to the country's social sectors has resulted in Pakistan being pushed to the very bottom of the assessments made in various reports of the United Nations Development Program (UNDP). Whether it is health, education, housing, drinking water, or women's empowerment, the country has been sliding down, even in comparison to countries far poorer and less endowed than Pakistan. Sadly, there appear to be only two things that are prospering in Pakistan. One is corruption, both of individuals and within institutions, and the other is population growth, with even official sites reporting an estimated 1.8 to 2.0 percent annual increase, which means a rough increase annually of about 3.3 million people. Given that about 40 percent of the population is already living below the poverty line and 5.6 percent of the population is unemployed, the rapidly increasing population is adding to the country's existing problems, steadily ratcheting up the pressure on a nation that already is under serious pressure. This alarming situation has been confirmed in the World Bank's Global Monitoring Report for 2010, which warns that political uncertainty and domestic turmoil arising out of militancy are likely to disrupt economic activity in Pakistan much more than in other South Asian countries.[3] Bad governance and, more often, no governance have contributed to religious, ethnic, and sectarian extremism and militancy. At the same time, the country's involvement in promoting the goals and objectives of foreign powers, occasionally at its cost, has also played an important role in furthering those tendencies.

A third worry is that the nation is fully armed, with one of the highest per capita gun ownership rates in the world. The government, which should be a source of security for its people, has instead become a source of insecurity. In many places, especially in rural Pakistan, the police, the courts, and the educational and health systems are either nonexistent or overwhelmingly inefficient and unreliable. The war on terror has also increased insecurity, rather than making people feel safer. As a result, instead of being able to depend on their government, the poor and uneducated have come to depend on tribal leaders, feudal lords, religious and political leaders, and increasingly on extremists and militants.

Pakistan's successful tests of its nuclear explosive devices in May 1998, in response to those of India, deeply angered and upset many countries, especially those in the West. Led by the United States, many of them imposed sanctions on Pakistan, demanding that the government satisfy their concerns. As if that were not enough, the reckless adventure of the chief of the army in the summer of 1999, in what came to be known as the Kargil episode, gave rise to serious alarm in world capitals at what was perceived to be a dangerous and provocative military campaign. That was followed soon thereafter by reports of the dubious role played by some of the country's nuclear scientists in pro- liferating nuclear technology and equipment, which deepened concern in many countries. The reports provided some countries the opportunity to accuse Pakistan's official agencies of involvement in that transgression, keep- ing the country under great pressure.

Since the 9/11 tragedy, Pakistan has found itself on the front line of the so- called "war on terror." Over the past few years, the country has been rocked by a wave of terrorist attacks and suicide bombings that have induced the expa- triate community to flee and discouraged foreign investment. Thousands of schools and other educational institutions have been destroyed by the mili- tants, and millions have been forced to abandon their homes. The attacks have crippled the economy and brought development projects to a halt. The government appears weak, confused, and ineffective, and neighboring India has tried to take advantage of the situation to disparage Pakistan, accusing the nation of involvement in acts of terror.

While General Musharraf's military regime had little interest in meeting the aspirations of the country's rapidly growing population, the restoration of democratic institutions in February 2008 raised huge expectations. Many Pak- istanis felt a genuine sense of joy and pride in the manner in which popular sentiment played a critical role in Musharraf's ouster. Some believed that nearly a decade of military rule had made the politicians wiser and more mature, convincing them that only a responsible and responsive government would be able to confront the massive challenges confronting the country. Sadly, the past two years plus have intensified the doubts and misgivings in large sections of the population, especially in the middle class and the poorer sections of society. These groups in particular have seen a dismal deterioration of governance by a confused and directionless leadership.

The current government, though elected, remains oblivious to the needs of the country and unaware of the sentiments of the common man. It has con- tinued to lurch from one crisis to another, causing disappointment and dis- may among the citizens, which is likely to weaken their belief in democracy and the rule of law. They have seen the essential commodities of daily use dis- appear from the market or become available only at exorbitant cost. They have also witnessed the virtual breakdown of the rule of law, with regular and sickening violence directed at schools, colleges, and even mosques, forcing millions to flee their homes. High food and fuel prices have increased poverty to unprecedented levels, while a weak economy means there is little hope of improvement in their lives.

However, this is the age of globalization. Growing links among nations and regions mean that Pakistan's future cannot be determined in isolation. Many of the challenges that young Pakistanis will face in coming decades will be similar to those faced by youth in other regions, where too the population is increasing at a phenomenal pace. For example, in 1960 the world's population was just 3 billion people. Since then it has more than doubled, and it will have tripled by 2050.[4] At the same time, there is an ineluctable power shift from the developed to the developing world, with Europe's and North America's share of global population shrinking and their citizens aging rapidly. Half of their citizens are over the age of forty, with recent migrants making up the growing share of their labor force. On the other hand, citizens in the developing world are much younger, at an average age of less than twenty-seven years old. Urban centers are growing rapidly. By 2030, there will be around 1.5 billion more urban dwellers in developing countries, and experts predict that half a dozen more "mega cities," with 10 million or more people, will have emerged.

But the rapidly increasing population in developing countries is likely to face enormous challenges, even in merely surviving. In addition to the religious, ethnic, sectarian, and tribal conflicts in many of these nations is environmental degradation on a scale that is beyond their comprehension. By 2030, the global demand for food is expected to grow by 50 percent and the demand for energy by 45 percent, which will necessitate massive investment and innovation to keep pace with needs. Pakistan's resources also have been impacted by climate change, a phenomenon that is having an adverse effect on the entire globe. It is likely to threaten the country's water resources, which will disrupt agriculture and increase the number and severity of natural disasters. Pakistan will also come under pressure to conform to higher standards of environmental protection, which will affect its industries and economic activities. That the richest 10 percent of the world's population owns 85 percent of its wealth means that even if the developing countries expand at unprecedented rates, it will take decades, possibly even centuries, for them to come close to the standards enjoyed in the developed countries. But if their economies were to stagnate, the situation would be much worse, particularly in countries in the midst of domestic violence and conflict.

The current portrait of Pakistan is that of a young and increasingly urban society, with half of its citizens under the age of twenty and two-thirds of that number yet to reach the age of thirteen. But most worrying is that the country's population has tripled in less than fifty years and is likely to grow by another 85 million in the next twenty years, primarily because birth rates remain high, even by regional standards, especially in rural areas. The economy must grow by 6 percent a year to meet the needs of its growing population. The country will also have to provide 36 million new jobs in the next ten years, which explains why Pakistan ranks 101 out of 133 countries on the Global Competitiveness Index. The current energy crisis has exposed the failure of the military regime to focus on this critical sector. That failure has led to power shortages for hours, with little prospect of any meaningful improvement in the coming years. In fact, by 2030, Pakistan will be more urban than rural, creating huge demand for infrastructure. Energy requirements are likely to quadruple. That could result in the shutting down of industries and factories, throwing millions out of their jobs, which would cause severe unrest and even social upheaval.

The challenges that Pakistan faces are not dissimilar to those faced by other countries in the developing world, though the current situation makes its predicament appear more serious and worrisome. Like other developing countries, Pakistan will be deeply influenced by global social, economic, security, and environmental factors. As Pakistan's Finance Ministry noted in a recent assessment of the country's future prospects:

> Pakistan's economy still faces pressures from an uncertain security environment, higher inflation, driven by a spike in food prices, acute power shortages, bewildering stock market, perceptible contraction in large-scale manufacturing and a slow-down in the services sector, lower than anticipated inflows, and growing absolute financing requirements.[5]

Even though growth was expected to pick up in 2011, it was forecast to be at a rate that barely exceeds the rate of population growth. Pakistan will remain heavily dependent on external assistance and remittances from its workers abroad.

The energy crisis is destined to get worse, with the result that industry will be further crippled and ordinary people's lives adversely impacted. Even though Pakistanis consume less than a quarter of the energy used by the average global citizen, by 2030, with annual economic growth above 6 percent, energy demand will be 4 times the current level. Water problems are also assuming alarming proportions, and Pakistan is now one of the world's most water-stressed countries. Sources of water are becoming depleted, and available water is deteriorating in quality as well, with the World Bank warning that Pakistan would be facing "outright water scarcity" in the coming years. That is on top of the increasing impact of changing climate conditions. That has been made evident by the fact that the period from 1995 to 2006 saw eleven of the twelve warmest years since 1850, which led to severe droughts. The glaciers on the Himalayas are retreating at between ten to fifteen meters a year and could disappear in about forty years.

Not surprisingly, these challenges have had a profound impact not only on the standard of living of the people but on the national morale as well. According to a recent survey, only one in ten expects the situation to get better in the near future, with most statistics indicating that the challenges faced by the country's coming generations will be far greater than today's challenges. That has led some political observers to claim that while Pakistan is a state, it is not yet a nation. Multi-ethnic states that evolve over a period of time into a nation-state are more united and cohesive. These observers believe that a common identity and mindset, shared sense of history, and common goals are missing from the equation. While Pakistan's genesis explains some of the current problems, it is only part of the story.

After the early death of the founder of the state, Mohammed Ali Jinnah, "feudal lords," in league with the country's civil and military bureaucracy, seized power. Their failure to overcome inequalities of wealth and opportunity, introduce effective democracy, and ensure a functional legal system combined to cripple the country in its very infancy. Pakistan was established in the name of Islam, but with the assurance that the religious, economic, and cultural rights of all other communities would be protected as well. However, Islam quickly became an instrument in the hands of the feudal lords and the clergy to deprive the provinces and smaller communities of their right to pursue legitimate demands and to express their own individual beliefs and views.

The breakup of the country in 1971 should have ended the illusion that common religious belief could hold people together in the face of oppression and injustice, even though common faith remains the strongest bonding factor in the country. A recent survey of 2,000 young Pakistanis in the eighteen-to-twenty-seven age group found that three-quarters identified themselves first as Muslims and only second as Pakistanis. Dejected and adrift, most see religion as their anchor. Pakistanis continue to hope that they can become a nation one day. How long will this process likely take? In Pakistan's case, it does not have to be centuries. Its people are diverse, but almost all understand Urdu. They watch the same television programs, listen to the same songs, support the same national heroes, deal with the same inefficient and corrupt bureaucracy, and suffer the same impediments and handicaps. They also have a strong and visible commitment to the country. However, if Pakistan is to chart a path to viable nationhood, a national dialogue on its most pressing problems is essential.

While the country faces major external challenges, its most serious ones are those at home. Therefore, while Pakistan has to devote its energies and resources to ending its raging internal wars, it also has to recognize that the long conflict with India has achieved nothing beyond creating a militarized security state that uses force as its first resort. Attempts to resolve the Kashmir dispute militarily have bled the country and left it dependent on foreign aid. First, the nation must begin to redefine the army's role so that it is limited to defending the country's frontiers. Second, Pakistan needs economic justice, which demands a social infrastructure that ensures decent employment and minimum income and benefits based on ability and hard work. In rural areas, where old structures of landownership remain intact, sweeping land reforms are desperately needed. India abolished feudalism upon attaining independence, but the enormous pre-partition land holdings of Pakistan's feudal lords were protected by the authority of the state.

Third, Pakistan must shed its colonial structure of governance. A huge, inefficient, and unconcerned centralized government sitting in the comfortable confines of Islamabad cannot effectively manage such a big and diverse country. Pakistan has to be reorganized as a genuine federation in which provinces and local governments hold economic and social powers and only a few critical areas, such as defense, foreign affairs, communications, and currency, remain the responsibility of the federal government. A welcome step in this direction was taken in April 2010, when Parliament approved an amendment to the Constitution that greatly expands the powers of the provinces, granting them authority over areas that had been denied to them in the past.

Fourth, Pakistan needs a social contract. This is the commitment that all citizens, irrespective of their religious, ethnic, and linguistic backgrounds, will be treated fairly and equally by the state and, in turn, will willingly fulfill basic civic responsibilities, as so categorically enunciated by the country's founder in his address of August 11, 1947. Fifth, Pakistan's education system needs a drastic overhaul, both in substance and form. The language of instruction, the syllabi, and the curricula have to be uniform in both private and public institutions. Finally, foreign policy has to be drafted and formulated by Pakistan's elected representatives to ensure that it is in consonance with the desires and wishes of the people. In other words, Pakistan has to end its role as a client state willing to offer its services to the highest bidder.

The challenges are so many and so formidable that it would be surprising if the reader did not reach the conclusion that the prospect of Pakistan emerging successfully out of its current difficulties and becoming a modern, moderate, and progressive Islamic state is bleak. Nevertheless, recent developments give ground for considerable hope. For one, the manner in which the people of Pakistan were able to rally round the chief justice of the Supreme Court after he was summarily dismissed by General Musharraf represented a welcome development in the growth of people's political awareness. In fact, Chief Justice Chaudhry's refusal to accede to Musharraf's demand that he submit his resignation was so unexpected and dramatic that it not only stunned the military ruler but also struck a chord of strong admiration among the people of Pakistan. It also triggered a massive protest movement among lawyers that soon extended to the entire country and brought thousands of young and old urban professionals within its fold. What was even more remarkable was the peaceful manner in which the protest movement reacted to the military regime's heavy-handed attempts to suppress it. In the process, the movement became nationwide, embracing all communities and virtually all political parties, which exposed Musharraf's isolation at home and his alienation from his people.

In the process, Pakistan saw, for the first time, a seemingly innocuous issue captivate the imagination of the people and galvanize them in an unprecedented manner. No one expected the poor, hungry, and uneducated to care about an issue of little direct interest to them. And yet, it gave birth to the nucleus of a civil society that had been nonexistent in the past. This mass awakening had a profound impact on the general elections held soon thereafter. For one, they took place with hardly any disturbance or violence, with the people rejecting the candidatures of many of Musharraf's cronies while giving a severe drubbing to religious figures, even in their traditional strongholds. The victory of mainstream political parties and the humiliation of the religious groups was a welcome confirmation of the inherent unpopularity of those who wished to use religion as a political tool.

Admittedly, the government that was elected has performed poorly. Politicians continue to show little commitment to good governance while remaining addicted to corrupt practices, actions that have not won them any praise. But that is not surprising, given that Pakistan has had long interludes of military rule and that even when elections have been held, they have been deeply influenced by the ethos of the authoritarian regimes. When the government has taken the initiative to reach out to the other political parties and bring them on board on issues of national importance, such as the issue of crafting a national policy aimed at confronting extremism and militancy, it has been successful. The best-known example was the creation of a national consensus that enabled the army to undertake massive operations against well-entrenched terrorists in some of the most inaccessible areas of Pakistan. In fact, the resolve and commitment with which the army conducted its operations and the skill and courage that it demonstrated earned it well-deserved praise at home and from senior U.S. military commanders. It helped to lay to rest the fears expressed in the West that the militants were about to overrun the state and possibly even capture its nonconventional weapons.

This success has given the country fresh hope and confidence and greatly strengthened its image and standing abroad. It also is a matter of deep gratification that Parliament has been successful, notwithstanding many doubts and misgivings, in doing away with many of the undemocratic measures and changes introduced into the Constitution by the military regimes of General Zia ul-Haq and General Pervez Musharraf. That the political parties were able to overcome their differences and resolve dozens of contentious issues is welcome evidence of the maturity and wisdom of the mainstream politicians. Another encouraging development has been the growing involvement of thousands of Pakistanis, in both urban and rural areas, who have pooled their resources and set up schools, colleges, clinics, hospitals, and similar facilities that are engaged in philanthropic and social work. This spirit of sacrifice and sharing in social uplift programs is not only commendable but also compelling evidence that the people remain committed to the state and also have both the will and the capacity to engage in nation-building tasks.

While there are many who would wish to pronounce, Cassandra-like, that an uncertain future is inevitable for Pakistan, its people have shown tremendous faith in their ability to overcome the many challenges confronting it. They have demonstrated an uncanny ability to surprise not only their enemies but their well-wishers as well by overcoming seemingly insurmountable hurdles and impediments, thus giving convincing evidence of their inherent resilience and inner strength. That was most dramatically revealed on two important occasions in the country's history.

The first was in the aftermath of the country's breakup in 1971. While the Pakistani political elite was primarily responsible for the anger and alienation that swept across what was then East Pakistan, there is no doubt that India contributed, in no small measure, to aiding and abetting in the breakup of the country. Recent revelations by prominent Indians have confirmed the initial widespread suspicion that had India not been instrumental in first nurturing the "separatists" and then militarily invading East Pakistan, the Bengali leadership may not have been averse to holding a dialogue with their West Pakistani counterparts, as many friendly countries, including the United States, had strongly suggested. That may not have prevented the breakup of the country, but it surely would have prevented violence and bloodshed. When East Pakistan succeeded in declaring itself an independent state, there was a deep sense of grief and anguish in Pakistan, with many convinced that its independence represented the death of the idea of Pakistan. Many scholars predicted that the other federating units would also seek to walk away, leaving the state subject to the ambitions of its larger neighbors. It was at that point that the people of Pakistan demonstrated tremendous strength and resilience in overcoming the trauma of the breakup and, in the words of Zulfikar Ali Bhutto, being able "to pick up the pieces" and rebuild the country with renewed vigor and resolve.

The second important occasion was India's nuclear weapon test in May 1974. Even though New Delhi chose to call it a "peaceful nuclear explosion," christening it the "Smiling Buddha," the Pakistani nation recognized that India's possession of this awesome weapon would have a critical bearing on the region and add greatly to India's ability to pressure Pakistan. Though a poor, underdeveloped country with limited resources and one that was under all kinds of external pressure, including sanctions, Pakistan was nevertheless able to initiate a comprehensive plan for the development of its own nuclear weapons. And, much to the surprise of the international community, it was able to regain strategic equilibrium by becoming a nuclear weapon state a few weeks after India conducted nuclear tests in May 1998.

Recent events in Pakistan have renewed the people's faith in themselves. Admittedly, the government has performed poorly, but the manner in which a military dictator was ousted, peaceful elections were held, and an elected government assumed power and, most important, the maturity with which the main opposition party and the ruling party are cooperating with each other on critical issues are evidence of the ability of the Pakistani nation to confront the challenges. Even the near-unanimity with which the political elite of the country has been pushing for "normalization" of relations with India is a welcome departure from the sterile, unproductive, confrontational policies of the past. There is every reason to believe that in another ten years, the parliamentary system will have taken root and become more durable, ensuring a stable and prosperous Pakistan. Those eager to write Pakistan's obituary, given that this strategically important country has become synonymous with terrorism and nuclear proliferation, are being much too hasty and presumptuous. It would be wrong to believe that everything about Pakistan is negative. After all, the country has weathered a savage civil war, resisted crude foreign pressure, and ousted a vicious military dictator. In fact, militancy and the horror that it created among the people of Pakistan has helped to bring an unexpected degree of unanimity and understanding among the people. Even the manner in which the common people of the country rallied around the victims of terror and helped look after millions of refugees is a glorious testimony to their inner strength and to their profound love and commitment to their country.

Postscript

Months after the Bellagio Conference, a horrible tragedy struck Pakistan that appeared to call into question some of the premises of this chapter. This was the gruesome murder of Salmaan Taseer, governor of the Province of the Punjab, by one of his own bodyguards. While it was a shocking and highly condemnable act, what rightly unnerved many people was the subsequent celebratory reaction among some in Pakistan. Many saw it as irrefutable confirmation of their fear that the country was suffering from the cancer of extremism and that this malaise had gone beyond the curable stage. While those concerns cannot be dismissed, the reality is far more nuanced. The curse of extremism, sanctified as part of state policy during General Zia's watch, had weakened in the nineties, when the country was governed by elected civilian governments. However, General Musharraf, although not a religious person himself, had no compunction about orchestrating a victory for the religious parties in the 2002 elections, primarily to defeat the mainstream political parties, the Pakistan People's Party and the Pakistan Muslim League–Nawaz, in order to perpetuate his own rule. That emboldened religious extremists all over the country, and as the dictator deferred military action to coddle his religious allies, large swaths of territory were lost to the militants. Since Musharraf's departure and, more specifically, since the coming together of the mainstream political parties on the issue of confronting militancy, much of that lost territory has been recaptured. The frequency of suicide attacks has also decreased, but their disruptive power and ability to frighten the public remains.

It is, however, doubtful that the extremists are in a position to win elections or to enhance their influence unless the government loses its nerve and fails to enforce the writ of the state, as appeared to be the case in the days after the death of Salmaan Taseer. Even if the current cast of characters in Islamabad is inefficient and corrupt, as it is widely perceived, it should have taken advantage of the widespread horror and revulsion at the behavior of the extremists to galvanize public opinion against them. Nevertheless, I am convinced that if the political leadership of the country demonstrates courage and conviction in confronting this menace—qualities that admittedly have not been in evidence so far—it will see the country's overwhelming majority step up and reaffirm its strong revulsion for extremism and militancy. After all, Pakistan today has a media more vibrant, a judiciary more independent, a civil society more influential, and federalism more effective than in the past.

Notes

1. Dominique Moisi, *The Geopolitics of Emotion: How Cultures of Fear, Humiliation, and Hope Are Reshaping the World* (New York: Anchor Books, 2009).

2. "Obama Confident of Pakistan Nuclear Safety," Associated Press of Pakistan, April 13, 2010 (www.app.com.pk/video/preview.php?id=24406).

3. World Bank and International Monetary Fund, *Global Monitoring Report 2010: The MDGs after the Crisis* (http://go.worldbank.org/8NMBGII280).

4. For a detailed discussion of these and following statistics, see the *Global Monitoring Report 2010* and recent UNDP reports on Pakistan at http://undp.org.pk/.

5. Ministry of Finance, Pakistan, "Pakistan Economic Survey 2008–2009", p. iv (http://finance.gov.pk/survey/chapters/overview09.pdf).

6

The China Factor

Of the factors shaping Pakistan's future, its relationship with the People's Republic of China (PRC) is the most enigmatic but possibly one of the most important. This chapter offers a brief overview of that relationship, whose importance is likely to increase in years to come as Pakistan's domestic order remains unstable and its relations with the West enter a new round of "ups and downs."

The Pakistan-China partnership was born at the height of the cold war, when the two countries were in opposite camps. The political systems in the two countries, one an Islamic republic and the other an avowedly communist and hence atheist state, should have made the two implacably hostile to each other even under normal circumstances. Pakistan and China are geographical neighbors, but they are joined together by extremely rugged, remote, and physically hostile territories, sparsely populated by potentially hostile ethnic minorities. They are not like France and Germany or even like China and Myanmar, with long and open borders and strong cultural and historical ties. So, it is not geography that binds them together. Yet China has poured in military supplies and has been unrestrained in providing nuclear weapons, missile technologies, and economic assistance to Pakistan. Pakistan, in return, has been an ever-grateful ally and even (at times) China's client state.

But the Pakistan-China relationship flourishes, as does the Pakistan-U.S. relationship. Is the only thing that binds Pakistan and China together an undisguised and implacable hostility toward India? With all three parties now nuclear powers and India rapidly rising as an economic and military power, will things change? In recent years we have seen a significant thaw in India-China relations. Both countries have put in a place a regular consultation process, with the heads of state and government exchanging annual visits. The two countries have acted in concert on many global issues. Their bilateral trade has been growing exponentially. The vexatious border dispute that was the cause of a war in 1962 and bitterness over the years is now on the back burner. Both countries have special representatives discussing solutions at regular intervals. Since 1967, not a shot has been fired across the Line of Actual Control (LAC). With India-China relations growing and taking a new color, will they have an effect on Pakistan-China relations?

"Higher than the Mountains and Deeper than the Oceans!"

Pakistan was among the earliest countries and the first Muslim nation to break relations with the Republic of China (Taiwan) and recognize the People's Republic in 1950. It established formal diplomatic relations with the PRC on May 21, 1951. But soon afterward, Pakistan joined both of the major U.S.-sponsored military pacts in the region, the Central Treaty Organization (CENTO) and the Southeast Asia Treaty Organization (SEATO), which were aimed at containing the communist threat posed by the Soviet Union and the PRC, then the Soviets' principal ally. However, it would seem that doing so did not inhibit Pakistan from maintaining a close and often cooperative relationship with the PRC. In an interview with a Pakistani journalist on July 29, 2009, the Chinese ambassador to Pakistan, Luo Zhaohui, said:

> Pakistan was one of the first countries to recognize New China. Ever since our diplomatic relations began in May 1951, we have enjoyed mutual understanding, respect, trust, and support and our friendship and cooperation have flourished. We are truly good neighbors, close friends, trusted partners, and dear brothers. When China was in difficulty caused by the Western blockades in the 1950s and 60s, it was Pakistan which opened an air corridor linking China with the outside world. In the 1970s it was Pakistan which served as a bridge for the normalization of China-U.S. relations.[1]

Pakistani diplomacy has always had a track record of deftness and alacrity in furthering perceived national interests, and there is no reason to doubt the ambassador's acknowledgment of Pakistan's assistance in overcoming the Western blockade.

Even while the Western blockade was on, China invaded the Chamdo region of Tibet in 1950, causing New Delhi to express its apprehension. China curtly told India that the invasion was no concern of India's and that it was an internal Chinese matter only. Pakistan surely took note of that. India's discovery of the Xinjiang-Tibet highway across the Aksai Chin in the early 1950s also would not have gone unnoticed in Pakistan, considering that it also shared a border with China in the region. Besides, the matter had caused some acrimony in the Indian parliament, among the Indian people, and in the Indian media. That could have provided Pakistan with just the motivation to seek a better understanding with Beijing, despite the military alliances that it had joined. Then as today, Pakistan's main foreign policy focus was India. That is what pushed it into the Western alliances and that was the inducement to seek rapport with China.

Even before India became independent and China became communist, there were visible tensions between the two countries. In March 1947, four months before independence, the Congress Party organized the Asian Relations Conference in New Delhi. The Chinese delegation expressed unhappiness that Tibet was invited separately; they then tried very hard to make the Tibetan delegation sit with them. Next, they protested the map of Asia that formed the backdrop to the main dais, which showed Tibet as an independent country. They wanted the painting modified immediately. The Chinese anxiety that the conference was part of India's plan to acquire implicit leadership in Asia came to the fore when the location of the secretariat of the proposed Asian Relations Organization, the apex body of the member nations, was being discussed. While India assumed that it would be in India, China objected. It was then decided to rotate the location half yearly between New Delhi and Beijing. Nothing was heard of the organization after that episode, and it died soon afterward.[2]

Whether the Pakistani opening with China was done with the tacit blessings of the United States is not known, but it is well known that the United States had established close ties with several top Chinese leaders, including Mao Zedong, during World War II. That included the establishment of a U.S. military mission to provide assistance to the Chinese communists in their war with Japan. Interestingly enough, much of the U.S. military aid to the Kuomintang (KMT)-led government and to the Chinese communists was air-supplied over the Himalayas from eastern India. The famous but now defunct Stilwell Road was specially built over the most hostile and inhospitable terrain to increase the quantity of that aid. Stilwell's U.S. Army training mission also trained KMT troops in eastern India's Ramgarh cantonment. Total aid during the WWII period to the two competing Chinese factions was close to $250 million, with about a sixth of it going to the communists.[3] Despite the Korean War, there were many, most notably Henry Kissinger, in the United States who wished to establish ties with Beijing and break its alliance with Moscow. That could very well have been possible, because by

1956 Chinese ties with the Soviet Union were souring because of Nikita Khrushchev's denunciations of Stalinist excesses and the personality cult that he had formed. In addition, India's 60th Parachute Field Ambulance Platoon had supported and had even taken part in the UN operations in Korea.[4] Its participation in the operation against China, however modest, would not have gone unnoticed in China, the main adversary of UN forces after the North Korean army folded after the UN landings at Inchon.

The events of 1948, which saw the accession of the principality of Jammu and Kashmir into the Indian Union, would strongly shape Pakistani policy. After Pakistan's failed attempt to seize Jammu and Kashmir by force, Pakistan had only one enemy, on which its energies were and are still fully focused. China, given its rivalry and tensions with India, was a natural ally for Pakistan. The 1962 India-China border war was the major turning point in Pakistan-China relations. In the immediate wake of the 1962 war, as India turned to the West for support, it soon found itself under severe pressure by the United States and the United Kingdom to "settle" the Jammu and Kashmir dispute with Pakistan, by accepting partition of the state or a UN-supervised compromise.[5] India balked at accepting either. Pakistan then turned to China, no doubt deriving moral and intellectual sustenance from the old Arab proverb "My enemy's enemy is my friend."[6] The Chinese have an even more apt proverb: "It is good to strike the serpent's head with your enemy's hand." It made sense to befriend Pakistan because it gave China a suitable stick to belabor India. It is still open to debate whether China's investment in its relationship with Pakistan is anything more than that.

Relations between China and Pakistan, which faced a common enemy, flourished. In 1963 Pakistan and China signed their first formal trade pact; the same year they also signed a border agreement in which Pakistan ceded the Shaksgam Valley in the disputed northern territories to China. In 1965, Pakistan and India went to war and China supported Pakistan diplomatically. It would seem that China was even readying a new front with India when it served India with a three-day ultimatum to dismantle certain posts on the contested Sino-Indian border. But before the Chinese could act, Pakistan accepted a UN call for a cease-fire. It is said that the Pakistanis told Mao Zedong that the cost of continued fighting was far too high, both diplomatically and economically. However, Mao pressed the Pakistanis to fight on, sending President Ayub Khan this message: "If there is a nuclear war, it is Beijing that will be a target and not Rawalpindi." But the Pakistanis could not oblige.[7]

The biggest step forward in bilateral relations came in 1970, when Pakistan facilitated the historic secret visit to China, via Islamabad, of Henry Kissinger, the U.S. national security adviser. The rest is history. Kissinger's and President

Nixon's personal animosity toward Indira Gandhi was well known.[8] Soon a U.S.-China-Pakistan troika came into being. The highpoint of this alliance came when India and Pakistan went to war in 1971 over Bangladesh. Despite the opposition of the United States, India inflicted a huge military defeat on Pakistan and succeeded in liberating Bangladesh from West Pakistan. The war was prolonged in East Pakistan because of the expectation that China would open a third front in the conflict.[9]

That the Pakistanis were banking on some Chinese action to subject India to military pressure is seen in the findings of the Hamoodur Rahman Commission. On December 5, 1971, in a message to Lieutenant General A. A. K. Niazi, commander of all Pakistan forces in East Pakistan, General Yahya Khan, president of Pakistan, assures him that there is "every hope of Chinese activities soon." The following day, Niazi, while briefing Governor A. H. Malik, breaks into tears and tells him that the Indian onslaught is relentless and advancing on all fronts. On December 6, the governor then sends a message to President Khan briefing him on the difficult position that they are in. However, he also informs him that "if help is coming, we will fight on whatever the consequences may be."

By December 9 the authorities in East Pakistan were ready to throw in the towel and sought the assistance of the assistant secretary general of the United Nations, Paul Mark Henry, to arrange a "peaceful transfer of power to the elected representatives of East Pakistan" and "repatriation with honor of armed forces of Pakistan to West Pakistan." But suddenly, on December 11, President Yahya Khan sends the following message to Governor Malik: "Do *not* repeat *not* take any action on my last message to you. Very important diplomatic and military moves are taking place by our friends . . . [it] is essential that we hold on for another thirty-six hours at all costs."[10] Clearly China promised more than it could deliver. Both the Americans and Pakistanis seemed to have believed that China's intervention was imminent and would save Pakistan from defeat. However, the Chinese failure to intervene beyond making a few noises did not dampen Sino-Pakistan relations.

In 1974 India tested a nuclear device, providing even greater impetus to Sino-Pakistan relations. China now began actively assisting Pakistan's nuclear program. Even though China and Pakistan reached a comprehensive nuclear cooperation agreement only in 1986, much was happening. "U.S. officials have said on many occasions since the early 1980s that Pakistan received a proven weapon design from China. It has been reported that this design was used in China's fourth nuclear weapons test in 1966 at Lop Nor. This test involved the detonation of a warhead carried by a missile."[11] These efforts fructified in the mid-1980s when Pakistan assembled and tested a Chinese-designed nuclear bomb in the Lop Nor testing grounds in northern Tibet.[12] In 1998 India tested a series of nuclear weapons over a period of two days. Pakistan followed soon afterward, testing five weapons. The weapons were now out in the open. There was little doubt that China and its North Korean ally had actively assisted Pakistan to develop not only nuclear weapons but also their missile delivery systems. That cooperation continues today.

In 1999, India and Pakistan again went to war following the occupation of the Kargil Heights by units of the Pakistani army. The ferocity of the Indian counterattack, which also involved India's air force, and none-too-subtle diplomatic pressure from U.S. president Bill Clinton forced Pakistan to withdraw to its pre-conflict position and to accept a cease-fire. But this time around China was much more muted in its support, in line with other countries and organizations that defended the inviolability of the Line of Control or supported India.[13] Did that signal any change in attitude toward Pakistan? Or was it just another phase in Chinese policy?

But then, what is Chinese policy? Why is China investing so much in Pakistan, even at the cost of earning global opprobrium as an irresponsible proliferator and even at the risk of poisoning its relations with India for all time to come? To put it very simply, China and Pakistan have traditionally valued one another as a strategic hedge against India. Since its economic reforms in 1976, China has shown great flexibility in conducting its international relations with all its neighbors, adversaries, and rivals. Japan is its largest trading partner and is a major investor in China's manufacturing sector. Taiwan, which China officially considers a renegade province, is its second-largest overseas investor. The United States is China's largest export market. China's annual bilateral trade with India has been growing exponentially and has now exceeded $40 billion. By 2012 that is slated to rise to $60 billion.[14]

China's cumulative foreign direct investment (FDI) is now close to $1 trillion. Up to 2007, it had received $750 billion, and it has received an average of $70 billion every year since then. FDI investors now account for 57 percent of Chinese exports.[15] Without exports, China's GDP growth would sputter to a halt. Also, without FDI, its export sector would not be able to sustain the frenetic pace of growth that Beijing has set for the Chinese economy. It is a testimony to Chinese pragmatism that three of its top four FDI investors—Japan, Taiwan, and the United States—are countries that it has troubled relations with. It is that pragmatism that leads China to believe that it can have much greater economic engagement with India and still hedge against its emergence as a strong rival in Asia and on the global stage.

Pakistan desisted from attacking India in 1962, when it was extremely vulnerable. Pressure from the West, particularly by the Kennedy administration, was a major factor. Before the second phase of the 1962 conflict between China and India, military supplies from the United States and the United Kingdom had started pouring in. The United States had even established a military aid group in New Delhi to process India's wish lists. In turn, the West began applying pressure on India to seek a speedy resolution of the Jammu and Kashmir dispute. The Americans were especially keen on settling the issue with a new line running slightly east of the existing Line of Control (LOC).[16] That moment soon passed. Neither side was ready for any major compromise. After inflicting another defeat in the North East Frontier Agency (NEFA), China unilaterally withdrew to the positions that it held before the conflict. India was quick to wind up the U.S. military aid group after the conflict and revert to its policy of nonalignment. By mid-1963, with the signing of an economic cooperation agreement, Pakistan-China relations were on the upswing.

Should such a moment of vulnerability ever arise again, Indian strategists generally agree that Pakistan will not let it pass. Pakistan will find seizure of Kashmir by force too tempting. Therefore, Indian military doctrine now emphasizes the capability to fight a two-front war.[17] Indian strategists also generally agree that because of the high costs involved, China will not seek to attack India in the event of a conflict with Pakistan. China has had the opportunity to do so three times since 1962, and it has not taken advantage of India's military preoccupation with Pakistan.

On the other hand, there are also significant Chinese concerns about the current unstable situation in Pakistan. In her testimony before the U.S.-China Economic and Security Review Commission, Lisa Curtis, a scholar based at the Heritage Foundation, a Washington, D.C., think tank, highlighted the issues of Chinese Uighur separatists and the safety of Chinese workers in Pakistan as two such sources of tension and concern that "could move the Chinese in the direction of working more closely with the international community to help stabilize the country."[18] This is also acknowledged by Andrew Small, of the German Marshall Fund:

> Chinese investment projects in the region are now important not simply in scale but in their strategic nature. The Gwadar port and the linked prospect of an energy corridor to China's northwest, for example, are valuable well beyond their economic worth. Yet all of these projects— including the much-touted Aynak mine—are go-slow until Chinese confidence about stability has returned. The Pakistani military is no longer able to ensure that Chinese interests are given a privileged and protected status. (...) Political tensions with the Pakistani government over these issues have grown markedly in the past year."[19]

The Chinese find the current situation in Pakistan uncomfortable, to say the least. They have time and again expressed concern over the domestic situation within Pakistan. In several recent track II dialogues with Chinese think tanks in which I have participated, Chinese scholars and officials have expressed concern about the deteriorating situation in Pakistan. They were even in full agreement with the Indian discussants that several militant groups now seemed to be acting independently of even the Inter-Services Intelligence agency and the Pakistani military.

Like many American and other Western scholars and writers, Chinese thinkers also privately express concern about the security of Pakistan's nuclear assets and fear the takeover of Pakistan by fundamentalist elements. Much has been said on this subject, and the Chinese authorities, who are as influenced by Western views on the subject as their international counterparts, would certainly be concerned about "loose nukes" in Pakistan.[20] Nevertheless, economic and military cooperation between the two countries proceeds unabated. China has been a steady source of military equipment for the Pakistan army, has helped Pakistan to set up weapons of mass destruction, and given it technological assistance and modernized its facilities.

In the last twenty years, for example, the countries have been involved in several joint ventures to enhance military and weaponry systems, including projects like the JF-17 Thunder fighter aircraft, K-8 Karakorum advance training aircraft, missile technology, Al-Khalid main battle tanks, and Babur cruise missiles. The armies have a regular schedule for organizing joint military exercises. China is the largest investor in the Gwadar Deep Sea Port, which is strategically located at the mouth of the Strait of Hormuz.[21]

China has become one of Pakistan's top five sources of imports. Major imports from China are machinery, chemicals, garments and other textile products, stationery, construction materials like tiles, sanitary wares, and crockery. Machinery and electrical appliances form the major part of overall exports. Bilateral trade reached about $7 billion in 2008. The balance, however, is tipped in favor of China due to far fewer Chinese imports of Pakistani goods.

Under the five-year program launched in 2006 to strengthen economic relations, existing trade is to be enhanced to $15 billion by 2012. In addition, the program has identified new projects for cooperation and investment in various economic fields. Some restrictions on free movement of goods and services are occasionally reported, but there have been discussions to remove them to further enhance the volume of trade and to significantly increase investment. Both countries can benefit greatly from further expansion in economic and trade relations under the five-year program. China also has been generous to Pakistan with financial assistance at crucial times. Recently, China agreed to extend $500 million in financial aid, according to a senior Pakistani official.[22]

The Pakistan-China relationship has been one of the world's most enduring relationships of the last five decades. It has stood the test of time, under some very difficult circumstances. President Zardari therefore noted that in spite of changes that occurred in the regional and international environment, the friendship between Pakistan and China is "time-tested" and has turned increasingly firmer and much more solid as time goes by and is "deep-rooted in the hearts and ethos of people of the two nations."[23] But most eloquent of them all was Chinese president Hu Jintao when he said that the relations between the two nations were "higher than the mountains and deeper than the oceans."[24] And indeed they are.

The View from China?

After having scaled the highest mountains and plumbed the deepest depths together and having so often expressed their feelings for each other with such mawkish sentimentality, where do Pakistan and China go next? The relationship between the Pakistan army's Inter-Services Intelligence agency (ISI) and several militant jihadist organizations is now well established. Internally, Pakistan has been wracked by sectarian strife, regional disputes, secessionist civil wars, a general breakdown of law and order, drug cartels, a struggling economy, and a severe water and environmental crisis. Its problems seem insurmountable and unending. Many Western scholars and policymakers have now increasingly taken to referring to Pakistan as a failing state.[25] There is a growing fear that its nuclear arms might be seized by ultra-radical elements, either through the collapse of the state or through an engineered takeover with the help of radical military officers.[26] In the past Pakistan has showed little compunction about selling and transferring nuclear technology to countries near and far. Its nuclear clients have included nations like Libya in North Africa, North Korea in the Far East, and even Iran in the immediate neighborhood, anathema to Pakistan's Arab friends such as Saudi Arabia. Its geography puts it at the fulcrum of the world's great struggle against radical Islamic fundamentalism and the terror that it has fanned. So how do policymakers in China see Pakistan?

They will have a few sleepless nights for sure. The Chinese treasure tranquility and order (Indians, who are probably more adept at finding order amid chaos, probably have far fewer sleepless nights than the Chinese). One can be sure that the Chinese will constantly be fretting about how to pick up the pieces if the Pakistani cookie crumbles. The jihadists, after all, give no special dispensations to anyone. Jihad is all-out war against all those seen oppressing the ummah, wherever in the world they may be. If Russia, with its Chechen problem, is considered a major enemy, then China, which has had possession of Xinjiang since 1949 and which is trying to swamp much larger numbers of Muslim Uighurs with unabated Han immigration, should be an even bigger enemy. Seminaries and jihadist training camps in Pakistan are reported to have trained several thousand Uighur militants.[27] Many are still in Pakistan, and many more lie in wait in Kazakhstan and Tajikistan.

That still leaves the question of why China continues to invest financially, politically, and militarily in a Pakistan whose future direction is uncertain. There is one ready answer. After investing so heavily in Pakistan since 1963, China is not ready to cut its losses and run. Then, of course, there is the real possibility that Chinese leaders do not share the pessimism of the Americans and the understandable optimism of many Indian analysts that Pakistan is ready to crumble into several new nation-states. All indications are that the Chinese recognize that Pakistan is in trouble. However, it seems that they believe that Pakistan is not a case like Somalia or even the former Yugoslavia, where age-old regional animosities released long-pent-up centrifugal forces. That is a fair assessment. As long as the Pakistan military remains a reasonably professional and strong institution, Pakistan will continue to exist. Incidentally, this Chinese assessment is shared by most analysts in India. And as long as the institution exists, Pakistan remains a relatively low-cost hedge for China against a rising India.

Finally, there is the simple fact that China is awash with foreign cash. It needs to put that cash to work, and project financing is its best option. It creates Chinese jobs and a market for Chinese capital industry. With project margins being what they are and over the long term (all project financing is long term), even if the initial principal is only partly recovered, it is still a worthwhile investment. It is much better than dumping the money in an American bank, where it would earn next to nothing. This is the Chinese way of making a virtue out of a necessity. And in some cases, like that of Gwadar in Balochistan on the Makran coast, it has other advantages as well.

Notes

1. Interview with Luo Zhaohui, ambassador of China in Pakistan (www.opfblog.com/8824/interview-with-honorable-luo-zhaohui-ambassador-of-china-in-pakistan).

2. L. C. Jain, "The Lost Heart of Asia," *The Hindu*, Sunday, February 7, 2010.

3. "China Defensive: 1942–1945" (www.history.army.mil/brochures/72-38/72-38.htm).

4. See "60th Parachute Field Ambulance Platoon" (www.korean-war.com/60thin-dian.html).

5. Office of the Historian, U.S. Department of State, *Foreign Relations of the United States: 1961–1963,* vol. XIX, *South Asia* (http://dosfan.lib.uic.edu/ERC/frus/summaries/960820_FRUS_XIX_1961-63.html).

6. In Matthew, Chapter 22, the Pharisees and the Herodians unite against Jesus. Even though they hated each other, they had a common enemy.

7. Jung Chang and Jon Halliday, *Mao: The Unknown Story* (London: Vintage Books, 2007), p. 606.

8. For a transcript detailing their views on Indira Gandhi and on India in general, see the BBC report "Nixon's Dislike of 'Witch' Indira" (http://news.bbc.co.uk/2/hi/4633263.stm).

9. In 2006, the Office of the Historian, U.S. State Department, released *South Asia Crisis: 1971,* volume XI of *Foreign Relations of the United States.* For a summary, see Claude Arpi, "1971 War: How the U.S. Tried to Corner India," Rediff Online, December 26, 2006 (www.rediff.com/news/2006/dec/26claude.htm).

10. These and the following messages quoted here are from the annex to the report of the Hamoodur Rahman Commission, which was appointed in December 1971 to inquire into the circumstances leading to the surrender by Lieutenant General Niazi. The full report is available at www.bangla2000.com/bangladesh/Independence-War/Report-Hamoodur-Rahman/default.shtm. This largely squares with the U.S. State Department history cited in note 9.

11. David Albright and Mark Hibbs, "Pakistan's Bomb: Out of the Closet," *Bulletin of Atomic Scientists,* vol. 48, no. 6 (July-August 1992), pp. 38–43.

12. For an overview of Pakistan's nuclear program and the Chinese role in it, see Thomas C. Reed and Danny B. Stillman, *The Nuclear Express: A Political History of the Bomb and Its Proliferation* (Minneapolis, Minn.: Zenith Press, 2009). For a more detailed perspective, see Carey Sublette, "Pakistan's Nuclear Weapons Program Development. The Eighties: Developing Capabilities" (http://nuclearweaponarchive.org/Pakistan/PakDevelop.html).

13. Elizabeth Parker and Teresita Schaffer note that "China has taken a more neutral position on India-Pakistan issues such as Kashmir and has begun to take the relationship with India more seriously," as exemplified in its "apparent disapproval of Pakistan's (1999) incursion into Kargil." See "India and China: The Road Ahead," *South Asia Monitor* 20 (July 1, 2008), p. 3.

14. Ananth Krishnan, "India-China Trade Surpasses Target," *The Hindu,* New Delhi, January 27, 2011 (www.thehindu.com/news/international/article1129785.ece).

15. "Cumulative FDI Exceeds $750b," Xinhua, August 8, 2007(www.chinadaily.com.cn/china/2007-08/28/content_6062409.htm).

16. See Office of the Historian, U.S. Department of State, *Foreign Relations of the United States 1961–1963,* vol. XIX, *South Asia* (http://dosfan.lib.uic.edu/ERC/frus/summaries/960820_FRUS_XIX_1961-63.html).

17. David Blumenthal, "India Prepares for a Two-Front War," *Wall Street Journal*, March 1, 2010.

18. Lisa Curtis, "China's Military and Security Relationship with Pakistan," testimony before the U.S.-China Economic and Security Review Commission, May 20, 2009 (www.heritage.org/research/testimony/chinas-military-and-security-relationship-with-pakistan).

19. Andrew Small, "Afghanistan-Pakistan: Bringing China (Back) In," German Marshall Fund Blog, October 23, 2009 (http://blog.gmfus.org/2009/10/afghanistan-pakistan-bringing-china-back-in/).

20. Thomas Donnelly, "Choosing among Bad Options: The Pakistani 'Loose Nukes' Conundrum," AEI Outlook Series, May 2006 (www.aei.org/outlook/24416).

21. Curtis, "China's Military and Security Relationship with Pakistan."

22. C. R. Jayachandran, "China Gives $500 Million in Aid Package, Pakistan Says," *Wall Street Journal*, November 14, 2008 (http://online.wsj.com/article/SB12266018 1953225067.html).

23. Quoted in "Pakistan-China Friendship Time-Tested" (http://english.people daily.com.cn/90001/90780/91342/6514759.html).

24. For Ambassador Masood Khan, the "gripping narrative of Pakistan-China relations [is unique] because it is all weather and time tested. There are many poetic expressions to describe it. It is deeper than oceans, higher than mountains, stronger than steel and sweeter than honey." From his remarks at a seminar at the Embassy of Pakistan, Beijing, March 18, 2010 (www.pakembassy.cn/statement_22.html).

25. "Pakistan 'Is a Top Failed State,'" BBC News, May 2, 2006 (http://news.bbc.co.uk/2/hi/4964934.stm).

26. "Gibbs: Obama Sees Loose Nuke Material as No. 1 Security Threat," Fox News, April 12, 2010 (www.foxnews.com/politics/2010/04/12/obama-appeals-world-powers-nukes-terrorist-hands/).

27. Huma Yusuf, "Effects of Uighur Unrest," originally published in *The Dawn*, July 13, 2009 (www.humayusuf.com/2011/01/effects-of-uighur-unrest/).

WILLIAM MILAM

7

Factors Shaping the Future

The list of negative factors that make Pakistan's future uncertain at best is long and depressing. Moreover, those factors, which are both complicated and interrelated, are relieved by almost no potential strengths that seem realistic. The few positive factors are mostly double edged: the so-called "demographic dividend," if not accompanied by a large investment in public education and reform of the educational curriculum as well as by a significant and sustained increase in the economic growth rate, makes the long-term prospects for the economy far less sanguine and the prospects for social upheaval and Islamization far more likely; the free media seem as likely to exacerbate the poisonous political culture as to constrain it; and the Lawyers' Movement, after its success against Musharraf, fizzled and splintered ideologically.

These positive and negative factors are both ambiguous in their impact and interrelated, and they will affect each other in negative and/or positive ways. Certainly, one can imagine virtuous circles; however, they do not come to mind as easily as the potential vicious circles that would drag the country slowly and inexorably downward toward some sort of failure.[1]

There are perhaps six major factors or variables by which we should be able to judge with some accuracy in the medium term—the next five to six years— what the long-term future holds for Pakistan and its people. These major factors/variables are both cause and effect: they can influence the direction of the many other factors and variables involved, which, in turn, can influence the direction of the major factors/variables. It is more difficult than it was a year ago to envisage the major factors/variables all moving in the right direction and leading to a virtuous circle, which would define a "good-case" scenario, by 2015–16.

By the same token, a less desirable future—either the "business-as-usual" or (less likely) a "bad-case" scenario—is easier to imagine. I hasten to add that I believe that there is a high probability that the endgame, whatever it is, will play out over many years. However, there is a caveat with regard to the timing—the occurrence of a "black swan" event (that is, one of low probability but high impact on a complex but fragile system—for example, a war with India), could accelerate the bad- and the worst-case scenarios and bring on a highly undesirable outcome much earlier.[2]

The India-Centricity of the Pakistani Mindset and Policy Focus

Pakistan's "India-centricity" is the most important and seemingly the least likely of the factors/variables that have to change if Pakistan is ever to reach a glide path to a sustainable virtuous circle. The bottom-line question is whether now or six years from now relations between the two countries are moving in the direction of sustainable normalization; their relationship is also, perhaps, the most measurable of the major factors that will shape Pakistan's future. The criterion by which to judge it is whether a sustained dialogue is under way—dialogue that has, depending on the time that it has been undertaken seriously, resolved one or two of the easier issues that divide the two countries. One issue that has been teed up for resolution for some time is Sir Creek, which is essentially a technical matter that lends itself to quick resolution. Another possibility is Siachen, which most Pakistanis and Indians (except perhaps the military) consider a piece of real estate that is not worth what it has already cost in lives and resources.

We should not expect dialogue to solve the more contentious issues in so short a period of time. Too much baggage is left over from previous conflicts to expect a miraculous turnaround in mindsets in either India or Pakistan. The Kargil conflict, the 1971 Indian intervention in what was then East Pakistan (which many Pakistanis still believe led to the separation of West and East Pakistan), the 1965 war, and the ongoing conflict over Kashmir remain neuralgic issues that may take a generation to detoxify.

The psychological resistance to establishing a normal relationship between the two countries goes even deeper than those issues, however, and it is an inhibiting factor overall. To read of the pain that people who lived through the 1947 partition still feel is to understand the deep-seated mutual enmity and mistrust of many Pakistanis and Indians.[3] Each move toward normalization meets with stubborn feelings of mistrust in the older generations of both countries. India and Pakistan may not be able to completely normalize their relationship for another fifteen years, when most of the generation that experienced partition is gone.

But, five or six years out, the continued absence of a dialogue that looks like a permanent feature of the diplomatic landscape will imply to me that Pakistan's India-centric mindset—the most critical issue, in my view—would negatively affect the other major factors. Without visible progress on normalization, it seems highly unlikely that the other major factors can be turned into a virtuous circle.

Yet signs were even stronger at the beginning of 2011 that the strategic mindset of the Pakistani military is deeply entrenched and unlikely to change in the next five to ten years without the kind of inducements from the United States and the West that are next to politically impossible. Statements by the Pakistani army chief (who has been given an unprecedented three-year extension) and the army's behavior toward its long-nurtured anti-Indian proxy militants as well as the Afghan Taliban, which shelters in the tribal areas between attacks on the International Security Assistance Force (ISAF) in Afghanistan, tend to bear this out.[4]

The Outcome in Afghanistan

It now seems almost certain that there will be a "political" resolution to the Afghan conflict. Whether the United States likes that outcome or not, both its domestic politics and those of its NATO allies are pointing in that direction, as are the political imperatives of President Karzai's government in Kabul. That is perhaps inevitable, as fewer and fewer see an end to the conflict as long as the Taliban come and go freely between the tribal area of Pakistan and the Afghan killing fields. The structure of such a political solution remains to be seen, and Pakistan's role in it is unclear.

President Obama clearly wants to be able to claim that the United States is winding down its involvement in Afghanistan by the time his campaign for reelection gets into high gear in the spring of 2012. Other Western governments pose even more immediate concerns. President Karzai, probably for reasons of his own, has shown his interest by calling a "Peace Jirga." He has also apparently authorized discussions with the Hizb-e-Islami of Gulbuddin Hekmatyar, an unlikely candidate with whom to share power if there ever was one. Even Mullah Omar, the reclusive Taliban supreme leader, has made statements that seem to reinforce the view that this is the likely way, eventually, to the exit for the U.S./NATO forces.[5]

This so-called "political solution," whether a good idea or not, is made more likely by increasing doubts that the war can be won without Pakistan's cooperation, which Pakistan has thus far withheld as it hedges its bets on the war's outcome and has used as a lever to gain a place, and a major one, at the negotiating table in order to counter the perceived Indian threat from the west. However, we are not near the negotiation stage yet, and the denouement in Afghanistan is probably several years away.

One very serious question that has had little serious discussion is how to structure a power-sharing hybrid political solution in Afghanistan to ensure that it is neutral in its effect on Pakistan's political development. The first principle of such a solution should be to promote Indo-Pak cooperation and not exacerbate their rivalry. This solution must avoid converting Afghanistan into another proxy battleground for India and Pakistan to continue their conflict.

That will be difficult in any case, and the less effective NATO's counterinsurgency strategy turns out to be over the next one or two years, the more difficult it will be. The Pakistan army is likely to see its interests best served by holding out for a power-sharing solution that gives it leverage over other interests, and it will likely work toward that goal. To the extent that it is successful, the army's own role in Pakistani politics is enhanced. It will then be even more able to portray itself as the sole guarantor of Pakistan's security interests, necessary to ensuring that the country's "strategic depth" against India in Afghanistan is maintained.

The army's links with the Afghan Taliban could become stronger, not weaker, although in the 1996–2001 period, when the Taliban ruled most of Afghanistan, Pakistan's influence over them waxed and waned. If, however, Pakistan feels that a political settlement gives India undue influence there, that would probably ignite a continuation of the proxy struggle, though perhaps a political, not a military one (at least initially). But this scenario would still maintain the army as primus inter pares in Pakistan's domestic politics. Its ability to run the state from behind a gauzy democratic curtain would certainly be enhanced. In such a context, the army is unlikely to wish to break its links with those Punjabi jihadists who maintain their focus on India/Kashmir and are not yet at war with the state of Pakistan.

However, the primary objection to an Afghanistan political solution that fully meets Pakistan's perceived political requirements is quite simple. It would tend to strengthen, not diminish, the India-centricity that is the key variable that must change if Pakistan is to develop along more positive lines. This is not to argue that Indian interests in Afghanistan should prevail either. That would also increase, not decrease, the India-centricity of the Pakistani army.

However, a negotiated solution to the Afghan war that is perfectly neutral in its political impact on Pakistan will be difficult to accomplish. The more complex the situation and the more parties involved, the more difficult it is to find a solution that does not break down because one or more parties see an advantage in cheating. Finding a political solution in Afghanistan that will, inter alia, not provide an incentive for Pakistan to try to game the outcome and control it to its advantage and the advantage of its proxy, could require a lot more time, determination, patience, and understanding than the United States and NATO have shown so far.

Though it may seem like "pie in the sky" (but most of the positives in a better-case scenario have a high content of wishful thinking), an Afghan political solution that is at least more likely not to intensify Pakistan's India-centric mindset would require a structure that would offset Pakistan's influence by inclusion of all the regional stakeholders. By including India, Pakistan, Iran, and the Central Asian states that border Afghanistan and by setting up a power-sharing system in which their proxies—the various Northern Alliance groups, perhaps a Shia party, possibly a second Pashtun party, and the Karzai government—share power equally with the Taliban, this goal could be achieved.

Given the history of these groups, a strong international overseer would be necessary both to initiate the process and to ensure that they are actually able to work together. If peacekeepers were needed at the beginning, it might be necessary to recruit a peacekeeping force of Muslim country troops (for example, Turkey). In any case, the United States, NATO, Russia, and China would have to stay politically, if not militarily, involved to ensure the success of the power-sharing system.

One objective should be for Pakistan and India to become aware over time of their emerging web of mutual interests in a neutralized Afghanistan that is under neither country's domination and therefore is not a threat to either. Would the two countries also discover a mutual interest in a more developed Afghanistan and cooperate in working to achieve that goal? In such a context, both countries might, over time, build up enough trust to tackle the other, long-standing and neuralgic disputes that are the root of their antagonism. India would come to recognize, I hope, that in the interests of its own economic and great-power ambitions, to which the United States could be of enormous help, it is necessary to accommodate the U.S. priority of building a stable, modern Pakistan. For Pakistan, peace and normalization of relations with India would become a sufficient as well as necessary condition if it is to build itself into a modern society and state.

The Army's Evolution

I suspect that there is a high probability that the civil-military balance in Pakistani politics will continue as it is for the next five to six years. The army, at this point, is in the catbird seat. Vis-à-vis a weak civilian government, it calls the shots for the most part on most policy issues, and it is unlikely to want its dominance weakened. However, it is also unlikely to be tempted into taking direct power, and there would be no reason to do so except in the case of a catastrophe such as war. It is looking these days to repair its image, which Musharraf's last two years tarnished badly, by refraining from getting in front of the curtain behind which it now exercises power. Its power seems equally unlikely to erode as long as the current government is in power.[6]

In the context of a continuation of the status quo in its relations with the elected civil governments, the primary question is how the army leadership—and the officer corps more broadly—will react to other possible changes in the political environment. Would tangible progress in an Indo-Pak dialogue be accompanied, over time, by a less intense India-centric mindset? Or would there be resistance to a change in outlook toward India, engendered by the perception that it would harm the army's vested economic and political interests? If there were palpable progress in a dialogue, accompanied by concomitant change in the mindset of the political leaders of Pakistan and its political class, would the army resist the political change that could imply?

A follow-on question is whether the army's praetorian mindset and tendencies would harden if what appears to be a sustainable and substantive dialogue between India and Pakistan takes hold. Would the corps commanders and the general officer corps view a substantive Indo-Pak dialogue as the beginning of a slippery slope to gradual subordination of the military to elected civilian rule? If so, how would they react? One possibility would be to repeat, more loudly and more publicly, the traditional military mantra that civilian political leaders cannot be trusted to fully protect Pakistan's national security interests. A rigid determination to remain the prime player in the political culture would certainly bring on the threat of direct intervention, though I believe that is not likely to happen in the time frame of our terms of reference.

The answers to these questions will be implicit in the army's behavior over the next five to six years. If the army continues to insist on calling the shots on all issues labeled "national security," and if it seems determined to keep the civilian government weak and a weak civilian government in office, the signs will not be good.

A possibly more important determinant of the army's attitudes and behavior over the next five to six years will be the changes, if any, in its demographic makeup. Traditionally the army has recruited primarily from the "martial" triangle in Punjab, a rural region demarcated on three corners by Rawalpindi, Attock, and Jhelum. At this point, even though the army has broadened its recruiting focus considerably over the past few years, a majority of its *jawans* still hail from this small part of Punjab. There is, among many families of that area, a strong tradition of army service going back generations, from grandfather, to father, to son. The second-largest number of army recruits is of Pashtun ethnicity.

As a majority of *jawans* begins to reflect the changed recruiting patterns, becoming much more urban in nature, there is an increasing probability that the *jawans* could be more resistant to the army's current policy of resisting militarily the predations of the extremist Islamist groups that challenge the writ of the state. The pool of young men that the army recruits, Punjabi or Pashtun, may be changing slowly, but they are increasingly from the same socioeconomic background as the young men that the jihadi organizations recruit. *Jawans* looking through their gun sights at their brothers or cousins may be more reluctant to shoot than at present.

Moreover, since 1980 there has been an increasingly deeper seepage of the Islamist narrative into Pakistani society's mindset, without an alternative competing narrative. This narrative has been fostered as a whole through the "soft power" activities of the large and active jihadi organizations operating both in Punjab and in the Pashtun areas. In addition, the pervasive activities of "apolitical" organizations such as Tablighi Jamaat, which have spread a strong Deobandi Islamist message, have inculcated that narrative even more deeply and widely.

Thus there is the possibility that the outlook of the army's half-million *jawans* will change in ways that will make it more difficult for it to continue the long-term conflict against Islamist extremists. A change in the attitudes of the army's enlisted ranks could also influence its behavior on other issues. They could, for example, enter the army with a far more negative image of India, the result of the undiluted Islamist narrative that they have learned at home or in school.

Thus, over the coming five to six years, the army's behavior will be affected primarily by the progress, or lack of it, on the Indo-Pak dialogue and by whether its recruits retain the same loyalties and attitudes as those that prevailed over the previous sixty years. It is not clear whether progress on the dialogue will cause the army to become more rigid in its attitudes and behavior or less so. Nor is it clear whether new generations of enlisted troops will cause it to back away from dialogue and/or a strong counterinsurgency policy.

The Lost Generation

The power of the fundamentalist Islamic narrative over the Pakistani public mindset became all too evident over the past year; in the massacre of scores of Ahmadis in May 2010, which provoked almost no public or political condemnation; in the ugly aftermath that followed the assassination of the governor of Punjab, Salmaan Taseer, which provoked high levels of public support for the killer; and, to a lesser extent, in the assassination of the Christian minister for minorities, Shahbaz Bhatti, a few weeks later, to which again there was no public outcry. The blasphemy law, which sparked the killing of both Taseer and Bhatti, has obviously become another third rail of Pakistani politics.[7]

Whether the power of the fundamentalist narrative extends over the intellectual and emotional mindset of Pakistani society or only over its political no-go areas is still open to question. Clearly the politicians and the public recognize the political power of the Islamic clergy when united for even a dubious cause, and they recognize the danger that can come from the armed, extremist elements that attach to some of the right-wing religious groups when the clergy perceives intrusion into issues that it believes it owns. It appears that the religious parties, from moderate to extreme, can control important aspects of the public political discourse and influence the political climate quite powerfully, even without having significant electoral success.

What has become even clearer is that the power of the fundamentalist narrative is more than just a public relations problem. It demonstrates a social toxicity that goes deep—perhaps deeper than we imagined. There remain scholars who have dug deeply into Pakistani society and still hold out hope that, ultimately, perversions of religious thought and practice, starting with the existing blasphemy laws, will be rejected as citizens begin to realize that they threaten those who might be considered religiously mainstream. The question may be whether this broad public awakening can outpace the growing grip that the narrative has on the public mind.

Exclusionary religious narratives have seeped into the pores of a generation of Pakistanis, and most of those born between 1980 and 2005 have heard no alternative. The elected governments of Benazir Bhutto and Nawaz Sharif did nothing to reverse the institutional and intellectual creep of religious fundamentalism into the mindset of Pakistani society after it was fostered and accelerated by Zia ul-Haq. General Musharraf's promises to reverse it with an appeal to "enlightened moderation" proved to be as hollow as his political vision. Pakistani scholars that I respect greatly have told me that "we have lost an entire generation."

To say that this generation is lost to these narratives, which purport to define who is a Muslim and especially who is not, is not necessarily to say that it is lost to Islamic extremism, though certainly the extremist organizations draw on it extensively for recruits. Most Pakistanis still reject violence (which is what defines an extremist) as a method of extending specific forms of religious thought and practice. But full-throated acceptance of zero-sum, intolerant, exclusionary Islamist narratives promotes many of the popular sentiments that inhibit progressive government policy and could inhibit the army in vigorously pursuing its counterinsurgency strategy.

It is difficult to define the fundamentalist narrative without being accused of Islamophobia. What I mean in this context is the narrative of an aggressively homogenizing Islam, which the West must keep separate from a narrative stemming from eclectic, mainstream forms of Islamic thought. The prevailing narrative in Pakistan emphasizes hostility between the West, primarily the United States, and the Islamic world and promotes the idea that the West in general, and the United States in particular, is out to destroy or subjugate Islam to Western ideas and values. This narrative blames the United States for most of the problems that beset Pakistan, and it promotes the idea that there is only one Islam—the one defined by the fundamentalist narrative. This is, in my view, aided and abetted by much of the curriculum of Pakistani public education as well as by the education of most madrassa students.[8] The public curriculum also tends to promote an ultranationalist sentiment that, inter alia, inhibits moderate leaders of Islamic thought from condemning the extremist tactics that religious extremist groups use with impunity.[9]

This narrative of Pakistani political Islam has elicited in the public an abstract sympathy with fundamentalist objectives and, sometimes, with the behavior of extremist organizations. The reasons for their sympathy are not well understood.[10] While few Pakistanis, if pressed, would voice general support of the extremists' use of violent methods to attain religious objectives, there is the ever-present tendency to blur the ends and the means. In some cases, sympathy extends to passive support for Islamist extremist organizations, which in some areas of Punjab and the frontier is clearly exacerbated by fear of the consequences of not extending support.

Nonetheless, we must be careful not to exaggerate this problem. Given better security, firmer and fairer law and order, and an effective government that Pakistanis believe in, sympathy with the extremists might dissipate and the credibility of the exclusionary religious narratives lose their force over time. Fundamentalist religious organizations, however, will continue to promote their narrative.

What is really the answer to this Islamist intellectual creep is for the Pakistani political establishment, collectively, to promote an alternative narrative, one that starts with and is based on the essentially tolerant message of mainstream Islam. This narrative would stress values that appeal to most Pakistanis, starting with economic stability and growth and the equitable distribution of the fruits thereof, universal public education that promotes tolerance, and the necessity of transforming Pakistani society to meet the demands of the modern world. Such a counternarrative would expose the core values espoused by the fundamentalist religious narratives as retrogressive, and it would, over time, be the most effective antidote to the negative Islamist narrative that now dominates the political dialogue.

In other words, the grip now held by the fundamentalist narratives on the mindset of Pakistani society will be best countered by effective governance and a state with a modern vision and persuasive narrative of its own. Again we come to the question of whether the feckless political culture that has characterized Pakistan almost from its inception can be detoxified by the democratization that has lately been its hallmark. The proof will be in the pudding.

The Imperative of Economic Growth and Reform

In Pakistan, the economic deficiencies are probably easiest to understand yet hardest for a democratically elected parliamentary government to deal with. Put simply, Pakistan has, as a country, lived consistently beyond its means for much of the past thirty-five years. The enormous structural problems that plague the economy and constrain policy reflect this history of generally financing the country's excess of domestic consumption over domestic production by borrowing from abroad. Pakistan's success at pulling this off for such a long time has led to almost automatic reliance on foreign capital for its inherent fiscal and balance of payments deficiencies. That has created a built-in political and social resistance to the fiscal reform that is necessary if this pernicious cycle is to be broken.

Unfortunately, successive Pakistani governments, both military and civilian, have relied on the country's geostrategic position to avoid reform and have always expected that their strategic allies of the moment will come to their rescue when there is a periodic payments crisis, as there inevitably is. This has been exactly the situation of the last two years, which required Pakistan to return to the International Monetary Fund for a large standby loan, bolstered by economic and military assistance and targeted budgetary support from the United States and other donors in the international community. That was, in great part, a result of the international economic meltdown of 2008–09, but Pakistan's dependence on foreign financing renders it especially vulnerable to international downturns.[11]

Previous crisis periods were interspersed with periods of windfall capital inflows from remittances or foreign assistance from allies or both. The windfall years enabled Pakistan's governments to avoid the kind of structural reform necessary to reduce Pakistan's dependence on foreign aid. Reform measures would need to include raises in the ratio of tax revenues to gross domestic product (GDP) and in the domestic savings and investment rates to levels that reduce Pakistan's need for foreign financing and increase its ability to finance growth and development from domestic resources. These failings were particularly characteristic of the military governments of Zia ul-Haq and Pervez Musharraf, which benefited from such windfalls but did not take advantage of them to initiate serious efforts at structural reform.

The era of windfall inflows of remittances and foreign investment that helped cloak structural weaknesses during those two regimes appear to be over. Large amounts of official flows will continue through the enlarged U.S. assistance programs, the Friends of Democratic Pakistan consortium, and the continued participation of other international financial institutions (the International Bank for Reconstruction and Development and the Asian Development Bank), but over the next few years the ability of the government to spur growth will be very limited given the need to implement serious structural reforms. This is not a comfortable position for a democratically elected government—or any government, for that matter. A sentence from the State Bank of Pakistan's first quarter 2010 statement is perhaps the best summation of the dilemma that the government faces: "[T]here is little doubt that the government cannot successfully stabilize the economy and simultaneously provide stimulus for growth."[12]

This economic paradox is both a short-term and a long-term factor in Pakistan's uncertain future. In the short term, there will be enormous pressure on the elected government to abandon stabilization for stimulus. That would be disaster in the long term because it would mean, inter alia, that Pakistan would not find the resources and the political will to provide increased educational infrastructure and jobs to accommodate the "demographic dividend." Thus the dividend would become a dangerous deficit, with possibly revolutionary implications. This is one area in which U.S. assistance, if targeted correctly, can make a difference.

On the other hand, a reformed and healthy economy that can, ultimately, produce steady sustained growth of 6 to 10 percent will be one of the bases for a strong alternative to the Islamist narrative and will, over time, reduce the pull of extremism. Sooner or later, that could reduce the India-centricity of society as well as that of political and military leaders.

The U.S. Factor—An Arranged Marriage?

The Raymond Davis affair illustrates that, despite the attempts of both governments over the past two years to bring it to a more mature level, the U.S.-Pakistan bilateral relationship continues to be fragile and, perhaps, synthetic.[13] It underlines the lack of trust on both sides and the fact that neither government as yet understands deeply the other's strategic culture, objectives, or redlines as well as how to work with a partner that is on a different and sometimes contrary strategic page.

The critically positive role that the United States had intended to play in a reforged political partnership with Pakistan has been set back significantly. It will take time and a sharpened recalibration of the U.S. approach to reinvigorate the relationship and move toward the partnership that the United States desires and that, I suspect, will be necessary for Pakistan as well if both countries are to achieve their strategic goals in the South Asian region. Both must work to diminish the constant mismatch of perceptions and misreading of interests that has led to conflicting policies and nontransparent actions and has bred mutual mistrust and anger. Over the next few years, the U.S. objective should be to convince the Pakistanis that the United States is a stable, reliable, transparent ally that understands where the two countries differ on issues and wants to find ways to work out or around those differences, an ally that knows that its long-term interests in South Asia are best served by a long-term, stable, and reliable relationship with Pakistan.

The difficulty is, indeed, formidable. The range of vested interests alone in Pakistan—the feudal and industrial elite, the military, and the Islamists—make this a long shot. A long-term commitment of resources as well as a huge reservoir of patience, pragmatic flexibility, and willingness to experiment will be required. Unfortunately, the United States has a very poor record of managing assistance efforts that require flexibility, pragmatism, and some semblance of timeliness.

In the end, it is the people of Pakistan who must be convinced that the United States is a reliable ally that can be trusted. They must come to believe that the United States shares their aspirations for a better life in Pakistan. The reform necessary to move these factors/variables in a positive direction must come from the bottom up. Segments, though not all, of the ruling elites—industrial and landed feudals, the military, the Islamists, politicians—will resist a change of direction as inimical to their vested interests.

In the meantime, the Kerry-Lugar bill, which provides for $1.5 billion in economic assistance over a five-year period, opens a window of opportunity to see whether the United States can target assistance in the right direction, to the higher-value economic and social targets, and whether doing so promotes movement toward reform of Pakistan's social, economic, and political institutions. The possibility that that much-heralded amount could be cut by Congress in these fiscally frugal times is alarming; any cuts would be another setback to the U.S. effort to strengthen the relationship.

The initial indication that Kerry-Lugar will emphasize supporting government efforts to increase, in the long term, institutional and productive capacity in the energy sector and education system is exactly right. More important in the context of this analysis, whether Kerry-Lugar appears in five to six years to have helped tip in the right direction the factors and variables that will determine Pakistan's future will be one test of whether a stable, long-term relationship is possible. In a sense, this five-year window for the Kerry-Lugar bill can be viewed as the diplomatic equivalent of the NATO deadline of 2014 for the beginning of serious troop withdrawals from Afghanistan.

Many analysts argue that more than large flows of economic assistance are needed to forge the organic partnership that the United States seeks. A "big idea" is necessary, they say, and big money is not necessarily a big idea. One often-mentioned "big idea" is for the United States to propose a nuclear agreement with Pakistan along the lines of, though not identical to, the nuclear agreement that the United States recently negotiated with India. I suspect that that avenue is a dead end, given domestic U.S. politics. Perhaps one way to approach the strengthening of the U.S. relationship with Pakistan and to move it closer to the kind of partnership desired is for the two countries to begin working closely together on the structure of a multilateral settlement for Afghanistan.

The Range of Possible Futures

It is likely that, in five to six years' time, Pakistan will look on the surface pretty much as it does now. Its future character and orientation will remain uncertain, although perhaps a bit more defined than at present. It will be necessary to look deeply below the surface—and to look carefully inside each of the determinants listed above—to estimate whether the country has moved closer to one of the three kinds of trajectories that I see as possible: a good-case trajectory; a business-as-usual-case trajectory; and a bad-case trajectory.

Evidence of moving toward a good-case trajectory would be provided if all of the six determinants listed above were moving in what could be persuasively argued were positive directions. Given the caveats set out above—and especially the caveat to the hope that Pakistan's India-centricity can be curbed over time—the good-case trajectory looks less and less likely. A second possible trajectory leads to a prediction of a business-as-usual Pakistan for the foreseeable future. This trajectory suggests that some of the determinants listed above would be moving positively (for example, toward a better, reformed economy), while others would show no positive movement (for example, no perceivable decrease in the India-centric mindset of the army, political leaders, and public). A bad trajectory would probably mean that none of the six determinants show any discernible positive movement in five to six years.

The judgments that can be made in this medium-term framework cannot be assumed to be definitive, but they will have a stronger predictive power than is possible today. For most of them, however, there is no simple criterion, and much will remain judgmental and subject to interpretation.

One thing that should be clear, however, is that these factors/variables feed on each other. That is true of all six variables, but the knock-on effect diminishes as one goes down the list, from India-centricity to a reformed economy. The point here is that each of these variables has a differential effect on all the others. All working in tandem toward one trajectory would be a powerful prediction of Pakistan's future. The more likely scenario is that some will work positively and some negatively. Where that leaves us in five to six years is highly uncertain—just like Pakistan's future.

Notes

1. The word *failure* is used here for a wide range of possible outcomes. Some would obviously involve a worst-case scenario, but others would emanate from what would have to be regarded as a "bad-case" scenario. The worst-case scenario differs from the bad-case scenario in that it involves apocalyptic outcomes—for example, balkanization, economic collapse, or Islamist takeover. The bad-case scenario implies non-apocalyptic outcomes in which Pakistan slowly proves itself unable to deal with its structural deficiencies and the challenges of the twenty-first century and slides inexorably into dysfunctionality, possibly involving a loss of government writ over a sizable chunk of the territory and/or economic stagnation accompanied by an increasingly intolerant and Islamist society. In the "good-case" scenario (but not the best), which is more of a long shot, Pakistan would, after two or three generations, overcome most of its many structural deficiencies and join the ranks of modern states and societies. There is also a business-as-usual scenario (not good but better than the bad alternative), in which Pakistan overcomes some of the deficiencies (for example, the stagnant economy), but not others (for example, "India-centricity") and stays in business pretty much as it has. That has a higher probability.

2 . See, for example, Niall Ferguson, "Complexity and Collapse," *Foreign Affairs*, vol. 89, no. 2 (March–April 2010), pp. 18–32, and Nassim Nicolas Taleb, *The Black Swan* (New York: Random House, 2010).

3. Yasmin Khan's recent book, *The Great Partition* (Yale University Press, 2007) and the first chapter of Alicia Albinia's book, *Empires of the Indus* (New York: W.W. Norton, 2008) are worth reading in this respect.

4. Some argue that the army chief is more fixated on the perceived threat of the large Indian presence in Afghanistan than on the usual neuralgic point of Kashmir, but that does not lead automatically to any change in the predominant India-centricity of Pakistan's strategic mindset.

5. In a series of contradictory and confusing statements that began with his September 2009 Eid al Fitr pronouncement and included a number of subsequent blog reports, Mullah Omar seemed to be distancing the Taliban from al Qaeda and limiting Afghan Taliban objectives to Afghanistan instead of pursuing the far broader objectives of al Qaeda. Reports in the April 18, 2010, *Sunday Times* of London quote him as indicating that the Taliban did not understand how difficult running a country is (implying that sharing power with parties more experienced at governance would be acceptable to them) and that the Taliban's only objectives in Afghanistan are the implementation of sharia law, the expulsion of all foreigners, and the restoration of security in the country.

6. What happens if Nawaz Sharif gets elected is another question, but I think that the army would wait to see if he had learned anything in the past ten years. Here is where it could be argued that the Eighteenth Amendment changes everything. As mentioned previously, an efficient and somewhat successful parliamentary government would provide reason to wonder whether the role of the army would erode or perhaps already had eroded. But only time will tell; it would contravene all historical evidence to assume such success at this time.

7. We had, perhaps, a foretaste of this when then–Chief Executive General Musharraf vowed publicly to change the blasphemy laws in early 2000 and had to back off because of push-back from the mullahs. In 2005, despite his tight grip on power, Musharraf had much difficulty pushing a rather tepid revision of the Hudood Laws through the National Assembly.

8. Although I think that the influence of madrassa education on the mindset of Pakistani society is much overstated.

9. Witness the recent gathering of Deobandi leaders in Lahore, which was called ostensibly to try to elicit a common message of condemnation of the tactics of Islamist militancy—suicide bombings and assassinations of innocent people—but which produced instead only the usual, time-worn charges that militancy is caused by the U.S. presence in Afghanistan and Pakistan, the lack of a true Islamist state in Pakistan, the Pakistani government's support of the United States, the drone strikes in the tribal areas, and so forth. In other words, these leaders said nothing about the extremists who promote violent means and train young men and women to carry out suicide bomb-

ings and assassinations. It was reported that the moderates who might have wished to condemn such tactics feared doing so.

10. See, for example, Jacob N. Shapiro and C. Christine Fair, "Understanding Support for Islamist Militancy in Pakistan," *International Security* (Winter 2009–10), pp. 79–118, which is an attempt, not all that satisfactory, at quantitative analysis of the question.

11. Pakistan is the outlier among the major South Asian economies in this respect. India, for example, has already begun to tighten monetary policy to restrain the possible inflationary effects of a resurgence of demand and economic growth; Bangladesh, which one would expect to have been equally, if not more, vulnerable than Pakistan, has maintained growth constant at about 6 percent and is now reflecting on what to do with a current account surplus that is about 3 percent of GDP—in other words, Bangladesh is exporting capital to the rest of the world!

12. The bank also notes that while the rate of growth in 2010 will be higher than in 2009 (when it was lower than the population growth rate, implying a decrease in GDP per capita), it will still not be "adequate to generate the required employment opportunities." Thus the government will face a growing unemployment rate even with improvement in the economy.

13. In the long run, the damage to the relationship may pale in comparison with the damage that the Davis affair did to the civilian role, on both sides, in strengthening and shaping the relationship. A weak government was further weakened; the paramountcy of the military/intelligence agenda was again reinforced. While the government stood by—perhaps "crouched down" is a better term—frozen by its fear of public reaction, the affair, which was really a conflict between the Inter-Services Intelligence Directorate and the Central Intelligence Agency, was settled by the two agencies. The outcome is perhaps a smoother, but even more militarized, relationship.

SHUJA NAWAZ

8

The Clash of Interests
and Objectives

Pakistan's future appears to be a spaghetti bowl of different interests and objectives: depending on what assumptions are made, different future scenarios unfold. Adding to the confusion is the fact that politics in Pakistan tends to be entirely short term, aimed at tactical advantage rather than strategic placement. As a result, Pakistan's economic future has become a matter of great concern—affected as much by what has happened in the past decade as by the emerging demographic shifts, which pose a huge challenge to the country—while offering tentative hope at the same time.

In 2009, the World Bank released its review of the development experience throughout the world over a thirty-year span, focusing on the bank's *World Development Report* and the issues that it had covered since its inception in 1979.[1] The accompanying World Bank Indicators produced a remarkable result. Over the period 1980–2007, Pakistan exhibited one of the developing world's highest average growth rates: 5.8 percent, second only to China's 9.9 percent. Of course, with a shorter time horizon, India and other rapidly developing economies would have made the top five and Pakistan would have been relegated to the lower rungs. But the important point is that Pakistan, despite its record of poor governance, produced a very high rate of growth. Clearly, there are sinews of strength in the country and economy that need to be identified and examined when calculating what is possible in the decades ahead. Pakistan has a middle class of some 30 million, with an average per capita income of $10,000 a year on a purchasing power parity basis. It has a huge and active diaspora that provides it large sums in remittances and that has the potential brain power to jump-start Pakistan's economy and society.

But overlying all the economic and social changes occurring in Pakistan is the regional political situation, which has a major effect on Pakistan's politics and economics. Pakistan is a prisoner of its geography. Sitting as it does on the cusp of South Asia and Central Asia, overlooking the Gulf and the Arabian Sea, it is subject to developments in and influences from its neighborhood and beyond. For the second time since 1979, it is coping with the aftereffects of a major invasion of Afghanistan, first by the Soviet Union and now by the United States and coalition forces. Its role as a frontline state imposes a heavy burden on Pakistan, even as it has to deal with the presence of a rapidly rising superpower to the east: India, its main rival since independence in 1947.

Basic Challenges

Pakistan's response to several basic challenges will determine its future path. One of those challenges is its demographics. Today, with a population of some 180 million, Pakistan has a population with a median age of eighteen years. Hence, it has some 90 million youth who need to be fed, educated, and given gainful employment lest it lose them to the lure of militancy, which already exists in the country. Pakistan's population distribution has a classic pyramid shape, with the younger generations at the bottom. For the next fifteen years, it will retain a bottom-heavy shape. That poses a challenge in terms of providing opportunities for the youth cohort, but it also provides a great opportunity in terms of a productive base for the economy, because a youthful population will continue to work and add value to the economy for the first half of the twenty-first century.

Moreover, Pakistan is fast becoming an urban country, with megacities like Karachi and Lahore and other urban centers displacing the weight of the countryside in the national economy. Traditionally, Pakistan has been an agricultural economy. It can no longer afford to be restricted to that sector alone; it will need to move up the value chain toward agriculture-based industries and then into manufacturing. Worldwide, the trend since the 1970s has been for developing countries to shift away from agriculture to manufacturing and services. On average, today agriculture accounts for only 20 percent of the gross domestic product of developing countries.[2] Future growth will more likely be in urban areas. That will be a huge challenge for Pakistani agriculture. If and when the 2011 census in Pakistan is successfully completed, it will validate those trends, dramatically shifting the political map of Pakistan as election boundaries are redrawn, giving more seats in parliament to the cities. Pakistan's feudal politics will suffer a body blow when that happens. Feudal cliques will resist such changes, and the result may be political turmoil.

The gradual emergence of provincial centers of power supported by a rising civil society that has found a voice through new mass media outlets had already led to a shift in Pakistan's power balance. In 2010, after seventeen years of debate, the National Finance Commission Award was ratified. In a realignment of power that will have long-term consequences, this law gives greater say in the use of revenue and resources to the provinces. The new rules for revenue sharing under this award promise to give the federating units greater say over state resources and returns the country to its original federal structure. This development alone may help in staving off the centrifugal forces that have been threatening the cohesion of the state. But the key will be implementation. Lack of action by the government has dashed some hopes.

A much-discussed topic in Pakistan in recent years has been a June 2006 article by Ralph Peters in an American publication, *Armed Forces Journal,* that raised the possibility of Pakistan being reduced to a rump of Punjab and parts of Sindh, with Balochistan and the North-West Frontier Province, now Khyber Pakhtunkhwa (NMFP/KP), breaking away. Peters suggested that Balochistan might become a free state including parts of Iran's own province of Sistan and Baluchestan, while the NWFP/KP would become a part of Afghanistan.

As Pakistan's provinces become stronger and if more provinces are carved out of the current four, the possibility of countervailing forces emerging inside the country emerges. This may reduce the enormous power of the Punjab, for example, with its 60 percent of the population, GDP, and armed forces.

The urban shift also has great meaning for the military. My own study of recruiting patterns in the Pakistan army between 1970 and 2005 indicates that there has been a major shift in recruitment from the countryside to the cities and within the Punjab from the north to south and central Punjab.[3] And in the decade ending 2005, more officers were recruited from Karachi than Jhelum. This trend also indicates that the growth of the urban share of the army is higher than in the country as a whole. This will have far-reaching effects on the nature of the officer class and its thinking as it becomes dominated by city dwellers. City dwellers, especially the petite bourgeoisie, are historically more religious and conservative than rural populations. Moreover, the shift into south and central Punjab means that the armed forces are recruiting in the same area as the emerging (predominantly Sunni) Punjabi militant groups such as the Lashkar-e-Tayyiba, Lashkar-e-Jhangvi, and Jaish-e-Muhammad. This will pose a huge challenge for provincial and central government leaders.

Pakistan also faces huge challenges in the energy and water sectors today. Continuing difficulties with India over the share of waters from rivers that have their source in Indian-controlled Kashmir has led to disputes over the construction of the Kishenganga Dam and other dams. Pakistan's own water resources have been badly managed. It needs energy from hydroelectricity as well as other sources, but its corrupt energy distribution system has created a major obstacle to its economic output. No immediate solution is evident for its longer-term energy needs. Apart from finding new sources of energy, it will need to resolve issues with India or risk another conflict.

Externally, Pakistan now faces hostility on both its eastern and western borders. The aftermath of the Afghan war has made Pakistan a frontline state again. Meanwhile, its hostility toward India continues to affect its military posture and economic development by drawing resources away from development to defense. Today some 150,000 of the 500,000-strong army are deployed on the western border. A raging insurgency in those border regions and even in the settled areas of Malakand and Swat has led to thousands of casualties, creating an insecurity that immediately affected both domestic and external investment. Meanwhile, India is emerging as a regional and global power, and its defense posture is mainly trained on Pakistan's eastern flank.

Tensions between the powerful and disciplined military establishment and the weak and disorganized civilian coalition government have added to political uncertainty and confusion. In the past, power centered in a troika: the president, the prime minister, and the chief of the army. Today, power has moved to the army chief, the president (despite his divestiture of power to the prime minister), and the chief justice of the Supreme Court, who represents the emergence of civilian society. Catching up are the media, especially the broadcast media, which are increasingly playing a major role in shaping public opinion. But the army—although, with its latent coercive capability, still most powerful—no longer has an alternative party waiting in the wings. The major opposition party, former prime minister Nawaz Sharif's Pakistan Muslim League (PML-N or "N" group) is not seen as pro-military and does not have the broad national base that the Pakistan People's Party has.

Pakistan suffers from a political system retarded by the belief among ruling elites that politics is a family business. Strong feudal groups and economic cartels have led to opportunistic coalitions of like-minded individuals, creating a predatory political class. Historically, the armed forces have been the only group able to counter the power of the ruling elites. As a result, Pakistan has suffered military or quasi-military rule for more than half of its life as an independent country. This prolonged military rule has left the nation's civil structure and political system stunted. Under the most recent long-term military ruler, General Pervez Musharraf (1999–2008), the army penetrated deep into the civil system, posting army officers in key institutions and ministries. And it has entered into the economic field too, crowding out private sector enterprises with its aggressive access to state resources. The end result has been a tentative return to democracy and a dysfunctional government that is largely bent on survival rather than on making the longer-term changes in the system that would allow democracy to survive.[4]

What Does the Future Hold?

A demographic time bomb is ticking in Pakistan today. Without coherent and effective family planning and urban planning, the rise of megacities will pose huge challenges for Pakistani society. According to one projection, another 80 million people will be added to the urban rolls between 2005 and 2030, a 140 percent increase over the 2005 baseline. Without proper devolution of fiscal and administrative authority to the cities, the ability of city managers to cope with urban poverty, unemployment, and demand for services will be seriously hobbled. The current trend is to wrest power back from local governments. If that continues, Pakistan risks having large cities that become ungoverned spaces and a cockpit of violence among different ethnic, language, and sectarian groups.

If the current lack of urban planning and zoning policies continues, urban growth will be haphazard, driven by short-term monetary gains rather than economic considerations. The education system will be unable to cope with the demands for services, and the health services sector will collapse. So too will Pakistan's infrastructure, which is already stretched to its limits. Provisions for water supply, sanitation and sewerage services, and transport systems will all be unable to meet demand, leading to chaotic and uneconomic growth of the cities. The central and provincial governments have failed to take advantage of community-based planning for urban development, which creates ownership among the users of services and could lay the basis for sound fiscal and financial policies. The desire of the Pakistan People's Party administration to gain power over all levels of government has short-circuited the little progress that was made under the Musharraf regime, when, despite shortcomings, some success was achieved in certain urban settings in providing services to city inhabitants. The current trends point to youth-led urban unrest and violence and missed opportunities for economic growth.

Pakistan has the potential to vastly increase its output and garner greater financial benefits from shifting to agri-businesses, moving up the value chain for its exports. As major shifts occur in India and China, Pakistan could easily move into the manufacturing sector, becoming, for example, the producer of spare parts for the growing automobile industry of Asia, as suggested by Shahid Javed Burki. Instead of relying on greater access to U.S. and European markets for low-end textile exports, it could move to higher-end products and hence higher revenues. But that will be unlikely if the current political system continues to give undue voice to the cartels that run the textile industry. Moreover, the energy shortage is likely to persist, creating further obstacles to the full employment of textile workers in current factories.

Regional disparities inside Pakistan will likely increase if the National Finance Commission Award is not implemented carefully. The devolution of central government powers to the provinces and the sudden abolition of the central government's concurrent responsibilities has created a bottleneck, as provinces lack the revenues and the manpower to handle their new mandates. That may well exacerbate provincial rivalries, unless a national consensus can develop on the best way to manage the transition to provincial rule. Pakistan has a well-integrated economy. If that can be further buttressed with modern infrastructure—roads, railways, and air links—it may be able to counter some of the tendencies toward separatism that have arisen over time. If the civilian government can produce consensus among the provinces on the national need for new dams and energy sources and on shifting nuclear efforts to power generation, Pakistan could easily meet its energy needs and provide for reform of its agriculture sector at the same time.

As an increasingly urban military officer corps emerges, the links between the military and business interests will deepen. It may be possible then to see more open discussion of the advantages of reducing hostility with India and the use of military power as a deciding factor in negotiations. Great potential exists for improvement of the economies on both sides of the India-Pakistan border with the rise of bilateral trade to its natural level at the time of partition (70 percent of their trade was with each other) between the areas that now form Pakistan and India. Research by Mohsin Khan of the Peterson Institute for International Economics and similar work by Adil Najam and Moeed Yusuf and by Mohan Guruswamy indicate that trade could well rise from its current $2 billion to $50 billion or even $100 billion, generating revenues for economic development. An important point is that such a rise in Indo-Pakistan trade would create vested interest groups in both countries that might inoculate both against war. A major potential spin-off benefit would be the opening of transit trade with Afghanistan and links to Central Asia that would allow both India and Pakistan to benefit from access to the abundant energy needed for their growth.

Economic ties and open borders for traffic between India and Pakistan would also be a major factor in helping to resolve water issues between the two countries. The economic incentives for resolving conflicts would outweigh the need to resort to threatening military postures. I see a growing civil society pressure on governments in both countries to open up relations, building on the momentum of the *Aman ki Asha* (Quest for Peace) initiative launched by the *Times of India* and the Jang Group of newspapers in Pakistan.

A key factor in all this will be the relationship between the military and the civil establishments. The transition to a new professional leadership circle in 2010 in Pakistan's army is a harbinger of future trends. A new military leadership that continues to eschew overt interference in civil matters should give the country's political system room to mature over time. If the military fails to do so, it may accelerate Pakistan's political and economic decline. For their part, the political parties will need to introduce greater democracy in their internal operations and broaden their base beyond family interests. The emergence of urban parties, building on the model of the Muttahida Qaumi Mahaz (MQM), without its cultish or violent behavior, would be a major new development. The attempts by the MQM to build an urban coalition across the country appear to be a good sign. It is natural to expect that urban parties will emerge and coalesce to counter traditional feudal interests as the country becomes more urbanized. But the forces of the ancien régime will oppose such progressive behavior.

Despite fears that the state of Pakistan will collapse, I do not see that occurring in the next five to seven years. Governments may come and go, but the institutions of the state are still able to function. The security establishment remains disciplined and ready to protect the country against internal and external threats. Civil society is coming into its own. The new media are adding transparency to governance. The general population supports the battle against extremism and militancy and is prepared to fight for its political rights and voice.

The different futures of Pakistan depend on how far and fast the country can imagine itself as a modern state, meeting the needs of all of its people, and escape from the thrall of religious conflicts. A Pakistan that wishes to provide an enabling environment for its young population and strengthen its economy so that it can also become militarily impregnable could have the confidence to settle differences with its neighbors without feeling paranoid about their aims. Pakistan needs specifically to restore financial stability through disciplined fiscal and monetary policies, shield its poorest citizens by providing resources for them as it adjusts its economy, and raise revenues from its own economic activities through taxes that are well designed and collected honestly. Its current tax-to-GDP ratio, at below 9 percent, is among the lowest in the world and is far below the revenue level needed to allow it to grow at more than 6 percent, which it must do in order to stay ahead of the curve of the expansion of its population.

All of this will require concentrated focus on economic and political policies that foster growth and create greater ownership of governance among the population. In such an atmosphere, the population could be critical in helping to fight militancy and end the insurgency that is threatening Pakistan today. A national debate is needed on what kind of Pakistan its citizens believe that they need. In other words, it is critical for Pakistan to set lofty targets for itself and to attempt to meet them with its own resources rather than be subservient to the interest of other states, near or far.

Notes

1. Shahid Yusuf and others, *Development Economics through the Decades* (World Bank, 2009).

2. Ibid., p. 47.

3. See Shuja Nawaz, *Crossed Swords: Pakistan, Its Army, and the Wars Within* (Oxford University Press, 2008), pp. 570–72.

4. Murtaza Haider, "Urbanization Challenges in Pakistan" (McGill University, 2006).

SHAUKAT QADIR

9

Still an Uncertain Future

Predicting the future is best left to soothsayers, palmists, and astrologists. However, since so-called analysts can't resist that temptation, they tend to attach several clauses of exceptions and conditions to safeguard their predictions against unexpected outcomes.

I would not like to attempt to predict the future of any people. To do so about Pakistan, beset with its myriad problems and many intangible factors, is an almost impossible challenge. However, since that is the objective of this conference and I have no alternative but to make an honest attempt, I intend to begin with the positive, negative, and intangible and unpredictable factors as I see them today before offering alternative scenarios for consideration. In conclusion, I offer a few words on the military and civil-military relations in Pakistan.

Positive Factors

—There is a democratically elected political government in place in Pakistan.

—The senior leadership in the military is making every endeavor to steer clear of politics, and General Ashfaq Parvez Kayani, the new chief of army staff (COAS) seems determined to reestablish the principle of supremacy of the civilian government.

—The military has swiftly recovered from the devastating effects of Musharraf's policies and has again molded itself into an efficient fighting unit under Kayani. It is also demonstrating its efficiency in dealing with insurgents in the recently renamed province of Khyber Pakhtunkhwa.

—Despite frequent terrorist attacks, the people of Pakistan continue to support the military in its efforts to root out this evil. Without their support, the military's efforts could never be successful.

—The efficiency of the domestic intelligence, police, and security forces has improved, and the people are becoming increasingly appreciative.

—The judiciary, having fought for its independence, is reasserting itself (perhaps overly so, but time will permit it to find the right balance).

—The recently approved Eighteenth Amendment to the Constitution has restored the balance of powers as envisaged in the original 1973 Constitution and has given greater political autonomy to the provinces. There are, however, a couple of clauses in this amendment that make the chairperson of each political party more powerful than he or she should be.

—The economy has begun to show signs of recovering and restoring the confidence of the people.

Negative Factors

—The political government may have been democratically elected, but it still fails to provide good governance to the people. There is increasing lack of confidence in the government and its representatives, visible in the increasing number of issues on which the people are taking to the streets and resorting to violence in demonstrating against the government.

—The unrest in the Hazara (the non-Pashtun portion of Khyber Pakhtunkhwa) could become increasingly difficult to handle and might snowball into a demand for a Saraiki province (also a simmering issue for many years) in southern Punjab. Personally, I have been in favor of increasing the number of provinces in Pakistan; however, that is another subject.

—Despite the military's success in the tribal areas, in this kind of "war," the military can only win battles; the war has to be won politically. There seems to be no recognition of that fact, nor is there a comprehensive political strategy to deal with it. The political leadership seems content to cede its authority over all matters remotely related to "security" to General Headquarters (GHQ). As a consequence, the administrative vacuum left by the exit of the Taliban is not being filled. The provincial government refuses to take over the Taliban captured by the army in Swat and Waziristan (numbering over 2,000, many of whom are minors), let alone initiate legal proceedings against them. The only plausible explanation is that the provincial political leadership is afraid of the Taliban's revenge. As a consequence, prisoners continue to languish in military custody—and by all standards of "human rights," in illegal custody. But the army has no options; it can hardly turn them loose again. What is more, the only effort to reclaim their young minds—corrupted by Taliban teachings and convinced of their "Islamic" duty to kill people through suicide attacks—is also being made under the aegis of the army, which has hired the services of child psychologists, who have had a remarkable success.

—However, it is a physical impossibility for the Pakistan military to maintain a credible deterrent force on its eastern borders, fight the Taliban, maintain sufficient presence in the recaptured areas to prevent the return of the Taliban, and simultaneously assume political and administrative control of the recaptured areas. What is more, the mere fact that the political leadership has not assumed its rightful duties in these areas is tantamount to voluntarily ceding political authority to the army, which the army does not want.

—Despite the efforts of the COAS to remain apolitical, he frequently has been left with little option but to interfere, albeit from behind the scenes. What is more, he has acquired a stature internationally that frequently forces him to take the lead role in a "strategic dialogue," as most recently with the United States, even if under the formal leadership of the foreign minister.

—Rampant government corruption continues. Not just the people, but even the military feel uncomfortable with Zardari and his cronies.

—Another political-judicial crisis appears to be in the offing on two major issues: the government's reluctance to obey the Supreme Court and to reopen the cases pending against Zardari in Switzerland for alleged money laundering; and the appeal filed in the Apex Court to consider the constitutional validity of certain clauses in the Eighteenth Amendment.

—Relations between the central government and the most important province, Punjab, continue to be strained. Punjab is governed by the Pakistan Muslim League–Nawaz (PML-N), which is the majority party in Punjab and the opposition party in the central government. The governor of Punjab, a staunch member of the Pakistan People's Party (PPP), continues to create hurdles for the provincial government. Admittedly, the Punjab government also is not performing as well as it was expected to, a failing that only aggravates the situation.

—Spiraling prices and energy and water shortages are all taking a toll of the common people, who are increasingly disillusioned.

—Balochistan is an increasing cause for concern. Indian involvement there and in Pakistan's tribal areas is now internationally accepted, at least by established (nonaligned) journalists, like Robert Fisk.

—India's ability to exercise control over two of the western rivers of Punjab, which were supposed to be Pakistan's under the 1960 Indus Water Treaty, is assuming alarmingly dangerous proportions for future relations between the two countries.

—Terrorism, insecurity, and resulting deaths of relatives, friends, and acquaintances are taking their toll, even as the people so far remain determined not to take to the streets. The question is how long it will be before they take matters in their own hands and the military is forced to quell vigilantes.

Intangible and Unpredictable Factors

The intangibles and the unpredictable factors are innumerable; here are a few:

—Will this political government complete its tenure? So far, it seems likely to do so, but unrest in the populace is spreading, and it is impossible to predict the outcome of even the mounting protests against electricity load shedding.

—How long will people continue to suffer from the scourge of terrorism without losing patience?

—General Kayani has accepted a three-year extension, but will his extension affect his personal performance or the army's in a beneficial manner or not? He has accepted his role as the real power behind the scenes and continues to perform creditably, in all humility, but until when?

—Although it seems unlikely and almost impossible so long as Kayani remains COAS, will the continuing failure of Pakistan's political masters again create a situation in which the military may be forced to intervene politically, albeit only as an interim measure?

—Is there still any link between the Pakistani intelligence agencies and the Pakistani Taliban? I know of the connection(s) with certain Afghan chapters, but this question keeps being raised domestically and by certain elements abroad. I am fairly certain that there is no longer any link, but I do not know. If there is one, it will have its own unpredictable ramifications.

—Will Pakistan's stuttering economy manage to stage some kind of recovery, despite power shortages? Currently, even if Pakistan is given preferential treatment by the United States for exports of its largest and best industry, textiles, I doubt if it could meet the export requirements with the prevailing energy shortage.

—Will India place Pakistan under greater pressure through its control of the timing of the flow of water?

—Will India continue its coercive diplomacy by creating unrest in Pakistan's tribal areas and Balochistan? Let me state unequivocally that if Indian friends choose to level counterallegations on Pakistan in this context, I have no intention of disputing them. Both countries would be better off by stopping this activity. The only reason why the issue raised here appears one-sided is because we are discussing Pakistan.

—How will the increasing numbers of the religious right in Punjab coupled with the growing unrest there shape up in the immediate future? Will the government be able to prevent the increasing growth of religious intolerance in Punjab?

The list of such factors is endless, but I will leave it here and move on to discuss possible scenarios.

Possible Scenarios

At least for the foreseeable future, it seems that there is no likelihood of a military takeover, even though the COAS may continue to be the most influential actor, behind the scenes.

While clauses of the Eighteenth Amendment have been referred to the Supreme Court for it to decide whether they are repugnant to the Constitution, I (a layman, not a constitutional lawyer) do not find any of those clauses unreasonable. The issue being talked about most is the new procedure for appointing judges to the high courts and the Supreme Court. In this context, their approval by a committee of elected members is not unreasonable. According to political science theory, "sovereignty" rests with the people; when they elect their representatives, the representatives become sovereign since, theoretically, they represent the people who elected them.

The clauses that give rise to concern for me have not been referred to the Supreme Court yet. The first clause is the amendment to article 63(A) of the Constitution, according to which an elected member who opts to vote against "party policy"—in effect, the wishes of the chairperson of his or her party—could be disqualified. In effect, Zardari could quit the office of president today and yet no member of his party could remain an "elected" member or hold any office intended for an "elected" member if he or she opposed Zardari's wishes irrespective of whether he continues as president, so long as he remains co-chairperson of the PPP.

The other, related cause for concern is the removal of the clause in the Constitution requiring periodical elections within each political party. In effect, an individual holding an office within the party could continue to do so for life. Coupled with the amendment to article 63(A), removal of this clause means that we are destined to have dictators as political party leaders, even if they are not elected as public representatives. This is the destruction of the very essence of any democratic system.

Scenario 1 (Best Outcome)

Following passage of the Eighteenth Amendment the prime minister begins to assert himself (with Zardari's blessing); attempts to grasp the complexity of Pakistan's security situation; and formulates a comprehensive security policy that not only deals with conventional threats requiring the use of force but also includes food security, health care, education, job security, energy security, water security, and every conceivable factor that affects the Pakistani citizen. Of necessity, such a policy must encompass a strategy of dealing with the growth of the religious right, particularly in Punjab.

It might also be in the national interest for General Kayani, the COAS, to be offered an extension, which he might accept. However, if he does, the central and provincial governments must ensure that there is no political-administrative vacuum that the army has to fill. The governments must not cede political authority to the military; they must leave the military to deal with its assigned role.

After handing over the administration of areas recaptured from the Taliban to the provincial government, the military clears the remaining tribal areas, where remnants of the Taliban still reign. The political leadership not only takes over administration but also absorbs the tribal areas into the mainstream of the Pakistani political system.

While employing force judiciously whenever necessary, the government also ensures that genuine grievances of deprived individuals and groups are addressed expeditiously. In this, Balochistan must have priority, second only to the tribal areas.

The governor of Punjab steps back to let the government function unhindered. In addition, the economy begins to strengthen and unemployment decreases while inflation is reduced. India and Pakistan cease fomenting unrest in each other's troubled regions, and India ensures the desired water flows to Pakistan from the Chenab and Jhelum rivers. Meantime, a mutually acceptable solution is found through a renegotiation of the Indus Water Treaty that offers Pakistan long-term assurances of a steady supply of water for irrigation.

In short, the central and provincial governments begin to perform the functions that they have been elected to perform and to deliver "good governance."

Scenario 2 (Almost-Worst Case)

A comment preceding presentation of the second scenario: Nawaz Sharif's party, the PML-N, has often been referred to as the "friendly" opposition. That is because despite the frequent refusals of Zardari to meet his verbal and written, publicly announced and unannounced agreements, the PML-N has not sought his ouster or attempted to force the issue of early elections, which many an analyst expected. However, that is not out of any love for the PPP or Zardari. Prior to the infamous "Swat Peace Deal," Nawaz Sharif was the strongest opponent to the use of force against the Taliban, insisting on a negotiated settlement as the only option. In fact, he and his party have themselves frequently been accused of soft pedaling on the rightists and even of being rightists.

When the Taliban demonstrated the kind of rule that they would impose on Swat, extensively covered by the media, the Pakistani nation suddenly united against the Taliban and strongly supported the use of force. The PML-N had no choice but to voice the people's demand as forcefully as it could. However, it is my considered opinion that the party in general and its leadership in particular is reluctant to come into power at a stage when it will have the responsibility of authorizing the use of force against the Taliban. It would far prefer to take over after military success has been achieved and to deal with the aftermath. That assessment is substantiated by the PML-N government's reluctance to face this issue in Punjab, the province that it governs. It is primarily for this reason that the PML-N does not want mid-term elections.

Whether the PPP-led government in the center lasts its remaining three years or not, it continues on its present path, bungling everything, failing to address the concerns of the people. Zardari continues to create one crisis after another, and the prime minister continues to try to bail him out.

In the event of a mid-term election or an election after the scheduled three years, the next government shows no radical improvement.

No comprehensive security policy is created, and the concerned political government continues not to fill the administrative vacuum left by the departure of the Taliban, leaving it up to the army to do what it can.

With the army spread thin on the ground, hamstrung by its commitment of resources to administer areas reclaimed from the Taliban, the Taliban reemerge in North Waziristan (as they already have, although they have carefully avoided running afoul of the military so far and have announced their intention of opposing terrorist attacks on Pakistani territory). They also regroup in the Aurakzai, Kurram, and Khyber agencies of the Federally Administered Tribal Areas (the order in which these are named is deliberate, since the Aurakzai will be the heartland and the other two, rim-land, protecting the heartland).

The possibility of a clash between the judiciary and the executive might be realized, further exacerbating the growing feeling of political insecurity.

In such an environment, if the military finds itself unable to deal with the spread of the Taliban with their multi-directional pincers, three subscenarios could emerge, all bad:

—The army might find that it has no option left but to intervene politically, either to respond to increasing public protests or, having foreseen that eventuality, to prevent them. However, judging from the current mood of the military, it is unlikely that it would like to take over the reins of government. It is far more likely to remove the political setup to hold another election immediately, if the PPP is still in power, or, if power has passed to another political party after elections and that has also failed, to instate an interim government of technocrats to run affairs for a year or two until elections can be held again. The latter course has been tried before and has not succeeded; in the event of the former course, the performance of the freshly elected government will decide the course of future scenarios. There is one more complication: in the event of either course, the Supreme Court will be asked to legitimize the action, which, under the Eighteenth Amendment, it has been prevented from doing.

—Before or after the first subscenario, people of the tribal areas could decide that enough is enough and take matters in their on hands. Anarchy will inevitably follow, and vigilantes, in the form of tribal *lashkars* (militias) are likely to mete out to the Taliban exactly what they have been receiving from them.

—In such an environment it is more than likely that the religious right will flourish. It is also likely that it will stoke further unrest among the people.

Scenario Three (Most Likely)

The political government continues its current course of "muddling through" with Zardari, creating crises where none need exist, and the prime minister keeps bailing him out. No comprehensive security strategy is worked out, and the provincial government continues to refuse to fill the administrative vacuum left in the areas reclaimed from the Taliban by the military. However, the central and provincial governments continue to "firefight" issues that arise, but the military remains the dominant actor, domestically and internationally.

General Kayani, the COAS, is offered an extension and accepts it. The army continues to influence policies to the extent that it can from behind the scenes, and Kayani (and the army) continue to be increasingly accepted internationally as the most reliable representatives of Pakistan. All international assistance continues to be negotiated with the army.

U.S. assistance in the form of the Kerry-Luger Bill, including help in resolving the energy crisis in the short term, alleviates the immediate shortfall. The International Monetary Fund and the World Bank, along with the countries that include the "Friends of Pakistan" group created in 2008, also punctually bail Pakistan out and improve its economic situation.

Military successes in the tribal areas continue but at a slower pace than in the previous twelve months or so, and, in two to three years, all the chapters of the Tehrik-e-Taliban Pakistan (TTP) are demolished. The army continues to attempt to assist in administering areas recaptured from the Taliban. However, the inactivity of the provincial governments permits the Taliban to resurface again and again, though no longer as organized as before.

While the Balochistan situation has been addressed partially by the central government, and the Eighteenth Amendment also should redress some of the Baloch grievances, no comprehensive policy is formulated. Indian interference continues, and the Baloch remain alienated. Occasional instances of violence in Balochistan and, indeed, throughout the country continue, though decreasing in number and intensity.

The relationship in Punjab between the local governor and the provincial chief minister continues to be uncomfortable.

The religious right, particularly in the Punjab, continues to gain strength, and only half-hearted efforts are made to bring it under control. With the passage of time, the Punjabi religious extremists become formidable enough for the military to be forced to initiate action against them, and the Punjab government reluctantly acquiesces.

Confrontation between the judiciary and the executive continues to erupt periodically and is dealt with on a case-by-case basis.

Corruption continues, but on a reduced scale. Inflation stays in the double figures.

India does not reduce the flow of water in the Jhelum and Chenab rivers by much. Pakistan's agriculture is not affected adversely.

After the completion of its tenure, the PPP government holds elections in 2012–13 in which no political party obtains sufficient seats to be declared a majority. The army assists in brokering a political deal to form a "national government" with representation from all political parties, which also are unlikely to be able to do much.

Analysis

Between scenarios 1 and 3 and between 3 and 2, there can be numerous others, relatively better or relatively worse. I am certain that the other, far more learned participants in the Bellagio conference who have contributed chapters to this volume can spell them out in far greater detail.

I would like to submit two conclusions that I have reached for the foreseeable future of Pakistan:

—However far the situation might seem to deteriorate, Pakistan is not likely to implode, as some of the doomsday specialists believe.

—There is no likelihood of a takeover of Pakistan by religious extremists. Pakistanis are a deeply religious people, but extremism is alien to their nature and, as they have proven, their tolerance for the Taliban form of government is very low while their tolerance for suffering in the cause of ridding themselves of this scourge is very high. The huge mass of the religious middle-of-the-roaders in Pakistan will not let this happen, at least for the next five years or so. However, if political leaders continue to fail the people with regularity, the future beyond five to seven years may be totally unpredictable.

The Role of the Military and Its Relations with the Current Pakistan Government

I confine myself here to the current role of the armed forces and the current state of what might be more appropriately termed "relations of the military with a nonmilitary (or political) government" than "civil-military relations," since the latter term should not be restricted to the government but should encompass the entire civil population.

The conventional role of the military is well known, but its current role is unusual. Much of it is covered in earlier paragraphs; however, some elaboration is essential to comprehend the current state of affairs. In 2007 Pakistan had an army that had reached its nadir; its name was mud with almost the entire civil population, and hundreds of soldiers were surrendering to a handful of Taliban. In one instance 208 soldiers, led by a lieutenant colonel, surrendered to two dozen Taliban without offering any resistance.

In an op-ed written immediately after that incident, I expressed the view that this was not an act of cowardice but one of extraordinary moral courage, since neither officers nor their soldiers were convinced that killing their own citizens in "America's War" was in their interest. This incident was in the aftermath of the Lal Masjid incident, in which President Musharraf, under siege by a self-created judicial crisis, sought to divert the people's attention by deliberately permitting terrorists to occupy this mosque, located in the Capitol, and letting things get so far out of hand that no alternative was left but for the military to take the mosque by force. The assault left several hundred children dead or wounded. Musharraf succeeded in creating the impression internationally that he was the sole bulwark between the extremists and the capture of Islamabad, but he did almost irreparable damage to the army. Mid-level officers and soldiers alike lost confidence in his leadership and in the tasks he assigned them.

I have known Ashfaq Pervez Kayani, the current COAS, for a long time and held him in very high esteem since I first came to know his particular qualities of command, leadership, and intellect, but even I underestimated him. Within months of taking over as COAS in November 2007, he switched a few of his division commanders (the division commander is the highest-ranking officer with direct command of troops) and went around each garrison talking to officers and troops, convincing them of the fact that Pakistan was actually fighting a war of survival against terrorists and that far from fighting "America's War," the army had to secure the future of the next generation.

Apparently he had also, through the mistakes of his predecessor, learnt two crucially important lessons. One is that the guerrilla warrior is far from a suicide bomber; the guerrilla believes that "he who runs away will live to fight another day." Consequently, if conventional forces are pitched against guerrillas, they can succeed only if the guerrillas are denied almost all avenues of escape, a strategy demonstrated with considerable success in the capture of Swat. Second is that to combat such an elusive force, initiative and the ability to survive without standard lines of communication, logistical support, and detailed orders at each stage will have to be inculcated down to platoon and section leaders.

The transformation was astounding. However, it would be unfair not to acknowledge the priceless contribution of the Swat peace agreement, an arrangement that I had opposed tooth and nail. However, I freely admit, with the benefit of hindsight, that without the disastrous consequences of this peace deal being visible to the entire nation, the military could never have succeeded.

The Taliban's form of justice and governance was visible to all through the media. This united the entire nation behind the military once again, and whatever vestiges of doubt might have lingered in the ranks of the military were put to rest. They went in committed soldiers, once again the well-oiled fighting machine that the army was before Musharraf's disastrous policies almost destroyed it.

I met with young officers and soldiers, without identifying myself, as they were preparing to enter South Waziristan. Their confidence, commitment, and sense of mission were inspiring. They were battle-hardened veterans who had seen the "enemy within" and were determined to eradicate it, and they included a large percentage of Pashtun. I also met with tribal Mahsud internally displaced persons (IDPs), before and after the operation commenced in their area. They were shamefaced at things having gotten that far, and they were immensely grateful to the military. I spoke too with ordinary people in Peshawar immediately after a suicide attack. One and all—even those who were weeping at the loss of loved ones (a young man had lost his wife and only daughter)—extolled the army and were determined to support it in its efforts to rid Pakistan of this scourge.

I will not repeat what has been stated earlier about how Kayani has become almost the most powerful individual in Pakistan. However, it needs to be pointed out that he is the most determined democrat of all the army chiefs that I have known personally or known of. It is therefore all the more astonishing that he should find himself saddled with this position. After assuming command of the army, he violated the established ritual of briefing the political leadership at GHQ and volunteered to deliver the briefing at the prime minister's office. Unlike some of his predecessors, Kayani has made it a point to receive and see off the prime minister whenever he proceeded abroad and to pay his respects, as he is supposed to.

Many analysts have questioned the army's resistance to placing the Directorate of Inter-Services Intelligence (ISI) under the Ministry of the Interior. My view is that it was a hastily made decision; the ISI should be where it is, under the prime minister. The fact that in the period after the Mumbai attack, the government made another hasty decision, agreeing to send the ISI's director general to India, and that it was advised to rethink that decision is not tantamount to military interference in political matters. I am fairly certain that that is all that Kayani suggested, in his own quiet way. Moreover, it is the duty of the COAS to advise the prime minister. (I believe that the ISI should be renamed, since it is not an inter-services organization, and it should be made a civilian agency, but that is another issue.)

I am reliably informed that when the historic "Long March" to restore the independence of the judiciary was approaching the Capitol, all that Kayani did was to visit the president and inform him that if the Long March reached the Capitol and Zardari wanted to call out the army in "Aid of Civil Power," in accordance with the Constitution, his orders might not be obeyed by the rank and file. Zardari caved in.

Zardari, however, continues to raise the possibility of a threat to democracy from the army and the judiciary (democracy being symbolized by the PPP!). His frequent references to the threat "from the pen and the sword" are not oblique. While the judiciary might pose a challenge to his continuity in power, the army has refused to dignify his utterances with any kind of response.

Kayani's first act that apparently violated his attempts to visibly demonstrate the principle of supremacy of the elected government was when a representative of the Inter-Services Public Relations Department (ISPR), a military spokesperson, issued a statement criticizing the Kerry-Lugar Bill.

I am convinced that Kayani must have made every effort to convey his reservations to the political leadership and had compelling reasons for going public. Nonetheless, that act took me by surprise, as did the fact that the day before Kayani left Pakistan for the "Strategic Dialogue" in the United States, five top bureaucrats, federal secretaries, came to GHQ to brief him, bypassing their respective ministers, the political leadership. When this issue was raised in Parliament by the opposition, the government denied all knowledge of it.

However, perhaps by then the government had acknowledged that Kayani would be the principal interlocutor for Pakistan as far as the United States was concerned, and Kayani was conscious of the inevitability of this fact. The last surprise for me was when Kayani called the chief minister of Punjab to his office and took him to task for a public statement in which he had, more or less, begged the Taliban to spare Punjab from more suicide attacks.

So what conclusions can we reach with regard to the relations between the military (primarily the army) and the current political government? I list some below:

—The government has voluntarily ceded all its responsibilities in any matter remotely related to "security" to the army.

—The provincial government has also left the army with no option but to govern the tribal areas retaken from the Taliban.

—The central government has also ceded (or accepted) the military's primacy in deciding issues related to foreign policy, at least those relating to the United States, India, and Afghanistan.

—On the other hand, the government is fully conscious that it faces no threat of a military takeover.

—The army chief's relations with Zardari might not be the best, but he seems to have fairly comfortable relations with the prime minister.

—However, Kayani has changed; once the committed democrat, he has accepted the realities and has pragmatically adjusted to the responsibilities thrust upon him, including those that demand political interference from behind the scenes. It is also obvious from his "dressing down" of the chief minister of Punjab that he is even handed and has now accepted the fact that he must perform his assigned role.

—When necessary, the COAS will increasingly play a role in political decisionmaking. In the immediate future and the short term it might be for the best; in fact, it could even be considered imperative for Pakistan that he do so. However, in the long run, it inevitably weakens democratic state institutions.

In conclusion, the military—specifically the army—has always had an extraordinary political role in Pakistan. Kayani offered the government a golden opportunity to reverse that state of affairs, but Zardari and his ilk squandered the opportunity. It is my considered view, despite opposing arguments from many quarters, that Kayani tried his best to "return to barracks" but could not. This time the army has been forced back into accepting a principal political role, which it did not seek. It appears that for the foreseeable future, the army will continue to remain politically active, though from behind the scenes.

10

Visualizing a Shared India-Pakistan Future

The religious extremism encouraged by the Pakistan army has turned into a double-edged sword. To some extent it did hurt the Soviet troops in Afghanistan in the 1980s and India after 1989, but it now hurts Pakistan more than India.

The consolidation of the presence of al Qaeda and its associates; the deepening of the roots of the Afghan Taliban in Pakistani territory; the growth of the Pakistani Taliban, called the Tehrik-e-Taliban Pakistan (TTP), in Pakistani Punjab and the tribal belt; and the ideological Talibanization of India-specific terrorist organizations such as the Lashkar-e-Tayyiba (LeT) and of growing sections of youth in the tribal belt and Punjab are the outcome of the army's encouragement of religious extremism. The army used extremism as an operational asset to achieve its strategic objectives of forcing a change in the status quo in Jammu and Kashmir (J&K), retaining the Pakistani presence and influence in Afghanistan and countering India's presence and influence.

The growth of religious extremism has made Pakistan a state of great concern not only to India (as it has always been), but also to other countries of the world. Al Qaeda and its associates, which have global ambitions, have established de facto control over north Waziristan. The noticeable surge in strikes by U.S. drone aircraft since President Barack Obama came to office in January 2009 might have weakened al Qaeda and its associates to some extent—as claimed by the United States—but the weakening has not significantly affected their ability to operate globally. They may no longer be able to conduct a 9/11-style terrorist strike, but they are still in a position to operate in a larger geographical area than they could before 9/11, although on a smaller scale.

What al Qaeda and its associates have lost by way of well-motivated and well-trained Arab and other foreign cadres has been made good to some extent by the increase in the number of motivated cadres and capabilities of Pakistani organizations such as the LeT. In the past, the LeT was essentially an asset of Pakistan's Inter-Services Intelligence (ISI)—raised, motivated, trained, and armed for use against India and against Indian nationals and interests in Afghanistan. While continuing to play the India-focused role assigned to it by the ISI, the LeT has gravitated into an organization with global ambitions and a global reach capable of compensating for the weaknesses of al Qaeda and its associates.

The TTP, which started essentially as an organization indulging in reprisals against the Pakistani security forces following their raid of the Lal Masjid in Islamabad by Pakistani military commandos in July 2007, has developed a larger agenda. It now assists the Afghan Taliban in its operations against NATO forces in Afghanistan and assists homegrown jihadis in the United States and other Western countries by training them in the areas it controls in the Federally Administered Tribal Areas (FATA).

The Pakistan army's policy of using the extremists and terrorists as operational assets where it can but countering them as adversaries where it should has created a dichotomy in its counterterrorism policy, thereby weakening the fight against terrorism emanating from Pakistani territory. While the Pakistan army can be expected to keep up its sporadic operations against the TTP, which poses an internal threat, it is unlikely to act effectively against the LeT and other India-specific terrorist organizations and against the Afghan Taliban. It has been avoiding action against al Qaeda due to lack of confidence in its ability to eradicate the group and fear that al Qaeda might indulge in acts of reprisal terrorism in Pakistani territory.

The internal security situation in Pakistan, already very bad, has been made worse by the activities of Sunni extremist groups such as the Sipah-e-Sahaba Pakistan (SSP) and the Lashkar-e-Jhangvi (LeJ) against the Shias, who constitute about 20 per cent of the population, against non-Muslim minorities, and against the liberal elements in the Sunni majority. The latter have taken up the cause of the minorities and advocate changes in the blasphemy law in order to prevent its misuse against minorities.

The religious parties that campaign in elections generally receive less than 15 percent of polled votes. There is no reason to believe that their number has increased. What has happened is that the terrorism-prone elements in these organizations (as well as in the general population) have moved toward the terrorist organizations for various reasons, including anger over the commando raid at the Lal Masjid and civilian casualties from drone strikes. Since the terrorist organizations do not run candidates in elections, it is difficult to quantify the support that they enjoy in the general population. However, the fact that they continue to have a regular flow of volunteers for suicide terrorism would indicate significant support for them, particularly in Punjab and other areas such as Khyber Pakhtunkwa Province and the FATA.

It would be incorrect to conclude from all this that there has been a radicalization of Pakistan as a state and society. What we are seeing is the radicalization of sizable sections of the population—particularly in certain areas of Punjab and the Pashtun belt—that have come under the influence of destabilizing ideas and are posing a threat to peace and security in Pakistan as well as the South Asia region and the rest of the world.

Despite pessimistic assessments by many analysts, I do not see any danger of radicalization of Pakistan as a state and a nation in the short and medium term. The army plays an important role in the governance of Pakistan—either directly, by taking over the reins of power, or indirectly, by having a say in matters concerning national security when duly elected political leaders are in power. There has been an increase in the number of radical elements in the army since the days of the late General Zia ul-Haq (1977–88). One finds an increasing number of students from the madrassas in the armed forces and other government departments. They are more prone to be influenced by radical ideas than students from nonreligious institutions.

Such radical elements are found mainly at the lower and middle ranks; the presence of radical elements at the higher command level is rare. However, there have been exceptions, the most prominent of them being General Zia himself, who was a devout Deobandi, and General Mohammed Aziz Khan, who retired some years ago. General Aziz Khan, who belongs to the Sudan tribe of Pakistan-Occupied Kashmir (POK), was considered a hard-core fundamentalist, in thought and action. Since his retirement, there have been no votaries of radical or fundamentalist ideologies at the level of lieutenant-general or general.

Despite the presence of radical elements at the lower and middle levels, the Pakistan army is not a radical institution in a religious sense. While the army and the Inter-Services Intelligence (ISI) Directorate, which consists largely of military officers, have no compunctions about using radical elements in society for achieving their strategic objectives, they have ensured that their institutions do not get infected with radical ideas at the senior level. During the war against the Soviet troops in Afghanistan in the 1980s, the ISI, in collaboration with the U.S. Central Intelligence Agency (CIA), used radical ideologies to motivate Afghan, Pakistani, and Arab volunteers to fight against Soviet troops.

At the same time, the ISI saw to it that those ideas did not affect the army as an institution. This is equally true in the case of the air force and the navy.

There are three destabilizing ideological influences in Pakistan: Wahhabized Islamic extremism, trans-ummah pan-Islamism, and countrywide anti-Americanism. Wahhabized Islamic extremism calls for the transformation of Pakistan into an Islamic state ruled according to sharia and the will of Allah, as interpreted by the clerics. It asserts that in an Islamic state, Allah will be sovereign, not the people. Trans-ummah pan-Islamism holds that the first loyalty of a Muslim should be to his religion and not to the state; that religious bonds are more important than cultural bonds; that Muslims do not recognize national frontiers and have a right and obligation to go to any country to wage a jihad in support of the local Muslims; and that Muslims have the religious right and obligation to acquire weapons of mass destruction (WMD) in order to protect their religion, if necessary. Anti-Americanism identifies the United States as the source of all evils afflicting the Islamic as well as the non-Islamic world. While religious anti-American elements look on the United States as anti-Islam, the nonreligious elements look on it as anti-people.

The geo-religious landscape in Pakistan is dominated by two kinds of organizations—fundamentalist parties and jihadi organizations. Fundamentalist parties have been in existence since Pakistan became independent in 1947 and have run candidates in elections although they are opposed to Western-style liberal democracy. Their total vote share has always been below 15 percent. They reached 11 percent in the 2002 elections, thanks to the machinations of the Pervez Musharraf government, which wanted to marginalize the influence of the nonreligious parties that opposed him, such as the Pakistan People's Party (PPP) of Benazir Bhutto and the Pakistan Muslim League of Nawaz Sharif (PML-N). In his overanxiety to cut Bhutto and Sharif down to size, Musharraf handed the tribal areas on a platter to the fundamentalists and the jihadis, thereby—more unwittingly than consciously—facilitating the resurgence of the neo-Taliban and al Qaeda.

So-called jihadi organizations misinterpret the concept of jihad and advocate its use against all perceived enemies of Islam—internal or external, non-Muslim or Muslim—wherever they are found. Their call for jihad has a domestic as well as an external agenda. The domestic agenda is to set up an Islamic state in Pakistan ruled according to sharia and the will of Allah. The external agenda is to "liberate" all so-called traditional Muslim lands from the "occupation" of non-Muslims and to eliminate the influence of the United States and the rest of the Western world from the ummah.

The jihadi organizations were brought into existence in the 1980s by the ISI and Saudi intelligence at the request of the CIA to be used against the troops of the Soviet Union and the pro-Soviet Afghan government. Their perceived success in bringing about the withdrawal of the Soviet troops and the collapse of the Najibullah government convinced the organizations that jihad, as waged by them, was a highly potent weapon that could be used with equal effectiveness to bring about the withdrawal of the Western presence from the ummah, to "liberate the traditional Muslim lands," and to transform Pakistan into an Islamic fundamentalist state. The Pakistan army and the ISI, which were impressed by the motivation, determination, and fighting skills displayed by the jihadi organizations in Afghanistan, transformed them after the withdrawal of the Soviet troops into a new strategic weapon for use against India to annex J&K and in Afghanistan to achieve a Pakistani presence.

The aggravation of anti-U.S. feeling in the Islamic world after 9/11 has resulted in dual control of the Pakistani jihadi organizations. The ISI tried to use them for its national agenda against India and in Afghanistan. Osama bin Laden and al Qaeda used them for their global agenda against "the Crusaders and the Jewish people." The jihadi organizations are now fighting on three fronts with equal ferocity—against India, as desired by the ISI; against the United States and Israel, as desired by al Qaeda; and against the Pakistani state itself, as dictated by their domestic agenda, to establish an Islamic state. The growing Talibanization of the FATA and Khyber Pakhtunkhwa Province (KP) and the Taliban's spread outside the tribal areas are the result of their determined pursuit of their domestic agenda. The acts of jihadi terrorism in Spain and the United Kingdom; the thwarted acts of terrorism in the United Kingdom; the unearthing of numerous sleeper cells in the United Kingdom, the United States, Canada, and other countries; and the resurgence of the neo-Taliban and al Qaeda in Afghanistan are the result of their equally determined pursuit of their international agenda. Members of the Pakistani diaspora in Gulf countries such as the United Arab Emirates and Western countries have been playing an increasingly active role in facilitating the pursuit of their international agenda.

The international community's concern over the prevailing and developing situation in Pakistan has been further deepened by Pakistan's status as a nuclear weapon state. The Pakistan army has repeatedly assured the United States and the rest of the international community that the security of its nuclear arsenal is strong and that there is no danger of its falling into the hands of the jihadi terrorists. Despite its reassurances, concern remains, due to various factors.

First, it is admitted even in Pakistan that extremist elements have infiltrated every section of the Pakistani state apparatus—the armed forces, the police, paramilitary forces, and the civilian bureaucracy. It is inconceivable, then, that Pakistan's nuclear establishment would not have been penetrated.

Second, the fundamentalist and jihadi organizations are strong supporters of a military nuclear capability so that the ummah can counter Israel's alleged nuclear capability. They consider Pakistan's atomic bomb not merely a national asset but an Islamic asset. They describe it as an Islamic bomb, whose use should be available to the entire ummah, and so support Pakistan's sharing its nuclear technology with other Muslim countries. In their eyes, A. Q. Khan, the so-called father of Pakistan's atomic bomb, committed no offense by sharing nuclear technology with Iran and Libya because both are Muslim states—or with North Korea as quid pro quo for its sharing its missile technology with Pakistan. They look on Pakistan's sharing its nuclear technology and know-how with other Islamic states as an Islamic obligation and not as an illegal act of proliferation.

Third, while scientists may be prepared to share technology and know-how with other Muslim states, there has been no evidence of a similar willingness on their part to share them with Islamic nonstate actors such as al Qaeda. However, the dangers of such sharing with nonstate groups were highlighted by the unearthing of evidence by U.S. intelligence after 9/11 that at least two retired Pakistani nuclear scientists—Sultan Bashiruddin Chaudhury and Abdul Majid—had been in touch with Osama bin Laden after their retirement and had even visited him at Kandahar. After being taken into custody and questioned, they admitted their contacts with bin Laden but insisted that their dealings with him were in connection with a humanitarian relief organization that they had founded after their retirement. Many retired Pakistani military and intelligence officers have been helping the neo-Taliban and Pakistani jihadi organizations, the most well-known being Lieutenant General Hamid Gul, director-general of ISI during Benazir Bhutto's first tenure as prime minister (1988–90). Are there other retired nuclear scientists who have been maintaining similar contacts with al Qaeda and other jihadi organizations?

The Pashtun belt on both sides of the Pakistan-Afghanistan border will continue to be under the de facto control of al Qaeda, the neo-Taliban, and Pakistani jihadi organizations. Neither the Pakistan army in Pakistani territory nor the U.S.-led NATO forces in the adjoining Afghan territory will be able to prevail over the terrorists in an enduring manner. NATO forces will not be able to prevail in Afghan territory unless and until the roots of jihadi terrorism in Pakistani territory are initially sterilized and ultimately destroyed. The

Pakistan army has so far exhibited neither the willingness nor capability to undertake that task. Its lack of willingness arises from its perception that it will need its own jihadis for continued use against India and the neo-Taliban for retrieving the strategic ground that it lost in Afghanistan. Moreover, the army fears that any strong action that it takes against the jihadis operating in the Pashtun belt could lead to a major confrontation with tribal groups, which contribute a large number of soldiers to the army. Next to Punjab, the largest number of recruits in the Pakistan army comes from the KP and the FATA.

The army's incapability arises from the fact that ever since Pakistan was born in 1947, the FATA has remained in a state of isolation and utter neglect, with no worthwhile development of its economy and infrastructure. It should be possible to root out the terrorist infrastructure in the area through NATO operations mounted from Afghan territory, but neither the current government nor any future democratically elected civilian government is likely to agree to that as it could aggravate anti-American feeling across the country and the entire political spectrum, discrediting the government in power at Islamabad. If the Pakistan government, including its military leadership, does not take vigorous action in time, there is the danger that jihadi extremism of the Taliban kind will spread from the tribal areas to the POK and to those areas of Punjab bordering the Pashtun belt. There are indications that it has already started to happen.

India and Afghanistan will continue to face the immediate impact of the uncontrolled activities of extremists and jihadis in Pakistan's territory. Jihadi terrorism in India's territory will ebb and flow, depending on the effectiveness of India's security forces and counterterrorism agencies in dealing with it. Occasional outbreaks of spectacular acts of terrorism will be followed by long spells of inactivity. In the first few years after terrorism broke out in J&K in 1989, it almost assumed the shape of a sustained insurgency. But the political, counterterrorism, and counter-infiltration measures (building of border fences) taken by Indian authorities have dented the terrorists' ability to sustain a wave of attacks. The total elimination of sporadic acts will not be possible until the state of Pakistan gives up the use of terrorism as a strategic weapon.

There will be continuing instability in Afghanistan, with the danger of Afghanistan reverting to its pre-9/11 position. Narcotics control measures and all measures to dry up the flow of funds to different terrorist groups will remain ineffective. The flow of funds from the international community to Afghanistan will not result in any significant economic development or improvement in the people's standard of living. On the other hand, there is some danger that those funds will leak into terrorist coffers through government sympathizers. The newly raised Afghan security forces and the civilian administration have been penetrated by the neo-Taliban.

The phenomenon of angry individuals in the Pakistani and other Muslim diasporas in the West taking to suicide terrorism and emulating al Qaeda's modus operandi will continue. Strong measures taken by Western governments against their own Muslim population as well as Muslim visitors to their country will add to the feelings of alienation and anger in the Muslim diaspora. That will hamper the integration of Muslims and aggravate the divide between Muslims and non-Muslims. Acts of reprisal terrorism against Western nationals and interests will continue to take place. A repeat of 9/11 in the U.S. homeland cannot be ruled out, however strong the physical security measures. A vicious cycle—more terrorism followed by more physical security measures and restrictions against Muslims followed by more alienation and anger—will continue unbroken.

The fire of jihadi terrorism started in the Afghan-Pakistan region. It can be extinguished only through appropriate measures in the region where it started, particularly in Pakistan, where the heart of the fire is located. Doing so requires a mix of immediate and long-term measures. The immediate measures would include pressuring Pakistan to stop using terrorism as a strategic weapon, effectively putting an end to the terrorist infrastructure created by the ISI, and to arrest and prosecute the leaders of jihadi terrorist organizations. Although those measures would weaken the Pakistani jihadi organizations, they would not end al Qaeda. It could be neutralized only by joint international action. The international community has not been successful because of lack of cooperation from Pakistan, which must be made to cooperate through carrot-and-stick policies. Another immediate measure required is a change in the current overmilitarized counterterrorism methods of the United States, which are causing considerable collateral damage and driving more Muslims into the arms of al Qaeda.

Long-term measures must include heavy investment in education in Pakistan and Afghanistan in order to make modern education available to the poorer segments of society at an affordable price. The madrassa system also must be reformed in order to make the madrassas serve the genuine religious and spiritual needs of the people without seeking to make jihadi terrorists out of them. Western countries should seek to erase the perception in their Muslim populations that Muslims are a targeted community. To do that, they must improve the interactions of intelligence and security agencies with Muslims. How can they be firm without seeming to be harsh? How can they avoid creating feelings of humiliation in Muslims under questioning? These are questions that need attention, immediately and in the medium and long terms. Eradication of the roots of terrorism will be a long, drawn-out process. It needs to be handled with patience and understanding of the feelings of Muslims. The economic development of the tribal areas on both sides of the Pakistan-Afghanistan border also needs attention.

India must be a frontline state in the political and ideological campaign against extremism and terrorism in the Afghanistan-Pakistan region. The threat originating from this area will continue to confront India, Afghanistan, and the international community as a whole for at least another ten to fifteen years. It has to be gradually diluted and the terrorist organizations demotivated before one can hope to see jihadi fatigue set in. Demotivation of the terrorism-prone sections of the population should be the first objective. Better education, better medical care, better infrastructure, better governance, and greater economic prosperity are important factors in any effort to achieve demotivation.

Nonetheless, attention to those factors alone will not achieve the level of demotivation required to roll back the jihadi threat. It is equally important to work simultaneously to change the motives of Pakistan's military leadership, whose reflexes are still largely influenced by memories of the defeat of the Pakistan army by the Indian army in 1971 and by fears of a possible repeat of 1971. The army's reflexes are governed not only by feelings of insecurity arising from fear of what India might be up to but also by the conviction that Jammu and Kashmir belongs to Pakistan and needs to be wrested from Indian control. Fears of India regaining its past influence in Afghanistan are another strong influence.

There is no possibility that India will hand Jammu and Kashmir over to Pakistan. No amount of terrorism and no increase in the strength and capability of the Pakistan army can shake India's control of J&K and its determination to fight for the territorial status quo. The recent attempts by Pakistan to bring China into Pakistan in a big way are an indication of its realization that it cannot achieve its strategic objectives against India through the use of terrorism alone. Pakistan also realizes that the United States is unlikely to help it achieve those objectives.

Having realized the likely futility of using either the jihadi card or the U.S. card against India, Pakistan is once again trying to use the China card by inviting Chinese troops into the POK and the Gilgit-Baltistan area and by encouraging China to diversify its economic and military stakes in Pakistan. China, which has been concerned over the implications for its status and security of the relationship between India and the United States, is showing greater willingness than before to let itself be used by Pakistan to buttress Pakistan's feelings of security vis-à-vis India.

In this web of geopolitical complexities, what are the policy options before India? Should it keep adding to Pakistan's feelings of insecurity and instability or take the initiative to lessen Pakistani concerns? Is it possible to lessen those concerns and help Pakistan rid itself of its anti-India reflexes without changing the status quo in J&K and without giving up India's growing links with Afghanistan?

Any exercise to demotivate the Pakistani state and help it to rid itself of its fears—which are seen by its army as real and by India as imaginary—has to start with frequent and sustained interactions between the institutions of the two countries: political parties to political parties, Parliament to Parliament, army to army, intelligence agencies to intelligence agencies, Foreign Office to Foreign Office, and Home Ministry to Home Ministry. Increasing institutional contacts is as important as increasing people-to-people contacts to dispel the two countries' imaginary fears of each other.

How should India and Pakistan increase their institutional interactions with each other? That is the basic question to be addressed, and it should be addressed in the context of an overall vision statement agreed to by the two countries. The imaginary fears are more in Pakistan's mind than in India's mind. India's prime minister should take the initiative by visiting Pakistan to set the ball rolling toward an agreed common vision.

11

At the Brink?

Pakistan's uncertain future is a widely shared cause of concern at the international level. That concern raises strong doubts about the long-term capacity of the Pakistani state to effectively fulfill its obligations: managing ethnic and religious conflict, guaranteeing internal peace and stability, and providing economic opportunities to youth. Internal failures would make it difficult for Pakistan to fulfill its responsibilities toward the international community as well, thereby further accentuating internal problems.

Pakistan's viability is not an entirely new concern. The issue was first raised before Pakistan was established. When the All-India Muslim League's demand for Pakistan as a separate homeland for the Muslims of British India gained popularity among Muslims during the mid-1940s, the issue of its long-term survival began to be debated in British India's political circles. At the time of independence in August 1947, most leaders of the Indian National Congress and a good number of British and other political analysts believed that the new state of Pakistan was not viable and that it would soon collapse under the weight of its problems.

Concerns about the Future of Pakistan

While accepting the partition plan on June 15, 1947, the Indian National Congress maintained that "when present passions have subsided, India's problems will be viewed in their proper perspective and the false doctrine of two nations in India will be discredited and discarded by all."[1] Maulana Abdul Kalam Azad maintained that Sardar Patel (one of the top leaders of the Congress Party of India) was convinced that "the new state of Pakistan was not viable and could not last. . . . Pakistan would collapse in a short time."[2] While commenting on the troubled political and administrative conditions in Pakistan in the immediate aftermath of independence, Keith Callard wrote, "There were those in India (and elsewhere) who had disbelieved the possibility of the survival of Pakistan even under favorable conditions. And actual conditions were far from favorable."[3]

In December 1971, Pakistan faced an acute crisis of confidence when East Pakistan broke away after Pakistan lost the India-Pakistan war. Many analysts were not sure that West Pakistan (present-day Pakistan) could overcome the shock of both military defeat and the loss of East Pakistan and survive as an effectively functioning state. In the midst of those concerns, the popular civilian leadership of Zulfikar Ali Bhutto managed to surmount the crisis of confidence and put the country on a democratic and constitutional path. However, the question of Pakistan's troubled and uncertain future continued to haunt Pakistani and other political analysts and historians.

In 1970, Tariq Ali argued for a socialist revolution to salvage Pakistan, writing that "the choice will be between socialist revolution—that is, people's power—[and] complete and utter disintegration" and underlining the need for building "the revolutionary vanguard which will enable us to achieve a socialist workers' and peasants' republic in Pakistan."[4] Thirteen years later, he returned to the question of Pakistan's future in his book *Can Pakistan Survive?* He attributed Pakistan's chronic instability to its internal contradictions and regional geopolitical factors. He went on to suggest that "the question which now increasingly haunts the new generation in Pakistan is not simply whether the country can survive but whether its existence was necessary in the first place."[5] The prescription he offered was a modification of his earlier suggestion. He wrote: "The survival of Pakistan as a state today does not depend on vested interests or the armed forces. Only a thoroughgoing social transformation and the institutionalization of democracy, together with the disbandment of the mercenary army, could offer Pakistan a future."[6]

Interestingly enough, now, in the first decade of the twenty-first century, Tariq Ali's suggestion to reshape the Pakistani society from top to bottom is advocated by Islamic orthodox believers and neoconservatives, albeit in an Islamic framework. They view militancy as an instrument for transforming society and warding off the enemies of Islam and their local agents. They talk of controlling the state machinery to transform the state and society along Islamic lines, as they define them.

In the early 1990s, the notion of a failed state emerged in the global political discourse, against the backdrop of a breakdown of state authority and internal strife in Somalia, Sierra Leone, Rwanda, Burundi, Liberia, Zaire, and the Sudan. A failed state is often described as a state that is unable to meet its obligations as a sovereign entity in both the domestic and international context. Its administrative and security structures, its economy, and its societal fabric are in complete disarray, making it impossible for the state to perform its basic functions. It is confronted by multiple, competing armed groups that prevent it from controlling major parts of its official territory. Such a state of affairs is seen as a threat to the international community. Robert D. Kaplan argued that "scarcity, crime, overpopulation, tribalism and disease are rapidly destroying the social fabric of our planet" and that the traditional boundaries of the state are losing relevance because of internal strife, migration of refugees, and the inability of the states to perform their basic responsibilities. "Henceforward the map of the world will never be static. This future map—in a sense, the 'Last Map'—will be an ever-mutating representation of chaos."[7]

Kaplan articulated Pakistan's problem as one that was "more basic still: like much of Africa, the country makes no geographic or demographic sense. . . . Like Yugoslavia, Pakistan is a patchwork of ethnic groups, increasingly in violent conflict with one another. . . . Pakistan is becoming a more and more desperate place. As irrigation in the Indus River basin intensifies to serve two growing populations, Muslim-Hindu strife over falling water tables may be unavoidable."[8]

During the 1990s, Robert Chase and his research associates identified nine developing countries that could be described as "pivotal states," those whose success or failure would have implications for regional and global stability. These states could go either way—emerge as successful states or decay and degenerate as state entities.[9] Pakistan is identified as one of the nine pivotal states facing serious internal threats and external challenges. It could go either way—succeed in coping with its challenges or fail. In either case, developments in Pakistan have implications beyond its borders.

Some writers have described Pakistan as a failed state; others believe that Pakistan is a failing rather than a failed state. Comparison of Pakistan with the African states of Somalia, Rwanda, Burundi, and the Sudan shows that the state system, economy, and society have not crumbled in Pakistan to the extent seen in those countries. Pakistan's state institutions and societal operations cannot yet be described as close to some ruinous end.

But if Pakistan cannot be described as a failed state, it is not a success story either. It is a troubled state that faces the threat of going under due mainly to internal problems and external pressures. However, it has the potential to overcome those challenges and shape up as a reasonably functional state. It can go either way: decline and fragment or emerge as a functioning democracy and a middle-level economy. However, Pakistan's turnaround is not possible without internal determination to address the issues that afflict the state and society and international support to meet those challenges. Pakistan alone is not in a position to overcome its currently troubled situation.

Different Scenarios

Writing in 1999, I articulated four future scenarios for Pakistan.[10] The most optimistic scenario projects Pakistan as adopting a participatory political process, offering ample opportunities to diverse interest groups to pursue accommodating and cooperative interaction with each other. Pakistan also makes significant strides in the economic domain by mobilizing domestic resources and international support. Further, participatory governance and an improved economy make it possible for the country to devote more resources to social sector development. The settlement of major India-Pakistan problems and improvement of their bilateral relations is also part of this vision of the future.

The second, more pessimistic, scenario visualizes Pakistan as becoming increasingly ungovernable, with the effective writ of the state being limited to the capital city and other major cities. Socioeconomic pressures and ethnic and regional cleavages fragment the political and social processes. As weapons are easily available in Pakistan, competing interests settle their scores with each other through armed conflict and challenge the tottering government. Those developments further undermine the economy, causing alienation and frustration in the populace, and create an anarchic situation that could trigger the rise of an authoritarian or dictatorial regime. The military is likely to establish such a regime, and if it does, it finds it increasingly difficult to keep the polity and the nation-state intact.

The third scenario visualizes internal strife in some parts of the country but life in other parts as stable and secure. Confusion and chaos provide a good opportunity to Islamic groups to win over the people in the name of an alternative Islamic ideology that they claim will solve the people's problems. A host of Islamic groups rather than a unified Islamic movement compete with each other and with "nonreligious" parties and elements. That adds to Pakistan's internal confusion, making it more vulnerable to both external penetration and intervention.

In the fourth scenario—described as the most likely—Pakistan does not fully overcome its socioeconomic, political, and other problems, but it does enough to prevent the country from collapsing. Pakistan is able to manage the situation, sometimes satisfactorily, sometimes poorly. It slowly moves along the road to fuller democracy; however, the process may freeze or face reverses from time to time. Much depends on how problems are kept within manageable limits. The struggle for survival is constant, and uncertainty about the future persists.

Writing in 2005, Stephen P. Cohen argued that "Pakistan will be a state-nation lodged between a weak democracy and a benevolent autocracy. . . . Barring a cataclysmic event or a conjunction of major crises such as military defeat, a serious economic crisis, and extended political turmoil, the failure of Pakistan as a state can be ruled out. However, failure can still take place slowly or in parts. Pakistan may be unable to maintain minimal standards of 'stateness.'"[11] He suggested six possible visions of the future of Pakistan, including the continuation of an establishment-dominated oligarchic system, liberal secular democracy, soft authoritarianism, Islamic state, divided Pakistan, and postwar Pakistan.[12] Though describing the breakup of Pakistan as "unlikely," Cohen suggests that it could take place in "at least four ways" because of internal conflicts and regional developments.[13]

Khaled Ahmed argued in 2008 that three broad narratives of political and security developments in and around Pakistan influence the visions of the country's future.[14] Those narratives, which overlap and can be subdivided into more narratives, show wide divergence in the interpretation of political and societal issues, thereby creating different visions of Pakistan's future. However, the common denominator is the confusion and uncertainty prevalent in Pakistan about the country's future and a confluence of internal and external factors that influence the narratives and visions.

The first narrative, described by Ahmed as the external narrative, is shared by the world outside Pakistan, especially by the states that are affected by Pakistan-Afghanistan–based militancy. This perspective views Pakistan as the center of militant groups such as al Qaeda, the Taliban, and other groups that use violence to pursue their ideological agendas beyond Pakistan. Consequently, the views of those states about the present and the future of Pakistan are shaped by their knowledge of and concerns about the militant groups and their activities.

The second narrative, labeled as the civil society narrative, focuses on the views of Pakistani society on militancy, al Qaeda, and the United States. Those views are based on their belief systems and ideologies rather than facts; thus they do not share the negative opinion of the non-Muslim world about Islamic militancy, al Qaeda, and the Taliban. Most people identifying with this narrative are alienated from the state and identify with Islamic movements or the notion of Muslim "ummah" (brotherhood or community). They think that the Muslim states and their rulers serve the interests of the United

States and the West, which they see as adversaries of Islam. According to Ahmed, they see "America's war against Al-Qaeda as a war against Muslims and [do not] take into account the global consensus behind this war."

The third narrative, described as the nationalist narrative, is purely India driven. In this narrative, India is viewed as a greater threat than al Qaeda or the Taliban. Some talk of two adversaries of Pakistan, which are India and the United States. This perspective is widely shared by Islamic groups and the political right. It is also shared by the military in Pakistan.[15]

The first narrative projects Pakistan as an epicenter of Islamic radicalism and terrorism and views Pakistan's future with a great deal of concern. The concern outside Pakistan is that if Pakistan cannot cope with radicalism and militancy, the state and society may disintegrate, with dangerous consequences for the rest of the world. Can the outside world salvage a country like Pakistan, where a large number of people entertain the second narrative, which views all domestic and external developments with reference to a religious ortho-doxy that maintains that Islam and Muslims are under threat from the non-Muslim world? To them, fighting the West rather than al Qaeda and the Taliban is the need of the hour, and they cannot trust their state system and rulers that serve Western interests. When we add the third narrative, which emphasizes a highly nationalist perspective, the dichotomy between this per-spective and that of the rest of the world becomes alarmingly conspicuous. In addition to the West, India also emerges as a threat to Pakistan. In fact, because it shares a border with Pakistan, India is seen as a more immediate threat than the West. For these people, the state is relevant to the extent that it enables them to achieve their objectives, which are based on religious and nationalis-tic beliefs. A rational and dispassionate approach based on the study of the dynamics of international politics is missing in most debates in Pakistan at the societal level on Islamic militancy, the current state of affairs in Pakistan, and the country's future.

Five Challenges

Pakistan's future as a coherent and stable state is threatened by five major challenges: religious extremism and terrorism, appallingly poor governance, a feeble economy, the misplaced priorities of the civilian political class, and the persistent efforts of the Supreme Court to expand its domain at the expense of the elected executive and legislature.

Religious extremism and militancy are the most formidable internal threats to political stability, societal harmony, and sociocultural pluralism.

Growing Islamic orthodoxy and militancy have not only imposed pressures on religious minorities but have also accentuated interdenominational conflicts among Muslims. There is less patience for religious and cultural divergence, and self-styled Islamic vigilantes threaten those who do not share their religious perspective.

Social, cultural, and religious intolerance and violence has caused irreparable damage to Pakistan's social fabric. There have been many instances of violence against the Ahmadis and Christians, in addition to conflict between the Shias and the Deoband Sunni. Pakistan is also witnessing intra-Sunni conflict, wherein the followers of the Deoband/Wahhabi Islamic tradition and the champions of the Barelvi Islamic tradition conflict with each other, either for control of mosques or by challenging each other's religious doctrine and rituals.

Since 2007, various militant Islamic groups, especially the Taliban, have been targeting major cities in mainland Pakistan with suicide and roadside bombings, with greater frequency. Pakistan experienced the maximum number of suicide attacks during April 2009–January 2010. According to data released by Pakistan's Ministry for Interior Affairs, there were 1,780 terrorist incidents (including suicide attacks), killing 2,072 and injuring 6,253 people, including 1,590 security personnel. That figure was higher than the corresponding figure for 2008.[16] The city of Peshawar experienced more suicide and car bombs in October–December 2009 than any other Pakistani city.

The troubled internal security situation and stepped-up violence have contributed to the extremely poor governance on the part of the federal and provincial governments, which are finding it difficult to effectively address the socioeconomic problems that afflict the state system and society. Corruption and mismanagement have greatly undermined government efficiency, and state patronage is being employed in a highly partisan manner, placing a greater premium on loyalty than on professionalism and performance. The federal and provincial cabinets have been unduly expanded to accommodate parliamentarians, multiplying the cost of administration without any increase in efficiency and performance.

The major disappointment is the economic domain, which is performing poorly in both micro- and macroeconomic affairs. The economy is heavily dependent on two foreign sources of revenue: economic assistance from foreign countries and international financial institutions and remittances from Pakistanis settled abroad. Pakistan's own economy is unable to generate enough resources to cover administrative, security, and other expenditures. Major social development programs rely on external assistance.

Ordinary people are hit hard by price hikes, shortages of essential food items, increased oil prices in the international market, and the continued neglect of their welfare, especially inadequate allocations to education, health care, and civic facilities. The economy is especially hurt by acute electric power and gas shortages, and the government does not have definite plans of action to cope with those problems.

The political class and other politically active circles have misplaced priorities. They pay more attention to advancing their partisan agendas than to working together to address the country's challenges. Even on issues of religious extremism and terrorism, the opposition parties are not forthcoming in supporting the government. They may condemn terrorism in principle, but they avoid condemning specific militant Islamic groups for involvement in specific terrorist incidents. They criticize the government for being what they describe as subservient to the United States with respect to terrorism issues in the region. Islamic parties openly sympathize with the Taliban and al Qaeda and oppose military action in tribal areas. The statements of political leaders on current issues and problems reflect their narrow partisan efforts to delegitimize each other. The key interests of the opposition parties, especially the Pakistan Muslim League–Nawaz (PML-N), include getting rid of President Asif Ali Zardari and increasing pressure on the federal government.[17]

Pakistan's democracy is threatened by the constant pressure generated by the Supreme Court on the elected executive. Since the restoration of the chief justice in March 2009 by the PPP government, after unnecessary delay and under pressure from the military and political interests, the Supreme Court has attempted to free itself from the influence of the elected executive and the legislature and stepped into the domain of the executive under the pretext of judicial activism.

Traditionally, the military has resisted civilian government influence in its affairs and has expanded its domain to pursue its self-ascribed task of saving the political system from major crises. Now, it seems that the superior judiciary (the Supreme Court and provincial high courts)—another nonelected institution—is endeavoring to free itself from the elected institutions and seems to have developed a military-like sense of self-righteousness that allows it to try to put every institution of the state on the "correct course" as the judiciary defines it. If that trend becomes established, the civilian political order, already under severe pressure, may cease to function.

The opposition parties and some lawyers support the Supreme Court's strident approach toward the PPP-led federal government in the hope that the court will either disqualify President Zardari or exert enough pressure to cause the collapse of the incumbent federal government.

In the past, some political leaders supported military intervention in the political domain, including dislodging of the government. Now the major opposition parties, especially the PML-N, are expected to support the Supreme Court if the latter decides to take a hard line toward Zardari or the federal government.[18] That will cause a serious blow to current efforts to put Pakistan on the road to democracy and civilian rule.

Is Pakistani Society Cracking Up?

If the Pakistani government and the state are finding it difficult to ensure good governance and function as a coherent and stable entity, the society is show-ing signs of cracking up, along multiple fault lines: ethnicity, region, and reli-gious sectarianism. Islamic orthodoxy and militancy have seeped deep into Pakistan's state system and society, weakening the attachment of the people, especially the youth that constitute the majority of Pakistan's population, to Pakistan as a nation-state. The notions of citizenship, civic obligations, and col-lective good have been replaced by the obligations of the individual as a Mus-lim who functions as a part of a transnational Muslim community. The state is relevant to the extent that it helps to achieve the radical Islamic transnational religious-political agenda.

In the early 1980s, Pakistan's military government inculcated Islamic ortho-doxy and militancy in the youth through the state education system and the mass media. The trend was strengthened by the traditional Islamic education many received through the madrassas that proliferated in the 1980s and the early 1990s with the encouragement of Pakistan's state policy. These policies created a one-dimensional and highly skewed Islamic worldview among youth, one that viewed national and global affairs in purely religious terms and defined world affairs in terms of "we, the Muslims" versus "they," the non-Muslim adversaries of Islam and Muslims. Such a narrow religious mind-set made them vulnerable to appeals by militant groups that advocated the pursuit of an Islamic religious-political agenda through violence.

These trends are more pronounced among the people subscribing to the Deobandi, Wahhabi/Salafi, and Ahl-e-Hadith (Hadees) Islamic traditions. Others are critical of the violent methods of the Taliban, but they do share their dichotomized worldview of Islam versus the rest of the world and the belief that Islam is under threat from non-Muslims and their agents among Muslims.

By September 2001, at least one and a half generations had been raised with religious orthodoxy and militancy as the favored mindset and basis for action. These people have reached middle-level positions in the government, the mil-itary, and the intelligence services and in the private sector. While most of them are not expected to get directly involved in violence, they have an inherited sympathy for Islamic militancy and a negative disposition, if not hostility, toward the West as the adversary of Islam and Muslims.

A Pakistani commentator described this phenomenon in these words: "Pakistan, aided to no little extent by Western funding, managed to arm an entire generation with not only guns but far worse, the ideological certainty of warriors of the faith, tireless defenders against the ungodly and evil. While the ungodly in those days [1980–1989] were Soviets, it is hardly surprising that the jihadi definition of the enemy expanded over [the] subsequent years and now appears to refer to practically everyone."[19]

Pakistan faces two sets of threats to its society. First, the Pakistani Taliban and other militant Islamic groups based in the tribal areas and several militant groups based in the Punjab pose a threat to social peace and stability. These groups have established a "jihadi" infrastructure in various cities of Pakistan, where they recruit young people to militancy.[20] Various Islamic political parties and groups sympathize with them, giving them enough space to flourish and multiply.

Second, the pro-jihad mindset split Pakistani society sharply along Islamic sectarian lines. It has caused two major problems for the country's youth, who find it difficult to link themselves positively to Pakistani society and the state. The first problem is that the concept of the nation-state and citizenship has been greatly undermined for them. Most of them are alienated from the Pakistani state and do not feel obligated to respect its primacy and or to honor their obligations as citizens. Their concept of religious affiliation has three levels. First is affiliation with Islam as a Muslim person with religious obligations to meet. Next is affiliation with nonstate national or transnational Islamic movements that uphold the primacy of Islam. Third is affiliation with the Islamic ummah, the universal Muslim community. As mentioned, the nation-state, Pakistan, is relevant only to the extent that it facilitates achieving the goals of Islamic orthodoxy and its radicalized worldview and the struggle against those who do not share those goals. The second problem is that the notion of collective good or social responsibility has been extremely weakened, except in purely Islamic terms. What matters most is a Muslim's obligation to God and the Muslim community, represented by Islamic movements. A radicalized Muslim may use violence without paying any attention to the consequences of his actions for other human beings or for Pakistan as a nation-state and a member of the comity of nations.

This worldview thus questions the legitimacy of the nation-state and the sociocultural and economic order. Rulers are viewed as corrupt, self-serving agents of anti-Islam political and economic forces and countries. Consequently, there is growing alienation of the people, especially the youth, from the Pakistani state and society (and from the state and society in the Muslim world in general). Islamic discourse emphasizes the need for total transformation of the state and society; however, radical Islamists have not developed any consensus on the operational norms and strategies needed to develop a new politico-social and economic order to replace the existing order; they speak in terms of broad generalizations and clichés. The process of delegitimization of the state and society in Pakistan is reinforced by the nonperformance of the Pakistani state in the social and economic sectors, which strengthens the perception that ordinary people cannot depend on the state to address their problems.

This has given rise to a culture of defiance and anarchy. Sporadic street protests by political parties, social groups, or disorderly crowds that are upset by some event like a road accident are quite common in urban centers. It has been observed for the last four to five years that the protesters seem most interested in making things difficult for others by disrupting ordinary business and city life, causing traffic jams, and ransacking property. There is an increased tendency to block highways to suspend intercity traffic, disrupt railway train services, and attack police stations and government offices. These mini-insurgencies have become routine.

Political leaders often encourage defiance of the government in order to paralyze it, hoping that will cause its collapse. The PML-N leadership, the main opposition party, has on occasion called on its supporters as well as government employees to defy government orders or has threatened to launch street protests. There is a lesser tendency on the part of the political leaders to use the Parliament for raising contentious issues; they appear to be more inclined to generate extra-parliamentary pressure.

These trends are indicative of the growing incoherence, divisiveness, and fragmentation in Pakistani society, which threatens the prospects of democracy and political stability. Several parts of Balochistan are experiencing insurgency-like situations by dissident Baloch groups. The targeted killing in Balochistan of people from other provinces has resulted in the loss of a large number of professionals, thereby further weakening the capacity of the provincial administration and the federal government to pursue development and modernization projects.

The Military and Pakistan's Future

Attention is now focused on the military as Pakistan drifts toward the edge due to multiple crises, especially the pressures generated by religious orthodoxy, extremism, terrorism, and the growing fissures in society. The military's importance has also increased because the administrative apparatus and para-military forces alone could not cope with the menace of terrorism. The perennial problem of troubled relations with India also sustains the primacy of the military for external and internal security.

The top brass of the military, especially the army, is focused on three major issues. First, they are attending to rehabilitation of the image of the military in Pakistan, which suffered a great deal in the last two years of Musharraf's rule, when the army's top brass faced virulent criticism from the public. Various efforts have helped to boost their image, including the 2010 army exercises, flood rescue and relief work in July-September 2010, rescue operations after a coal mine collapsed near Quetta in Balochistan in March 2011, rescue work when a strong tornado hit some villages in the Sialkot area of the Punjab in March 2011, and more recruitment of Baloch youth to the army in 2010–11.[21]

Second, the military is paying full attention to dealing with terrorist groups based primarily in the tribal areas. The present series of encounters between the military and the militant groups began in the last week of April 2009, following which the army, the air force, and paramilitary forces dislodged the Taliban from Swat/Malakand and South Waziristan. Currently security forces are taking tough action against various militant groups in other tribal areas, especially in Orakzai, Khyber, Bijaur, and Kurram. Their successes have improved the image of the army by showing that the top command has the determination and capability to challenge the terrorist groups that have become the major threat to Pakistan's internal peace and stability and to the military's primacy in the country. The operations have also contributed to improving the military's image abroad as a task-oriented force for counter-terrorism operations.

Third, the army chief has devoted much attention to improving service conditions and facilities for officers and other ranks. Greater attention is being given to improving the quality of life for the junior commissioned officers, noncommissioned officers, and other ranks that did not benefit from the Musharraf government's favors to the military.

The army's highest priority is counterterrorism and counterinsurgency operations; therefore, its top brass is not expected to knock out civilian rulers in the near future. They are cognizant of the problems of the state and society outlined here, which force them to avoid direct assumption of power. Their preference is to improve their image inside and outside Pakistan and to protect and promote their professional and corporate interests from the sidelines.

The experience of last three years shows that the top brass gave enough space to the civilian leadership in governance and security policy management. After the 2008 election, they looked to the civilian leadership to provide policy guidelines. Meetings between the president, prime minister, and the army chief take place quite frequently. However, the civilian government has found it difficult to provide leadership for two main reasons.

First, lack of confidence and professionalism are the major obstacles to the civilian government in assuming a leadership role in the security and foreign policy domains. There are hardly any professionals in the government dealing with security- and terrorism-related issues. Most of the time, the political leadership does not come up with a well-thought-out discourse on internal and external security. Civilian leaders invariably engage in rhetoric on security issues and examine those issues, including terrorism, in a highly partisan manner; they prefer to rely on the army for professional advice. There have been more security-related briefings by the army and intelligence top brass to the federal government and the Parliament than ever in the past.

Second, while the military expects the civilian leadership to provide policy guidelines, the military's top brass is not giving the latter a free hand. There are certain policy areas where they accept no civilian interference; in the case of other issues, the top brass favors shared decisionmaking, albeit with the military having the stronger role.

The top brass is opposed to civilian interference in its internal organizational matters, including appointments, promotions, transfers, and postings, and in its commercial and business activities. They think that civilian interference in these matters undermines the military's discipline and professionalism. The policy areas in which they prefer shared civilian-military decisionmaking rather than having civilians decide matters unilaterally include defense expenditures, service conditions, perks and privileges, and the key foreign policy and security issues such as India (including Kashmir), Afghanistan, military-related affairs with the United States, weapons procurement, and nuclear policy. Civilians are not expected to exclude the top brass from policymaking in these areas.

The military also resists civilian efforts to weaken the army chief's role in managing the affairs of the Inter-Services Intelligence Directorate (ISI), although its director general is appointed by the prime minister on the recommendation of the army chief. Another domain where the military has acquired reasonable autonomy is counterterrorism and counterinsurgency operations. The key policy decisions are made jointly by the civilian and military leadership, and the military wants civilian political leaders to build political support for counterterrorism activities. However, actual security operations and related activities are the exclusive concern of the military.[22]

The key concern is the disposition of the military toward civilian affairs and governance if the political and economic situation continues to deteriorate in the future. Several difficult situations may arise: the current degeneration of the political process may continue unabated and state institutions may be unable to perform their basic functions; Pakistan's economy may stumble further because of internal mismanagement or the absence of internal support; socio-cultural and political conflicts and political revolts and insurgencies may cause a total breakdown of the state system in large parts of the country.

There are two other negative scenarios for the future. One concerns open conflict between the overactive Supreme Court and the federal government that leads the opposition parties to launch street protests against the government and in favor of the Supreme Court. Some opposition parties, including the PML-N, have hinted at supporting the Supreme Court in the event of a government–Supreme Court conflict. That would be a highly destabilizing development.

Another issue of concern relates to political and administrative follow-up to military operations in Swat/Malakand, South Waziristan, and other tribal areas and rehabilitation of the internally displaced people. Civilian authorities have hitherto shown limited capacity to undertake administrative, security, rehabilitation, and reconstruction responsibilities, making it difficult for the army to withdraw its personnel from the areas cleared of the Taliban and other militants. If the capacity and performance of civilian authorities remains far below expectations, that can become an irritant in civil-military relations.

The strains and tensions caused by such situations would have far-reaching implications for the future of democracy and the nature of civil-military relations. The military has several options to affect the weak and divided civilian institutions and processes. One, it can publicly support a weak and divided government, thus enabling it to gain the confidence to take the political and administrative initiative and assert its authority. That would also send a message to the opposition groups that the military wants the government to stay on, at least for the time being. Another option is to build pressure on the government, either by making its displeasure known on policy matters or forcing it to change its policies. Still another is to displace the government by bringing in a new combination of political leaders.

The military will continue to function as an autonomous political player, building alignments with civilian leaders from time to time but not seeking a permanent arrangement with a particular political leader or group. It will make and break partnerships with civilians in keeping with its professional and corporate interests.

It can pursue its political agenda through Inter-Services Intelligence and Military Intelligence (MI). For example, it viewed the direct references to the military and the intelligence agencies in the Kerry-Lugar bill (September-October 2009) as a deliberate attempt by the Pakistan government to interfere in its internal organizational and service matters. It invoked the ISI links with the political right and the media to launch a massive campaign against the proposed law. The PML-N adopted a tough stand against the Kerry-Lugar bill after the Punjab chief minister and the leader of the opposition in the National Assembly met with the army chief in the last week of September 2009. The military thus demonstrated its capacity to exert pressure on the civilian government through the intelligence agencies.

The military's capacity to support some factions and put pressure on others is expected to become crucial if the confrontation between the executive and the Supreme Court reaches the breaking point. If the Supreme Court decides to reprimand the civilian government, the government will not be able to resist without the backing of the military. If the top brass of the military decide to back the Supreme Court, the civilian government is likely to collapse.

The military can impose a government of its choice if internal chaos paralyzes the existing government. The military may also decide to assume power directly as a last resort to salvage the collapsing state and society. That may happen if various crises threaten the state system, society is highly factionalized on various counts, and internal violence intensifies when various terrorist outfits and armed groups attempt to overwhelm the state and society. The military's direct role in governance and politics will be facilitated if large sections of politically active circles in urban centers become indifferent to the military's direct political role or support it against a backdrop of decay of civilian governance and political management.

However, much will depend on the internal state of affairs in the army. How far will it continue to insulate itself from societal polarization and religious cleavages? Some evidence suggests that subtle sympathy for Islamic militancy exists in the lower echelons of the army and the intelligence agencies. If some of the divisive trends that characterize society penetrate the military, its internal coherence may be adversely affected, compromising its ability to undertake a swift and peaceful takeover of the state apparatus. This issue is becoming increasingly important because the army's recruitment pool is expanding in terms of area, ethnicity, and orientation of new recruits. Education and socialization within the army have thus gained greater importance for promoting internal coherence, discipline, and professionalism. Further, the military's direct intervention is discouraged by the proliferation of civil society social and political groups and organizations, political activism, and complex socioeconomic forces. In future coups—if any—the top brass will have to take into account more factors to ensure a swift, orderly, and gentle takeover.

Concluding Observations

Pakistan is slowly drifting toward greater political and social fragmentation. Most threats to its future are internal, the result of the sharpening of multiple fault lines, a weak and dispirited civilian leadership, an overconfident superior judiciary bent on establishing its superiority over the elected executive and legislature, and the threat of religious extremism and militancy. Pakistani society is more fragmented than ever before, and the economy is unable to develop enough resources internally to sustain the state system. If these trends continue, Pakistan may lose efficacy and become a nonperforming state in most sectors of society.

If left alone by the international community, the Pakistani state may go under. If it does, the negative ramifications will extend far beyond its territorial borders. However, if the international community can devote resources to human and social development, focusing mainly on education, health care, and economic development that benefits the common person, the situation may be salvaged. Unlike a number of African states, Pakistan has sufficient educated, highly trained human resources, and its institutions, such as the bureaucracy and the military, continue to function effectively. Some sectors of the economy, such as communications, information technology, and several scientific and technical fields, also continue to do well. Agriculture has much potential. If immediate attention is given to these areas, Pakistan can be pulled back from the brink.

This calls for a thorough review of Pakistan's current political and security profile. Pakistan needs to learn to live in peace with itself and improve its relations with neighboring states, especially India, to ensure peace and stability at its borders. It should also seek to relax relations with Afghanistan.

Pakistan needs to look inward in order to promote internal political harmony and stability, strengthen the economy, and create a knowledge-based rather than a religious belief–based society. All is not lost in the case of Pakistan; there is some hope left. Can Pakistani leaders and the international community work together to pull back Pakistan from the brink?

Notes

1. K. Sarwar Hasan, *The Transfer of Power* (Karachi: Pakistan Institute of International Affairs, 1966), p. 261.

2. Abdul Kalam Azad, *India Wins Freedom* (Calcutta: Orient Longmans, 1959), p. 207.

3. Keith Callard, *Pakistan: A Political Study* (London: George Allen & Unwin, 1957), p. 14.

4. Tariq Ali, *Pakistan: Military Rule or People's Power* (New York: William Morrow, 1970), pp. 243–44.

5. Tariq Ali, *Can Pakistan Survive? The Death of a State* (Harmondsworth, Middlesex, UK: Penguin Books, 1983), pp. 9–10.

6. Ibid., p.161.

7. Robert D. Kaplan, "The Coming Anarchy," *Atlantic Quarterly,* February 1994, pp. 44–76.

8. Ibid.

9. Robert Chase, Emily Hill, and Paul Kennedy, *The Pivotal States: A New Framework for U.S. Policy in the Developing World* (New York: W.W. Norton, 1999), pp. 1–11.

10. Hasan Askari Rizvi, "Pakistan," in *The Pivotal States*, edited by Chase, Hill, and Kennedy, pp. 64–87.

11. Stephen P. Cohen, *The Idea of Pakistan* (Lahore: Vanguard Books, 2005), p. 296.

12. Ibid., p. 297.

13. Ibid., pp. 291–92.

14. Khaled Ahmed, "Three Terminal Narratives of Pakistan," *Friday Times* [Lahore], July 16–24, 2008, p. 8.

15. Ibid.

16. *Daily Times* [Lahore], January 26, 2010.

17. Hasan Askari Rizvi, "The Political Class and Democracy," *Daily Times* [Lahore], December 1, 2009.

18. Hasan Askari Rizvi, "Towards Instability?" *Friday Times* [Lahore], April 23–29, 2010, p. 2.

19. Hajrah Mumtaz, "Reforming the Unrepentant," *Dawn* [Karachi], January 10, 2010.

20. See the editorial "Jehadi Infrastructure," *Dawn*, May 12, 2010. See also Zahid Hussain, *Frontline Pakistan: The Struggle with Militant Islam* (Columbia University Press, 2007), pp. 89–101.

21. See Umer Farooq, "Operation Image Restoration," *Herald* [Karachi], May 2010, pp. 43–45.

22. Speaking at a public meeting in Swat, Prime Minister Yousaf Raza Gilani said that the government would not "bow down to extremism and terrorism" and that it would launch military operation "anywhere that served as a safe haven for terrorists." He also declared that the army chief would decide about the military operation in North Waziristan. *Daily Times* [Lahore], May 30, 2010.

AQIL SHAH

12

Security, Soldiers, and the State

Social scientists consider themselves lucky when they can adequately explain an important social phenomenon ex post facto. Crystal-balling the future, however, is a perilous undertaking, not least because it involves making somewhat static extrapolations from a highly dynamic social world that often unfolds contingently and without much forewarning. Any forecasting of the future can at best be a cautiously probabilistic estimate, subject to history's many twists and turns.

The question that this chapter seeks to answer calls for such peeping into the future: what will Pakistan look like in five to seven years? It is safe to argue that it will probably become neither Sweden nor Somalia. But given history's sticky footprints and barring any tectonic economic or political shifts, Pakistan is unlikely to extricate itself from its "path dependent" pattern of tolerating a gross imbalance of power between the military and civilians.[1] This imbalance is an enduring legacy of the country's birth as a ramshackle postcolonial state under conditions of warfare and territorial conflict with a politically and militarily stronger neighbor, India. Those initial conditions drastically empowered the military relative to civilian political institutions, enabling it to achieve autonomy from the civilian government and to dominate national security policymaking. Over time, the military has developed both an institutional culture legitimizing its intervention in, influence on, and control of the state and a vested corporate interest in maintaining its dominance. The military's political power has been reinforced by successive strategic alliances between Pakistan and the United States, which have provided the generals with military assistance, financial largesse, and diplomatic support. The result: a powerful and autonomous military that not only "defends society" but "defines it."[2]

Since independence in 1947, Pakistan has cycled between civilian and military regimes of an almost predictable duration with an almost predictable frequency. The country has yet to experience a peaceful and democratic transition of power from one civilian government to another. In fact, Pakistan is one of the few countries in the world where the military continues to defy democratic civilian control and where military intervention is still a plausible, if not widely considered legitimate, mechanism of regime change. If anything, Pakistan's particular political trajectory exhibits the effect of path dependence with a vengeance. The lesson is clear: unless the state's institutional configuration is set right at the outset of statehood, changing or reversing course can be quite difficult at a later stage. But history is not destiny, and a confluence of human agency and structural change has disrupted seemingly entrenched legacies of the past in many states across Asia, Africa, and Latin America. Pakistan is not condemned to repeat its past, even though its future looks quite bleak at present. Like many other states, Pakistan too might take a future path quite different from those indicated by typical prognostications, a possibility that I explore in the discussion that follows.

An Out-of-Control Military

At present, Pakistan's domestic economic, developmental, and political problems are undoubtedly many and enormous. An economy trapped in a cycle of debt and deficits, a rapidly growing population, a low literacy rate, chronic energy shortages, and pernicious levels of poverty—to name a few of its economic-developmental woes—are interwoven with and complicated by the fragility of the state, which is afflicted by internal challenges to its monopoly on the means of legitimate coercion. Its transnational interactions (Afghanistan-Pakistan, India-Pakistan, United States–Pakistan) are complex and fraught with consequences for its domestic stability and international security.

But running through both the domestic and foreign dimensions of Pakistan's past, present, and future is one connecting factor: an out-of-(civilian)-control army. Civil-military relations are not just one of many "structural problems" faced by Pakistan.[3] In fact, civil-military relations are central to and inseparable from center-province relations, ethno-regional conflict, internal political stability, Islamist influence in the polity, the prospects of warfare with India, nuclear security and proliferation, and regional and global terrorism.

It would be an understatement to say that Pakistan's current predicament and future options cannot be adequately understood without recognizing the influence, motivations, and norms of the army, an institution that has directly ruled the country for thirty-three years and unrightfully exercised behind-the-scenes influence and vetoes over key national security and foreign policy areas in most of the other years. The military also consumes a lion's share of unaccounted-for expenditures, which not only are wasteful but also divert precious resources from socioeconomic development. The military is thus both unaccountable to Pakistanis and unaffordable for Pakistan. Space constraints prevent any lengthy treatment of the military institution in this chapter.[4] Suffice it to pose a counterfactual: had the Pakistan army been under democratic-civilian control, might Pakistan and its neighborhood have been a different place? Given that civilian control of the military is a necessary condition for democratic rule and democratic dyads rarely fight each other, it would be reasonable to answer that question in the affirmative.

Will the military continue to behave badly? The military staged a voluntary extrication of itself from power in 2008, and subsequently the generals took a number of steps to signal their intent to stay out of civilian politics. Under Chief of Staff General Ashfaq Pervez Kayani, who replaced Musharraf in that post in November 2007, the military remained more or less politically neutral during and after the 2008 elections. The army high command reportedly disbarred officers from meeting politicians and closed down the notorious "political cell" of the Inter-Services Intelligence Directorate (ISI) tasked with "political management." General Kayani also ordered the withdrawal of hundreds of active-duty army officers whom Musharraf had placed in the civilian bureaucracy.

But appearances can be deceptive. If the past is any guide, the Pakistani military's disengagement from power does not necessarily mean its exit from politics. Given the deadweight of institutional habits, the military's behavior is more likely to mimic the "garbage can" model of bureaucratic behavior, which posits that hierarchical organizations tend to respond to changed conditions or the need for adjustments to their policies by employing a set of learned and routinized responses rather than looking for alternatives.[5]

At Least Three Futures

Pakistan's long-term stability and that of the surrounding region rests in good measure on a democratic pattern of civil-military relations, meaning a military that is subordinate to civilian politicians and politically neutral. So, what might the future of civil-military relations look like? There are at least three possible future outcomes: an unstable hybrid regime; a stable democracy; and an unstable military autocracy.[6]

Unstable Hybrid Regime

The first future for Pakistan would be a "freezing" of the political system in the intermediate, gray zone between full-fledged democracy and military autocracy. While exerting sustained civilian control over the military poses a formidable challenge for any transitional democracy, the coalition government led by the Pakistan People's Party (PPP) faces the additional burden of resolving a complex array of economic, political, and security challenges, most of which are immediate legacies of Musharraf's military authoritarian rule. In this scenario, in which the civilian government is responsible for and under pressure to squarely tackle multiple problems, including a tottering economy and the menacing threat of terrorism, the military will be happy to operate in the shadows while civilians nominally reign.

It is this latent military power that will likely make the consolidation of democracy difficult. New, emerging centers of power, such as the assertive higher judiciary, could exert countervailing pressures to deepen democracy and help ensure the rule of law. Given the renewed moral and legal authority that it acquired after the restoration of Chief Justice Iftikhar Chaudhry and other judges who had defied the Musharraf regime,[7] the judiciary is in an especially auspicious position to counterbalance the other branches of the government, including the military. However, in the absence of agreed rules of the game for resolving political and constitutional conflicts, an activist court can also easily become an independent source of political instability. While the Supreme Court has typically avoided offending the military for fear of defiance and/or reprisal, it has kept the civilian government on a short leash and doggedly encroached on executive functions—from fixing basic commodity prices to hiring and firing civilian officials.

The Court is also developing the habit of "legislating from the bench," most glaringly reflected in at least two cases: first, in its obstruction of constitutional amendments reducing the powers of the chief justice in appointing senior judges and subjecting judicial appointments to approval by a parliamentary committee; second, in its quashing of the National Reconciliation Ordinance (indemnity law), which opened the way for its zealous pursuit of corruption cases against President Asif Ali Zardari. This ongoing skirmishing between the executive and judiciary could culminate in an institutional showdown between them, one that might open the door for another military mediation of civilian crises.[8] But beyond the danger of civilian institutional clashes, deteriorating economic conditions and increasing lawlessness and ethnic violence in Pakistan's commercial hub, the port city of Karachi, could provide the military an additional opportunity for a limited political incursion.[9] That would only reinforce the depressingly familiar (but unstable) pattern of civil-military relations in which the military formally stays out of power but stands ever ready to chasten civilians when they fail to meet the generals' exacting expectations for political and economic performance.

Stable Democracy

A second possible future is the slow and steady stabilization of democracy. Consolidating democratic procedures and practices is at best an uncertain process, one that might degenerate especially if an anti-system group or institution mobilizes sufficient resources against it.[10] In the medium term, one of its necessary, if not sufficient, conditions will be at least two or more peaceful turnovers of power following relatively free and fair elections.[11] The gradual "routinization" of elections as the only legitimate mechanism of regime change will help make democracy the only game in town and limit the scope for military political intervention.The prospects of democratization will hinge on the behavior and attitudes of several politically significant actors, including political parties, the middle classes, and the military.

Political Parties. Democratic consolidation will require political parties to perform the intermediary role of linking state and society through public interest aggregation and representation. Pakistan's two main parties, the ruling PPP and the Pakistan Muslim League–Nawaz (PML-N), are under-institutionalized and may even be akin to unreconstructed "family fiefdoms."[12] But party system weaknesses are not so much the cause of Pakistan's democratic weakness as they are a symptom of the military's sustained and systematic short-circuiting of the process of competitive politics. Ironically, the hold of the Bhuttos over the PPP and of the Sharifs over the PML-N may be one of the main reasons that these parties have survived the military's divide-and-rule repression and may consolidate democracy in the future.

There are other reasons to be hopeful about the future of democracy. Pakistan's three-year-old Parliament has removed military-era prerogatives—such as the infamous Article 58(2)B, which empowered the president to arbitrarily dismiss an elected government—from the Constitution; abolished the concurrent legislative list, which includes subjects on which both the Parliament and provincial assemblies can enact legislation, thereby passing exclusive control of federally run ministries (such as those for education, food and agriculture, labor, and minority affairs) to the provinces; enhanced provincial authority to collect revenues; and created parliamentary committees for appointing top judicial and election officials. The government has also raised the provinces' share of resources in the federal revenue pool through the Seventh National Finance Commission Award.

By and large, the two main parties have lived up to the pledge, made in the Charter of Democracy signed by the late Benazir Bhutto and Nawaz Sharif in 2006, that they would not use extra-constitutional methods to acquire power. They appear to have learned from experience that their zero-sum rivalry in the 1990s played into the hands of the military. The real question is whether the two parties will continue to play the democratic game. While their coalition at the center proved transitory, they were able to sustain a coalition in the Punjab for almost three years. But in February 2011, the PML-N expelled the PPP from the provincial cabinet, ostensibly due to the PPP-led federal government's failure to implement governance reforms (including the reduction of government expenditures, enactment of new accountability laws, and removal of corrupt officials). More worryingly, it seems that the PML-N, or at least powerful elements within it, are getting impatient and are ready to "knock on the garrison's doors" to oust the PPP government and pave the way for snap elections.[13] But goading the generals for partisan ends is fraught with danger. The military trusts neither party's leadership, so a PML-N victory at the polls does not mean that the generals will treat its government any differently.[14] The lesson is straightforward: unless the politicians show a unified commitment to the democratic process and tolerate their opponents in office, the military will always find the opportunity to deceive, divide, and dominate them.

How will democracy shape the behavior of the Islamist parties? It will likely blunt their potential to act as democratic "spoilers"—that is, to use democratic means to capture power and then disband democracy, an oft-expressed concern of democratic skeptics, especially outside Pakistan. If the past is any guide, this much-dreaded "one man, one vote, once" scenario is unlikely to materialize in Pakistan. And while, on average, Islamist parties perform better in elections in Pakistan than in other Muslim-majority countries,[15] their disproportionate leverage over politics and policymaking is linked more to their mutually beneficial ties with the military than to their mass following.[16] For instance, their electoral success in the 2002 elections was a direct result of military electoral manipulation and repression of more moderate political parties, not a resounding public rejection of the latter.[17] When the two main parties contest elections without authoritarian restrictions, the Islamists are sidelined. Twice, once in 1970, and again in 1997, non-Islamist parties have electorally stalled the Islamists. And while the Jamaat-e-Islami boycotted the most recent ballot in 2008, even the relatively more successful Jamiat Ulema-e-Islam–Fazl-ur-Rehman (JUI-F) won only 6 of the 108 national assembly seats that it contested.

What about their "illiberal" influence as pressure groups within a democratic framework? The traditional hold of the PML-N and the PPP in the largest province of Punjab (and of the PPP in rural Sindh) and the vote banks of regional, ethnic parties—for instance, the Muttahida Qaumi Movement (MQM) in urban Sindh and the Awami National Party in Khyber Pakhtunkhwa—can act as a barrier against disproportionate extremist influence on legislation relating to women's rights, minorities, and so forth. But the Islamists have a major political stake in protecting heinous religious laws already in the statutes, such as those that prohibit and punish blasphemy, and they have the capacity to mobilize street mobs against their reform or repeal. In other words, the Islamists wield political influence far in excess of their popular following, and that is primarily because of military patronage. For instance, the existing illiberal laws are not the expression of the popular will but the outcome of autocratic fiat underwritten by a pact between the military and the mullahs in the 1980s.

Democratic Middle Classes? What about the role of social classes? For instance, will the urban middle class act as an agent of democratization? The logic behind the middle class as democracy's cheerleader is that it stands to benefit from trade with India, which would entail greater civilian control over bilateral relations and domestic resources.[18] First, that assertion is rooted in the Eurocentric and historically inaccurate view of "no bourgeoisie, no democracy."[19] There is no inherent connection between an urban middle class and pressure for democracy. Rarely unified or motivated by collective social interests, the middle classes across Asia (for example, in Indonesia under Suharto and in present-day Thailand) and Latin America have shown themselves to be quite capable of backing illegitimate autocratic governments for their narrow economic and material interests. Pakistan, where the middle classes appear to have a historically low threshold of tolerance for "corrupt" politicians and a preference for order rather than democracy per se, has been no exception. Moreover, any prospective material benefits of trade with India will not necessarily accrue to a particular class; they could easily be counteracted by the anti-India psychosis that permeates popular media and the public education system, in which the middle class tends to be schooled.

At the societal level, the real issue is not merely whether this or that class champions democracy but whether there is broad-based public support and attachment to the practice and institutions of democratic rule. But democracy does not necessarily need natural-born democrats, and the causal chain can also run in the opposite direction. Democracy can create democrats.

Professional Praetorians and Ways to Control Them. Ultimately, democratic institutionalization will require more than balancing just the civilian side of the equation. It will also require a military committed both "behaviorally" and "attitudinally" to a subordinate role in a democratic framework.[20] The military's changed behavior in the immediate post-transition period could easily be interpreted as a shift from military politicization under Musharraf to military professionalism under General Kayani. But the Pakistani army's problem has never been "professionalism" per se. Rather, it is a particular brand of tutelary professionalism that gives it a sense of both entitlement over the polity and superiority over civilians. It is this misguided but deeply rooted cult of guardianship that leads it to believe that it can govern the country far more efficiently than "corrupt" politicians.[21]

More specifically, democracy is unlikely to become "the only game in town" if the military withdraws from power but considers itself above the rule of law and believes in its right to take actions independently of the duly constituted civilian government. Both supra-legality and relative autonomy continue to shape military behavior: consider the army's not-so-covert attempts to protect military officers from scrutiny in the Benazir Bhutto murder case and its "democratically" objectionable public reaction to the Kerry-Lugar-Berman bill (declaring it a threat to national security) despite the civilian government's acceptance of the aid proposed in the bill.

At a minimum, a democracy needs an elite consensus on procedures, including free and fair elections, and a civilian government free of unconstitutional and unaccountable veto powers over its authority. Pakistan appears to be meeting the first condition; there is an evolving civilian elite consensus on a federal parliamentary democracy as the most appropriate form of government for Pakistan. But can civilian politicians reverse the military's prerogatives and establish civilian supremacy in the near future?

The scholarly literature on civil-military relations identifies at least three ways of achieving civilian control of the military: institutions, interests, and ideas.[22] First, strong institutional rules and channels (legislative oversight, civilian-controlled ministry of defense, and the like) can induce military subordination by enforcing sanctions for irregular behavior. Second, satisfying military corporate interests by providing adequate resources and allowing legitimate professional autonomy may dissuade the military from meddling in politics. Third, the military may feel obligated to comply with civilian authority because it believes in the norm of civilian supremacy.

How do these mechanisms fare in Pakistan? Saying so risks stating the obvious, but institutions need time and space to develop. Existing channels of civilian oversight are frail because of military intervention and influence, which helps the military place itself above any kind of meaningful reproach or call for accountability. Given military threat perceptions, military interests have rarely gone unheeded in Pakistan. Similarly, civilians have rarely interfered with military autonomy in its internal affairs, except in rightful (if not always deft) control of top-level promotions and appointments. If neither of the two mechanisms works, voluntary military subordination to civil power may be a viable option, one that is typically ignored in the policy and scholarly literature on Pakistan. Military subversion of democratic procedures is much less likely when the military accepts that it is an instrument of the state, subject to the authority of democratically elected representatives. Changes in the military belief system may require either internally led reform or a sustained process of democratization that facilitates positive unlearning of beliefs about the military's role in politics. Neither is likely in the short to medium term.

There is truth to the claim made by some observers of Pakistan that the military's undue political influence is linked to the acquiescence—or worse, collaboration—of civilian groups.[23] But it misses an important point. Militaries may rely on and benefit from the cooperation of sections of civilian society to enhance their domestic power and/or legitimacy, but military power is not the product of their consent. Historically, civilian governments have not failed to extend their authority over the armed forces in any sustained manner because they accept or prefer the military's supra-political role. Instead, many civilian politicians have, in their own self-interest, come to function within the constraints set by "military prerogatives" in defense allocations, foreign and defense policies, and even internal security[24] and to "anticipate that deviations . . . are likely to be counterproductive."[25] Some civilian leaders have vigorously contested such prerogatives (for example, Z. A. Bhutto in the 1970s and Nawaz Sharif in the 1990s) when they had the opportunity. But decisively swift military retaliation against them cast a heavy shadow on future civilian expectations of military institutional behavior.

If the military's influence cannot be eroded in the short to medium term, can it be more positively channeled? One solution favored and peddled by the generals is to "bring the army in to keep it out" through such arrangements as the National Security Council (NSC). The logic is that civil-military integration would prevent the military from going it alone, create the need to achieve a broad civil-military consensus on all important strategic issues, and in the process train civilians in the complex art of defense policymaking. Besides being patently anti-democratic, conceding to the military an institutionalized role in national policymaking has not been a source of stability anywhere, not even in the archetypical model, Turkey. Besides, the main problem in Pakistan's civil-military relations is not the lack of civilian capacity to formulate national security policy, and regularly rubbing shoulders with the military top brass is unlikely to make civilians more capable. That will require, in the first instance, loosening the military's hold over the state rather than tightening it more severely, so that civilians can wield the authority needed to develop the confidence and skills necessary for managing the state's primary coercive apparatus.

Inducing the military to stay away from politics permanently and to submit to civilian control is complicated by the country's complex geopolitical environment and threat perceptions, which historically reinforced the military's political role and continue to provide the basis for its monopolistic influence over national security policy.

Comparatively speaking, one of the most potent mechanisms for eroding the domestic political power of the army is a defeat in war, as in Greece in 1974 after the Turkish invasion of Cyprus and in Argentina in 1982 after the Malvinas/Falklands war. In Pakistan, however, the military's humiliating defeat in the 1971 Bangladesh war was not sufficient to bring about a lasting institutional retrenchment from interference in politics and civilian affairs, in good measure because its defeat (and dismemberment) by India exacerbated Pakistan's security dilemma and made jingoistic nationalism more, not less, politically appealing. Whether another defeat in a war with India (regardless of the nature or extent of such a defeat) would reorient civil-military relations (and with them, military autonomy and expenditures) therefore is unknown. In any case, the potentially devastating presence of nuclear weapons makes war too catastrophic to contemplate. Not war per se, but civil-military conflict over "who governs" war and peace may in fact prompt military intervention (for example, in Kargil in 1999). Defeat on the battlefield could still have the effect of increasing military insecurity and putting a political premium on nationalist demagoguery rather than reorienting the Pakistani state in a civilianized direction.

A negotiated settlement of the conflict with India, which has eluded the two sides for over sixty years, may remove the territorial/nationalist drivers of military leverage over civilians. But vested interests on both sides would rather continue the conflict than upset the status quo, and the international community appears unwilling or unable to break the enduring impasse. There are some indications that the United States sees stabilizing the "Indo-Pak" relationship as a way to redirect Pakistan's military machine to fight Islamist militancy on its western border with Afghanistan. But any serious or sustained effort to engage the two sides in a meaningful, results-oriented effort appears unlikely in the medium term.

In addition, given the internal security challenges emanating from militancy, Pakistan's threat environment is likely to become more, not less, dangerous. In regions like South America, the ouster of the military from power and, crucially, a lasting reduction of military autonomy were linked to the cessation of the internal threats (from insurrectionary communism) that had originally induced the military to turn inward and take control of politics. Hence, depending on how the overlapping external and internal threat environments evolve, the military may have less or more incentive to cede ground to civilians.

Unstable Military Autocracy

The third and most drastic outcome is, of course, a military coup d'état followed by military-led authoritarian rule. Both domestic and international factors may counteract, if not eliminate, this option. At the moment, the "military-as-institution" has little reason to take on the burden of the "military-as-government" because it can get what it wants by exerting its authority from behind the scenes without assuming responsibility for decisionmaking.[26] Consider the immediate reversal of the civilian government's decision to place the ISI under the Interior Ministry in July 2008 and the three-year tenure extension awarded to General Kayani, ostensibly for the sake of "continuity" in the fight against terrorism.

If history is any yardstick, the military usually waits at least a decade or so for the next full-blown intervention, when the memory of its previous intervention has all but faded in the public mind and civilians are sufficiently discredited. In fact, the PPP-led civilian government's perceived incompetence, highlighted during last year's devastating floods, in which the military provided (and was seen as providing) quicker humanitarian relief than the civil authorities, might have already helped it regain the public trust eroded during Musharraf's military rule.

However, public trust in the military does not mean support for military intervention or rule. And Pakistan's "reactivated" civil society (lawyers' associations, human rights groups, and sections of the media) has shown itself to be capable of reversing authoritarian encroachments—for instance, as it did when it took on the Musharraf regime for attacking the judiciary. But directly challenging the generals could become more difficult when the military has concealed its iron fist in the velvet glove of democracy.

If domestic factors do not entirely bind the military, the external costs of military rule may act as an inhibitor. The Kerry-Lugar-Berman bill, passed into law as the Enhanced Partnership with Pakistan Act of 2009, ties the continuation of U.S. aid to both verifiable civilian control over the military and the latter's abstention from politics, conditionality that could help restrain the army's praetorian proclivities. But the threat of external sanctions and even international opprobrium has not dissuaded the army from taking costly autonomous decisions in the past (for example, regarding nuclear proliferation and the 1999 military coup). Moreover, despite its pro-democracy rhetoric,

Washington typically has preferred "order" to "liberty." The long U.S. practice of "getting things done through the generals" means that it is likely to continue to treat the military as a separate entity within the Pakistani state. This geopolitical support reinforces the military's distorted self-image as a globally indispensable force in possession of a strategic piece of territory that it can leverage to gain domestic and external influence. In fact, the United States has funneled untraceable funds through under-the-table deals to the ISI, a process that undercuts the civilian-led state and erodes the rule of law, both of which are crucial to fighting terrorism and militancy in the medium to long run.[27] A classic example of this covert dealing is the sudden release of the CIA contractor Raymond Davis by a local court less than two months after he fatally shot two Pakistanis in Lahore in January 2011. Davis was exonerated of murder charges in exchange for "blood money" paid to the families of the victims. The release was orchestrated by the ISI reportedly after the CIA agreed to limit its spy operations inside Pakistan.[28]

The episode strained the CIA-ISI relationship, which reached a new low after the May 2, 2011, U.S. raid in which Osama bin Laden was killed. The raid—which was carried out, ostensibly without the knowledge of the Pakistan military, on Pakistani territory (and in the garrison town of Abbottabad, some 70 miles from the capital, Islamabad)—humiliated the generals. Either way, whether bin Laden was able to find sanctuary in Pakistan due to military incompetence or connivance, the military's carefully constructed myth of invincibility was at least temporarily shattered. Increased domestic criticism and calls for military accountability seemingly provided a "window of opportunity" for bringing the military under greater democratic scrutiny. But entrenched institutional arrangements can be hard to break. The military deftly diffused some of the negative attention from itself through the use of both carrots and sticks. For instance, the generals agreed to go through the motions of accountability by presenting themselves before Parliament in an "in camera" briefing. At the same time, they decided to signal to the media and others in civil society that criticizing or exposing military ineptitude or collusion with militants would have high costs. That was amply demonstrated in the alleged abduction, torture, and murder of the maverick journalist Saleem Shehzad, who had exposed al Qaeda's infiltration of the Pakistan navy in the wake of a daring militant attack in May 2011 on an important naval base in Karachi.[29] The raid, apparently carried out with "insider help" deeply embarrassed the military once again, this time for failing to dislodge a handful of terrorists from a vital military installation for almost a day.

Given the military's current less-than-stellar public standing, a blunt military coup may not be a feasible option for the high command. But as noted above, given the military's entrenched praetorian norms and interests, some form of authoritarian backsliding with at least a hidden hand from the generals cannot be ruled out, especially if civilian institutions (like the judiciary and the executive) were to openly clash or if economic and internal security conditions were to reach (or be seen by the generals as reaching) crisis proportions. In fact, the military's civilian proponents have been advocating a "soft coup" as in Bangladesh circa 2006–08. In January 2007, the Bangladeshi army intervened to suspend an increasingly violent competitive political process and installed a technocratic front regime to carry out radical reforms. But the generals had to retreat to the barracks within two years because they failed to "cleanse" politics and could not offer a credible political alternative to the country's two traditional political parties, the center-left liberal Awami League of Sheikh Hasina and the center-right Bangladesh National Party, headed by Khaleda Zia. In other words, the failed Bangladesh experiment is a cautionary tale, not a model to emulate.

Conclusion

Pakistan is not condemned to repeat its past. But the medium-term course is most likely to be more of the same, not internal fracturing or spectacular stability. In the likely absence of a sustainable solution to the decades-long Indo-Pak territorial rivalry, Pakistan's India-focused security concerns will continue to provide a powerful driver for its geopolitical behavior, including its not-so-deniable support to radical Islamist groups in Afghanistan. The threat from Islamist militancy inside Pakistan, which by default implies more, not less, military influence over national security policy, is likely to further reinforce the pathologies of civil-military relations.

At the level of domestic politics, Pakistan is likely to remain a formally civilian-led regime governing under the watchful eye (and elbow) of a politically influential and autonomous military. Crucial to the country's longer-term political and economic stability will be the evolving commitment of both civilian and military actors to play by the "rules of the game." While civilians need to keep their own house in order, the persistent trend of recurring military regimes has habituated the military to professional norms and prerogatives that are ill-suited to consolidation of democratic institutions. Those norms will have to undergo sustained erosion and the military brought under firm democratic civilian control if democracy is to be put on a firm footing.

In addition to factors like favorable geopolitical and threat environments, a sustained process of democratization might induce the military to stay away from politics. But democratization itself is an uncertain process, fraught with the threat of erosion and reversal. Even if democratic procedures and conventions consolidate and the military threat to civil supremacy is thwarted, democracy is not a panacea for the economic and political problems that afflict Pakistan. However, it is a first and necessary step in the right direction, without which Pakistan is more likely to remain stuck in a vicious trap of political and economic instability, erratically lurching from unstable democracy to unstable authoritarianism and back.

Notes

1. "Path-dependent" means that institutional change is constrained by past choices and structures. Once a country embarks on a certain institutional path, reversal can become difficult due to a variety of reproduction mechanisms, such as powerful interests wedded to its continuity. For a good review of the concept and its applications to politics, see Kathleen Thelen, "Historical Institutionalism in Comparative Politics," *Annual Review of Political Science* 2 (1999), pp. 369–404. See also Paul Pierson, "Increasing Returns, Path Dependence and the Study of Politics," *American Political Science Review*, vol. 98, no. 4 (2000), pp. 251–267.

2. Richard Kohn, "How Democracies Control the Military," *Journal of Democracy,* vol. 8, no. 4 (October 1997), p. 142.

3. Jonathan Paris, *Prospects for Pakistan* (London: Legatum Institute, 2010), p. 6.

4. I discuss the institutional foundations of military politics and intervention in my forthcoming book, *Out of Control: The Pakistan Military and Politics in Historical and Regional Perspective.* Existing scholarly accounts of civil-military relations in Pakistan include Saeed Shafqat, *Civil-Military Relations in Pakistan: From Zulfiqar Ali Bhutto to Benazir Bhutto* (Westview Press, 1997); Hasan Askari Rizvi, *The Military and Politics in Pakistan: 1947–1997* (Lahore: Sange Meel, 2000); and Mazhar Aziz, *Military Control in Pakistan: The Parallel State* (London: Routledge, 2007).

5. See Michael Cohen and others, "A Garbage Can Model of Organizational Choice," *Administrative Science Quarterly* (1972), pp. 1–25.

6. The following discussion draws on but contests and extends Jonathan Paris's discussion of civil-military issues.

7. Justice Chaudhry was sacked and put under house arrest by General Musharraf in March 2007 for his refusal to obey the military regime's commands. He was finally restored to office in 2009 by the current PPP government after a military mediation spurred by the lawyer-led civil society movement.

8. Amid intensified tensions between the Supreme Court and the PPP-led government in 2010, the Court was reportedly considering the option available to it under Article 190 of the Constitution, which makes it incumbent upon state institutions (in this case, a thinly veiled reference to the military) to implement the Court's decision. But according to media reports, the military rebuffed the Court, indicating the high

command's reluctance to take sides in the duels between the executive and the judiciary. Tariq Butt and Usman Manzoor, "SC Says Article 190 Is Mandatory," *The News* [Rawalpindi], February 10, 2010.

9. The generals have already expressed in a press communiqué their impatience with the civilian government's apparent inability to restore law and order. The message was clear: "Clean up the mess, or we will be forced to do it ourselves." See "Corps Commanders Concerned over Karachi Situation," *Dawn* [Karachi], August 22, 2011.

10. Guillermo O'Donnell, "Illusions about Consolidation," *Journal of Democracy*, vol. 7, no. 2 (1996), pp. 34–51.

11. At a minimum, democratic consolidation requires a country to pass the "two-turnover test," which indicates that political leaders and parties are sufficiently committed to democracy to surrender office peacefully. See Samuel Huntington, *The Third Wave: Democratization in the Late Twentieth Century* (University of Oklahoma Press, 1993), p. 267.

12. Paris, "Prospects for Pakistan," p. 6.

13. Party president and Punjab chief minister Shahbaz Sharif's call for including the military (and the judiciary) in a proposed all-parties' conference to tackle Pakistan's multiple crises was seen by many observers as an indication of the party's permissive attitude to a temporary intervention. See, for instance, "Call for Intervention," *Dawn* [Karachi], March 9, 2011.

14. Leaked U.S. diplomatic cables show that the army chief of staff, General Kayani, and his corps commanders distrust Nawaz Sharif even more than President Asif Ali Zardari. In fact, in March 2009, when Kayani was planning to oust Zardari in order to prevent a showdown between the government and the Sharif-led protest movement over the reinstatement of judges fired by General Musharraf, he planned to keep the government of prime minister Yousaf Raza Gilani in place to avoid a new election that would likely bring Sharif to power. See cable sent by U.S. ambassador Anne W. Patterson, "Little Movement on Reconciliation," March 12, 2009 (www.guardian.co.uk/world/us-embassy-cables-documents/196412 [March 30, 2010].

15. Charles Kurzman and Ijlal Naqvi, "Do Muslims Vote Islamic?" *Journal of Democracy* (April 2010), pp. 50–63.

16. See Hussein Haqqani, *Pakistan: Between Mosque and Military* (Carnegie Endowment, 2005). See also Vali Nasr, "Military Rule, Islamism, and Democracy," *Middle East Journal* (Spring 2004), pp. 195–209.

17. See Aqil Shah, "Pakistan's 'Armored' Democracy," *Journal of Democracy*, vol. 14, no. 4 (October 2003), pp. 26–40.

18. Paris, *Prospects for Pakistan*, p. 25.

19. Barrington Moore Jr., *Lord and the Peasant: Social Origins of Dictatorship and Democracy* (Beacon Press, 1966), p. 418. While the phrase is Moore's, his own analysis is much more complex than it suggests. In general, however, the bourgeoisie-liberalism-democracy teleology has trouble accounting for the role of authoritarian state actors in fragmenting and depoliticizing the bourgeoisie.

20. On the "attitudinal" and "behavioral" dimensions of democratic consolidation, see Juan Linz and Alfred Stepan, *Problems of Democratic Transition and Consolidation* (Johns Hopkins University Press, 1996).

21. This observation is based on my doctoral dissertation research, which included interviews with several dozen (mostly former) senior and mid-level military officers in 2006–09, analysis of military writings, and archival research in and outside Pakistan.

22. For a concise discussion of these three approaches, see "Introduction," in *Civil-Military Relations in Latin America*, edited by David Pion-Berlin (University of North Carolina Press, 2001), pp. 1–35. The seminal work focusing on the ethic of military professionalism and to a lesser degree on civilian institutions to ensure civilian control of the military is Samuel Huntington, *The Soldier and the State: The Theory and Politics of Civil-Military Relations* (Belknap Press of Harvard, 1957), especially pp. 80–87. Samuel E. Finer emphasizes the military's internalization of the norm of civilian supremacy, rather than generic professionalism, as a check on its intervention in politics in his classic, *The Man on Horseback: The Role of the Military in Politics* (London: Pall Mall, 1962), pp. 25–32.

23. See, for instance, Christine Fair, chapter 4 in this volume.

24. Military prerogatives are areas "where, whether challenged or not, the military as an institution assumes they have an acquired right or privilege, formal or informal, to exercise effective control over internal governance, to play a role within extra-military areas within the state apparatus, or even to structure relationships between state and political or civil society." See Alfred Stepan, *Rethinking Military Politics: Brazil and the Southern Cone* (Princeton University Press, 1988), p. 93.

25. Guillermo O'Donnell, "Delegative Democracy," Working Paper 172, Kellogg Institute for International Studies, Notre Dame University, March 1992, p. 7.

26. The government-institution distinction in the military is Stepan's. See his *Rethinking Military Politics*, pp. 30–32.

27. The CIA reportedly has given the ISI funds that equal up to one-third of the agency's budget as well as hundreds of millions of dollars in "bounty" money for the capture of wanted al Qaeda militants. See Greg Miller, "CIA Pays for Support in Pakistan," *Los Angeles Times*, November 15, 2009.

28. See Chris Allbritton, "ISI Gains Most from CIA Contractor's Release," Reuters, March 17, 2011.

29. Elisabeth Bumiller, "U.S. Admiral Ties Pakistan to Killing of Journalist," *New York Times*, July 7, 2011.

HILARY SYNNOTT

13

Looking at the Crystal Ball

It is a mistake to look too far ahead. The chain of destiny can only be grasped one link at a time.

—Winston Churchill

It is a truism that there can be no adequate understanding of Pakistan without a knowledge of its past. If that is true of the present, it must also be true of any attempt to look into the future. But where in Pakistan's complex historical narrative should one make a start?

Perhaps in the period of the great movement toward politicized religion led by Zia ul-Haq, so effectively supported by the CIA, in the 1980s? This would encompass two of Pakistan's four experiences of military rule, the to-ing and fro-ing of elected but scarcely democratic governments, the development and proliferation of nuclear weaponry, and a couple of tumultuous bouts of activity in Kashmir. But that would be to omit the three wars with India and what many in Pakistan regard as the first two U.S. betrayals, in 1962 and 1971, as well as the loss of Pakistan's east wing to Bangladesh.

So maybe it would be more useful to start with the birth of the country itself, in 1947? That would take in the specter of Pashtun separatism, the brutal suppression of dissent in Balochistan by the first of the Bhutto dynasty, and the collapse of the Constitution. But even beginning at the beginning of the nation would not allow adequate consideration of the wellsprings of Pakistan's putative identity and the reasons for its separation from the larger part of the former Raj. To take due account of the arcane qualities of the Durand

Line and the influences of differing religious narratives, we would have to start the clock even earlier.

All of these momentous circumstances before and after the dawn of Pakistan had profound and to a great extent debilitating effects on the country's progress, both within Pakistan itself and in its relationships with the wider world. Most if not all of those effects may be relevant to the state of the nation today as well as to its state in the future; they must therefore be borne in mind. Among specialists (there can be no true "experts"), it perhaps goes without saying that they will be. But it is a tedious idiosyncrasy of the South Asian region that the recounting of the supposed lessons of history tends to supplant consideration of a way forward. It is easier to dwell on past grievances than to devise, still less to implement, action to improve prospects for the future. It will be best not to fall into that trap.

So why not consider the past and the future within a similar time frame and broadly confine the period from which we seek to extrapolate to, say, seven years? This period has the advantage of falling within the direct experience of current actors and analysts, and it has witnessed more than enough challenges that echo the characteristics of earlier periods. In the years after 2003, a military autocrat, losing his bluster and with much external encouragement, sought to cut a deal with a detested political foe and was ultimately tripped up by his own expedient gymnastics. In contrast to the blatant military interference in the 2002 electoral process, the outcome of the elections in 2008— perceived as adequately free and fair despite routine shortcomings over electoral rolls and the like—dashed the hopes of Panglossian ideologues and confirmed the fears of the weary Pakistan-watching realists: the two all-too-familiar national parties prevailed yet again, despite the appalling records of their previous two terms in office. An apparently flawless indirect electoral process produced a president of world-class notoriety who persisted for nearly two years in reneging on solemn pre-electoral pledges for which his assassinated wife had vigorously campaigned. And, again confounding the over-optimists, the apparent trouncing of the religious parties' coalition in the northwest by a more secular ethnic-based party did nothing to prevent the eruption of violent tension in the region.

If the elections and unpopularity caused the army to beat a tactical withdrawal to barracks, the fecklessness of the political leadership re-endowed them, by default, with authority to conduct politico-military operations as they saw fit against an insurgency that was belatedly recognized as a threat to the nation, having been homegrown from nearly nothing in 2005.

But if internal statecraft during this period was stagnant, contaminated by political rivalries, self-seeking, and crass incompetence, the external situation assumed increasing importance and relevance. Having ignored Musharraf's repeated warnings in 2002 and onward not to lose sight of the challenges in Afghanistan, the U.S.-led coalition, contrary to its hopes and what passed for its plans, was sucked into a politico-military quagmire in Iraq, which had ancillary costs in terms of popular revulsion on the part of Pakistanis. As the "surge" in Iraq began to take effect in 2007, U.S. attention belatedly reverted to Afghanistan and, all too much later, toward Pakistan. But it was only after Barack Obama's election that the elements of a U.S. policy started to emerge, first in March 2009 and then in a more refined form in December. That policy, at last, appeared to recognize the intrinsic significance of Pakistan, a nuclear-armed country with a population some six times that of Afghanistan and a highly politicized army whose interests were very different from those of the United States.

By 2010 it had become clear that the U.S. efforts since October 2001 to forge a transactional partnership with Pakistan had failed: Pakistan's army had suffered more losses than the whole of the International Security Assistance Force; it felt no gratitude for U.S. attempted inducements; it declined to do U.S. bidding over the Afghan Taliban, still less in relation to "freedom fighters" such as the Lashkar-e-Tayyiba, which was implicated in the outrages in Mumbai; and the opening of U.S. military markets allowed the army to purchase big-ticket weapons to feed its fixation with India at the expense of the nation's social welfare. The Pakistani population had further reasons to resent the United States: for what they saw as attempted bribery; for diminishing their security and well-being; for increased violations of the sovereignty of a declared ally; and, in anticipation, for the "fourth betrayal" when, as they fully expected, the U.S. started to pull out of Afghanistan in 2011.

The above pictures are, perhaps, drawn somewhat starkly. But perceptions about such matters, both in the region and among many Western commentators, also are stark—and when elections approach, perceptions are often what count. Just as the last seven years has seen two elections in the United States and two very different governments in Pakistan, so the next seven years will see another two U.S. presidential elections and who knows what political shifts in Pakistan. More to the point, the two processes are likely to impinge greatly on each other. The significance of the Afghanistan campaign, and hence of Pakistan's role in that connection, on U.S. mid-term and presidential elections in 2010 was inescapable, as it will be in 2012. And the success or failure of U.S. efforts in relation to Pakistan will have a profound effect on Pakistan. If things go badly, there may be knock-on effects within the region.

So, the last seven years encapsulates much of the nature of Pakistan and many of the realities within and around it: the strength, power, and cunning of the army; the irresponsibility of the nonmilitary body politic; the limitations and ineffectualness of the institutions; the absence of hope for the future on the part of Pakistan's swelling population; the interplay of interests between Pakistan and Afghanistan; and the constant concerns of and about India.

At the same time, these very evident shortcomings and challenges have become so serious that they are now widely acknowledged, and that arouses the hope that change, being so desperately needed, might at last prove possible. What follows therefore explores such possibilities. Of course, change could go either way. But since there is almost no limit to a possible descent, even if the road is, as at present, paved with good intentions, let us focus particularly on the more difficult of the two directions and consider the feasibility of positive change and how it might be brought about. What follows, therefore, is not a prediction. Nor is it simply an expression of hope. It is a recognition that progress will require both enlightenment and effort and that without effort any movement will be backward.

Extrapolation into the Future

The following list of "variables," which are more susceptible to change, and "constants," which are more enduring, is a provocation to discussion. Each component could, to varying degrees, profoundly affect Pakistan's future, in terms of the country itself and its relationship with others. Some discussion follows the list, leading to consideration of courses of action that could be conducive to securing desired outcomes. The variables include Pakistan's body politic; the economy; the role of the state; the judiciary and the police; the status of insurgents; Afghanistan and the United States; potential "friends of Pakistan"; and the degree of optimism in and about Pakistan. The constants include the role of the army; India; China; Kashmir; the lingering question of the Durand Line; nuclear issues; corruption; sectarianism; and the degree to which pessimism about the future overwhelms Pakistan.

Variables

The Body Politic. Zardari's presidency will not continue through the next seven years, even as the role of the presidency becomes titular, although it is fruitless to speculate whether he will survive his current term of office or depart sooner. Prime Minister Gilani should last until elections due in 2013, although those could be brought forward. But the Pakistan People's Party (PPP) will most likely suffer electorally from the departure of the last of the Bhuttos (assuming that the next generation is too young to assume power) and the nasty aftertaste caused by Zardari and his coterie. The Pakistan Muslim League–Nawaz (PML-N) will gain national ascendancy, but its ascent will not be tidy and its influence will not apply equally around the country. If Nawaz Sharif becomes prime minister, he will assuage the religious factions, thereby annoying the United States, and he will capitalize on that domestically. His propensity to make himself the center of things, together with patronage, will not allow much room for strategic thought, planning, or execution. Governance will therefore be characterized by inefficiency, unpredictability, and pork-barrel opportunism. The army could intervene. An alternative political leader might be more effective but would be politically weak. In any case, there is no sign of a plausible alternative, just as, contrary to all hopes and efforts, no contender has emerged in the past. If Nawaz were to fall under the proverbial bus, his brother Shahbaz Sharif might take the reins. In any event, provincial governance in Punjab and Khyber Pakhtunkhwa will gain importance. Tensions will rise between the center, and Sindh, and Balochistan. Local governance is unlikely to prosper.

The Economy. The economy will depend crucially on political as well as economic leadership and on the extent to which necessary medium- to long-term economic considerations are allowed to prevail over shorter-term political desiderata. The International Monetary Fund will not be able to cope with outright irresponsibility, and if that occurs the poor will become poorer and the gap between rich and poor will widen. External development assistance from the United States and donors who subscribe to the Tokyo Conference will no doubt fall short of their impressive pledges, as it has so far. Much will be provided in the form of budget support and thus lack transparency, but outside assistance will be an essential part of social welfare funding, which will otherwise continue to be neglected. Foreign direct investment will depend on assessment of political risk. To the extent that risk diminishes, the country's natural resources, especially gas and coal and other minerals, might be better exploited and the energy deficit might be tackled. The availability of water will depend mainly on the management of thorny domestic issues, including water storages, interprovincial disputes, and the renovation and maintenance of neglected distribution networks. Disputes over water with India will assume disproportionate importance as blame for the consequences of internal mismanagement will increasingly be lumped together with grievances about external water diversion. The durability of the Indus Water Treaty, under threat in 2001–02, cannot be taken for granted.

The Role of the State. The relationships between the central, the provincial, and the district governments will remain fraught because they are affected by the allocation of financial resources and hence by patronage and corruption. Although the National Finance Commission has introduced positive changes recently and despite the preponderance of representatives from Punjab in parliament, the allocation system may be made still more equitable, so as to take better account of relative disadvantage. The center will, however, continue to be beholden to or to promote local power brokers, which will lead to unhealthy compromises. Crucially, the relative roles of the army and any elected government will remain grossly unbalanced, with the army playing a dominant role in strategic and foreign policy issues. That will change only if there are, first, significant improvements in the effectiveness of the political class, which is unlikely to become apparent in the time frame under consideration. Nonetheless there may be scope at the edges to reduce some of the army's grosser privileges and incursions into the civilian domain.

The Judiciary and the Police. Each of these important institutions is in a state of flux, which risks arousing over-optimism. Judicial independence is a great prize, as would be a truly independent and effective Electoral Commission. But there are signs of an unhealthy overconcentration on settling old scores rather than implementing much-needed reform of these institutions and enhancing public respect for them. Increasing the pay and improving the working conditions of the police, including correcting disparities between, for example, Punjab and Khyber Pakhtunkhwa, are necessary but not sufficient for reducing corruption, which may be so ingrained as to take decades to control.

Insurgency. Efforts to eradicate the homegrown "Pakistani Taliban" insurgency are likely to be broadly successful as a result of attrition and the elimination of militant leadership. But a trail of resentment will follow in their wake, arising from concomitant injustices, damage to property, and displacement. The major potential variables concern the army's attitudes toward the Afghan Taliban, the Haqqani and Hekmatyar networks, and "freedom fighters" such as Lashkar-e-Tayyiba, which at present remain largely unchanged.

Afghanistan. The management of Pakistan's thorny relationship with Afghanistan could be put on a sounder footing by the establishment of an Afghanistan-Pakistan "composite dialogue," which Pakistan currently eschews. Karzai's presidency is an obstacle, for familiar reasons, as is the low representation of pro-Pakistani Pashtuns in the Afghan army and police. Similarly, suspicions surrounding India's role in Afghanistan (and Balochistan) will continue to infect Afghan-Pakistan relations unless and until they are addressed head-on.

The United States. The role of the United States will be crucial, if not determinant. The tension between the U.S. domestic political imperative to begin to draw down military forces in Afghanistan in mid-2011 and the perception that doing so is "cutting and running" is the most significant political challenge. Because of the many uncertainties, at present Pakistan insists on the necessity of "waiting and seeing," which amounts to political paralysis. Pakistanis' deeply negative attitude toward the United States is a major impediment to positive action. Successful administration of nonmilitary aid will take time to become apparent, but attitudes in Pakistan could become more favorable in advance of significant actual progress on the ground if the view developed that the United States is sincere in its beneficial intentions and is prepared, unprecedentedly, to become an all-weather friend. That would depend as much on the reactions of Congress to inevitable failures and backsliding as on actual progress in Pakistan. The United States will also need to address the issue of greater access by Pakistan to U.S. markets, especially in the textiles and garment sector, and consider whether it should continue to facilitate big-ticket arms purchases unrelated to counterinsurgency operations. The issue of drone attacks also merits careful and constant assessment, as there is the increasing risk that the attacks are making more enemies than they destroy.

Potential "Friends of Pakistan." The Tokyo Conference in 2009 provided a vehicle for pledges of help while the Friends of Democratic Pakistan aims to supply a policy framework for external help. There is a possibility that such instruments might assuage Pakistani confusion and justifiable irritation over dealing with a multiplicity of donors who understand little about the country, demand a lot, and relish offering unsolicited advice. The challenges will be to ensure that actions speak louder than the words; to bring pledges closer to the amount needed to meet Pakistan's needs and serve donors' self-interest in securing a stable Pakistan; to turn the pledges into actual disbursement (seldom achieved in the past); and to guard against Pakistan's using foreign aid to free up its own resources to fund the army and India-related arms procurement.

Optimism. Optimism is a major variable that will color or, when it proves unfounded, darken relationships. It is not to be confused with the frequently expressed but seldom justifiable Pakistani plea, "Trust us." It will have little basis if it is not accompanied by a determination to bring about change and to ensure that mutual trust is underpinned by evidence to justify it.

Some Constants

The Army. Rich in resources and confidence, despite the temporary humiliations at the tail-end of the Musharraf era, Pakistan's army will continue to see itself as the guardian of its idea of the nation. It therefore stands ready to intervene in political life again should it consider that necessary, but it will be reluctant to do so without strong cause. Continuing U.S. assistance, including reimbursement of declared costs of operations in western Pakistan and modern equipment such as helicopters, will add to its strength and capabilities, further distancing it from an underresourced and incompetent civilian regime. Continued access to arms sold by the United States that are not relevant to counterinsurgency operations will help the army maintain its fixation on India. There is some scope for change at the margins, for instance by reintroducing and enhancing periods of study abroad for promising officers, although those might include some future autocrat. An area to watch is the recruiting pattern and the possibility of greater religious conservatism within the army. The greater readiness of senior army and ISI officers to meet and interact with representatives of the United States and certain other countries, which has emerged only in the last few years, is an opportunity that should be built on.

India and Kashmir. Policy on Kashmir will continue to be dictated by the army. It will take strong political leadership and resolutely independent-minded foreign ministers (hitherto conspicuously absent) to secure any significant shift in approach. A true "solution" to the Kashmir issue is nowhere in sight (the so-called progress of the track II process between Tariq Aziz and S. K. Lamba has been exaggerated). But a reasonable aspiration is to manage the issue through a modus vivendi no worse than that of the last few years. If Indian political sentiment were to allow it, there is scope for rapid adoption of some Kashmir-related confidence-building measures. But a real and permanent change of Pakistani attitude will require a radical reduction of the role of the army and possibly generational shifts of sentiment. The effects of further terrorist incidents like Mumbai are unpredictable, but severe heightening of tension and even conflict (with all the accompanying dangers of escalation) cannot be excluded. In this respect the broad relationship is likely to remain constant.

The Nuclear Dimension. Pakistan will continue to enhance its nuclear capabilities, in terms of warheads and delivery systems, vigorously. It will maintain a high level of security, no doubt with some external assistance. The risk of nuclear material falling into the hands of terrorists is remote but, as always, cannot be totally excluded. It emphatically cannot be assumed that the absence of major conflict with India during recent periods of high tension proves that nuclear weaponry will never be used in South Asia.

China. China will remain an all-weather ally and continue, not least for its own strategic and commercial purposes, to contribute to the development of Gwadar and transport networks. That is of concern to India. But China's support will not be limitless: it will not condone violence or conflict with India; it will vigorously protect the interests of its citizens in Pakistan; it is concerned about the proliferation of militant groups and their association with Uighur militants; and it will encourage moderation in Pakistan's relations with Afghanistan.

The Durand Line. This border issue with Afghanistan will not be "resolved" in the foreseeable future. Nor would agreement about the Durand Line resolve the range of other Afghan-Pakistan differences and tensions. As with Kashmir, an agreed and durable resolution will require a sustained period of stability and the consolidation of mutual confidence, which does not exist at present. External efforts to facilitate or impose a resolution will accentuate other difficulties. For the time being, the complexities of the Durand Lind will have to be worked around.

Corruption. Corruption will be always with us. A good example set at the highest level, hitherto elusive, would be helpful in combating corruption, though even unfounded rumors of corruption would be undermining. However, greater transparency with respect to military expenditures and the use of external development funds will be essential if external support is to be maintained.

Sectarian Violence. Sectarian violence too is likely to remain a common feature of life in Pakistan, and it may increase as other domestic tensions increase. It will affect the governability of some areas, especially Karachi and the Northern Areas. Improvement in relations with Iran is unlikely to have much effect.

Pessimism. The factors described above and the absence for so long of any positive trend nourishes and enhances pessimistic and fatalistic sentiment. Well-educated youth and the scions of feudal and entrepreneurial families will continue to emigrate. Inward migration of talent and expertise, such as appears to be happening in India, will first require significant improvements in security, opportunity, and general welfare.

What Next?

The foregoing analysis might encourage the conclusion that Pakistan is well on the way to failing as a state and that there are few if any reasons to expect that it will pick itself up, turn the corner, and cease to be a source of major international concern. That may be. But, just as the future is unforeseeable, so such a conclusion is not inevitable. Assumptions to that effect by other countries are most likely to become self-fulfilling. As always, the condition of Pakistan is affected not only by its own actions and nature but also by external actors—for better or, perhaps more often, for worse.

A crucially important challenge for external actors, therefore, is to avoid assiduously actions that are likely to aggravate an already fragile situation.

While that may seem obvious, the repetition of strategic errors committed in the interest of short-lived tactical advantage suggests that overarching control of policy toward Pakistan has been seriously deficient and has too often taken second place to operational expediency.

Thereafter, the imperative is to take actions that enhance the effectiveness and sense of responsibility of elected governments; to help such governments bring about visible improvements in the welfare of ordinary Pakistanis; and to improve Pakistanis' perception of the United States and of democratic values (without being too prescriptive about the nature of democracy).

Securing the most appropriate mix of action will require considerable subtlety, patience, persistence, and forbearance. There can be a tension between the objective of strengthening elected governments, for example, and that of improving the image of the United States. It will do no Pakistani government any good to be seen as overdependent on a foreign power, but it could be salutary to take actions that bring benefits for which Pakistani leaders can take credit. Overconcentration on the military, although desirable for operational reasons, will further undermine the democratic process and risk exacerbating regional tensions. But if Pakistan is ever to flourish in the longer term, the relative strengths and resources of the army and the civilian body politic must be rebalanced.

MARVIN G. WEINBAUM

14

Regime and System Change

When a country continually experiences the ebb and flow of crises, as is the case with Pakistan, its future becomes more difficult to chart. Challenges to Pakistan's economy, constitutional order, political integration, and national security leave open a wide range of potential outcomes. During its sixty-four-year history, the country has experienced the trauma of wars, territorial dismemberment, loss of top leaders, economic shocks, and more. Yet little appears to change. The political, economic, and social establishment that was ensconced decades ago is still largely intact. Whatever the regime, military authority continues to eclipse civilian rule in critical policy areas, and Pakistan's regional and international allies and adversaries remain mostly unchanged. The public's disappointment and frustration with governance under successive leaders as well as its hopes and aspirations also are basically unaltered.

Even with this seeming resistance to basic changes, there exists the potential for gradual and even abrupt transformations of Pakistan's political system. This chapter identifies six scenarios of varying probability for the country's political future over the next five years. These scenarios reflect changes in the distribution of power, class relationships, and supporting ideologies. None of the scenarios is entirely exclusive of the others, and there are alternative forms of the same scenario.

A number of factors are poised to influence which scenario Pakistan experiences in the medium term. Most are part of the country's political and economic landscape and are subject to mitigation by government policies. Others are regional or global and largely beyond the control of any Pakistani regime. Whether internal or external, the precipitating factors are likely to be interactive

225

and mutually reinforcing in promoting change. One of these factors, involving the outcome of the ongoing insurgency in Afghanistan, is explored more closely for its implications for Pakistan's own insurgency and its potential as a game changer for the country. The chapter concludes with a separate discussion of leadership as a key determinant of Pakistan's political future.

Main Domestic Factors

Performance of Democratic Government. An elected government that falls far short of popular expectations of its ability to address the country's pressing economic and social issues creates disillusionment and mistrust in a democracy and readiness for change. Rampant corruption, political victimization, and a failed judicial system have in the past led to a greater societal willingness in Pakistan to accept authoritarian government. Four of five coups against elected governments took place to bring an end to political chaos and domestic unrest, for which previous political governments were held responsible. At some point, disenchantment with establishment rule, whether civilian or military, may leave the public more amenable to radical solutions to the country's governance.[1]

The Military's Interests. At issue is the willingness of the military to resist direct intervention in democratic politics and to curb any ambitions that it may harbor to again assume the reins of the government. Most regime changes have come about as a result of the army's direct or indirect involvement in politics, usually to protect its preferential status and valued prerogatives. Politicians are ordinarily viewed as corrupt, unprofessional, and lacking the capacity to deal with the country's problems. Finding a sustainable balance between civilian and military institutions is critical to a democratic outcome in Pakistan. For now the Pakistani army shows little interest in assuming the responsibility of formally exercising power. Yet the weakness of the current elected government has elevated the military leadership, especially its army chief, to an increasingly visible and assertive role in forming both domestic and foreign policy. And few doubt the readiness of the military to intervene directly in the event of a severe breakdown of public order.

Economic and Social Deficits. Most often, popular pressure for regime change in Pakistan and elsewhere is a reflection of worsening economic conditions. Energy deficits affect not only the country's industry but also the public's overall satisfaction with the government. Joblessness and rising economic disparity more subtly undercut a regime's acceptance. Sharply rising inflation, however, probably is the single most important driver of anti-incumbency sentiment, especially in Pakistan's cities, whose populations are less prepared than those in rural areas to cope with higher food prices.

The inadequacy of Pakistan's basic government services—including health and education, which are generally either rudimentary or badly degraded—undermine support not only for the government in power but also for the political system. High levels of unemployment are endemic and contribute to the estrangement of large parts of the public from their government. A political movement able to vent the country's growing social and economic grievances could become a strong force for change. The potential for class conflict increases with Pakistan's youth bulge: 62 percent of the population is below the age of twenty-five, and a large number of young people are unemployed. Meanwhile, the country is undergoing rapid urbanization. Civic disorder is more likely to occur among a more easily mobilized urban population than in the countryside.

Conflicting Identities. Pakistan has a troubled history of ethnic feuds, sectarian bloodshed, and linguistic politics that has kept 180 million individuals from fully forming one nation. The country's dominance by Punjab's ruling elite has alienated the smaller provinces and ethnicities. Separatist Sindhi, Baloch, and Pashtun movements feeding on feelings of economic exploitation and political discrimination have questioned the viability of Pakistan's federal framework. The long-standing rebellion by Baloch tribesmen, ethnic clashes between Muhajirs and Pashtuns in Karachi, and attacks on Shia by radical Sunni groups all put in doubt the writ of the state and a regime's capacity for governance. While none of Pakistan's fissures immediately threaten national disintegration, they weaken the country's ability to withstand future crises.

The Challenge of Insurgency. The commitment of military and civilian policymakers to sustain and expand efforts to curb militant and extremist groups can have a profound effect on the survival of a democratic government. A recently greater resolve to move aggressively against the Pakistani Taliban requires continued popular support for the army's actions in the tribal areas. Failure to confront fully the existential threat presented by long-favored jihadi organizations as well as insurgent forces may in time force Pakistan's military and civilian establishments to share power with extremist groups. The more religiously doctrinaire and aggressively nationalistic state that is then likely to emerge is bound to increase tensions with India and the likelihood of armed conflict.

Main External Factors

Relations with India. Every sign of improvement or serious strain in relations with India has unsettling political consequences. Even while the idea of reconciliation with India draws popular approval, indications of progress in negotiations with New Delhi over Kashmir and other issues have repeatedly triggered terrorism or military adventurism. Periods of crisis not only strengthen nationalist sentiments in Pakistan but also heighten the credibility of the country's jihadi and other extremist groups. The management of Pakistan's relations with India has proven to be a source of discord between the country's civilian and military leaders and a leading source of regime change. Pakistan's ethnic cohesion is strained by differences among the provinces in the priority given to Kashmir and other issues with India. A humiliating military defeat of the Pakistan army, as occurred with the loss of East Pakistan in 1971, and an accompanying economic and humanitarian crisis could test the very integrity of the Pakistani state.

The Conflict in Afghanistan. Pakistan has a considerable stake in the outcome of the current counterinsurgency campaign in Afghanistan and the staying power of the international community. Success has the potential to stabilize not only Pakistan's neighbor but also the entire region. In the event of a failed counterinsurgency campaign and the inability to achieve political reconciliation with the Taliban, Pakistan can be expected to call on its sheltered Taliban to provide a friendly Pashtun force to protect its interests in a disintegrating Afghanistan. However, an outcome that leads to the re-Talibanization of all or even parts of Afghanistan could also have an unsettling political impact on Pakistan. The success of Islamic forces in Afghanistan could give Pakistan's own Taliban strategic depth and energize its fight against the Islamabad government and the country's constitutional system.

Partnership with the United States. A severe trust deficit has for some time defined the relationship between the United States and the Pakistani elite and public, and it threatens the future of the much-advertised strategic partnership. Fueled by media commentary, belief in conspiracy theories alleging that the United States, in collusion with India and Israel, seeks to weaken Pakistan and seize its nuclear weapons is widespread, even at the highest echelons of the civilian government and military. Despite the growing appreciation of the threat posed by the country's militants, most Pakistanis are convinced that the radicalization of the frontier is a direct result of U.S. counterterrorism policies and military operations in Afghanistan. Less than a tenth of the public holds a favorable view of the United States, and almost twice as many Pakistanis see the United States as a threat to Pakistan's security as see India as a threat.[2]

Despite such feelings, Pakistan can ill afford a serious breach in its partnership with the United States. There is no ready substitute for the advanced weapons and training that the United States provides the Pakistani military. Islamabad governments have periodically relied on U.S. diplomacy in times of crises with India. Pakistan's economy can ill afford the loss of U.S. budgetary assistance and development aid for the country's economy. U.S. assistance is also instrumental in attracting support from other sources. A more liberal U.S. trade policy in coming years could have an enormous effect on private direct investment and job creation and serve to strengthen democratic government in Islamabad.

Although the ability of the United States to influence the course of Pakistan's domestic politics is limited, Washington's policies are regularly the subject of domestic debate that can result in strengthening or weakening a regime. National figures ready to assert issues of sovereignty and otherwise stand up to U.S. pressures have, especially in recent years, been able to gain wide popular support. Conversely, those government officials and others who are seen as too closely identified with U.S. policies are put on the defensive and are likely to see their electoral prospects threatened.

The Global Economy. The severe global economic downturn since 2009 has placed a great strain on Pakistan and called into question the government's ability to manage a hard-pressed economy. Stabilization has required returning to the International Monetary Fund (IMF) for budgetary support, and international financial institutions and donors have helped Pakistan to stave off a more serious economic crisis. But if continued international backing has strengthened the country economically, it has also called for conformity to IMF-dictated policies, which leaves those in power trying to implement unpopular fiscal and budgetary measures vulnerable to political attack. In general, externally imposed conditions invite conspiracy-based explanations of foreign motives that weaken the confidence of Pakistanis in their own government.

Six Scenarios

The following six scenarios differ on how power is exercised as well as in their supporting ideologies. Each has been assigned an independent probability of materializing in the next five years.

Fragile Democratic State. This particular outcome is distinguished by its continuity with the current political dispensation. In this scenario Pakistan experiences only incremental changes in its politics and its economy. Although faced with periodic constitutional and economic crises, the country manages to muddle through. The country's ruling elites and the relationships among its leading institutions would remain mostly unchanged. Civil society may experience growth and judicial activism may continue to play a larger role, but there will be no new balance among the pillars of the state. Most of the same cast of civilian leaders will still hold power or be contenders for power. Corruption will continue to be the focus of political debate, and any reforms will have marginal effect. Although the military avoids taking the reins of power, it is not constrained from intervening to protect its prerogatives and interests in foreign and domestic policy areas. (Sixty percent probability.)

Authoritarian State. Such a regime is a likely consequence of disappointing, dysfunctional civilian rule that leads the public to demand more decisive leadership. Domestic issues most often drive public discontent, above all resentment against regime corruption and ineptitude. Under military rule, civilian institutions are suspended or strongly subordinated, and military personnel assume key positions in both the government and private sector. A civilian-led authoritarian regime exercising arbitrary rule would come about if an elected executive is able to centralize and personalize power at the expense of other institutions, including the military.[3] This scenario would leave intact the country's civilian and military establishments and not seriously disrupt economic and social class relations. (Forty percent probability.)

Jihadist-Oriented State. This outcome describes the ascendance of extremist religious organizations, probably in coalition with other parties and possibly the military, enabling it to set the national policy agenda. It will most likely have features associated with authoritarian rule but remain distinctively ideological and normative. It may be infused with strong nationalism and could conceivably seek to alter social class relations. Pakistan's fractured society, disgruntled provinces, uneducated and unemployed youth, failed system of education, and shattered economy set down the conditions for a jihadi scenario.[4] This outcome is most likely to result from a combination of regional and international developments, such as Taliban ascendance in Afghanistan and a sharp deterioration in relations with India. (Twenty percent probability.)

Democratically Progressive State. Such an outcome is marked by a more responsive and responsible democratic government. Elected regimes complete their constitutional terms of office, transfers of power occur regularly and peacefully, and there is substantial growth in civil society. A progressive scenario is probably contingent on a changed mindset among many Pakistanis characterized by an appreciable gain in respect for individual and minority rights. It would most likely be accompanied by policies directed at the improvement of social welfare across the population. Much of the improvement would be made possible by a stabilized economy and improved relations with Afghanistan and possibly India. (Twenty percent probability.)

Radically Redistributive State. Such an outcome is made possible by a catastrophic implosion of the economic system and a dramatic discrediting of the country's establishment. While democratic in character, such a scenario is more likely to tend toward authoritarian rule, whether secular or Islamic. It would be likely to address issues like economic inequality and poverty allevi-ation. This scenario would probably require the emergence of leadership and secular organizations capable of mobilizing a large-scale popular movement. (Twenty percent probability.)

Fragmented State. This outcome may arise as the result of a major trauma to the federal system, causing nationalist forces in the smaller provinces to form either substantially autonomous relationships with the federal govern-ment or to become independent national entities. It carries elements of a more serious national disintegration along multiple ethnic, sectarian, and cultural lines. Like the previous scenario, it assumes that the military and fed-eral civilian establishments are deeply discredited, most probably in the event of a disastrous economic and/or military failure. Fragmentation within the army potentially frees elements to align with radical forces, putting the con-trol of Pakistan's nuclear arsenal at risk. (Ten percent probability.)

Insurgency and Pakistan's Future

Pakistan has for some time pursued a dual set of policies toward Afghanistan. On the one hand, many Pakistani government officials acknowledge that as long as it is not strategically aligned with India, a stable, peaceful Afghanistan can serve Pakistan's national interests. A secure, self-absorbed Afghanistan under the current Kabul regime can possibly defuse sources of Pashtun nationalism and reduce radical influences in Pakistan's tribal belt. It can also benefit Pakistan in its quest for trade opportunities and energy transfers with Central Asia. On the other hand, Pakistan has another line of policy that pro-vides sanctuary to Afghan insurgent groups dedicated to overthrowing the Kabul government and ousting international forces from the country.

Pakistan's military and political classes have been publicly critical of the counterinsurgency strategy pursued by the Obama administration. Pakistan makes the claim that a successful military surge could push militants from Afghanistan across the border. But a more serious possibility is that in the event that the Taliban regain their hold on Afghanistan, they would in time align their forces with domestic insurgents in Pakistan to fight against the state. Until now the Afghan insurgents have refrained from any involvement in anti-state actions in Pakistan. Under the protection of Pakistan's military, the Afghan Taliban have found safe haven in the tribal areas and Balochistan. Yet Pakistan has good reason to be concerned that it would have little control over the Tal-iban leaders should they achieve military success in Afghanistan.[5] Repeatedly in the 1990s, Mullah Omar's Taliban demonstrated their independence and defied their Pakistani patrons. Even while enjoying sanctuary in Pakistan after 2001, the Taliban leadership is believed to resent being manipulated by the Pakistani intelligence agencies.

While the military and political aims of the Afghan Taliban differ at present from those of their Pakistani counterparts, their shared ideology makes them natural partners in seeking to install sharia governments in both countries as well as elsewhere in the region. They also cooperate closely with the Islamic Movement of Uzbekistan, which found sanctuary in Pakistan in late 2001 and earlier had been able to conduct military operations against the Uzbek regime from Taliban-controlled Afghanistan. Mullah Omar's Taliban and their allies, the Haqqani network and Gulbuddin Hekmatyar's Hizb-e-Islami, together with the Pakistani Taliban, retain links of various strengths to al Qaeda as well as militant jihadi organizations inside Pakistan.

Failure of the U.S. current counterinsurgency strategy is almost certain to promote civil conflict in Afghanistan and set the stage for a regional proxy war. Ethnic minority Tajiks, Hazaras, and Uzbeks in Afghanistan can be expected to resist any outcome that restores the Taliban to power. They learned a decade ago that the Taliban will not be satisfied with control of just Pashtun-majority areas but will want to extend their authority over the entire country. With Pakistan as the Taliban's patron, Iran, Russia, and the Central Asia republics will similarly seek spheres of influence in Afghanistan. For all of Pakistan's current concerns about Indian involvement in Afghanistan, a civil war in Afghanistan is only likely to increase Indian activity. The possibility of Indian military advisers and arms transfers to Afghanistan cannot be ruled out. Saudi Arabia will also exert influence through client groups, mostly in order to minimize Iranian gains.

Predictably, with civil war in Afghanistan, millions of refugees fearing retribution, ethnic cleansing, and economic deprivation are likely to flee again to Pakistan and Iran, creating a humanitarian crisis that dwarfs that of any previous exodus. In the aftermath of its 2010–11 floods, Pakistan's ability to absorb a new wave of refugees is almost nonexistent; so too is its capacity to handle the resulting financial burden. In the face of high inflation and unemployment and a weak government, the potential for civil unrest in Pakistan would increase. The most likely outcome would be a full-fledged return to power of the Pakistan military. Instability could also create conditions for a radical transformation in which the county's civilian and military leaders are forced to accommodate radical Islamic elements in the government—with all the implications that carries for the control of nuclear weapons and the possibility of armed conflict with India.

Pakistan's leadership has concluded that the best way to minimize an Indian presence in Afghanistan and to avoid civil war is to promote a negotiated settlement between the Afghan Taliban and the Karzai government. Above all, Pakistan is determined that any talks with the Taliban should not ignore its interests, particularly its concerns about Indian activities in Afghanistan. Ideally, the inclusion of the Taliban in a compromise deal with other ethnic groups will serve to check the ideological and territorial ambitions of the Pashtun Taliban while retaining them as an asset should Afghanistan disintegrate following NATO's planned 2014 departure. Pakistan's insistence that it can deliver the major insurgent groups for a political settlement is, however, open to question.

Leadership and Radical Change

A fragile democracy and a largely benign military form of authoritarianism have alternated as Pakistan's predominant forms of government in the recent past. They are likely to continue to define Pakistan over the next five years. Notwithstanding widespread disillusionment with the democratic government elected in February 2008, for the time being at least most Pakistanis are opposed to a return to military rule. For its part, the Pakistan army appears anxious to give the impression that it is deferring to the democratic institutions of government. The army's traditionally low opinion of elected politicians has not changed, but it would rather let the civilian government exercise the formal responsibilities of power, especially given the country's many intractable problems. Though ostensibly subordinate to democratically elected representatives, the military has never ceded its control of areas of foreign and domestic policymaking that directly impinge on its institutional interests. If the military does seek full power over the next five years, it will probably be in response to domestic instability so palpable that military rule would be welcomed by most of the public.

Even while a repeat of the past cycles of military and civilian governments remains the most predictable course of events, a transformation of Pakistan's political system cannot entirely be ruled out. It is often observed that class disparities and inequities that exist in the absence of a social safety net leave Pakistan with the basic constituency needed for political and social upheaval. Pakistanis have reason to doubt that either the current civilian regime or a successor military-led government is interested in addressing their discontent. Yet the kind of transformations depicted by Pakistan's alternative scenarios face long odds. The status quo continues to be bolstered by a political leadership bound to patronage and by the absence of program-based parties or an energized civil society that could mobilize the population.

Periodically, political figures have emerged able to inspire and arouse the public in pursuit of a progressive scenario for Pakistan, but all have eventually forfeited the public's confidence. For a time in the early 1970s, Z. A. Bhutto transformed the country's political discourse and reconfigured politics, but he soon jettisoned his progressive agenda to rule as a parochial, self-aggrandizing feudal politician. After 1998, Benazir Bhutto and Nawaz Sharif acquired popular electoral mandates that might have broken the familiar mold of democratic politics. Instead, they succumbed to establishment politics, tolerating corruption and incompetence or, in the case of Sharif, became addicted to enhancing their personal power. General Musharraf was initially widely welcomed in the expectation that he would use his presidency to create a fresh political ethos and attract a new breed of politicians. That he placed greater value on furthering the army's and his own personal agenda soon became evident.

The mass support received in 2007 and 2008 by a lawyers' movement that championed an independent judiciary and democratic government does, however, suggest that a normally politically passive population can be activated by an impelling cause. The judiciary's recent assertiveness, together with constitutional changes bolstering the parliamentary system, improves chances for a government of checks and balances. Some observers see in these developments an important step toward the realization of a progressive democratic scenario. Others worry that an arrogant, arbitrary judiciary in league with the military or an autocratic party leader can become a powerful instrument of repression. More immediately threatening to a more open society has been the success of extremist groups in intimidating political leaders and evoking intolerant attitudes across society following the 2011 assassinations of the Punjab chief minister and the leading spokesperson for the Christian community.

Any radical scenarios for Pakistan seem to await the galvanizing effects of leaders with good organizational skills who are able to evoke wide popular sentiment. They can tap the frustrations growing out of severe energy and water shortages, high food prices, and high unemployment among the country's youthful population, which creates a potentially volatile body of followers. Demagogic leaders could mount emotional appeals to nationalism, class, and religious values. The advent of liberalized print and electronic media able to fan strong opinions can potentially rally large numbers of people. For the time being, however, ethnic differences, still powerful patron-client relations, and vigilant security forces handicap nascent national movements. Pakistan's political complexion could change profoundly were the military to fracture or the educated middle class to lose its confidence in the constitutional system. But at least for the next five years, despite the existence of conditions that could lead to far-reaching political and social change, resiliency and inertia are likely to be featured and a scenario strong on continuity remains most probable.

Notes

1. The largest percentage of Pakistan's population, its youth, is confused about democracy being a viable system for the country. According to a survey of Pakistani youth conducted by the British Council in 2009, one-third believe democracy is the best system of governance, one-third support sharia law, and 7 percent think that dictatorship is a good idea (www.britishcouncil.org/pakistan-next-generation-report-download.htm).

2. See BBC World Service Poll, "Global Views of the United States Improve While Other Countries Decline," conducted by GlobeScan/PIPA, April 2010 (http://news.bbc.co.uk/2/shared/bsp/hi/pdfs/160410bbcwspoll.pdf).

3. Z. A. Bhutto might have moved in this direction had he survived politically into a second term of office. Nawaz Sharif in his second round as prime minister sought to centralize power in the executive by using heavy-handed tactics with the legislature and intimidating the judiciary.

4. According to the Pew Global Attitudes survey "Pakistani Public Opinion," released in August 2009, which claimed to cover 90 percent of Pakistan's adult population, 83 percent supported stoning people who commit adultery; 80 percent favored punishments like whippings and cutting off hands for crimes like theft and robbery; and 78 percent supported the death penalty for people who leave the Muslim religion. Percentages were never this high, even after Zia ul-Haq's decade-long Islamization movement. See http://pewglobal.org/2009/08/13/pakistani-public-opinion/.

5. That concern is an indication that Pakistan's strategies for a future Afghanistan may also be evolving and becoming more nuanced. In saying that "we can't have Talibanization . . . if we want to remain modern and progressive," army chief General Ashfaq Kayani has in fact suggested that Pakistan is better served if the Taliban does not fully prevail in Afghanistan. Pamela Constable, "Pakistan's Army Chief Seeks Stable Afghanistan," *Washington Post,* February 2, 2010.

ANITA M. WEISS

15

Population Growth, Urbanization, and Female Literacy

The first glimmer of light appears, seeping through the darkness. Dawn is finally breaking after what has felt like a very long, dark night. The warmth of a new day engulfs those who awake early. As the lilting a capella voice, gently yet firmly, eases into one's sensibilities, it intones the sanctity of the day, declaring the greatness of God. Hope soars. Gradually, that voice is joined by others, from other mosques, calling the faithful to prayer. But that lone voice gets drowned out by others using loudspeakers, creating a cacophony of now indistinct sounds whose timings are just off from one another. The intensity increases, and a listener now hears only yelling and shrieking, too much competition between one voice and another, and no clarity.

That's not the way the story should go. Pakistan has been through this so many times before. How many times will there be a new beginning, just to be overcome by the unrelenting jockeying for power and position that has come to characterize life in Pakistan? A general once at the helm of the government is gone, the Eighteenth Amendment has been enacted, and it seems that the army will not be able to take over again, at least within the bounds of the prevailing Constitution. However, afflicted by nearly daily bomb blasts and suicide attacks, major cities throughout Pakistan are subject to twelve to fifteen hours of daily electricity load shedding while rural areas must endure living with even less electricity. Energy consumption is at an all-time high, and there

I am deeply indebted to the many people who kindly met with me in Pakistan in the past few years and shared their views and insights about the challenges confronting Pakistan, to Miangul Hassan Aurangzeb and Saba Gul Khattak for their helpful comments, and to Aruna Magier and Patrick Jones for their assistance with data research.

236

is not enough to go around. It is, therefore, not just a contest between communities for power and influence but for diminishing resources too. The promises of economic growth, of external investment, and of commitment of major companies to Pakistan's future are mitigated by the recognition of the need for internal calm. There is still little said about social investment, aside from increasing the base number of literates, and no discussion of the components necessary to be considered literate here. There is no national consensus in Pakistan today on such things as how to share water, women's inherent rights, what a "good education" comprises aside from having served time as a student, what kind of political system is most desirable, or even a vision of civil-military relations. What indeed does the future hold for Pakistan when its demographic profile tells us that its annual population growth rate remains over 2 percent but that it does not have the requisite development of natural resources, the economy, and the human potential that must accompany such growth if the state is to be viable and robust?[1]

What transpires domestically is now intrinsically related to myriad global concerns in a variety of ways and for a variety of reasons. However, in this chapter, I do not consider how external factors will affect Pakistan's future. Rather, my aim is solely to examine domestic factors with an eye toward understanding how Pakistan's changing demographic profile may affect its future options. Toward that end, I focus on three critical areas: first, the rise in population growth and heightened demand for resources (for example, education, healthcare, energy, and employment); second, the effects of urbanization and related environmental challenges brought about by the demographic shift; and finally, what it will mean for Pakistan's future to have a significantly greater number of educated women than ever before.

It is sobering to reflect on how Pakistan has transformed since 1947, when British India was partitioned and an independent homeland for Muslims was carved out of its northern corners. Questions, debates, and mistrust of a shared vision by its leaders arose from the outset. Mohammed Ali Jinnah—a British-trained lawyer who rose to be the founding father of the country, the Quaid-e-Azam—and other Western-oriented professionals envisioned a multiethnic, pluralistic, democratic state free from the hegemony of any one group. That hope was evident in Jinnah's inaugural presidential address to the Constituent Assembly of Pakistan three days prior to independence, when he declared that "if we want to make this great State of Pakistan happy and prosperous, we should wholly and solely concentrate on the well-being of the people, and especially of the masses and the poor."[2] Jinnah encouraged the rise of a vigorous civil society, one in which ethnic and religious divides would be set aside to promote the overall well-being of the new country.[3] He regarded Pakistan as the culmination of what had finally become a grassroots movement, encompassing partisans from a range of ethnic, class, regional, and religious backgrounds—a profusion of groups working together for the overall well-being of the state regardless of its divisions.

Differences between leaders and groups were to be resolved within a constitutional context, as Jinnah and other leaders shared the conviction that a popular consensus existed on the necessity, viability, and structure of the new state. Most citizens of Pakistan, whether existing residents of areas designated in the 1947 partition or immigrants (muhajirs) who left everything behind in the areas ceded to India to board the trains for Pakistan, shared the conviction that they had achieved something pivotal for the Muslims of South Asia. The havoc and social chaos that became the legacy of partition kindled a unifying spirit among much of the citizenry of the new state. According to the mainstream, populist narrative, Pakistan's future held great promise. While substantive political and economic challenges confronted the new state, most shared the conviction that they would be surmounted over time.

Pakistan's promise remains unfulfilled even today. Pakistan has failed to invest in its people, notably its women. Too often people use the trope that tradition is largely responsible for Pakistan's challenges in lowering its population growth rate. That is fallacious. The lack of priority given to female education, combined with the lack of priority given to developing sectors in the economy to support the economic empowerment of women, is fundamentally responsible for Pakistan's not lowering its population growth rates significantly—especially between the 1970s and 1990s, when Pakistan's population doubled.[4] Experiences worldwide attest that educated women have smaller, healthier families and that only when women come to enjoy economic security and a sense of economic justice can they turn their focus to becoming involved in civil society and political groups.

Pakistan's Population Growth and Urban Expansion

Pakistan is the sixth-most-populous country in the world—soon to become the fifth most populous—with a mid-2010 population estimated at 184.8 people (up from 175 million just a year earlier).[5] Its land area, however, is only thirty-second in size in the world. Since independence, Pakistan's population has increased fivefold from the 34 million counted in the first census in 1951;[6] its population in 2030 is projected to be 265.7 million.[7] The United Nations estimates that the population will nearly double by 2050, when Pakistan will become the world's fourth-largest country, with 335 million people.[8]

Table 15-1. *Population by Province and Urban-Rural Residence*
Millions

Province	Total population	Urban population	Percent urban	Rural population	Percent rural
National	147.1	51.9	35.3	95.2	64.7
Balochistan	8.5	2.0	23.5	6.5	76.5
KP	20.9	3.4	16.3	17.5	83.7
Punjab	84.8	31.1	36.7	53.7	63.3
Sindh	32.9	15.4	46.8	17.5	53.2

Source: Federal Bureau of Statistics, *Pakistan Demographic Survey 2006*, pp. 39–43, table 1.

Pakistan's population is not evenly distributed throughout the country. It ranges dramatically from sparsely populated Balochistan to parts of Karachi and the old city of Lahore, which have some of the highest densities in the world. As shown in table 15-1, two-thirds of all Pakistanis, on average, still live in rural areas. The share is higher in Balochistan and Khyber Pakhtunkhwa (KP), formerly the North-West Frontier Province, where over three-quarters of the population resides in rural areas, but the distribution is changing in other parts of the country. In particular, the urban population in Sindh has nearly surpassed the province's rural population, due in large part to migration to the city of Karachi, where the population surpassed 15.5 million in 2010. Pakistan's urban annual growth rate has averaged 3.82 percent since 1950 (see table 15-2), with slower growth experienced only in the first half of this decade.[9]

Pakistan's cities continue to experience significant growth. Seven other cities (Faisalabad, Gujranwala, Hyderabad, Lahore, Multan, Peshawar, and Rawalpindi) have populations of over a million, and Lahore's population is well over 5 million. An international think tank, City Mayors, now lists Karachi as the largest city in the world, with a population of 15.5 million as of 2010. (However, the population of its total metropolitan area, at 18 million, makes it smaller than a number of others in this comparison.)[10] Roughly one-third of all urban dwellers live either in Karachi or Lahore.

City size is but one factor to consider when envisioning how to create livable cities in Pakistan. At least one-third of urban residents live in *katchi abadis* and other slums lacking basic services.[11] Megacities today have tremendous infrastructure problems. In Lahore, for example, the city has expanded so far—Defense, Iqbal Town, and Township now being common residential areas—that it has lost its sense of having a center. The deterioration of public transit

Table 15-2. *Population of Major Pakistani Cities*
Thousands

City	2000	2005	2010	2015
Faisalabad	2,140	2,482	2,833	3,260
Gujranwala	1,224	1,433	1,643	1,898
Hyderabad	1,221	1,386	1,581	1,827
Karachi	10,019	11,553	15,500[a]	14,855
Lahore	5,448	6,259	7,092	8,107
Multan	1,263	1,445	1,650	1,906
Peshawar	1,066	1,235	1,415	1,636
Quetta	614	725	836	971
Rawalpindi	1,519	1,762	2,015	2,324

Source: Population Division of the Department of Economic and Social Affairs of the United Nations Secretariat, *World Population Prospects: The 2006 Revision and World Urbanization Prospects: The 2007 Revision* (http://esa.un.org/unup).

a. According to the City Mayors database, which lists the Karachi metropolitan area with a population of 18 million (www.citymayors.com/statistics/largest-cities-mayors-1.html).

networks and the proliferation of automobiles and private minibuses have caused unprecedented traffic congestion, bottlenecks, and pollution. The Ravi River receives so much hazardous and untreated waste daily that the city of Lahore is now essentially encircled by poison.[12]

Politics and ethnicity are uniquely intertwined in Pakistan. The family, a primary social concern in Pakistan, functions as the fundamental source of ethnic identity, which is a key influence on political attitudes. Ethnic identity is the primary source of provincial divisions in Pakistan, although a province is by no means the exclusive domain of only one distinct ethnic group. Indeed, some of the greatest initial political disputes occurred over the question of which province distinct districts should join. For example, many Balochs had championed having Dera Ghazi Khan be a part of Balochistan, although it ended up being in Punjab. Numerous Pashtuns (called "Pakhtuns" in Pakistan) live in villages abutting G. T. (Grand Trunk) Road between Rawalpindi and Attock, but one does not enter Khyber Paktunkhwa until the bridge is crossed.

One of the key reasons for the delay in conducting the 1991 census (it was finally held in 1998, seven years late) was that popular knowledge held that the influx of millions of Afghan Pashtun refugees into Balochistan had caused the majority ethnic group in the province to change; however, stating definitively that Balochs no longer constituted the majority ethnic group in Balochistan would provide further fuel for open conflict between groups in the province. In addition, clearly stating that the city of Karachi had indeed experienced a very high growth rate would have brought demands for commensurate representation in the national parliament and higher quotas for government jobs, university admissions, and so forth, further aggravating hostility between the Muttahida Qaumi Movement (MQM) and other groups. Punjab, the most populous province, would have seen its share of federal jobs and funding affected—whether its count was too high or too low—further antagonizing groups in other provinces and fueling anti-Punjabi sentiment or anger from Punjabis who considered that they were undercounted.

An associated outcome would be that rural landholding elites would lose seats in the national assembly if the census proved that there had been significant population growth in urban areas. Furthermore, it was feared that sectarian disputes between Sunni and Shia groups would escalate further (as they did, regardless) because each group would certainly decry the overcounting of the other, thereby fueling the widespread, random, and ravaging acts of terrorism that those disputes have wrought. Finally, showing a population growth rate that hovered around 3 percent would have undermined economic growth by fueling pessimism in the country as well as serve to underscore the state's failure to raise the status of women. That, in turn, would have further antagonized the brewing "culture wars" between Western-oriented groups demanding that the state actively pursue the empowerment of women versus Islamist groups demanding that the state suppress those forces that seek to exploit women and lead them away from their prescribed roles as commonly perceived within the conservative religious tradition.[13]

Ethnic groups are not symbolic, imagined communities, either. Ethnic orientations toward social hierarchies, toward the state, and even toward Islam differ markedly between some groups. Being cognizant of the primary ways that ethnicity influences individuals' political and economic stances enables us to gain a fuller view of the interaction of the different segments that Pakistan comprises. There also are significant cultural differences between major ethnic groups in Pakistan that contribute to misunderstandings and very real tensions between provinces.

Separatist movements and ethnic crises have plagued Pakistan since its inception, although the nature of the conflicts and the adversaries have changed over time. At independence, there was a definable fear that Pakistan might cease to exist; East Pakistan's secession in 1971 further aggravated that anxiety. More recently, separatist movements in what was the North-West Frontier Province (now KP), Balochistan, and Sindh have given way to demands for greater power and autonomy, recently realized through the devolution that resulted from the Eighteenth Amendment. Perhaps one of Pakistan's greatest challenges today lies in how to create a sense of citizenship among communities that have not historically regarded each other as being of the same people, apart from most being adherents of the same religion. That, of course, is interwoven with the myriad economic difficulties and development concerns that Pakistan is facing.

Pakistan's four major provinces—Balochistan, Khyber Pakhtunkhwa, the Punjab, and Sindh—were initially created to reflect language divisions within the country. In early 2010, the Northern Areas became a fifth province, Gilgit Baltistan, and in March 2010 North-West Frontier Province was officially renamed Khyber Pakhtunkhwa. Provincial residence no longer denotes either ethnicity or language, particularly because Punjabis and Pashtuns have settled outside of the provinces associated with their respective languages. For example, nearly half of all Pakistanis (48 percent) speak the provincial language Punjabi while over two-thirds identify as being ethnically Punjabi. Therefore, a sizable number of ethnic Punjabis do not speak the Punjabi language. We must presume that, in this case, many who identify as being ethnically Punjabi and who do not speak the Punjabi language are Saraiki speakers (who constitute 10 percent of the population).

In response to the creation of the new province, Gilgit Baltistan, from the former Northern Areas, there have been demands not only for renaming other provinces but for carving out new ones. The Punjabi language distribution is important here. The population of the province of Punjab (84.8 million) would make it the fifteenth-largest country in the world if it were a separate national entity.[14] A political movement is gaining strength in southern Punjab to separate that area from Punjab and thereby create a Saraiki-speaking province. In addition, riots have broken out in Abbottabad and other non-Pashtun, Hindko-speaking areas of Khyber Pakhtunkhwa because Hindko speakers feel divested of their provincial citizenship under the new name and are agitating to carve out a separate province of their own.

Political dissent and control is a key factor in demands for restructuring FATA (the Federally Administered Tribal Areas). This legacy of British colonialism, which can be traced to the Frontier Crimes Regulation Act of 1901, is composed of seven tribal agencies and six frontier regions. While administered directly by the federal government, it enjoys a great deal of local autonomy. Here, tribal leaders hold sway over their members' lives to a considerable extent, and federal institutions and constitutional laws are essentially irrelevant. Political agents, representatives of the federal government, rarely wield even limited influence; they are essentially couriers. A common sentiment in FATA is the disdain with which most residents regard the federal government. Projects to build modern roads, schools, and new kinds of economic enterprises are often viewed locally as insidious efforts to dominate the tribal areas. It is erroneous to assume that the federal government of Pakistan maintains effective power and influence in FATA.

Where will this sense of provincial citizenship lead as Pakistan's population increases? Will it strengthen Pakistan to have smaller provinces, especially given the devolution of administrative oversight from the federal center to the provinces, or will it further dilute any sense of national identity, displacing loyalty to the center with provincial loyalty?

The Position of Women in Pakistan

Two perceptions characterize the basic understanding of traditional gender relations in Pakistan: women are subordinate to men, and a man's honor resides in the actions of the women of his family. Throughout the country, gender relations differ more by degree than by type. Physical space is allocated to and used differently by men and women. Traditionally, a woman was seen as needing protection from the outside world, where her respectability—and therefore that of her family—is at risk. Women in many parts of the country live under the traditional constraints associated with purdah, under which women are separated from men both physically and symbolically, thereby creating highly differentiated male and female spheres.

In the past, most women spent most of their lives physically within their homes, venturing outside only when there was a substantive purpose. While greater numbers of women venture into public spaces in Pakistan today than in the past, in most parts of the country—except perhaps Islamabad, Karachi, and wealthier parts of a few other cities—people still consider a woman (and by extension, her family) to be shameless when no restrictions are put on her mobility.

Two major factors determine the degree to which women's mobility is restricted: class and rural or urban residence. Poor rural women in Punjab and Sindh traditionally have enjoyed a greater degree of mobility than women in the western parts of the country if for no reason other than sheer necessity. Typically these women are responsible for transplanting seedlings and weeding crops, and they often are involved in activities such as raising chickens (and selling eggs) and stuffing wool or cotton into local blankets (*razais*). When its level of prosperity rises and a family begins to aspire to a higher status, often the first social change that it adopts is to put a veil on its women and place them into some form of purdah.

Marriage is a means of cementing alliances between extended families. There remains a preference for marriage to one's patrilineal cousin, otherwise to kin from within the *biradari* (clan). The pattern of continued intermarriage coupled with the occasional marriage of nonrelatives creates a convoluted web of inter-locking ties of descent and marriage, resulting in the perception by many non-Pakistanis that all the Pakistanis that they know are related to one another.

Social ties are defined in terms of giving away daughters in marriage and receiving daughters-in-law. To participate fully in social life, a person must be married and have children, preferably sons. The percentage of women who get married and have children in Pakistan is overwhelming: in 2002, 98 percent of all women aged thirty-five to forty-nine were married or had been married at one time. Fertility rates are finally declining: a mere two generations ago, an average family consisted of eight to ten children; a generation ago (in the early 1990s), it was six children; and today the norm is four, even among many rural families.[15]

Overall literacy rates in Pakistan have been steadily rising. The last census in 1998 reported that 43.9 percent of Pakistanis over the age of ten were literate (54.8 percent of males but only 32.0 percent of females).[16] This has occurred even though there has never been a systematic, nationally coordinated effort to improve female primary education in the country. One cannot decry cultural reasons for the low female literacy rates, as the South Asian regional norm is over two-thirds.[17] Research conducted by the Ministry for Women's Development and a range of international donor agencies twenty years ago revealed that *access* was the most crucial concern that parents had. Indeed, reluctance turned to enthusiasm when parents in rural Punjab and rural Balochistan could be guaranteed their daughters' safety and, hence, their honor.

Today this scenario is changing remarkably. The World Bank reports an overall literacy rate of 79 percent for young men age fifteen to twenty-four; the figure for females in the same age group is 61 percent.[18] This bodes well for the emerging generations of Pakistan's workforce because both males and females will have unprecedentedly high levels of education. While overall literacy rates are rising, the state has established distinct quotas to promote women's greater participation in public arenas of society: 10 percent for women in government service; 17 percent for women in the national and provincial parliaments; and 33 percent for women in most tiers of local government. However, it has been less successful in forging economic opportunities for women outside of government service. Of a total labor force of 51.78 million in 2007–08, only 10.96 million were women.[19] Even those sectors commonly associated with women as nurturers, such as teaching, have been dominated by men. Just over a third (37.9 percent) of all primary school teachers are women. That figure climbs to nearly half (48.4 percent) for middle school teachers, then decreases to just over a third (34.9 percent) for high school teachers and only 30 percent for university teachers.[20] Issues related to obligations for women, mobility, economic self-sufficiency, the primacy of domestic obligations for women, and "male honor" when a family lives off the labor of its women serve to prevent women from entering the most nurturing professions, which they dominate elsewhere in the world—but not in Pakistan.

Implications

Pakistan's economy has grown much more than that of many other low-income countries, but the country has failed to achieve social progress commensurate with its economic growth. The educated and well-off urban population lives not so differently from its counterparts in other countries of similar income range. However, the poor and rural inhabitants of Pakistan have been left with limited resources, clamoring for jobs and decent schools for their many children, plagued by inflation, and living—quite literally—in the dark. Pakistan's ranking in the United Nation's Development Program's Human Development Index slipped from 120 in 1991 to 138 in 2002 and to 141 in 2009—worse than that of the Congo (136) and Myanmar (138) and only just above that of Swaziland (142) and Angola (143), all countries with far weaker economies.[21]

With greater numbers of people demanding goods and services in the country and many of them living in densely populated cities that are difficult to navigate (physically as well as politically), the government of Pakistan must give priority to creating economic opportunities for the masses and to ensuring both economic and political justice. As greater percentages of citizens become more aware through better education and the expansion of media coverage of what transpires elsewhere in the world, they will naturally expect—and demand—more. We have already seen the violence that emerges from narrow views of community—a divisive cleavage that ostensibly pits Western-oriented, wealthy groups against the poor, the disempowered, those who cannot afford a government education, and those who know that receiving one will not alleviate their poverty and disenfranchisement. These are the people who identify with their groups wholly, whether through tribal identity, sectarian identity, kinship, locale, or other factors.

An important change that results from urbanization is the nuclearization of the family, which is occurring today in a large number of families in Pakistan's cities. The old *havelis* have given way to self-contained flats, and it is now common not to know one's neighbors. This has a substantive effect on the country's social character as values now are imparted in schools, through the media, and on the streets. Younger generations of Pakistanis, especially children of the elite, are now questioning the priorities of their elders in wholly unprecedented ways. Yet the failure of government schools to provide a viable education has unduly harmed the children of the poor—the very group that it claims to be dedicated to serving. The forthcoming Five-Year Plan has the goal of achieving universal primary education and 75 percent enrollment in secondary education, although the overall development budget is facing a 40 percent cut. Can that goal be achieved? Pakistan's future will continue to be precarious if it is not.

Pakistan's high population growth rate, combined with current fertility levels, certainly constrains Pakistan's economic prospects. As high popula-tion growth rates and rampant urbanization create greater challenges than opportunities for Pakistan's future, the opposite must be said for the increase in the absolute number of literate women. In research that I have conducted in a wide variety of areas in Pakistan—from the Old City of Lahore to met-ropolitan Islamabad and Peshawar and small towns in Swat in 2010–11—I have found educated women the most secure about their future. As I was told more than twenty years ago by one impoverished widow in the Old City of Lahore, who saved every rupee that she earned from sewing *panchas* (the weighted hem at the bottom of *shalwars*, traditional pants) so that she could educate her daughters: "Land and gold can always be taken away, but no one can steal a good education."[22]

The draft National Population Policy recognizes that a huge societal shift is now under way:

> Societal changes such as rapid urbanization, increased female achieve-ments in education and employment market, related expansion of opportunities for women, proliferation of information through elec-tronic and other media, and improvements in economic situation have set in a process of changes in social values. Demographic surveys show that fertility level has declined but has slowed during the last few years.[23]

An increase in the absolute number of educated females will confront Pak-istan with different kinds of challenges. The gender and development literature contains numerous examples of such women demanding cleaner neighbor-hoods, better schools, and legal reforms to support their economic participa-tion (such reforms are already under way in Pakistan),[24] and, important for Pakistan, they are enjoying lower population growth rates. Might we see more political accommodation as women become more active in political office, as I saw in the North-West Frontier Province government earlier this decade, when it was women from various political parties who crossed party lines to find solutions to the problems plaguing their children's schools and healthcare options? They considered it their *amanat* (a kind of sacred obligation) to fulfill their duties as parliamentarians despite having been elected to reserved seats. In interviews that I conducted recently with women in Swat, I saw a self-confidence among educated women; they will certainly stand up, in larger numbers, to the obstructionist forces seeking to keep them down. Bella Abzug, the late U.S. congresswoman and founder of WEDO (Women's Environment and Development Organization) once said,

> It's not that I believe that women are superior to men; it's just that we've had so little opportunity to be corrupted by power. . . . I'm one of those who has always believed that women will change the nature of power, rather than power changing the nature of women.[25]

If there ever was an ideal ground on which that will occur, it is Pakistan today.

Notes

1. United Nations Development Program (UNDP), *Human Development Report 2010. The Real Wealth of Nations: Pathways to Human Development* (2010), p. 186, table 11. If taken as a whole from 1947 to 2010, Pakistan's total population growth rate has been 2.74 percent.

2. Reprinted in C. M. Naim, *Iqbal, Jinnah, and Pakistan: The Vision and the Reality*, South Asian Series 5 (Syracuse University Maxwell School of Citizenship and Public Affairs, 1979), p. 212.

3. Ibid., pp. 212–13.

4. Ministry of Population Welfare, Government of Pakistan, "Draft National Population Policy 2010," January 18, 2010, p. 1.

5. UNDP, *Human Development Report 2010*, p. 186, table 11. The 2009 figure, which is debated, is the estimate of the CIA *World Factbook* (www.cia.gov/library/ publications/ the-world-factbook/geos/pk.html). The UN Population Division estimated it at 180.8 million. However, figures in the Ministry of Population Welfare, "Draft National Population Policy 2010," estimated Pakistan's population at the same time as 171 million.

6. Ministry of Population Welfare, "Draft National Population Policy 2010," p. 1.

7. UNDP, *Human Development Report 2010*, p. 186, table 11.

8. This estimate by the UN Population Division was reported in "Pakistan Faces Population Time Bomb; Whom to Blame?" *News Blog* (www.thenews.com.pk/blog/ blog_details.asp?id=208).

9. Population Division of the Department of Economic and Social Affairs of the United Nations Secretariat, *World Population Prospects: The 2006 Revision* and *World Urbanization Prospects: The 2007 Revision* (http://esa.un.org/unup). The urban growth rate was highest in the country's first decade as *muhajirs*, migrants from India, relocated in the country's cities. It again averaged over 4 percent growth between 1975 and 1990, presumably due to the influx of Afghan refugees into Pakistan's cities.

10. City Mayors, "The Largest Cities in the World and Their Mayors" (www.city mayors.com/statistics/largest-cities-mayors-1.html).

11. Government of Pakistan, Planning Commission, *Ten-Year Perspective Development Plan: 2001–11 and Three-Year Development Programme: 2001–04* (Islamabad: Printing Corporation of Pakistan Press, September 2001), p. 249.

12. Ali Raza, "Ravi Receives 1,307 Tonne Toxic Waste Daily," *The News*, April 20, 2010 (www.thenews.com.pk/TodaysPrintDetail.aspx?ID=235023&Cat=5&dt=4/24/2010).

13. For further discussion of the various factors that constrained the Pakistan government from holding a census, see Anita M. Weiss, "Much Ado about Counting: The Conflict over Holding a Census in Pakistan," *Asian Survey* (July/August 1999), pp. 679–93.

14. CIA, *World Factbook*. That would place Punjab between number 14, Ethiopia (85.2 million), and 15, Germany (82.3 million).

15. Government of Pakistan, *Pakistan Integrated Household Survey 2002*, p. x, and UNDP, *Human Development Report 2010*.

16. Government of Pakistan, "1998 Census Demographic Indicators" (www.census.gov.pk/DemographicIndicator.htm).

17. UNDP, "Country Brief, South Asia Region, Pakistan," 2003, compares Pakistan's female literacy rate with that of other countries in the region with similar per capita income levels.

18. Figures are for 2009 (www.data.worldbank.org/sites/default/files/gstable 12.pdf).

19. Finance Division, Government of Pakistan, "Population, Labour Force, and Employment," *Pakistan Economic Survey 2008–09*, p. 183.

20. These figures are for 2007–08. *Compendium on Gender Statistics in Pakistan*, Government of Pakistan, March 2010 (www.statpak.gov.pk/fbs/content/compendium-gender-statistics-pakistan-2009). The primary, middle, and secondary school data are from the Academy of Educational Planning and Management, Islamabad; data from different universities were used to compile the information at the university level.

21. UNDP, *Human Development Report 2010*.

22. For more information on women's survival strategies in the Old City of Lahore, see Anita M. Weiss, *Walls within Walls: Life Histories of Working Women in the Old City of Lahore*, 2nd ed. (Oxford University Press, 2002).

23 Ministry of Population Welfare, "Draft National Population Policy 2010," p. 7.

24. For further discussion of these ongoing legal reforms, see Anita M. Weiss, "Moving Forward with the Legal Empowerment of Women in Pakistan," USIP Special Report (forthcoming).

25. As quoted in Tennessee Guerilla Women, "Bella Abzug: 'Women Will Change the Nature of Power' (Video)," July 19, 2009 (http://guerillawomentn.blogspot.com/2009/07/bella-abzug-women-will-change-nature-of.html).

JOSHUA T. WHITE

16

The Perils of Prediction

Predicting Pakistan's future is risky business. Just a few years ago, no one would have expected the emergence of a robust Lawyers' Movement, challenging the Musharraf government and agitating for judicial independence. Few would have predicted the rise of a bafflingly multifaceted Taliban movement in Pakistan's western frontier that brought together a wide array of Pashtun and Punjabi militants. And who could possibly have predicted an outbreak of deadly rioting in the historically peaceful Hazara division in the newly named Khyber Pakhtunkhwa Province? Clearly one should have humility when gazing into the future, particularly with respect to a country about which there are relatively few reliable data.

Key Factors

What are the key factors that are likely to determine Pakistan's future course? Many deserve attention: demographics, energy demand, state spending on social welfare, state patronage of militant Islamist groups, and foreign policy toward neighboring countries, to name just a few. Here, with no pretense of being comprehensive, I have chosen to focus on three particular factors: Islamism, fragmentation, and blowback from terrorist attacks.

Islamism

The trajectory of Islamism in Pakistan is a critical determinant of the future. Political Islam is often framed as a competition between radicalism and liberalism. One common formulation pits dangerous Deobandism against benign Barelvism, each group challenging the other ideologically for the soul of the state. An even more hyperbolic formulation sees a battle between a secularist vision that seeks to roll back the institutional expressions of Pakistan's state Islamism—the sharia courts, Hudood ordinances, Council on Islamic Ideology, and others—and the Ahl-e-Hadith/Wahhabist ideologies of a Saudi-like sharia state.

Although political and military elites have long publicly supported the idea of an Islamized Pakistan—so much so that only a handful of politicians and public intellectuals will question the need for an "Islamic state"—there is little to suggest that they have an interest in promoting a wholesale alternative narrative. That is to say, the future of Islamism is not likely to be contested at the extremes. The Pakistani people, by most measures, support a relatively benign sharia and are unlikely to countenance either the establishment of a robust Islamist state or the dismantlement of existing Islamic state institutions.

The real debates over Islamism are likely to be more subtle, focusing on differentiation among Islamist groups. What kind of distinctions will the public make between the Taliban "over there" (Afghanistan, Kashmir, India) and the Taliban "over here" (Pakistan) or between groups that participate in elections and those that reject the democratic process? What distinctions will be made between groups that engage in relatively popular jihads (Kashmir) and relatively unpopular ones (sectarian violence) or between those that support the Pakistani army and those that target it?

These distinctions are in part ideological, and they may be shaped in the coming years by media debates, academic conferences, clerical fatwas, and so forth. But such debates do not occur in a vacuum; they are driven by interests and incentives, and in Pakistan, those interests and incentives are largely those of the state. It is the state, its institutions, and its leadership that will most significantly shape the debate about Islamism. Recent research by C. Christine Fair and others shows that the public already differentiates among Islamist organizations and does so in ways that appear to mirror state "messaging" about those organizations. Even so, they often fail to understand the links between and common operations of groups that, at first blush, appear to be distinct.

A focal question then concerns what incentives the state will continue to provide to Islamists. Will the military continue to feed the narrative that links Pakistan's strategic situation—its disadvantages vis-à-vis India and the United States—to a larger story about the disadvantages of the Muslim ummah? Will it continue to provide succor to militant groups operating in Afghanistan and Kashmir, which in turn pressure mainstream political parties and religious movements to condone militancy? Will it continue to invest little in protecting political and religious leaders who speak out against violence? Will political elites continue to find it useful to ally with religious parties that are opposed to any retrenchment of state sharia laws and institutions? And will they continue to make concessions to extremists?

Unfortunately, the political incentives for both military and political leaders are mixed. Both find advantage in encouraging public support for militant Islamists "over there." Both find it useful to portray the Islamist narrative as a response to U.S. hegemony. And both are inclined to respond to groups that claim an Islamic mantle with accommodations such as peace deals (for example, by the army), sharia concessions (for example, by the liberal Awami National Party), and even preemptive strategies (for example, Chief Minister Shahbaz Sharif's suggestion that the Taliban find another, less sympathetic target than his home province of Punjab).

The future of Islamism in Pakistan, at least in the near and mid-term, is likely to depend in large part on which groups the state chooses to support and how it differentiates (to itself and to the public) between those that are legitimate and those that are not. Those decisions, by and large, will be shaped by the extent to which Islamist groups threaten the military and political elites.

Fragmentation

A second factor in determining Pakistan's course is the likelihood of subnational fragmentation. As an ethnically and linguistically diverse state, Pakistan has long been concerned about its cohesiveness and integrity. In the 1950s and 1960s it dealt with agitation by the Afghan government and Pashtuns within the North-West Frontier Province (NWFP) for a greater "Pashtunistan" that would reach from eastern Afghanistan to the Indus River. In the 1960s it faced an uprising of Bengali nationalism in East Pakistan—a consequence of near-sighted linguistic and political dominance by West Pakistan. It has dealt with ethnic Baloch nationalism for decades, and more recently there have been calls for a "Seraikistan" to be carved out of Punjab and Sindh and a Hazara province out of Khyber Pakhtunkhwa.

Can the state contain these fissiparous forces? With the exception of the Bengali nationalist movement in 1971, when West Pakistani elites disastrously calculated that they could crush an uprising by half the country, Pakistan's leaders have been able to contain nationalist movements, albeit harshly at times. Pashtun nationalism, though troubling, never represented a pressing strategic threat to the state.

Baloch movements were a thorn in the side of the military, but they have been diminished through a combination of bribery and brutality. The demand for a Saraiki province has slowly gained momentum but remains inchoate. And the Hazarawals demanding a province, historically allied as they are with factions of the weak Pakistan Muslim League, have little political leverage. If, however, there is to be demarcation of new provinces, it is likely to be part of a grand political bargain that—like India's internal reorganization along linguistic lines in the 1950s and 1960s—ultimately strengthens rather than weakens the state.

While these examples of ethnolinguistic nationalism seem unlikely to flare up in ways that would seriously endanger the state, they could nonetheless undermine the legitimacy of the government and the army. Somewhat more likely is the possibility that Pashtun nationalism would be revived—not from the left, in the tradition of the secular Awami National Party, but from the right, using the rhetoric and organization of new Pakistani Taliban groups. The Pakistani Taliban have emerged as a new vehicle for the expression of Pashtun grievances, but they have been careful to portray themselves solely in religious rather than ethnic terms. This is perhaps because they consider religious mobilization to be more effective than ethnic mobilization or perhaps because their ranks are increasingly supplemented by Punjabis from Kashmir- and sectarian-oriented organizations.

If the Pakistani or U.S. militaries expand their operations in Khyber Pakhtunkhwa or the Federally Administered Tribal Areas (FATA) over the coming years, Taliban groups could leverage local discontent to promote a hybrid religious-ethnic narrative of resistance against the Pakistani government. That would not necessarily "splinter" the Pakistani state, but it could result in deep antagonism toward the government and the loss of peripheral areas in Khyber Pakhtunkhwa, FATA, and Balochistan to Taliban control.

Blowback from Terrorist Attacks

The third factor is the likelihood of another major attack on the United States or India by organizations linked to Pakistan. This may not fit the typical definition of a "core variable" underlying Pakistan's future development, but it is arguably a fundamental one. No other factor could so dramatically shake up Pakistan's relationship with its key interlocutors—the United States and India—and spark internal instability.

A Pakistan-linked attack on the United States admittedly has a ripped-from-the-headlines quality, but it is one of the few events that could precipitate a major restructuring of the U.S.-Pakistan relationship. Nothing else is likely to be a game-changer in the bilateral relationship because the United States is wary of participating in negotiations over Kashmir, a nuclear deal for Pakistan is improbable (or would be heavily diluted), and U.S. efforts to extract concessions from India on issues related to its military posture or activities in Afghanistan would almost certainly fall flat.

By contrast, a high-casualty attack on the United States could spark any number of U.S. responses: ultimatums to the Pakistani military about dealing decisively with militant networks, unilateral drone strikes across Pakistan, overt U.S. troop movements into the tribal areas, or threats to withhold military supplies and economic aid. Such actions could force the opening of new avenues of cooperation, particularly if militant groups had also increased their targeting of the Pakistani state; however, they could also push Pakistan in dangerous new directions, encouraging both elected and military elites to cast about for alternatives to a U.S. partnership. (While in today's geopolitical environment they may find few takers, in ten to twenty years China or Russia may be willing to forge new relationships.)

We have already seen, on multiple occasions, what can come of Pakistan-linked attacks within India. The 2001 attack on the Indian Parliament brought India and Pakistan close to war. Following the 2008 Lashkar-e-Tayyiba attack in Mumbai, India demonstrated remarkable restraint, leaving the United States to lean on Pakistan (which it did, rather unsuccessfully). Future attacks—when, not if, they happen—could easily bring both countries to war. With a more open and aggressive media than at any previous time in Pakistan's history, a major war could serve as a referendum on the Pakistani military—either buttressing its legitimacy as the de facto guarantor of the state or exposing its recklessness in engaging in asymmetric warfare against India.

Future Predictions

There are good reasons to reject the most dire predictions of Pakistan's future. It may be a dysfunctional state, but it is not a failed one. The bureaucracy, for all its problems, retains not inconsiderable capacity and expertise. The army, as guarantor of the state, is relatively professional and disciplined. The political class, venal as it may be, generally holds to basic democratic principles (though not with respect to internal party workings). The media, though often shrill, is increasingly influential and confrontational. And the public at large, while quick to embrace an abstract Islamist narrative, has shown limited appetite for strict sharia or violence within Pakistan in the name of religion.

These are positive factors, and ones that should temper any assessment of Pakistan that is uniformly gloomy. Keeping these and other relatively stabilizing factors in mind, however, there seem to be three scenarios that could play out in the next five to seven years. Each, while somewhat pessimistic, falls within the realm of the possible and points to the prospect of new dynamics in the U.S.-Pakistan relationship.

A Center-Right Government

One relatively likely scenario would be the emergence of a center-right government, such as one led by the Pakistan Muslim League–Nawaz, that constrained but did not reject cooperation with the United States. The contours of such a government are not difficult to imagine. It would run on a mildly Islamist platform—promising Islamic values, protection of Pakistani sovereignty, and less deference to the West. It would form a coalition with Islamist parties in Khyber Pakhtunkhwa and Balochistan and garner informal electoral support by Sipah-e-Sahaba and other militant groups in Punjab. It would, along with the religious parties, adopt mild but troubling sharia measures at the provincial level, enabled by the devolution reforms of the Eighteenth Amendment.

Moreover, it would seek to limit the scope of U.S. operations in Pakistan and publicly challenge U.S. drone strikes. Behind the scenes, Pakistan's cooperation with the United States would not change dramatically, but the presence of a center-right government would give the army an excuse for acting haltingly on U.S. demands and deflecting decisions to the Parliament as a way of rendering them moot. Compared with its center-left predecessors, such a government would be considerably more resistant to military or paramilitary operations against militant groups within Pakistan, and it would have an especially hard time taking action against popular social welfare organizations that are linked to, or serve as a front for, extremist groups.

Overreach

A second potential future could emerge in the wake of a major attack on the United States for which there was clear evidence of complicity by organizations in Pakistan. The government of Pakistan, facing another "Armitage moment" of decision, weighs its options and realizes that it would face severe military and economic losses if it were to break off its strategic relationship with the United States. Neither China nor Saudi Arabia could provide an adequate substitute for U.S. largesse. Then, as after 9/11, it chooses to cooperate with a new wave of U.S. demands to crack down on militant groups.

Those demands are sweeping, and they include insistence on actions against popular social welfare groups affiliated with militant organizations—groups known for their jihadi activities in Kashmir—as well as on large-scale military operations in the tribal areas. The Americans also take the prerogative to expand the area of operations of their drone strikes and begin using them on a near-daily basis against training camps in Khyber Pakhtunkhwa, southern Punjab, and the Pashtun slums in Karachi.

The combination of the Pakistani army's reluctant actions against militant groups and the unilateral U.S. response provokes an intense reaction in the country. The elected government, unable to construct a narrative to explain its actions to the public and unwilling to take the blame for unpopular army activities, is consumed by a wave of resignations. There are days of violent street protests led by a broad-based political coalition opposed to "violations of Pakistani sovereignty." The bar associations openly question the decision of the government to cooperate with the U.S. requests, and the Supreme Court, using its sweeping *suo moto* powers, calls serving army officers from General Headquarters to justify the arrest of Jamaat-ud-Dawa activists and explain the U.S. use of drones in Karachi and Bahawalpur.

Sensing an opportunity amid the chaos, Pakistani Taliban groups led by the Tehrik-e-Taliban Pakistan begin a coordinated campaign against the government in Islamabad, which the Taliban accuses of being subservient to the Americans. In an attempt to take the Pakistani military off guard, teams of Taliban soldiers advance simultaneously into a number of settled districts in Khyber Pakhtunkhwa and Punjab, setting up "shadow nazims (mayors)" and driving out civil servants and police forces. They declare that areas under the control of the Pakistani government are *dar-ulharb* (that is, "under the abode of war," in which Muslims can wage jihad against the state) and promise to expand sharia in accordance with the wishes of the people.

By the time that the Americans realize that they may have overplayed their hand by demanding too much, too quickly, the government's credibility has been severely diminished, anti-Americanism has reached a feverish pitch, and the Taliban have made limited but significant territorial gains across the frontier.

A More Political Taliban

After several years of ineffective counterinsurgency operations in southern and eastern Afghanistan, the United States eventually draws down its military presence significantly in 2014 and finds a face-saving solution whereby a Taliban-affiliated political party enters into a power-sharing agreement in Kabul. It is an unpleasant situation, but some measure of calm has returned to the country, and Pakistan is relatively pleased that pro-Islamabad Pashtuns are again at the helm in Afghanistan.

Unfortunately, even the half-hearted political victory by the Taliban in Afghanistan encourages Pakistani Taliban groups to press for concessions within Pakistan. Some Taliban factions, particularly in Waziristan, keep up their violent confrontation with the Pakistani army. But others, emboldened by their counterparts in Afghanistan, adopt a politically shrewd strategy of declaring sharia in pockets of Pakistan, making a show of force, and then extracting political concessions from the government, leaving them in control of those regions.

The Pakistani Taliban also learn, again from the Taliban in Afghanistan, that "kindler, gentler" Taliban rule—less exploitative and more focused on providing quick justice—is more likely to take root in local communities and less likely to provoke the Pakistani army. They begin partnering with social welfare organizations (linked, naturally, with militant outfits and religious parties) to deliver basic social services in areas under their control.

The army, for its part, feels relatively secure about the evolving situation in Afghanistan and sees little reason to act decisively against these Taliban groups, which are increasingly providing a wide range of services to disenfranchised communities. But as the Taliban become more sophisticated, they gradually but consistently encroach on the influence of the government—first only in the border areas but eventually in pockets across the country. The slow, seemingly benign expansion of these Taliban groups happens without much fanfare, but before long results in the weakening of the state and the creation of militant safe havens in virtually every region of the country.

MOEED W. YUSUF

17

Youth and the Future

Hardly anyone questions the importance of Pakistan to future global security. Pakistan's importance is tremendous, and it has spurred voluminous research. However, most studies are narrowly focused on immediate concerns regarding Pakistan's role in the U.S. mission in Afghanistan and in battling militancy within its territory. This microscopic focus is of little value in understanding Pakistan's potential trajectory beyond three to five years. Virtually no one has attempted to understand the perceptions and outlook of the real custodians of Pakistan's future—that is, its young generations. This is an obvious void, because it will be the orientation of Pakistani youth, not present-day leaders, that determines what kind of state Pakistan becomes over the next decade or two.

This chapter focuses on Pakistani youth's perceptions and preferences and attempts to analyze them in light of the socioeconomic realities that their country is likely to face over the projected period. The premise is that youth preferences will be tempered by those realities and that the manner in which that dynamic plays out will determine what Pakistan looks like in a decade or more from now. Much of the discussion benefits from fresh data obtained from three recent high-profile surveys that seek to capture opinions of youth on various personal, community, national, and international issues.[1] I begin by analyzing selective aspects of the data sets and discuss where the current mood of Pakistani youth may lead their country. Next, I look at the projections for Pakistan's performance across certain key socioeconomic variables. Third, I posit how socioeconomic trends and youth preferences are likely to impact each other and where that dynamic is likely to lead Pakistan. Finally, policy interventions are identified that would allow Pakistan to progress toward becoming a stable, prosperous state.

Why Bother about Pakistan's Youth?

Focusing on young people has special significance in Pakistan's case, given that the country possesses one of the largest youth populations in the world. Pakistan is a country of 180 million people, 101.95 million (59 percent) of whom are young men and women below the age of twenty-four—a proportion of youth that is exceeded only by that in Yemen. Another 13.95 million fall within the twenty-five- to twenty-nine-year bracket, bringing the under-thirty tally to 67.1 percent of the total population.[2] What is more, Pakistan is only halfway through its democratic transition, and the current rate of 3.9 births per woman is set to carry Pakistan's youth bulge well beyond 2025.[3] Pakistan's fifteen- to twenty-four-year-old population will expand by 20 percent during the 2020s, and in 2030 the country's under-twenty-four population, projected to number over 130 million, will still form the majority of the population.[4] The sheer numerical strength of Pakistan's upcoming generations implies that the direction in which the critical mass of this segment chooses to push the country will inevitably become the destiny of one of the world's most populated states.

The Minds of Young Pakistanis: What the Data Show

Summarized below are the opinions of Pakistani youth identified by three recent national surveys: the British Council's "Pakistan: The Next Generation," the *Herald*'s "Youth Speak," and the Center for Civic Education's "Civic Health of Pakistani Youth."[5] Table 17-1 provides a summary of selected questions from the three surveys. Rather than presenting data from each survey separately, I have created seven broad functional categories, each combining information from one or more surveys. The discussion that follows, based largely on responses in table 17-1, analyzes each functional category and posits what kind of Pakistan those responses and preferences may bring about.

Views on Pakistan

Young Pakistanis remain patriotic at the core, but their religious identity supersedes their affinity with the country. In terms of their trust in Pakistan to provide for them, they display a rather schizophrenic mindset: they realize that the desire for upward economic mobility may best be served by emigrating (75 percent would prefer to do so), yet they retain a sense of optimism

Table 17-1. *Youth Preferences in Pakistan from Selected Data
from the Three Quoted Surveys*[a]
Percent of respondents

Issue	Yes	No	Author's observations
How youth view Pakistan			
What do you see yourself as?[b]			
Muslim	75		
Citizen of Pakistan	14		
Are you proud to be a Pakistani?[c]	79	12	Figures from Balochistan were the positive bleakest. There was a weak positive correlation between religiosity and pride.
If you had the chance to leave Pakistan, would you opt for it?[c]	75 (yes/maybe)	23	
In five years, do you think your life will be better, worse, or the same?[c]	79 (better)	5 (worse)	
Are you optimistic about finding employment?[c]	57	16	Education positively correlated with optimism about finding a job.
The role of religion			
Do you think Pakistan should be an Islamic state?[c]	64 (Islamic)	22 (secular)	People who were more religiously inclined were more likely to answer yes.
Should the Pakistani legal system have punishments like flogging, stoning to death, and cutting off of limbs?[c]	33	47	Even some who were not strictly observant supported such punishments.
How religious are you?[c]	81 (very or moderately observant)	15 (rarely observant)	

(continued)

Table 17-1. *Youth Preferences in Pakistan from Selected Data
from the Three Quoted Surveys*[a] *(continued)*
Percent of respondents

Issue	Yes	No	Author's observations
How important is your religious sect to your identity?[c]	86 (very or moderately important)	11	
How important is your ethnic identity?[c]	86 (important/ somewhat important)	9 (unimportant)	

Pakistan's problems

What is the single most important issue facing Pakistan?[c]

Inflation	40
Unemployment	20
Terrorism	14

Who is to blame for the political problems that Pakistan faces?[c]

Politicians	37	People from Balochistan tended to blame the military much more than people from other provinces did.
United States	25	
Military	19	

Who is most to blame for the economic problems that Pakistan faces?[c]

Politicians	41
United States	23
Military	13

The political system

Which political party do you support?[c]

PPP	28	Fifty-nine percent of PPP voters responding wanted Pakistan to be an Islamic state.
PML-N	13	
MQM	8	

Issue	Yes	No	Author's observations
Do you prefer democracy or military rule?[c]	76 (democracy)	21 (military rule)	Preference correlated with the source that youth get most of their information from.

(continued)

Table 17-1. *Youth Preferences in Pakistan from Selected Data from the Three Quoted Surveys*[a] *(continued)*
Percent of respondents

Issue	Yes	No	Author's observations
How much confidence do you have in Pakistan's institutions?[b]			
Great deal of confidence in the military	60+		
Great deal of confidence in religious institutions	40+		
Great deal of confidence in the national government	<10		
Do you cast your vote?[d]	52.8	Not reported	
Do you think your vote can bring change?[d]	61.8	Not reported	
Do you take an active part in politics or political activities?[d]	21.9	78.1	
Lifestyle			
What are the three activities that you spend most of your free time doing?[c]			The top three choices may have varied in relative importance but they were the same across the socioeconomic spectrum.
TV	51		Political news on tele-
Reading	45		vision was most
Going out with friends	33		watched by twenty-four- to thirty-year-olds.
What are the three places where you spend the most time with your friends?[c]			
Home	66		
Who are you closest to?[c]			
Parents	52		The richest cohort was closer to friends.

(continued)

Table 17-1. *Youth Preferences in Pakistan from Selected Data
from the Three Quoted Surveys*[a] *(continued)*
Percent of respondents

Issue	Yes	No	Author's observations
Do you think it's appropriate to be friends with members of the opposite sex?[c]	31	47	Females were less likely to approve. More religiously oriented respondents were less likely to approve.
Should women work?[c]	61	23	The higher the number of children that a respondent desired, the less likely the respondent was to support women working.
Would you opt for an arranged marriage?[c]	52 (yes/maybe)	31	
Do you financially support any organization?[d]			
Religious organizations	21		
Social organizations	14.8		
Political organizations	7.2		
On what platform, in your view, can youth freely express their point of view and ideas?[d]			
Friends	70		
Internet	30		
Educational institute	34		
Religious institute	5		
Extremism/radicalization			
Do you think that extremist tendencies are on the rise in the younger generation?[d]	69.6	Not reported	
Can youth play a positive role in combating the increasing level of extremism?[d]	85.4	Not reported	
Should the Pakistan army be fighting in the tribal areas?[c]	42	33	The rich were far more likely to support the fighting.

(continued)

Table 17-1. *Youth Preferences in Pakistan from Selected Data
from the Three Quoted Surveys*[a] *(continued)*
Percent of respondents

Issue	Yes	No	Author's observations
Whose war is Pakistan fighting in the tribal areas?[c]			
United States	51		The more educated
Pakistan	18		Pakistanis were more
Both	26		likely to blame the
			United States.
Should the Pakistan govern-	47	29	
ment negotiate with the			
Taliban?[c]			
What should the United States do in Afghanistan?[c]			
Pull out instantly	34		
Pull out but give financial	16		
and political assistance			
Are madrassas radicalizing	44	25	Those who were reli-
the youth of Pakistan?[c]			giously inclined were
			less likely to say that
			madrassas are radi-
			calizing Pakistani
			youth.
What are the main reasons for violence and terror in Pakistan?[b]			
Injustice	28		
Poor economic conditions	27		
Lack of education and	20		
awareness			
Who started the 1965 war?[c]			
India	75		
Pakistan	13		
How did West Pakistan treat East Pakistanis?[c]			
Don't know	40		
Unfairly	38		
Fairly	19		
Who is responsible for the Kargil conflict?[c]			
India	38		
Pakistan	22		
United States	25		

(continued)

Table 17-1. *Youth Preferences in Pakistan from Selected Data
from the Three Quoted Surveys*[a] *(continued)*
Percent of respondents

Issue	Yes	No	Author's observations
Do you think Kashmir should be . . .?[c]			
Part of Pakistan	50		
Part of India	2		
Independent	40		
Do you think there should	60	18	
be closer economic ties be-			
tween India and Pakistan?[c]			
Do you think there should	45	37	
be an open-visa regime			
between India and Pakistan?[c]			

a. For questions with multiple choices, only popular answers and their respective percentages are shown. The unpopular choices are included only if they are relevant to the analysis.
b. Question from the British Council survey.
c. Question from the *Herald* survey.
d. Question from the Center for Civic Education survey.

about their future in Pakistan that defies most projections. Seventy-five percent believe that the next five years will be better, and the majority expect to
find a job; the more educated are more hopeful about that. This mindset may
perhaps be explained as a coping mechanism for those who want to leave
Pakistan but are unable to do so.

   This implies a future Pakistan in which
   —religious and national identities remain intrinsically linked
   —difficulties and challenges are psychologically (not operationally) neutral-
ized by a coping mechanism that provides hope and resilience even when it defies
reality.

Role of Religion

The data reinforce the fact that separation of church and state is a principle
that Pakistani youth do not subscribe to. Religion remains central in the lives
of Pakistanis, with 81 percent of youth being strictly or moderately observant.
Sixty-four percent seek an Islamic state; support wanes only among a minority of youth educated in elite schools. Strong support for Islam's role notwithstanding, unpacking the notion of an Islamic state is not easy. Existing
literature shows that there is no agreement on just what kind of Islamic state
Pakistan should be. In fact, the surveys quoted here hint at the failure of the

Pakistani state to impose Islam—the same Islam for everyone—as a unifying bond. Young people seem to give tremendous importance to their religious sects, and sectarian identity has led to more discord than agreement in Pakistan in the past. Moreover, ethnic identity continues to be extremely important—86 percent say that it is "important" or "somewhat important"—despite the state's efforts to subdue ethnic divisions by imposing Islam as the overarching identity.

Next, so acute has been the deterioration in the country's delivery of public services, dispensation of justice, and maintenance of law and order that the youth are losing trust in the efficacy of the current system altogether. Although a minority, a substantial 33 percent supports harsh punishments that are derived from the traditional Islamic narrative but are antithetical to the modern concept of human rights. Important to note is the fact that this preference transcends individual levels of religiosity. As the *Herald* survey comments, "For a significant chunk of young people disillusioned with the country's judicial system, these punishments have gone beyond being religious tenets and may have become representations of justice itself."[6]

This implies a future Pakistan that is
—highly conservative but not to be confused with extremist
—aware of its sectarian identity
—aware of its ethnic identity
—increasingly frustrated by and dissatisfied with service delivery and dispensation of justice.

Pakistan's Problems

As surprising as it may be to Western audiences, terrorism is a distant third when it comes to the proportion of people who consider it to be Pakistan's biggest problem. Their two top concerns, inflation and unemployment, strike at the heart of governance and economic management and put a high premium on government performance. Arguably then, young people are likely to become increasingly impatient if economic pressures on their everyday lives are not eased in years to come. Politicians remain the single most loathed group in the minds of youth; they are considered most culpable for the political and economic problems that bear on average Pakistanis. Rather interestingly, the military is perceived as being less culpable than both the politicians and the United States, which is ranked after the politicians in terms of exacerbating Pakistan's political and economic problems. Anti-U.S. sentiments permeate deep among the Pakistani youth—even more interesting is the fact that the more educated tend to be more critical of the United States—and are not likely to be easily reversed.

This implies a future Pakistan that
—demands better performance from its leadership
—simultaneously remains impatient with the failures of its discredited leadership
—is avidly anti-U.S.

The Political System

Feelings among Pakistani youth about the country's political system are mixed. Bouts of unsuccessful military rule seem to have convinced them that democracy is the way forward for Pakistan. A clear majority supports civilian rule. That said, the long-standing puzzle associated with Pakistani voting behavior holds true for youth as well: despite the importance of religion and support for an Islamic state, youth favor mainstream, "secular" political parties. The Pakistan People's Party (PPP) remains the most popular outfit, followed by the Pakistan Muslim League–Nawaz (PML-N) and the Muttahida Qaumi Movement (MQM). No Islamic party is featured among Pakistani young people's favorites; national, regional, and ethnic parties are decisively more popular than Islamic ones. That does not mean that Pakistan's military has been delegitimized in the eyes of the youth. Despite support for democracy, their trust in democratic institutions is far lower than their trust in the military. Over 60 percent express confidence in the military (the poorer a respondent, the less likely he or she is to buy into the merits of democracy) while more than 40 percent do so in religious institutions. Institutions associated with the national government receive support from less than 10 percent of respondents. Such mindsets leave room for an acceptable political role for the military, whether from behind the scenes or through direct intervention. This is one of the contradictions that Pakistani citizens have failed to resolve for years, and Pakistani youth seem to have fallen into the same trap.

Perhaps most alarming is how averse Pakistani youth are to direct political activity. Although they are ardent followers of national politics and often are seen as part of mass civil society movements, most recently the 2007 lawyers' movement against President Pervez Musharraf,[7] the data reveal dismal figures regarding their participation in politics and their inroads into power structures. Nearly half of young people do not vote, about 40 percent have no confidence in the utility of their vote, and a shocking 78 percent are categorical in their rejection of active politics. Less than 1 percent see an active political role as desirable. Even philanthropic tendencies, otherwise strong, gravitate toward religious and social organizations, not political ones. That raises yet another contradiction: Pakistani youth desire change, and they are pessimistic about the ability or willingness of the current political class to bring about positive change, but they are averse to becoming part of the political process themselves. They remain politically disillusioned and disengaged.

This implies a future Pakistan that

—is supportive of democracy but retains some level of hope in the military

—is ruled by moderate political parties

—has youth who are politically disengaged but remain desperate for political change.

Lifestyle

Pakistan's society remains traditional at its core. Although trends are changing, the social life of a majority (66 percent) of young men and women still revolves around the home. Except those in the highest socioeconomic strata, youth report being closest to their parents (52 percent even when the highest strata are included). Arranged marriages are popular. Young people—especially females—are averse to friendship with members of the opposite sex, and although a majority support working women, that support is inversely correlated with the number of children desired. Since childbearing is an important consideration, in reality a majority of women end up staying at home. Most youth also feel constrained in expressing their views freely with those to whom they are closest (parents) and can do so only with friends. Religious institutions are one of the least hospitable in terms of allowing freedom of expression; only 5 percent of the respondents in the Center for Civic Education's survey believed that they could express themselves freely at religious institutions.

One of the most profound changes in the lives of Pakistani youth has been the advent of free media. Television has surpassed radio, newspapers, and books to become the principal source of information for the country's rising generation. While entertainment remains popular, youth between the ages of twenty-four and thirty prefer to consume political news. Moreover, an overwhelming majority prefers the vernacular press and media, with English media a distant second. There is ample evidence in the disaggregated data from the surveys studied (not mentioned in table 7-1) that the type of information received from television has a deep impact on youth perceptions. The preference for particular channels is strongly correlated to youth views on, among others, religiosity, democracy, and key foreign policy questions like Kashmir.[8] Television thus stands out as one of the principal avenues of influence on young minds in Pakistan.

This implies a future Pakistan that

—is traditional and, while modernizing (according to the Western point of view), remains obsessed with holding on to traditional values and lifestyles

—uses television, which has the power to mold views and opinions, as the principal source of information.

Extremism and Radicalization

A majority of young Pakistanis see rising extremism among youth as a growing concern, and almost 86 percent believe that they can and should play a role to stem the tide. The majority see madaris as part of the problem, although the view is not as simplistic as it is often portrayed in Western discourse. A slim majority supports the Pakistan military's operations in the tribal areas—the richer the respondent, the more likely the person is to support the operations, perhaps an indication that he or she has more to lose—but use of force still remains unpopular overall. A majority believe that the Pakistani state should negotiate with the Pakistani Taliban. That sentiment holds irrespective of where on the political spectrum the respondent lies. Sizable proportions of supporters of even the mainstream and ethnic parties like PPP and MQM support negotiations.[9] Underlying that support are two perceptions evident in the survey findings: first, that the root cause of terrorism in Pakistan is injustice as well as failure of governance and service delivery, which cannot be tackled by use of force, and second, that Pakistan is ultimately fighting "America's war" (51 percent believe that to be the case) and that the situation will get better if the United States packs up and leaves Afghanistan. The latter suggests significant uptake of the popular narrative repeated on Pakistani television, in addition, of course, to the failure of Western policies to win Pakistanis' "hearts and minds."

This implies a future Pakistan that is

—opposed to extremist forces but still remains opposed to heavy-handed solutions to the problem unless they become an absolute necessity

—susceptible to conspiracy theories and popular discourse that strikes an emotional chord even if it defies strict strategic logic.

Reading of National History vis-à-vis India

When it comes to national history, especially vis-à-vis India, Pakistan's textbooks seem to have retained their influence. Over 50 percent still want Kashmir to be part of Pakistan while another 40 percent support an independent Kashmir. Questions regarding India-Pakistan wars receive factually inaccurate responses. A majority blame India for initiating the 1965 war as well as for Kargil, and as many as 40 percent claim ignorance on how the Pakistani state treated East Pakistanis. That said, a positive trend is obvious from the fact that a comfortable majority support closer economic ties and a visa-free regime with India. There is an obvious desire to move on despite what they believe are Indian transgressions of the past.

This implies a future Pakistan that is
—influenced by state-sponsored historical narratives.

Future of the Pakistani Federation

There is one other important conclusion that can be drawn from these surveys. The findings do not bode well for the Pakistani federation in the coming years. The much-discussed discontent among the lesser provinces has carried over to the next generation. Baloch youth stand out as most distraught with the federation. Except for a minority, they are least enthusiastic about being part of Pakistan and are least proud to be Pakistanis. They also are the keenest to leave Pakistan, and they oppose the military and state institutions more staunchly than youth in other provinces.

This implies a future Pakistan in which
—barring institutional transformation, today's youth will inherit a federation that is held together tenuously and in which the fundamental terms of coexistence remain undetermined.

The Realities That Youth Will Have to Contend With

Current opinions of Pakistani youth can be analyzed to predict what Pakistan may look like in the future if young people carry those sentiments into their adult lives. In reality, however, what they can achieve for Pakistan will be affected by the socioeconomic realities with which they have to contend. The literature argues that a youth bulge can become a blessing or a curse, depending on how a society channels the energies of its youth. Empirical evidence suggests that youth outcomes strongly correlate with, among other factors, socioeconomic conditions, educational standards, access to opportunities for social and economic advancement, and cultural polarization. The discussion below outlines the current projections for Pakistan in these areas in order to predict the future conditions under which its youth may live.

Education

Educational attainment is the fundamental prerequisite for a country looking for a positive channel for youth energies. Unfortunately, education trends in Pakistan remain worrisome. Access to education indicators have improved constantly, and youth literacy, at 69 percent, is 15 percentage points higher than adult literacy. Yet in absolute terms, those figures are abysmal. Gender disparity is high as well: while 79 percent of young males are literate, a mere 59 percent of young females are.[10] In the coming years, quantitative education indicators such as literacy rates and school attendance are projected to improve. However,

Pakistan is all but certain to miss the target of universal primary education by 2015 set under the Millennium Development Goals and even its own educational goals under the current medium-term development framework. To be sure, even as indicators such as enrollment rates and average years of schooling improve, there will still be an extremely large number—in absolute terms—of children out of school for the foreseeable future. Moreover, the gender gap is unlikely to shrink significantly. Since current adult female literacy levels are very low and mothers' education is found to be strongly correlated with daughters' education, the next generation of girls is at a disadvantage.[11]

Quality of education is an even greater concern. The projected quantitative improvements will be largely ineffectual if educated youth are not trained well enough to find a respectable place in the economy. Pakistan's education system is stratified; as a result, only the urban, elite private schools, which cater to less than 15 percent of school-going children, exhibit decent quality. Quality of the public education system and the religious madaris remains abysmal. This is a potentially explosive situation since over 60 percent of youth attend public schools.[12]

The danger from stratification of the education system extends beyond qualitative concerns; there is a socioeconomic dimension to the equation as well. Madaris cater to the poorest classes, public schools to the lower-middle class, and private schools to the upper-middle class and elite segments of society. There also are differences in the messages that they impart to their students. Madaris produce graduates with narrow-minded, conservative (though not necessarily radical) ideological beliefs, public school graduates have a vision that is only slightly more tolerant, and private school students are fairly liberal in their thinking. The differences in their outlook are so severe that the elite students harbor extreme disdain for their counterparts while poorer youth see the elite as surrogates of the West whose extravagant lifestyles are much to blame for economic inequality in Pakistan. Over time, youth in the three systems have become so isolated from each other that they can, and do, pass through the school system without having to engage in any meaningful interaction with each other.[13]

Virtually all these qualitative problems are recognized, and education reform policies discuss them in detail. The forward-looking strategy, however, is realistic and acknowledges that restructuring of the education system will be a gradual process. The future then promises improved access to education, but the problem remains that over 65 percent of school-going children in Pakistan who attend public schools and madaris are still being poorly educated. Moreover, they will continue to develop divergent outlooks across the three parallel systems and remain antagonistic toward each other's vision. All this points to much internal societal friction and polarization.

This implies a future Pakistan in which
—quantity of education and gender disparity improve, but overall levels still leave much to be desired
—the overwhelming majority receives poor-quality education
—the three parallel education systems create divergent world visions that are difficult to reconcile
—different socioeconomic strata are increasingly isolated from each other and continue to harbor disdain and antipathy for each other
—society is increasingly polarized.

Economic Security

Adequate economic opportunities commensurate with an individual's level of educational attainment are the single most important requirement if youth energies are to be channeled positively. Pakistan is likely to fall short on this count, too. Although Pakistan's macroeconomic growth over the years has been respectable (average growth has been just above 5 percent over the past two decades), the task of keeping up with Pakistan's burgeoning labor force is too monumental. Official estimates suggest that Pakistan will have to grow at a rate of 6.35 percent on average to keep unemployment at the current, rather impressive level of 5.32 percent but that the expected growth over the next five years will be, at best, 5.5 percent. In fact, any attempt to push growth rates above 5.45 percent would be unsustainable and expected to result in a balance of payments crisis at some point.[14] Unemployment is therefore certain to grow in the medium term.

Pakistan's natural resource crunch may make it difficult to achieve India- or China-like growth rates even over the longer term. Pakistan will be an increasingly resource-starved country in the coming years. The water table is falling by 2 to 3 meters a year in some regions. The renewable water supply per capita halved in the last quarter of the twentieth century and is projected to reach just above the "water scarcity" level of 1,000 per capita cubic meters of internal renewable water by 2025.[15] Energy shortages are currently causing havoc with the economy. Current supply lags demand by approximately 6,000 megawatts a day. Fresh plans to increase supply are likely to reduce this burden in the next three to five years, but in order to create a sustainable supply, Pakistan will have to invest in a variety of local ventures in addition to finding feasible and dependable import options. That in itself is a tall order and requires a huge amount of investment in the next decade.

Pakistan's economic problems are compounded when one considers that its growth model has persistently benefited the rich more than the poor, even though poverty levels have declined in the past decade. Today a little less than a quarter of the population is below the poverty line. The income ratio of the highest to lowest income quintiles has increased persistently since 1970 and stands at a staggering 4.2.[16] Malnourishment, another measure of the deprivation among the marginalized segments of society, has increased since the mid-1990s despite the fact that Pakistan has traditionally been a food-secure country. Using the youth development index (YDI) that they created to examine the level and determinants of youth development in Pakistan, Faizunnisa and Ikram argue that the development of Pakistani youth varies significantly depending on gender, location, and socioeconomic status.[17] Youth from higher socioeconomic strata have a development score that is twice as high as that of those from the lower socioeconomic strata.

In light of the fact that the richest 20 percent of the population continue to get richer and live luxurious lifestyles that are comparable to those of elites in developed countries, poor youth are bound to feel increasingly alienated from the system. With unemployment and underemployment tipped to continue nagging the economy, Pakistani youth, especially the non-elite, are likely to face an uphill battle in matching the optimism about finding employment and having a better future that they report in the surveys quoted here. Rising inequality implies a high level of underemployment for young people who possess relatively less marketable skills. Children of the poor, who have generally little access to the corridors of power and already are disadvantaged due to the poor skill sets that they develop in public schools, are invariably the first ones to be denied respectable employment. A disproportionate number of entry-level positions thus end up going to the already rich, which leaves others from lower socioeconomic classes underemployed. For educated (even if poorly educated) young men, underemployment ends up having just as much of an alienating effect as unemployment. This is the fate that the underprivileged segment of Pakistani youth is staring in the face.

This implies a future Pakistan with
—higher unemployment (it may still be low in absolute terms)
—growing underemployment
—increasing resource scarcity
—higher inequality.

The Disconnect between Expectation and Reality

The challenges faced by the Pakistani state in the education sector have been discussed. Pakistani parents and youth, however, are increasingly cognizant of the importance of education. Parents are generally supportive of facilitating education for their children, and that is true even for poor households, among which it is becoming increasingly common to save or take loans for children's schooling. Young people themselves show great interest in obtaining an education. According to a 2002 Population Council Survey, 80 percent of the male respondents and over 70 percent of their female counterparts expressed a desire to be educated at the secondary and tertiary levels.[18] The more recent surveys confirm that sentiment.

Theoretically, a strong desire for education ought to be considered a positive attribute. A deeper look, however, suggests that educational attainment is a double-edged sword. Churning out youth who are educated and therefore expect a bright future without providing them opportunities for employment and economic gain can backfire. That is especially true if, like Pakistani youth, the majority wants to work, provided that suitable opportunities are available.[19]

Realities on the ground hint at an impending crisis. If the quality of public and rural private sector education and the madaris remains poor and the labor market continues to favor the children of the elite, the disconnect between expectation and reality could result in added discontent among the youth. The surveys quoted here point to educated youth already feeling extremely disgruntled by the lack of meritocracy and absence of a level playing field. Half of working youth surveyed by the British Council had taken more than six months to find a job, and many pointed to corruption and discrimination as disrupting their work lives.[20] One can find ample empirical validation of the expectation-reality disconnect on urban streets in Pakistan as well, where increasing numbers of reasonably articulate holders of post-secondary degrees are seeking financial help—that is, begging. My discussions with such individuals reveal their great contempt for a state that cannot provide opportunities. There is also envy and resentment toward the elite, who are believed to deliberately create entry barriers for the poor, and there is a sense of alienation from the larger society.

This implies a future Pakistan in which
—expectations of those entering the workforce remain unfulfilled
—the underprivileged may become increasingly disillusioned and disgruntled with the system.

Migration

Migration often is seen as an obvious outlet for countries that have a bloated labor force and are unable to provide sufficient internal employment opportunities. Emigration eases the pressure on domestic resources and provides an avenue for potent foreign exchange as overseas workers send remittances home. Traditionally, Pakistan has used the migration option to good effect, with thousands of unskilled and semi-skilled Pakistanis finding employment in the Gulf and the skilled force finding opportunities in Europe and North America. With the labor force projected to grow and lingering socioeconomic problems at home, Pakistan is desperate to export labor. As already mentioned, the majority of Pakistan's young population is willing to leave the country. All this, however, is academic in the face of projected trends. Net migration rates are set to decline after a rather successful period in terms of labor export between 2000 and 2010. Migration will begin to taper off at the modest rate of less than 150 emigrants per 1,000 population by 2020.[21] In short, for the most part, Pakistani youth will have to find productive endeavors within their country.

This implies a future Pakistan with
—declining and later stagnant emigration.

Urbanization

Opportunities to migrate abroad for Pakistanis may dwindle, but that will not slow internal migration. Pakistani youth will be living in an increasingly urban Pakistan and will have to contend with the changing power structures and social realities that come with it. Currently, 37 percent of Pakistan's population live in cities. By 2030, urban dwellers will have equaled the rural population.[22]

The urbanization trend will produce mixed results. It will present all the challenges usually associated with the process—higher population density, poor living conditions, health and environmental hazards, and greater possibilities for crime, sectarianism, and so forth—but there will be significant positives as well. Urbanization will inevitably alter the power balance between the urban bourgeoisie and rural landed elite. The hold of the feudal mindset that has traditionally plagued Pakistani politics and is widely believed to have stifled growth of the urban classes and perpetuated a patronage-based political system will loosen. A move toward more educated and entrepreneurial urban dwellers thus augurs well for the future of democratic politics in Pakistan. As Faizunnisa and Ikram (2004) shows, young urban males and females fare much better on the youth development index than their rural counterparts.[23] Migrants from rural areas will therefore become associated with youth who have attained higher levels of development. The net result could be constructive in channeling productiveness.

This implies a future Pakistan
—that is increasingly urbanized
—in which political contours and power structures begin to change in favor of urban dwellers.

Pakistan 2025

The Pakistan of 2025 will depend on just how youth preferences and socio-economic realities affect each other. Table 17-2 paraphrases the attributes listed above that Pakistan is likely to possess based on youth preferences and socioeconomic realities.

Barring any unforeseen game-changers, some of the current trends are almost certain to hold as Pakistan moves forward. The Pakistani identity seems set to continue being one based on religion; there will be no meaningful division between church and state. Islam will also maintain its centrality as a faith and the society will continue striving to retain its traditional values and conservative core. That, however, will not be without a constant tussle with the forces of modernization, to which more and more young men and women will be exposed as the country urbanizes. Notwithstanding, the "traditionalists" are likely to retain the upper hand—certainly for the next ten to fifteen years and perhaps for years beyond.

Signs are ominous for Pakistan's prosperity as a state. Current trends suggest that Pakistan may be transformed into a society that is highly fractured and polarized—even more so than at present. Combine modest economic performance, rising inequality, underemployment as the norm for youth from lower socioeconomic strata, an expectation-reality disconnect, and dwindling resources over the longer run, and the story becomes obvious. The underprivileged segment that is the overwhelming majority of Pakistan's population will inevitably become more and more disgruntled at the absence of a level playing field and will look for channels to vent its frustration. Urbanization in this case may play a negative role, bringing thousands of resentful youth together with little opportunity to engage in constructive behavior. Crime is an obvious outlet. In Pakistan's case, extreme sectarian, ethnic, and provincial affiliations may create additional cleavages. Most likely, all of these factors will create a complex milieu of coexisting points of friction, interacting with one another in unpredictable and largely counterproductive ways. The state's capacity to maintain order will be severely tested.

Underlying the predicted frustrations of Pakistani youth is the state's inability to provide adequately for its people. Historically, Pakistan's citizens have been extremely impatient with that inability, and poorly performing governments are not tolerated for long. In fact, Pakistanis have remained indifferent to abrupt changes in rulers, and they have shied away from opposing undemocratic governments openly. The overwhelming support for democracy in Pakistan has never translated into a popular consensus on the

Table 17-2. *Summary of What Pakistan Would Look Like on the Basis of Current Youth Survey Responses and Projected Socioeconomic Trends*

Attributes of the Pakistan of 2025	
Based on youth responses	*Based on projected socioeconomic conditions*
Religious and national identities will remain intrinsically linked.	Quantity of education and gender disparity in this realm will improve, but overall levels will still leave much to be desired.
Difficulties and challenges will be psychologically (not operationally) neutralized by a coping mechanism that provides hope and resilience even when it defies reality.	The overwhelming majority of people will still be receiving poor-quality education.
It will be a highly conservative country—this is not to be confused with extremism.	The three parallel education systems will create divergent world visions that are difficult to reconcile.
It will be a country that is aware of its sectarian identity.	Different socioeconomic strata will become increasingly isolated from each other and thus may continue to harbor disdain and antipathy toward each other.
Pakistanis will also be ethnically aware.	Society will become increasingly polarized.
Today's youth will become increasingly frustrated and discontented with service delivery and dispensation of justice.	Unemployment levels will rise although they may still be low in absolute terms.
They will demand better performance from their leadership.	Underemployment will also rise.
They will simultaneously remain impatient with the failures of the already discredited leadership.	The country will become increasingly resource starved.
Pakistanis will be avidly anti-United States.	Inequality levels will rise.
The population will be supportive of democracy but will retain some level of hope in the military.	Expectations of those entering the workforce will remain unfulfilled.

(continued)

Table 17-2. *Summary of What Pakistan Would Look Like on the Basis of Current Youth Survey Responses and Projected Socioeconomic Trends (continued)*

Attributes of the Pakistan of 2025	
Based on youth responses	*Based on projected socioeconomic conditions*
The country will be ruled by moderate political parties.	The underprivileged segments of society may become increasingly disillusioned and disgruntled with the system.
Today's youth will be politically disengaged while remaining desperate for political change.	Outbound migration trends will decline and later stagnate.
It will remain a traditional society, and while it will continue to modernize (according to Western standards), its people will remain committed to maintaining traditional values and lifestyles.	The country will be increasingly urbanized.
Television will be the principal source of information; it will hold the power to mold views and opinions as it desires.	Political contours and power structures will begin to change in favor of urban dwellers.
It will be an anti-extremist polity but one that will still remain opposed to heavy-handed solutions to the problem of extremism unless such a course of action becomes an absolute necessity.	
The society will remain susceptible to conspiracy theories and popular discourse that strikes an emotional chord even if it defies strict strategic logic.	
Pakistanis will be influenced by state-sponsored historical narratives.	
Barring institutional transformation, today's youth will inherit a federation held together tenuously and in which the fundamental terms of coexistence are yet to be settled.	

rules of the political game. Looking ahead, Pakistan faces an irreconcilable conundrum because what the country is really suffering from is a crisis of the state system that transcends any particular government.

Democratic failure becomes a self-fulfilling prophecy if the population's desires are impossible to meet in a prescribed term in office and if citizens themselves are not fundamentally opposed to a nondemocratic alternative. As the situation stands, the economic and educational constraints identified in this chapter cannot be turned around without persistent good performance over the next decade or two. That means that no ruling government will be able to perform "well enough" in the interim. The lack of credibility of the political elite and the extreme desire to see positive change among the youth are likely to keep the discourse viciously anti-incumbent, pushing for quick changes in government rather than allowing for continuity of the political process and maintaining faith in a particular government's policymaking ability. The relatively high confidence in the military may kick in sooner or later. In essence, should large segments of the youth continue to be alienated, democratic consolidation will remain an uphill task.

A ray of hope for the future of the political system is provided by changes in the power structures that will shift the balance in favor of the urban bourgeoisie. Even if a philosophical commitment to democracy is lacking over the next decade or so, the vacuum created by those changes could theoretically be filled by a new, urban class of politicians who do not carry the baggage of the current political elite and are likely to receive greater leeway and maneuvering room from the average citizen. Unfortunately, here the upcoming generation's averseness to active participation in politics is inherently counterproductive: the very segment that is to craft Pakistan's future and seek positive change is willing to leave power in the hands of the same elites in whom it has seemingly lost hope.

It is important to note that neither the potential for greater polarization and internal discord nor risks to the future of democracy necessarily point to a rise in support for extremist forces. Even as youth acknowledge rising extremism among their ranks today, support for political parties lies convincingly with the mainstream parties. In fact, if there is any shift, it is toward ethnic and regional outfits largely opposed to the "Islam-as-unifying-factor" agenda. The consensus against a Talibanized Pakistan is also very strong among young men and women. Their extreme concern about extremism, reflected in the survey data presented earlier, reflects this sentiment. Even the argument that frustration and discontent with the present system may make the Taliban a likable alternative does not hold. Ironically, increased ethnic and sectarian awareness is likely to be at odds with Talibanization in the case of Pakistan; the ethnic and sectarian diversity in the country will not allow a pro-Taliban consensus. In fact, far more realistic is that a strong anti-Taliban commitment will temporarily pacify other subnational groups as Pakistan fights to survive, much as it does in present-day Pakistan. This is reassuring given the recent developments in Pakistan in which street support has been seen for acts of extremist violence. Perhaps the most shocking was the support among the religious right for the assassin of the governor of Punjab Province, Salmaan Taseer, allegedly killed due to his vocal opposition to Pakistan's controversial blasphemy law.[24]

That said, a contradictory trend may coexist with opposition to extremist forces. Over the next decade, the conflation of Islamic principles, radical discourse, and anti-West sentiment will linger. The Pakistani popular narrative will not change drastically until the Pakistani media have gone through their learning curve and textbooks are revised to present a more objective view of history. Until then, Pakistan's population will remain susceptible to conspiracy theories that strike an emotional chord. Deep-rooted anti-Americanism will always leave the window open for the Islamist enclave to couch their message within an anti-West and pan-Islamist narrative. U.S. policy toward the region therefore is a critical factor. Any Western policy that allows the Islamists to paint the national leadership as surrogates of the West will backfire. It will keep the present Pakistani mindset entrenched; Pakistanis will remain anti-extremist and anti-West at the same time. All said and done, Pakistan's youth seem to have learnt the lesson from recent developments in Pakistan that the Taliban are not an attractive alternative.

Turning Pakistan Around

The analysis presented here paints a fairly bleak picture for Pakistan over the next ten to twenty years. A turnaround is possible only over the longer term, and for it to occur, the two upcoming decades must be viewed as a corrective phase in the country's history during which difficult policy choices are made for the greater good of the country and its people. Pakistan will have to adopt a corrective course of action in the immediate future and implement it sincerely. It will have to persist without any major politically motivated reversals.

Many of the concerns for Pakistan's future flow out of one fundamental shortcoming: the country's poor socioeconomic and educational prognosis. Pakistan requires an inclusive macroeconomic growth model and sound economic management over the next decade. Projections suggest that if corrective policies are persistent (including not only economic policies but also ones that address the need for better natural resource management), Pakistan will be able to rid itself of the structural anomaly whereby it cannot sustainably grow above 5.45 percent a year in the short term. As the macroeconomic fundamentals improve, higher growth rates would become possible. Should that happen, the size of the economic pie will increase, and the economy will be able to cater to a greater number of entrants into the labor market.

The inclusionary model is also required to address the persistent increase in inequality. More inclusive economic policies combined with the loosening of the hold of the feudal classes will gradually lead to lower inequality. More inclusive growth would also imply that Pakistan's less-developed provinces, like Balochistan, would become fully integrated in the mainstream economy and thus have little incentive to opt out of the federation. Furthermore, an improved socioeconomic scenario will automatically eliminate the expectation-reality disconnect and dampen some of the negative effects associated with urbanization and the concern about internal polarization. A greater number of young people will find avenues to channel their energies positively. Luckily, the latest economic policy documents suggest that the future vision about macrogrowth is in fact leaning toward a more inclusive model. Inequality is explicitly recognized as a major social and economic threat that ought to be tackled at all costs.

A positive spin-off of improved socioeconomic performance can also be envisioned in terms of support for democracy. If the system begins to deliver, more patience may be exhibited toward leaders, which in turn may provide greater room for policy continuity and some sort of consensus on the rules of the game.

On the educational front, quantity—in terms of the numbers of Pakistani children having access to education—is set to rise. The qualitative aspect of the education offered, however, needs immediate attention. Even if qualitative gains must follow quantitative improvements, the stratification of the school system and the poor quality of public schooling ought to be addressed through a concerted policy effort starting now. Again, the government's 2009 education policy recognizes the need to maintain a special focus on these two failings over the next decade. Next, textbook reform is long overdue. A conscious effort needs to be made to present a more objective and less paranoid historical narrative to Pakistani children. Pakistan's internal problems will be dealt with more effectively through enhanced civic consciousness and awareness of society's responsibilities toward the state rather than by creating a siege mentality that makes a security-centric vision inevitable.

The above said, if Pakistan is, realistically speaking, to produce better results, the current lot of Pakistani youth will have to rid themselves of their political inactiveness and strive to become part of the power structure. A new class of politicians is a virtual prerequisite to move Pakistan away from the entrenched patronage-based political model. Moreover, a more tolerant and strategically adept polity is also a necessity in an increasingly globalized world. Perhaps the single most important factor in molding young Pakistani minds is television. The television industry's learning curve needs to be accelerated by hiring professionally trained individuals who are visionary in their thinking. The narrative would have to move away from mere populism to provide a fresh discourse on Pakistan's strategic compulsions and future potential. Greater debate on civil-military relations and resource allocation priorities is also long overdue. Much more emphasis is also warranted on civic education of the citizens.

Western—that is, U.S.—policies hold paramount importance. Looking ahead, Western policy must be extremely careful about Pakistani sensitivities. For one, Pakistan is set to remain a highly conservative, Islamic state that is opposed to forced modernization or moves that could be construed as an attempt to impose Western values. All dealings must be conducted without any ambitions to alter that framework. The Western military presence in and overall policy toward the Muslim world will also influence the narrative in Pakistan; to shy away from that fact serves no purpose. Further, the ability of the Islamist enclave to sell their viewpoint to Muslim societies is strongly correlated with how those societies perceive Western policies. If short-term interests continue to dictate the Western agenda and the people of Pakistan see themselves being left out of the bargain, Western policy will continue to fuel the very discourse and mindset that it seeks to eliminate. Western engagement will have to be much more patient, long-term, transparent, and sensitive to Pakistani concerns. Such engagement, combined with more visionary political leadership, provides the best hope for the future of Pakistan; it will allow Pakistani leaders greater room to challenge entrenched narratives about the West and the tendency of the ultra-right to deliberately conflate anti-Western sentiment with extremist rhetoric.

Some of what has been suggested above finds space in Pakistan's youth policy. Issues discussed in this paper that have not been dealt with in policy should be incorporated so as to formulate a holistic policy vision for channeling Pakistani youth energies constructively. Most important, the vision articulated in a holistic youth policy must be implemented swiftly and sincerely. Should Pakistan persist on its corrective course, the Pakistan of 2050 may well be more stable, progressive, and developed than the Pakistan of 2025. It may never be a secular, liberal democracy, and it may still possess contending narratives about the Pakistani identity; yet it will be a Pakistani federation in which the question of an internal rupture would have become moot and the youth will not feel the disillusionment that their parents did. Make no mistake, however. Getting to the Pakistan of 2050 envisioned here will be a tall order, and the margin for error in the corrective phase is minimal.

Notes

1. The data are based exclusively on responses from youth who reside in Pakistan. Therefore, the views and potential role in shaping the country's future of youth among the Pakistani diaspora are not examined in this chapter.

2. Center for Civic Education, "Civic Health of Pakistani Youth" (Islamabad: 2009), p. 1; United Nations, "World Population Prospects: The 2010 Revision."

3. World Bank, "World Development Indicators" (http://data.worldbank.org/indicator/SP.DYN.TFRT.IN/countries/PK?display=graph).

4. Michael Kugelman, "Pakistan's Demographics: Possibilities, Perils, and Prescriptions," in *Deepening the Dividend: Overcoming Pakistan's Demographic Challenges*, edited by Michael Kugelman and Robert M. Hathaway (Washington: Woodrow Wilson Center, 2011), p. 6.

5. The British Council, "Pakistan: The Next Generation" (Islamabad: November 2009); "Youth Speak," *The Herald*, vol. 41, no. 1 (January 2010), pp. 52–105; Center for Civic Education, "Civic Health of Pakistani Youth" (Islamabad: 2009). All three surveys were conducted at the national level. The British Council survey drew on a sample of 1,226 of young men and women between the ages of eighteen and twenty-nine. The *Herald*'s sample was 845, and targeted ages were fifteen to twenty-five years. The scope of the Center for Civic Education survey was narrower than that of the other two surveys, focusing mainly on questions relating to civic education. Its sample size was 1,855, and targeted ages were late-teens to thirty years.

6. "Youth Speak," *The Herald*, p. 57.

7. For a succinct journalistic account of the lawyers' movement, see James Traub, "The Lawyers' Crusade," *New York Times*, June 1, 2008 (www.nytimes.com/2008/06/01/magazine/01PAKISTAN-t.html?pagewanted=print).

8. "Youth Speak," *The Herald*, p. 59.

9. Ibid., p. 88.

10. UNICEF, "Pakistan Statistics" (www.unicef.org/infobycountry/pakistan_pakistan_statistics.html#77); UNESCO Institute for Statistics (http://stats.uis.unesco.org/unesco/TableViewer/document.aspx?ReportId=143&IF_Language=eng).

11. Rana Ejaz, Ali Khan, and Karamat Ali, "Bargaining over Sons' and Daughters' Schooling: Probit Analysis of Household Behavior in Pakistan," Working Paper 01-05, Islamia University of Bahawalpur, 2005, pp. 7–8, 13; Minhaj ul Haque, "Discrimination Starts at Home," p. 2 (www.popcouncil.org/pdfs/Pak_AYP004.pdf). The analysis is based on results from the Population Council's Survey, "Adolescents and Youth in Pakistan: 2001–02: A National Representative Survey" (UNICEF, 2002).

12. Academy of Educational Planning and Management, *Pakistan Education Statistics 2007–08* (Islamabad: Ministry of Education, Government of Pakistan, 2008).

13. For a slightly more detailed discussion on this issue, see Moeed Yusuf, "Prospects of Youth Radicalization in Pakistan: Implications for U.S. Policy," Analysis Paper 14 (Brookings, 2008), pp. 3–5.

14. Planning Commission, *Medium-Term Development Imperatives and Strategy for Pakistan*, final report, Panel of Economists, Government of Pakistan, April 2010, p. 26.

15. C. Christine Fair and others, "Demographics and Security: The Contrasting Cases of Pakistan and Bangladesh," *Journal of South Asian and Middle Eastern Studies*, vol. XXVIII, no. 4 (Summer 2005), p. 66.

16. Ministry of Finance, *Pakistan Economic Survey: 2007–08*, Islamabad, p. 218; Planning Commission, *Medium-Term Development Imperatives and Strategy for Pakistan*, final report, Panel of Economists, Government of Pakistan, Islamabad, April 2010.

17. Azeema Faizunnisa and Atif Ikram, "Determinants of Youth Development in Pakistan," *Lahore Journal of Economics*, vol. 9, no. 2 (2004), pp. 125–26.

18. Population Council, "Adolescents and Youth," p. 56.

19. Ibid., pp. 67–68.

20. British Council, "Pakistan: The Next Generation," p. 15.

21. United Nations, *World Urbanization Prospects: The 2007 Revision Population Database* (http://esa.un.org/unup/).

22 United Nations, *World Population Prospects: The 2008 Revision Population Database* (http://esa.un.org/unpp).

23. Faizunnisa and Ikram, "Determinants of Youth," pp. 125–26.

24. Carlotta Gall, "Assassination Deepens Divide in Pakistan," *New York Times*, January 5, 2011 (www.nytimes.com/2011/01/06/world/asia/06pakistan.html?pagewanted =all).

STEPHEN P. COHEN

18

Afterword

Just before and after 9/11, the official and establishment Pakistani narrative was that the country could, with outside assistance, surmount its economic difficulties, take its rightful place as an ally of the West, and become an anchor of the moderate branch of the Islamic world. Pakistan would be a bridge: the gateway to modernity for other Muslims and a gateway to Islam for the West.[1] This was also the view of the George W. Bush administration, which had begun to rebuild relations with Islamabad.

That optimistic narrative has recently been challenged by gloom-and-doom scenarios that portray Pakistan as an already failed state, a malign supporter of radical Islamic causes, and the epicenter of global terrorism. "Failed," "flawed," and "unraveling" are adjectives that are now widely used to describe the country. It is typically described as having failed, as being in the process of failing, or as a "monster state" of one sort or another.[2] Many Western states see Pakistan as so close to failure—and so important—that assistance is essential because of its weakness, not because of its strength.

Several analyses of Pakistan completed before Musharraf's departure anticipated the current crisis. Perhaps the toughest was the view of a group of experts on Pakistan convened by the National Intelligence Council (NIC) in 2000 as part of its projection of global developments in the year 2015.[3] The passages on Pakistan and India are worth quoting in full, because the predictions were presumably gathered before 9/11 and at the peak of President Musharraf's popularity.

The collective judgment of those experts was that by 2025, the South Asian region's strategic relations would be defined by the growing gap between India and Pakistan and their seemingly irreducible hostility. The experts were wary of the possibility of small- or large-scale conflict:

India will be the unrivaled regional power with a large military—including naval and nuclear capabilities—and a dynamic and growing economy. The widening India-Pakistan gap—destabilizing in its own right—will be accompanied by deep political, economic, and social disparities within both states. Pakistan will be more fractious, isolated, and dependent on international financial assistance.

The threat of major conflict between India and Pakistan will overshadow all other regional issues during the next 15 years. Continued turmoil in Afghanistan and Pakistan will spill over into Kashmir and other areas of the subcontinent, prompting Indian leaders to take more aggressive preemptive and retaliatory actions. India's conventional military advantage over Pakistan will widen as a result of New Delhi's superior economic position. India will also continue to build up its ocean-going navy to dominate the Indian Ocean transit routes used for delivery of Persian Gulf oil to Asia. The decisive shift in conventional military power in India's favor over the coming years potentially will make the region more volatile and unstable. Both India and Pakistan will see weapons of mass destruction as a strategic imperative and will continue to amass nuclear warheads and build a variety of missile delivery systems.

That assumes that at best, India will be able to translate its new global status into regional hegemony or that at worst, a rising India and a declining Pakistan are likely to clash. As for Pakistan itself, the conferees concluded that by 2050,

[i]t will not recover easily from decades of political and economic mismanagement, divisive politics, lawlessness, corruption and ethnic friction. Nascent democratic reforms will produce little change in the face of opposition from an entrenched political elite and radical Islamic parties. Further domestic decline would benefit Islamic political activists, who may significantly increase their role in national politics and alter the makeup and cohesion of the military—once Pakistan's most capable institution. In a climate of continuing domestic turmoil, the central government's control probably will be reduced to the Punjabi heartland and the economic hub of Karachi.

A few years later, despite the experts' concerns, the NIC barely mentioned Pakistan, and then only in the context of one of three global-change scenarios.[4]

In 2004 a project by the Center for Strategic and International Studies (CSIS) came to a cautiously optimistic conclusion about Pakistan.[5] Completed after Musharraf's third year in power, it looked at the prospects for change and reform in Pakistan, dealing mostly with macro-political and economic factors and stressing the importance of rebuilding Pakistan's institutions. Pakistan's external relations and U.S. interests were the framework for the analysis:

> The two and a half years since the attacks on New York and Washington in 2001 have intensified the internal pressures Pakistan faces. The U.S. decision to start its antiterrorism offensive by seeking Pakistani support was based on the presumption, widely shared in policy and academic circles in the United States, that Pakistan is central to the prospects for stability in South Asia. This study bears out that assumption. Every major aspect of Pakistan's internal stresses that we examined—the economic prospects, the role of the army and of political parties, the role of Islam and of the militants, and even the tensions between states and regions—is linked to developments outside Pakistan's borders. Positive scenarios from the point of view of key U.S. interests—regional stability, diminution of terrorism, reduced risk of conflict with India, and nuclear control—all involve a stabilized Pakistan and a strengthened Pakistani state. If one adds U.S. economic interests and hopes to the list, the importance of a Pakistani revival is even greater.[6]

The CSIS study suggests that to have any kind of impact on Pakistan, the United States will have to increase the level of attention and resources that it devotes to South Asia in general and to Pakistan in particular—noting that the U.S. has a number of objectives in that country, all of which must be taken seriously. The project reflected the thinking behind the Biden-Lugar legislation, which urged massive U.S. economic assistance for Pakistan in addition to the growing amount of military aid.[7] The CSIS report also urged support for India-Pakistan dialogue and support for civil society, noting that the "social development Pakistan so badly needs cannot be supplied entirely by the government."[8] Above all, the report emphasizes the weakness of Pakistani institutions, civil and governmental, and indicates that they—notably the judiciary, educational institutions, and agencies that deliver power and water to the Pakistani people—should be the focus of reform efforts and assistance from the United States. As part of the project, a simulation exercise was run to test two scenarios, one in which Musharraf slowly rebuilt Pakistan and a second in which political turmoil overtook his regime; however, the dependent variable was India-Pakistan relations, not the future of Pakistan.

My own study, published in 2004, warily concluded that Pakistan may have reached the point of no return along several dimensions and that extreme scenarios were no longer inconceivable. I gave the establishment-dominated system a fifty-fifty chance of survival but specified no time line, and I also set forth a number of indicators, all of which were blinking bright red by 2006. The book anticipated Musharraf's demise and outlined the problems that would be faced by a successor government.

There is also an Islamist narrative, which sees Pakistan as the vanguard of an Islamic revolution that will spread from Pakistan to India and then to other lands where Muslims are oppressed.[9] The language is eerily reminiscent of the Marxists of the 1970s, who saw Pakistan as a vanguard of an Islamic-socialist revolution. As Hasan Askari Rizvi notes:

> Tariq Ali's suggestion to reshape the Pakistani society from top to bottom is [now] advocated by Islamic orthodox believers and neoconservatives, albeit in an Islamic framework. They view militancy as an instrument for transforming society and warding off the enemies of Islam and their local agents. They talk of controlling the state machinery to transform the state and society along Islamic lines, as they define them.[10]

There is a strong similarity between the totalitarian vision of orthodox Marxist-Leninists and that of the extreme Islamists. In many countries, the dislocated and angry intellectual class that would have turned to Marxism in the past now finds comfort in radical Islam.

Of the serious studies of Pakistan written over the last few years, none predict failure or success; most opt for some intermediate "muddling through" scenario. Most also identify certain factors as determinative and one European study emphasizes the importance of the coherence and integrity of the Pakistani state.[11]

Jonathan Paris, an American analyst based in Great Britain, has written the most comprehensive study in the prediction genre, *Prospects for Pakistan*, published in 2010.[12] He had not visited Pakistan before completing the study but traveled there just after it came out. His methodology and analytical patience set his work apart. His time frame is one to three years, and he looks at both challenges to Pakistan and "topics" that seem to be of particular importance; the latter are roughly equivalent to the factors or variables discussed in the Bellagio project. Paris's list of challenges contains no surprises:

—state fragmentation and loss of control over various territories, which undermine the integrity, solidarity, and stability of the country

—insecurity and terrorism throughout Pakistan

—the economy
—governance issues, including corruption
—rebuilding the Pakistan "brand."

The last item in the list is also used by Shaukat Aziz, a former finance minister and prime minister of Pakistan, and it is not clear whether it refers to Pakistan's image abroad or to the nature of Pakistanis' allegiance to the state and the purpose of Pakistan—what I have termed the "idea" of Pakistan. Paris's list of "topics" includes:

—the economy
—civil-military issues
—trends in Islamism
—the future of Pashtun nationalism
—the future of the Pakistani Taliban
—Pakistan's relations with three countries: India, China, and the United States.

The study also includes a discussion of demography, the insurgency in Balochistan, and other factors. Notable for their absence are discussions of the role of the media, the rise of civil society, the new role of the courts, and constitutional developments, although some of the latter, such as the Eighteenth Amendment, were still being formulated while the study was under way.

One of the most useful aspects of this study is Paris's exploration of a range of futures for the main topics or variables. For the economy, he examines both a "glass half full" and a less optimistic "glass half empty" scenario; for civil-military relations, he discusses three futures: a return to military dominance, continuation of the current status quo, and movement toward democratic consolidation. There is less scenario-building regarding Islamic trends in Pakistan, but he rules out either the emergence of religious parties as a dominant factor in Pakistani politics or a Taliban takeover. Those are eminently reasonable predictions for the short time frame of the study.

In his summary evaluation of Pakistan's expected challenges, Paris argues that the country will "muddle through," but he notes that the "unexpected challenges" are what make it so difficult to predict even the next one to three years in Pakistan. He points out that the spike in food costs, the rise of the Pakistan Taliban, the military's push against militants in Swat and Waziristan, and the Mumbai attack were all unpredicted and perhaps unpredictable. Ultimately, he concludes that Pakistan is likely to "muddle through or slightly worse. Absent a major unexpected shock, it is not destined to become a 'failed state.'"

Bearing in mind the one- to two-year time frame, this is sensible, but the uncertainties are still considerable. The phrase "muddling through," has become the standard optimists' characterization of Pakistan, although it remains undefined and the time frame is always short term. One senior U.S. official with extensive contacts in Pakistan, notably the military, remarked to me in 2010 that Pakistan may be below the waterline as defined by "muddling through."

A team of Indian experts organized by the government-funded Institute for Defence Studies and Analyses, using a methodology similar to Paris's, came to approximately the same conclusions.[13] After a general discussion of recent events and trends, *Whither Pakistan,* written just after Paris's study, identifies six "key drivers" that will "decide the direction in which Pakistan is likely to evolve in times to come": "political dynamics," radicalization of Pakistani society, the military, the economy, relations with India, and foreign policy.[14] All are seen as critically important, and all are seen as very uncertain. The drivers are not sequenced or ranked in terms of importance, and some factors, such as demography, are not considered at all.

This study develops three scenarios, "Lebanonization," a stable Pakistan, and a sharp downward slide and implosion. The authors note, unhelpfully, that there are several intermediate scenarios, in which "some drivers pan out and others do not," but those scenarios are not listed or discussed. The analysis concludes with the observation that Pakistan's stability and democratization is in everyone's interest but that "the big question is whether Pakistan can succeed in holding itself together against various fissiparous tendencies that afflict it today." Pakistan's relations with other countries, notably India, are not central to its future, as domestic trends and developments are the independent variable. From the perspective of this Indian report, India is blameless regarding Pakistan's plight; it is the victim of Pakistani misdeeds and miscalculations.[15]

Another scenario-building approach was taken by one of Pakistan's most distinguished retired generals at a 2009 Canadian conference on Pakistan's future.[16] Lieutenant General Talat Masood, a former secretary in the Ministry of Defense and now an active participant on the Track II and seminar circuit, posited three scenarios—best-case, worst-case, and nuanced—but provided no probability estimate.[17] The best-case scenario is one in which both civilians and the military see the need for change and discard outdated policies; rule of law is reestablished, especially in the frontier region; the military returns to the barracks; and economic reform begins to take hold. Relations with India improve, and Pakistan regains its prior international status as a progressive state with continuing good relations with the United States, China, and the Muslim-majority world.

In Masood's worst case, none of that happens. The Taliban problem continues to fester; Pakistan-based militants continue their activity in Kashmir and elsewhere in India, leading to another India-Pakistan crisis; as a result of security problems foreign investment ceases to flow to Pakistan; and, ultimately, the military again comes to power in a new coup d'état.

The "nuanced" case predicts continued domestic disorder, but the economy is kept afloat by remittances from overseas Pakistanis, the international economy continues to aid Pakistan, and dialogue with India is restored, with the Inter-Services Intelligence Directorate (ISI) and the army restraining themselves. Of course, other outcomes are possible, and General Masood's mixed outcome could have several permutations.

One of Pakistan's most thoughtful scholars, Pervez Hoodbhoy, attempts a five-year projection, warning of the consequences for the country if reform does not happen quickly.[18] B. Raman, India's leading Pakistan-watcher and a former intelligence officer, concludes by arguing that India has a stake in the survival of a moderate Pakistan.[19] Two liberal Pakistani journalists, Najam Sethi and Ahmed Rashid, have also expressed their concern about a failing Pakistan.[20]

Farzana Shaikh, a Pakistani scholar resident in Great Britain, dismisses the rhetorical flourishes of "country on the brink" or "failed state," arguing that Pakistan's problems stem from its very origins and that the identity of Pakistan has never been clear nor has a consensus been developed on the purpose of Pakistan.[21] The failure of the economy, political incoherence, separatism, corruption, and the rise of extremists are all problems—or in Paris's term, "factors." However, underlying them are the absence of a national purpose, notably the ambiguous but generous role accorded to Islam since the founding of Pakistan, which has restricted its progress ever since.[22] She remains somewhat optimistic, buoyed by the rise of the new media, an active judiciary and legal community, and human rights activists who have tried to imagine Pakistan in a new way. As Benedict Anderson has argued, nations are "imagined" communities: at bottom they are ideas, and they can be reimagined. However, Pakistan the nation resides uneasily alongside Pakistan the state. Not only is the nation in deep trouble, as it has been since independence, but the state of Pakistan also is crumbling, raising the question of whether the state can support the idea or the idea can sustain the state.

Bruce Riedel, a former U.S. intelligence analyst with long contact with Pakistan, examines but does not predict an Islamic militant victory in Pakistan. He points to Pakistan's creation of and collusion with militant groups, which he believes has left Islamabad vulnerable to an Islamic coup.[23] Riedel dates the crisis back to the war against the Soviet Union, then occupying Afghanistan, but the collusion began much earlier, with state patronage of militant Islamic groups going back many years. Riedel sees Pakistan as ripe for change, "but it could be radical change for the worst"; he believes that the battle for the soul of Pakistan has never been so acute. He develops a scenario in which Islamist and Taliban forces push to the East and establish an Islamic Emirate of Pakistan, virtually dividing the country between Islamists and moderate Muslims and anchoring Pakistani influence in the Pashtun parts of Afghanistan. Pakistan's nuclear arsenal would be at stake, and relations with India would also worsen, as would relations with the United States. Riedel's policy recommendation is that this is a future to be avoided at all costs, and that the United States must work with remaining moderate elements in Pakistan to prevent it.

Riedel's "Emirate of Pakistan" is a fictional device. He does not specify the time frame in which it might come about, but there is no mistaking the urgency and depth of his concern about Pakistan's future. He seems to assume that the United States at least still has an opportunity to deflect Pakistan from a dangerous and self-destructive course, one that would turn it into a major enemy of the United States, not an ally.

Even more pessimistic is the analysis by John R. Schmidt, a U.S. diplomat who served in Islamabad. He traces Pakistan's problems to its feudal political culture, in which the wealthy refuse to tax themselves; the parties are arrayed around powerful families, not ideas; and it matters little who governs, so deep is the decay in Pakistani political institutions.[24] With the rise of the Islamists, who do not constitute a unified body but are able enough to challenge Pakistan's crumbling establishment, the state faces a threat to its very existence. The "muddling through" preferences of the establishment were only confirmed by such events as the attack on Sri Lanka's cricket team. The establishment is not likely to engage in serious reform; instead it will kick the proverbial can down the road. There are solutions to Pakistan's many problems, and Schmidt, writing in 2009, observes that it is probably "not too late" if the government undertakes the struggle against the Islamist threat and the army treats the Taliban insurgency seriously. He warns that the day of reckoning is coming and that the more time that is taken to address the rot, "the bloodier and more protracted the confrontation is likely to be." And, of course, the fall of Pakistan to radical Islamic forces would be calamitous for the rest of the world, even though there is probably "little that the rest of the world can do to prevent this. . . . The matter rests, as it always had, with the Pakistani people and the political class that rules them."

Hasan Abbas, a former Pakistani police officer now resident in the United States, offers, along with Paris, a comprehensive assessment of Pakistan's multiple crises; he is more optimistic than Riedel and others about a positive transformation.[25] After a comprehensive assessment of recent threats to the state and to the very idea of Pakistan—including a detailed study of the rise of terrorism, sectarian violence, and political and criminal extremism—he suggests that both the lawyers' movement and the rise of the new media offer an opportunity for Pakistanis and outsiders to save Pakistan from what could be comprehensive failure. Noting that Pakistan ranks ninth among 177 of the world's weakest countries, he says that "the challenges of militancy, weak governance, and economic insecurity are feeding each other in a dangerous cycle, which must be broken if Pakistan is to be saved."[26] He makes seven recommendations each to Pakistani and U.S. policymakers. The agenda suggested to the Pakistanis includes a new social contract between the government and the people; the removal of colonial-era laws; major investment in education and health care reform; the reconfiguration of the state's governance structures; bringing in the Army Education Corps and Medical Corps to meet educational and health targets; providing support for progressive religious groups in order to help defeat the "idea of Talibanization"; defeating the communications strategy of the Taliban; closing down militant madaris; overhauling the police, law enforcement, and intelligence services; reviving the peace process with India; and enhancing the security of the nuclear weapons establishment while enhancing civilian oversight of the entire nuclear establishment.

The United States is offered a similarly comprehensive agenda, including developing a more comprehensive strategy toward Pakistan; avoiding condition-heavy aid packages; addressing the Kashmir problem and India-Pakistan relations; accepting Pakistan's status as a nuclear weapons state; stressing education and health in U.S. aid to Pakistan; helping Pakistan improve its civilian law enforcement capabilities; replacing drone attacks in Khyber-Pakhtunkhwa with a humanitarian aid package; and, finally, creating an effective oversight mechanism for Pakistani aid and assistance programs.

The scope of Abbas's recommendations is breathtaking, and they point to a complete transformation of Pakistan to be led by Pakistanis themselves with the full support of the United States. This is also the case with the recommendations, written by Abbas, of a study group organized by the Asia Society. His writings acknowledge the deep problems facing Pakistan and the urgency of the reform agenda, as seen by a thoughtful and expert former member of Pakistan's police force. Abbas is cautiously optimistic. While the indicators are increasingly negative and there are credible "gloom and doom" scenarios, "many things are going well," notably the slow and sure transition to democracy since the January 2008 elections.

As he notes, the politicians are settling down; however, if they do not deliver, they will be out of a job. The army's non-interference posture in relation to the political arena also deserves to be acknowledged although it will take a while for the civilian and democratic leadership to assume complete control and be in a position to decisively define the overall direction of domestic and foreign policy. Two of the "signs of hope" that he discusses are the lawyers' movement of 2007–09 and the rise of the new media. Left unsaid is Pakistan's future if such a reform program is not initiated and carried out successfully. Abbas does not consider the shape and timing of failure.

In one of the most comprehensive overviews of Pakistan yet published, Anatol Lieven expresses little doubt that Pakistan will survive as a state and stresses the great strength of Pakistani society, as opposed to the sometimes incompetent state.[27] But he warns against two trends. One is environmental degradation, inexorably progressing because of changing climate conditions. While many countries are adversely affected, Pakistan will be hit worse than most. The other threat that would lead to major changes in Pakistan would be a mutiny within the otherwise stable army in case of a U.S. (or joint Indian-U.S.) incursion into Pakistani territory.

Finally, the distinguished diplomat-journalist Maleeha Lodhi assembled a group of Pakistani scholars and former officials who, in an edited volume, present another "to do" list that assumes that the present extended crisis can be surmounted. The volume never grapples with the critical questions of whether it is too late to reinvent Pakistan and what paths, besides the restoration of Jinnah's liberal idea of Pakistan, are possible for a Pakistan that is now immersed in identity and governance crises.[28]

Notes

1. The one country that has taken the latter very seriously has been China, which from the 1960s used Pakistan as the jumping-off point for the expansion of its diplomacy and military assistance programs in the Middle East. However, because China has developed direct economic, diplomatic, and military ties with the Gulf, the Arab world, and Africa, Pakistan is less useful today.

2. I deal with the "failure" syndrome in chapter 1 of *The Idea of Pakistan.*

3. National Intelligence Council, *Global Trends 2015: A Dialogue about the Future with Nongovernment Experts,* NIC 2000–02 (Washington: National Intelligence Council, December 2000), pp. 64 and following.

4. Pakistan is barely mentioned in another major NIC publication, a scenario-building exercise that posits three future worlds, and only in the context of an Islamic caliphate, in which it is one of the battlegrounds between the forces of the caliph and the "crusaders."

5. Teresita C. Schaffer, *Pakistan's Future and U.S. Policy Options* (Washington: CSIS Press, 2004).

6. Ibid., p. 36.

7. It was titled the Enhanced Partnership with Pakistan Act and passed the Senate in 2008.

8. Ibid., p. 5.

9. For prime examples of this rhetoric, see Simon Henderson, "Pakistan on the Brink: Implications for U.S. Policies," May 4, 2009, Washington Institute for Near East Policy (www.washingtoninstitute.org/print.php?template=C05&CID=3050). The website of the Jamaat-e-Islami is a good source for the Islamist narrative (http://jamaat.org/beta/site/index), and the authoritative study of the Jammat is by Vali Nasr, *The Vanguard of the Islamic Revolution: The Jama'at-i-Islami of Pakistan* (London: I. B. Tauris, 1994).

10. See chapter 11 in this volume. Tariq Ali has written that "the choice will be between socialist revolution—that is, people's power—[and] complete and utter disintegration" and underlined the need for building "the revolutionary vanguard which will enable us to achieve a socialist workers' and peasants' republic in Pakistan." Tariq Ali, *Pakistan: Military Rule or People's Power* (New York: William Morrow, 1970), pp. 243–44.

11. Marco Mezzera and Safiya Aftab, "Country Case Study: Pakistan, State–Society Analysis," Clingendael, Netherlands Institute of International Relations, January 2009 (www.initiativeforpeacebuilding.com/pdf/Pakistan_State_Society_Analysis.pdf).

12. Jonathan Paris, *Prospects for Pakistan* (London: Legatum Institute, 2010).

13. Institute for Defence Studies and Analyses, *Whither Pakistan* (www.idsa.in/book/WhitherPakistan).

14. Ibid., p. 135.

15. An earlier Indian attempt to develop scenarios for Pakistan's future was done at a leading Delhi think tank, the Observer Research Foundation. Wilson John, *Pakistan: Struggle Within* (New Delhi: Longman Pearson, 2009).

16. Johannes Braune, *Pakistan's Security: Today and Tomorrow* (Ottawa: CSIS, April 2004).

17. Ibid.

18. See Pervez Hoodbhoy, "Whither Pakistan? A Five-Year Forecast," *Bulletin of the Atomic Scientists,* June 3, 2009 (www.thebulletin.org/web-edition/features/whither-pakistan-five-year-forecast), and Pervez Hoodbhoy, "Pakistan: The Road from Hell," June 9, 2009 (www.opendemocracy.net/article/pakistan-the-road-from-hell).

19. B. Raman, "Pakistan: Quo Vadis?" Raman's Strategic Analysis Blog, May 13, 2010 (http://ramanstrategicanalysis.blogspot.com/2010/05/pakistan-quo-vadis.html).

20. Ahmed Rashid, "The Scary Unraveling of Pakistan," *The Daily Beast,* November 30, 2009 (www.thedailybeast.com/blogs-and-stories/2009-11-30/gunning-for-zardari/), and Najam Sethi, "Islam and the West: Dilemmas of a Failing Pakistan," *New Age Islam,* June 25, 2010 (www.newageislam.com/NewAgeIslamIslamAndWest_1.aspx?ArticleID=3048).

21. Farzana Sheikh, *Making Sense of Pakistan* (London: Hirst, 2009).

22. See the review of Shaikh by Andrew Buncombe, "Review of *Making Sense of Pakistan,* by Farzana Shaikh," *The Independent,* June 21, 2009 (http://license.icopyright.net/user/viewFreeUse.act?fuid=NDQ1NTI1NQ%3D%3D).

23. Bruce Riedel, "Armageddon in Islamabad," *National Interest*, June 23, 2009 (www.nationalinterest.org/printerfriendly.aspx?id=21644).

24. John R. Schmidt, "The Unraveling of Pakistan," *Survival: Global Politics and Strategy* (June–July 2009) (www.iiss.org/publications/survival/survival-2009/year-2009-issue-3/the-unravelling-of-pakistan).

25. Hassan Abbas, *Pakistan Can Defy the Odds: How to Rescue a Failing State*, Institute for Social Policy and Understanding (Clinton Township, Mich.: ISPU, May 2009).

26. Ibid., p. 28.

27. Anatol Lieven, *Pakistan: A Hard Country* (New York: Public Affairs Press, 2011).

28. Maleeha Lodhi, *Pakistan: Beyond the "Crisis State"* (Columbia University Press, 2011).

Contributors

Kanti Bajpai
Lee Kuan Yew School of Public Policy, National University of Singapore

Laila Bokhari
Research Fellow, Norwegian Institute of International Affairs and Norwegian Defence Research Establishment (FFI); Associate Fellow, International Centre for the Study of Radicalization and Political Violence, Kings College, United Kingdom; currently based at the Royal Norwegian Embassy in Islamabad

Stephen P. Cohen
Senior Fellow, 21st Century Defense Initiative, Brookings Institution

C. Christine Fair
Assistant Professor, Center for Peace and Security Studies, Edmund A. Walsh School of Foreign Service, Georgetown University

Tariq Fatemi
Ambassador (retired), Pakistan Foreign Service

Mohan Guruswamy
Chairman, Centre for Policy Alternatives, New Delhi

William Milam
Senior Policy Scholar, Woodrow Wilson Center; former U.S. Ambassador to Pakistan

Shuja Nawaz
Director, South Asia Center, The Atlantic Council

Shaukat Qadir
Brigadier (retired), Pakistan Army

Bahukutumbi Raman
Additional Secretary (retired), Cabinet Secretariat, Government of India, New Delhi; currently Director, Institute for Topical Studies, Chennai, and Associate of the Chennai Centre for China Studies

Hasan Askari Rizvi
Professor Emeritus, Department of Political Science, University of the Punjab, Lahore

Aqil Shah
Postdoctoral Fellow, Society of Fellows, Harvard University

Hilary Synnott (1945–2011)
Sir Hilary Synnott, Knight Commander of the Order of St. Michael and St. George, joined the British diplomatic service in 1973, after a career as a naval officer. He served in India as Deputy High Commissioner and subsequently as High Commissioner to Pakistan. In 2003, Sir Hilary became the Coalition Provisional Authority coordinator for Southern Iraq, and he later wrote a classic diplomatic memoir, *Bad Days in Basra* (2008), based on his experiences there. At the International Institute for Strategic Studies, where he was Consulting Senior Fellow in recent years, he wrote *The Causes and Consequences of South Asia's Nuclear Tests* (1999) and *Transforming Pakistan: Ways out of Instability* (2009).

Marvin G. Weinbaum
Scholar-in-Residence, Middle East Institute; Professor Emeritus, University of Illinois

Anita M. Weiss
Professor and Head, Department of International Studies, University of Oregon

Joshua T. White
Ph.D. Candidate, Johns Hopkins School of Advanced International Studies

Moeed W. Yusuf
South Asia Adviser, United States Institute of Peace, Center for Conflict Management

Index

Abbas, Hasan, 291–93
Abzug, Bella, 247
Afghanistan: and India-Pakistan relations, 37, 38, 103, 137–38, 220, 233; political solution effects, 136–38, 255–56; population growth, 15; as trade route, 155; and U.S.-Pakistan relations, 14, 36, 39–41, 102–03, 136–38, 217
Afghanistan, in future scenarios: balkanized/fragmented state, 51; Islamic revolution, 74–75; as key change variable, 35–38, 60–61, 220, 231–32; muddling-along version, 80; as regime change pressure, 228; state collapse, 71
Agricultural sector, 19, 21, 116, 151, 154
Ahl-e-Hadith, 83
Ahmed, Khaled, 186–87
Ahsan, Aitzaz, 5
Al Huda, 96
Ali, Tariq, 183, 287
Al Qaeda, 11, 37–38, 42, 85–86, 172–73, 176, 177, 210. *See also* Islamic *entries*
Aman ki Asha initiative, 156
Anderson, Benedict, 290

Angola, Human Development Index, 20, 245
Anti-Americanism. *See* United States–Pakistan *entries*
Apex Court, 160
Armed Forces Journal, 152
Army. *See* military *entries*
Army Education Corps, 16
Asian Relations Conference, 124
Asian Relations Organization, 124
Assassinations, 11, 75–76, 120, 141
Aurakzai agency, 164
Authoritarian regime scenarios, 51–53, 230–31
Awami National Party, 95
Ayub Khan, 1, 18, 35, 52, 99, 125
Azad, Maulana Abdul Kalam, 182–83
Azhar, Masood, 100
Aziz, Shaukat, 288
Aziz Khan, Mohammed, 174

Bahawalpur, police effectiveness, 101
Balkanized/fragmented state scenarios, 51, 72–73, 79, 152, 231, 251–52
Balochistan/Balochs: ethnolinguistic foundation, 240–41, 242; governance